Face to Face Advisories

BRIDGING CULTURAL GAPS IN GRADES 5–9

Linda Crawford

All net proceeds from the sale of *Face to Face Advisories* support the work of The Origins Program, a nonprofit educational organization whose mission is to promote an equitable and humane multicultural society through quality education for all.

The stories in this book are all based on real events in classrooms. Names and many identifying characteristics of students and situations have been changed to protect the privacy of students.

Worldwide Web sites mentioned as citations and/or sources for further information may have changed or terminated since this book was published.

ISBN: 978-0-938541-20-2

Library of Congress Control Number: 2013916188

Cover photography by Karl Herber

Interior photography by Karl Herber, Jennifer Bush, and Elizabeth Crawford

Cover and book design: Heidi Neilson

The Origins Program
3805 Grand Avenue South
Minneapolis, Minnesota 55409
800-543-8715
www.developmentaldesigns.org

17 16 15 14 13   5 4 3 2 1

ACKNOWLEDGMENTS

I am eager for the opportunity to acknowledge the many educators, students, friends, and family it took to make this book a reality. They contributed by their willingness to be interviewed, by sharing stories, by reading parts of the manuscript, and by actually trying out some of the advisory meetings with their own students and providing generous feedback. Your candor makes this book ring true.

Interviewees:

Steve Hasti	Terrance Kwame-Ross	Lourdes Ramirez
Ralph Crowder	Diana O'Donnel	Genta Hayes
Robert Litvak	Tracine Asberry	Leya Cooper
Lars Carlson	Roxanne Hable	Sarah Klouda
Gina Kundan	Ana Knapp	Maria Pia
Jo Devlin	Jitenrapal Kundan	Kandace Logan
Tara Thuckral	Kay Arndt	Scott Tyink
Sharon Greaves	Todd Bartholomay	Christopher Hagedorn

Ann Ericson (Community of Peace Charter School, St. Paul, Minnesota) and Steve Hasti (Richard E. Green School, Minneapolis, Minnesota) led many *Face to Face Advisories* meetings with their advisory groups and provided valuable information about seventh, eighth, and tenth grade student reactions. I also thank Ann's students who shared with me firsthand about their experience thinking and talking together about the often sensitive issues of cultural differences.

Readers of the book are crucial to its authenticity. Our thanks go to Barbara Glaser for her careful read and commentary, and to Eleanor Sears' for invaluable feedback that kept our focus on the educators who would make these advisory meetings real.

Heidi Neilson, our graphic designer, turned these thousands of words into orderly, readable, friendly pages that are easy to use as a teaching guide, meeting by meeting. Images of Ven Anderson's sixth, seventh, and eighth grade advisory group at New City School (Minneapolis, Minnesota) grace the cover and interior, thanks to their generous and patient participation in two (not one!) photo shoots. They are, indeed, a healthy community in action!

Finally there was our own Origins team of people who nurtured *Face to Face Advisories*. Consultants Chris Hagedorn and Scott Tyink provided crucial guidance to keep the book right for adolescents. Executive Director Dr. Terrance Kwame-Ross supported the project from its inception, never doubting that we could do it well. Jo Devlin edited the book multiple times with skill, wit, and a deep commitment to a world enlivened by cultural variety. Publications Director Elizabeth Crawford, a partner in this enterprise of communication across cultures since 1989, has carefully considered every word. The book is deeper, clearer, more honest, fair, and useful than it ever would have been without her leadership.

TABLE OF CONTENTS

Authentic Advisory Conversations about Culture

"Schools in societies with democratic ideals are obligated to cultivate enlightened and engaged citizens. Helping young people form the habits of listening to strangers, at that very public place called school, should advance this work."[1]

Engaging in teacher-led conversations in school gives students practice in the citizen's task of talking and listening to people who differ from you in significant ways. This book provides both meat and method for leading conversations with and among adolescents about their differences. It is designed to help educators teach young adolescents habits of listening carefully to and actively supporting each other, so differences are less likely to become bias, indifference, prejudice, and discrimination. These are the forces that weaken society, and in school they make learning more difficult, especially for students with other disadvantages.

Some demographic groups have much more success in school than others. Exactly what is the nature of the gaps between them? In the United States, the differences between the successful and unsuccessful groups could be described as cultural. High performers tend to be European American or Asian American, from middle- or upper-income families; low performers tend to be Native American, African American, or Latino American and from poor families.[2] Those differences have prevailed in the statistics for years. Culture appears to be deeply entwined with school performance. It is "at the heart of all we do in the name of education.... Even without our being consciously aware of it, culture determines how we think, believe, and behave, and these, in turn, affect how we teach and learn."[3] By reducing the cultural gaps between students who succeed and those who do not, between students of color and in poverty and their usually white, middle class teachers, we can create a positive school culture and perhaps we can also reduce the performance gaps.

Goal: Open-mindedness and respect through perspective-taking

The outcome we seek is school communities built on honest and open communication among students and between students and teachers about matters deeply important to them: the cultures that make them who they are. The more students get to know and appreciate one another across their differences, the more included and connected to school they become. Included and connected, all students are far more likely to succeed.

My advisory group was able to do only the meetings in Perspective One, but those conversations seemed to draw the group together. At the end of the year, when I saw the statistics on referrals and suspensions for all the middle school homerooms, I was surprised at the low number of referrals and suspensions that my kids had compared to all the other advisory groups. The only way I can explain the difference is all those conversations we had about our various cultures and how they had influenced us. For a whole year we had listened to each other share and learned about each other's home lives and what we cared most about. (Seventh-eighth grade language arts teacher who implemented Face to Face Advisories)

Social outcomes

The advisory experiences in this book guide students toward participation in society with respect and appreciation for others, including those very different from them. We want students to be able to see our complex society from multiple perspectives, completing their secondary education with the following outcomes:

- I understand and appreciate the ways our cultures shape us differently (Perspective One).

- I perceive that we are all connected and interdependent, no matter how diverse our cultures (Perspective Two).

- I can describe the price that humanity pays for ignoring that interdependence and engaging in cultural conflicts with one another (Perspective Three).

- I understand that life is varied and constantly changing, and I am able to be flexible and see a person or situation from multiple perspectives (Perspective Four).

- I am willing to take a stand for cultural understanding and justice (Perspective Five).

The Illinois Learning Standards: Social/Emotional Learning, one of the most comprehensive sets of social-emotional learning (SEL) standards in the country, include target outcomes that, for example, relate to both Perspective Three ("I can describe stereotyping and its negative impact on others; I can identify negative depictions of differences among people; I can explain how lack of understanding of social and cultural differences can contribute to intolerance") and Perspective Five ("I can describe situations where minority groups have been respected at school or in the community; I can identify ways individuals and groups overcome social and cultural misunderstandings; I can describe situations where minority groups have been respected at school or in the community"). [4] The Illinois standards align with the SEL skills defined by the Collaborative for Academic, Social, and Emotionall Learning (CASEL). See Social-Emotional Learning in Face to Face Advisories, page 343, for more examples of skills practiced.

Moving Students into Action

In addition to heightened awareness and shifts in perspective about multicultural issues and the bias and discrimination that often characterize them, student outcomes from the *Face to Face Advisories* conversations also include deeper shifts in the way they perceive and think about the world and their role in it. Three mindset shifts can emerge from these conversations and empower students to engage positively with diversity:

Action mindset: Empowered students have an action mindset. Awareness comes first. Then students who have deepened their understanding of the challenges of our multicultural society can do what adolescents do best—spring into action. They can support each other, make requests for specific improvements in school, protest acts of discrimination, and interrupt bullying and the conditions that lead to bullying. They can reach out and get to know students outside their usual group, and they can have cultural conversations, read about cultural issues, and take stands for justice outside of school. In schools that utilize the *Developmental Designs* approach, they can apply what they have experienced in goal-setting, making agreements, practicing skills ahead of the need to use them, using reflection for self-guidance, problem-solving together, and using language that empowers others to understand and take action for justice, or at least confront cultural bias and exclusion (learn more on page 10).

Growth mindset: Empowered students have a growth mindset. They know that small steps can lead to success. They use failure as a starting place to learn what they need for success. They keep their eyes on the prize, and partner with teachers and fellow students to help them succeed. Many students lack this crucial mindset; the *Face to Face* advisories help them replace habits of hopelessness and defeat with belief in their own possibilities. We adults learn to believe in the future *for* them until they can see it for themselves.

Objective mindset: Empowered students have an objective mindset. They are not thrown off by setbacks. From work in these advisories on perspective-taking, they can identify biased language, verbal manipulation, and logical fallacies. They can think clearly and can construct their own understanding, even in the presence of put-downs, disrespect, or bias.

Method: Advisory provides the setting to accomplish the goal

What needs to happen to build open-mindedness, respect, and appreciation for others? Students need to experience their differences and think about social diversity in the context of a safe, inclusive community. The advisory period or homeroom, where students begin their day, can be a time for authentic, relationship-building and community-building conversations and activities. The advisories in this book expose students to diverse perspectives and guide them to understand those perspectives, and to critically and honestly analyze ideas from a variety of perspectives. It all happens through safe, engaging, guided peer-to-peer activities that build social-emotional skills and connections across differences. Teacher support—background, research, references for further reading, educator stories, and reflection questions—help teachers lead each advisory.

Day by day, students greet each other respectfully, then share interesting, meaningful activities that draw them together. Through purposeful conversations; learning both formal and light-hearted social skills; reflecting on their own ideas, identities, and beliefs; and games that bring out the best in everyone, they open to diverse people and cultures. They learn to take a stand for inclusiveness and openness by engaging in these activities.

In *Face to Face Advisories*, students contemplate whether equity is lacking in their school, and actions they could take for equity in school and in the larger society, on both the individual and institutional levels. The connections and understandings they gain in these conversations help create the optimal inclusive social-emotional conditions for learning. They help close cultural gaps and prepare the way for academic success for all.

Evidence for Benefits of Culturally Responsive Education

There is evidence that when there is positive contact and understanding among adolescents with diverse cultural profiles and between students and teachers who differ culturally, school environments are more conducive to learning. A safe, friendly, and respectful school culture benefits all—students and teachers.

CASEL has compiled a large body of research that substantiates the connection between improved academic performance and social-emotional skills developed through:

- cultivating warm, supportive, respectful relationships among students and teachers
- exposing students to a high-quality curriculum drawn from diverse cultures
- utilizing active ways of learning, high participation, and honest exchange of ideas through
- socially-skilled cooperative learning techniques
- integrating social and emotional learning and academic instruction in activities that call for perspective-taking and problem-solving[5]

Using the *Developmental Designs* approach, *Face to Face Advisories* meetings are designed to contribute to a healthy school culture. Within a safe, inclusive community, the content of the discussion is diverse, the ways of learning varied and broad-based. The focus is on replacing bias with equitable community, and students are encouraged to think for themselves. The advisories include all the dimensions cited by multicultural education specialist Dr. James Banks and other scholars and educators as necessary for culturally inclusive and responsive learning: content integration, equity pedagogy, knowledge construction, and prejudice reduction—all within an empowering school community.[6]

1. Content integration: We need to include many cultures and multiple points of view when we read literature or study history or geography or current events. Study of readings from diverse cultures contributes to the improvement of school performance.[7]

Seth Agbo and Gloria Ladson-Billings investigated the effect of culturally relevant teaching on the success of Native American and African-American students. Agbo urges inclusion of materials and styles from students' cultures: "[U]nless there is a genuine effort to mobilize Native resources and direct learning as far as possible toward Native identities and ideologies, the standardized test scores for American Indian children will remain mediocre in quality."[8] Ladson-Billings writes that to help students from ethnic minority backgrounds to learn effectively, teachers must be aware of cultural and value differences and the linguistic variables that are likely to affect teaching and learning.[9]

2. Equity pedagogy: We must employ pedagogy that attracts all students to learning—ways of instructing that engage through diverse ways of learning and knowing. Interactive learning that emphasizes active student participation and exchange of ideas between and among learners decreases behaviors that interfere with learning[10] and fosters high engagement.[11]

3. Knowledge construction: We need to understand how a student's point of view is constructed, recognizing the huge role that culture plays. Students need to learn to distinguish real thinking from shallow rhetoric, analyzing events or literature to understand diverse perspectives, to develop a critical consciousness about power differentials, and to solve problems contributes to improvement in school performance.[12]

Conversations that encourage students to construct their own understanding of the world stimulate their motivation to learn.[13] Richard Ryan and Edward Deci's research shows that experiences that allow adolescents to consider the validity of ideas and critically examine perspectives are likely to increase their endorsement of learning in general.[14] Ladson-Billings agrees: "Rather than the voice of one authority, meaning is made as a product of dialogue between and among individuals."[15]

Ladson-Billings also points to the importance of developing a "critical consciousness" of both school culture and the culture of society: "Beyond those individual characteristics of academic achievement and cultural competence, students must develop a broader sociopolitical consciousness that allows them to critique the cultural norms, values, mores, and institutions that produce and maintain social inequities. If school is about preparing students for active citizenship, what better citizenship tool than the ability to critically analyze the society?"[16]

4. Prejudice reduction: We must name the bias that permeates our society and explore ways to reduce it. Experience with peers considering relevant topics, expressing ideas and emotions, solving problems, addressing conflict, and understanding others' perspectives improves school performance.[17] When students experience their school climate as biased against their culture, they are less likely to engage. Conversely, in a school climate that is supportive of and congruent with positive beliefs about minority groups, students are more motivated to learn. For example, when African-American youths experience a positive, inclusive climate that promotes positive connections, they are more likely to be fully engaged in academics.[18]

5. Empowering school culture: We must create school environments that support and encourage students to construct their own understanding of the world, and that provide safe environments for discussions that may challenge the status quo.

- Adolescent learning competency is greatly enhanced when learning is socially interactive.[19]

- "According to theories of self-efficacy, choice theory, and self-determination, educators cannot teach young people the skills, concepts, and facts they need to become lifelong workers and learners unless they do so largely in a way that feeds the youthful need to relate to others."[20]

- African-American students in a suburban school were willing to study and engage in school when "[t]hey came to prefer being in the Honor Roll as a result of hard work [rather] than to achieve popularity among their peers for nonacademic activities." Eventually, these African-American students came to consider it worthwhile to work hard to do well in school, and they began to enjoy popularity *because* of their academic success.[21]

- Positive, trusting social relationships and interactions among school staff and with students' families improve school performance.[22]

- Students' perception of teachers as warm and supportive improve their school performance.[23]

- The Centers for Disease Control and Prevention report that if students feel more connected to school, they are healthier and perform better in school; they are "more likely to attend school regularly, stay in school longer, and have higher grades and test scores." In addition, opportunities to do critical and reflective thinking, work effectively with others, and identify and express their feelings all help provide youth with "the academic, social, and emotional skills they need to engage in school."[24] In general, a positive school climate is related to improved school performance.[25]

CULTURALLY RESPONSIVE INSTRUCTION IN ADVISORY

The advisory meetings in *Face to Face Advisories* lead students through conversations about cultures using all the methods proposed by the five dimensions cited above as well as other tools of culturally responsive teaching. The meetings expose students to ideas and information from many cultures. They help students analyze the mistakes of the past and inspire them to take action for equity. They show that we tend to think in the ways of our cultures, and that we must work to improve the fairness and quality of our thinking. During these advisories, students are likely to become aware of their biases and identify the sources of those biases. They are also likely to begin developing a critical consciousness about culture, which will help them understand power differentials and how they operate in school and in society.

As the meetings work toward these understandings, they also address adolescents' developmental needs for a sense of their own competency and autonomy, for positive relationships with peers and adults, and for fun that sustains them and draws them together. When these needs are met, adolescents are much more likely to engage in challenging cultural conversations which are critical for peace and prosperity in their lives. (See more about creating an inclusive advisory community, page 19-24.)

A good day at school

In these advisories, students learn to use multiple perspectives to examine culture in lively, fun, and friendly ways. They help students interact with each other and with adults successfully. In short, *Face to Face Advisories* meetings set the tone for a good day at school.

Content Integration: Diverse cultural content in advisory

In these discussions of culture, discrimination, and related topics, we build on the fact that students engage and participate more when they are invited to learn in ways that appeal to them. The work that has been done in culturally responsive teaching strongly indicates that student interest in school increases in proportion to the degree that content and instruction feel relevant to them. "Thus, culturally responsive pedagogy validates, facilitates, liberates, and empowers ethnically diverse students by simultaneously cultivating their cultural integrity, individual abilities, and academic success."[26]

Educator and philosopher Maxine Greene writes, "If there is to be a truly humane, plague-free community in this country, it must be one responsive to increasing numbers of life-stories, to more and more 'different' voices."[27] American school curricula have inadequately regarded the lives and cultural histories of minorities, or relegated them to slots in the calendar (for example, MLK Day or Cinco de Mayo). We can do better!

"In the United States, the prescriptive view can be seen in the use of standard English, Eurocentric ways of knowing and learning, a Eurocentric literary canon, and a conventional, unproblematic rendering of U.S. history. This form of the cultural/prescriptive view marginalizes the pluralistic composition of U.S. society by devaluing the language, contributions, and histories of some groups."[28]

The advisories in this book engage the content-integration challenge through stories and resources drawn from and relevant to the many cultures of America.

Definition of culture in this book

In these conversations, we call the shared values, beliefs, attitudes, and practices—the sum of the influences in the place, time, and environment in which a group of people live—culture. Examining culture—including our own—helps us understand why a person or a group of people are the way they are and do the things they do. Sometimes subtly and sometimes obviously, culture influences the choices and decisions we make and the style and direction of our lives.

For the purposes of this book, a useful definition of culture includes the following:
1. Culture is not genetically determined but socially learned, passed on from generation to generation.

2. Culture does not belong to an individual—it is shared.

3. Culture is integrated. It is like a webbed system, in which many elements of life are interconnected.

4. Culture is dynamic and changing, as people constantly change.

5. Culture subsumes values, knowledge, and beliefs that affect behaviors.[29]

Culture is an integrated web of ways to be that keeps changing as people change. Everything that affects the lives of our cultural group or groups comprises our culture: our environment, social class, "race"/color, gender, family and friends, current events, education, values, technology and commerce, food, fashion, the media, and more. Factors like physical and mental abilities and sexual orientation, insofar as they place us in a group that shares our qualities, become part of our culture. Ask a blind or deaf person about the culture of visually- or hearing-impaired people she is part of, and you will learn about a culture. Ask a gay, lesbian, bisexual, or transgender person about the influences in his or her life, and you will likely hear about the culture of GLBT people. We are drawn to people like us, and we are in turn shaped by our associations with them.

Equity Pedagogy: Diverse ways of learning include everyone

The way we present content is as important as the content itself. If we address only some of the ways our students can learn, only some of them will engage and learn. Equity pedagogy calls for teaching approaches that optimize opportunities for academic achievement of students from diverse groups. When we teach a variety of learners in a variety of ways, everyone has a chance to learn, at least some of the time, in a way that is accessible and appealing.[30]

The advisory meetings in this book frequently have students work with partners or in small groups. There are hands-on projects, and sometimes we learn by playing a game. Students make choices about how to respond to a question or express themselves. We use art, poetry, drama, and more to draw everyone into learning. We do not always teach students of a particular color or ethnicity or gender in a particular way, since students have multiple intelligences and learn in multiple ways, and every cultural group, although it may be characterized by certain strengths, contains a wide range of learning preferences. The important thing is to mix it up so we reach all students.

Connected learning

We contextualize learning to make it more meaningful and to deepen student understanding. We continually ask, "What is the connection between this content and the lives of these students?" Sometimes in order to do justice to a topic, you'll stay with it longer than you planned. Sometimes you may take a side road which will deepen understanding, even though you know your students will never be tested on the material. "Ironically, the key lever in this standards-based reform strategy—the use of high-stakes external tests—has unwittingly provided teachers with a rationalization for avoiding or minimizing the need to teach well, that is, to teach for in-depth understanding."[31]

It is crucial that students see connections between their lives in school and outside school, between the content of their learning and their daily lives. To build such connections in these advisories, we invite guests (see page 25), we read and discuss literature, and we examine documents from a variety of cultures. Most important, we ask students to reflect on these resources and experiences by making connections to their own lives and their own ways of thinking. Many meetings in *Face to Face Advisories* include reflection questions and other ways of reviewing experiences and content.

Knowledge Construction: Critical thinking to construct cultural understanding

It is not enough to merely expose students to content from diverse cultures. We must also help them reflect on and assess the content, discern underlying assumptions and points of view, look for evidence that supports conclusions, and the other skills of critical thinking. Paying attention to whether and how students construct their knowledge brings rigor to the advisory discussions. Students are invited to share their thoughts and experiences, but they can be guided to do so in a way that uncovers assumptions, points of view, and biases—their own and others'. Everyone is taught and expected to reveal his or her perspective and to cite evidence for statements presented as facts. Such intellectual rigor is fundamental to educational success and to good citizenship. The work we do in advisory will reverberate in other classes and will make more astute readers and thinkers of our students.

The advisories also ask students to express their feelings. Adolescents are imbued with many and strong emotions, and requiring them to ignore or suppress that part of themselves weakens any interaction. Sharing the emotional effects of dealing with individual and institutional bias may be an opportunity for some to feel genuinely known and accepted. Our job is to maintain a healthy balance between emotional self-expression and evidence-supported factual statements.

Sources for work on perspective-taking

See Perspective Four for advisories that introduce and discuss perspective-taking. They help students look at life from more than one angle, seeing what previously may have been hidden. Additional resources can be found at the following Web sites:

- Conflict Resolution Education: http://www.creducation.org/resources/perception_checking
- Third Side Perspective-taking: http://www.thirdside.org/3S_Perspective_Taking_Exercise.pdf

Bias Reduction

Careful examination allows us to uncover biased thinking. Students decide whether a statement reflects a skewed point of view. By naming distortions they see and hear, identifying bias when and where they find it—in current events, in literature, in history, in everyday encounters in school—students learn to assertively name and take action against bias.

In support of his "prejudice reduction" dimension of multicultural education, Banks describes some of the research on the prevalence of "racial" awareness, identification, and preference in young children in our society, and the crucial need to help them develop more democratic attitudes while they are still young.[32] Prejudice does grave damage. The more we expose it, the less power it has.

I can be pretty blunt sometimes. If there is language in our texts that might confuse students, I name it: "This is racism." If a bully says something, I call him out. It works to name it in front of the whole class. It's kind of weird, but it works. The point is: We're all watching this and we're not having any of it! (Seventh-eighth grade language arts teacher)

Advisory is a time to build relationships and talk about what matters most to us in real life. It creates a ready, supportive context for openly discussing cultural differences, bias, and prejudice with our students and inviting them to take a stand for what they believe is right. The year's worth of advisory meetings in this book outline engaging and respectful conversations about our relationships with one another across cultures.

[P]eople usually get uncomfortable with a conversation about race, class, or religion. It doesn't just come up. When it does, people avoid it, or they talk about it but don't do anything. You don't talk about it unless you push into it. It's hard to accept that we're biased, that we're all perfectly imperfect. We need to teach kids how to have these conversations at school and with their own families. (Youth worker)

Empowering School Culture

Banks recognizes that since school itself is a complex culture, creating a healthy, empowering school climate requires us to examine the entire system—curriculum, instruction, materials and equipment, and the adult community.[33] The *Developmental Designs* approach directs efforts toward the social-emotional climate of the system, considering the quality of relationships among staff, among students, and between students and staff. The following practices in advisory meetings provide an integrated, comprehensive approach to creating a school climate in which each person is likely to feel valued.

Developmental Designs practices in advisory

Goals and Declarations: everyone in the advisory, including the teacher, declares a personal stake in the group. "If things went really well for you in this advisory, what would it look like? What is the best outcome for you personally that you can imagine?" The group converts those goals into a declaration: *What will you personally do in advisory to make that happen?*

Social Contract: an agreement among all the stakeholders in the advisory that draws from their personal goals and binds the advisory community to rules for respect of all individuals and cultures

Modeling and Practicing: the routines and activities of the advisory are modeled and practiced by all so that all know the expectations and competencies essential to their success

The Loop: a two-step reflective process that includes thoughtful planning of activities and assessment afterward of the content and the process, the ideas and opinions generated in the activity, and how they relate to a student's own life and opinions, so students can detect when they are worthy and when they are ill-founded

Empowering Language: student and teacher self-expression respects guidelines that ensure that communication in advisory is respectful of many points of view, never debasing

Pathways to Self-control: students are guided to be authentic during the meetings without demeaning others. If they disrupt the community, the Pathways provide techniques for correction that maintain the individuality and dignity of the rule-breaker

Collaborative Problem-solving: diverse groups learn to make decisions through a consensus process that includes everyone

Power of Play: the use of games to create bonds throughout the diverse advisory community, with no one left out

Practices for Motivating Instruction: everyone has opportunities for leadership and self-direction during meetings. Conversations are relevant to students' home and neighborhood lives, and activities are designed to appeal to a variety of learning styles.

See The Origins Program publications *The Advisory Book*[34] and *Classroom Discipline*[35] to support implementation of *Developmental Designs* practices.

HOW THIS BOOK IS ORGANIZED

The more than 125 meetings in *Face to Face Advisories* present five perspectives on culture.

1. **Identity and Diversity:** We get to know one another culturally and personally, have fun together, and begin to understand how we are all shaped by our cultures.

2. **Interdependence:** We come to see that we depend deeply upon one another.

3. **Us versus Them:** We examine our tendency to choose sides, to bond with people like us, to be wary of those who are different, and to ignore our connections and interdependence at great cost. We discuss specifically and honestly the issues of a diverse society by critically engaging in conversations that acknowledge and address bias and discrimination.

4. **Open to Change:** We see that the world is not static, but constantly changing, and there is hope that we can guide the future so we do not repeat the mistakes of the past.

5. **Taking a Stand:** We become willing to take action against bias to help create a just, inclusive world in which everyone counts.

Each advisory meeting description is accompanied by guidance on how and why to implement with maximum effectiveness. There are explanations of how to guide the greeting, share, game, or other activity, and there are tips to support their implementation. Each advisory is augmented by a "Keep in Mind" section with background information, research, related ideas, and a variety of points of view to deepen the leader's understanding of the topic and provide enrichment possibilities. The topics are also enriched with stories from the classrooms of middle-level and high school teachers and from students. By reading the "Keep in Mind" section for an advisory before leading it, teachers can prepare quickly.

How to Lead Face to Face Advisories introduces the *Developmental Designs*™ structure for advisory meetings. There are two developmentally appropriate meeting formats:

- The Circle of Power and Respect (CPR) format, with four elements: a welcoming message, a greeting that includes everyone, person-to-person/partner/whole-group sharing and listening carefully to one another, and a wide variety of activities, many of them playful, often followed by reflection.

- The Activity Plus (A+) format, with three elements: a welcoming message, a greeting that includes everyone, and a longer activity, always followed by reflection.

Community-building Advisories provides fifteen meetings especially designed to build positive relationships and prepare the group for effective *Face to Face Advisories* conversations. Lead these meetings before the perspectives advisories, to start the year, or whenever you begin this work.

An **Appendix** provides additional resources useful in leading various meetings.

Conversations about Cultural Issues Can Change Lives

Some conversations are ritual exchanges that you might hear anywhere: *Hello. How's it going? How are you? Good morning. Hi. Yo! Can you tell me where the office is? What time is it? Fine, thanks. How are you?*

A lot happens in such exchanges: we acknowledge each other's presence; we show that we are friendly; we accept, at least on the surface, differences between us. This is the social hum of an orderly school, and it's a good thing—but it isn't enough. This level of communication does not prevent cliques, exclusion, or profound loneliness, and it's certainly not enough to prevent bullying. It also isn't sufficient to help teachers and students get to know one another across their differences. For that, we need to model authenticity and truthfulness, inviting students to do the same. We can set a tone of honesty, frankness, and good humor about ourselves. When the adults around them are authentic and occasionally vulnerable, students are more likely to take a chance to do so.

The bonus for the adults is that they may gain important understandings for themselves:

I enjoyed leading these advisories. I gained insights about myself in the conversations. This is the wonderful thing about these topics: we all have work to do—it is a lifelong journey. Many of the ideas that we were discussing, especially the dealing with differences continuum, are areas that I am continually reflective about in terms of my own interactions with people. I thought deeply about the conversations. (Seventh-eighth grade science teacher)

If we really want all of our students to succeed in school, we must build understanding and support across our differences, or many students—most likely those of color, or living in poverty, or with disabilities, or immigrants, or those struggling with sexual orientation, or who are not fluent in English—will feel disconnected from school and will underperform or simply give up.

The conversations in these advisories are opportunities to address some of the culture-based factors in the failure to learn, such as language issues, lack of connection to school, bias, and cultural differences in style that become behavior issues or learning disablers. To close academic gaps, we must first communicate well enough to close the cultural ones. The conversations in *Face to Face Advisories* help mitigate some of the causes of those gaps.

---

[1] Walter Parker, "Listening to Strangers: Classroom Discussion in Democratic Education," *Teachers College Record* 112, no. 11 (2010): 2815-2832, http://www.tcrecord.org/library. (ID Number: 15794).

[2] Susan Aud, Mary Ann Fox, and Angelina KewalRamani, "Status and Trends in the Education of Racial and Ethnic Minorities," *National Center for Education Statistics (NCES)*, July 2010, http://nces.ed.gov/pubs2010/2010015.pdf. See Appendix, page 345, for more information.

[3] Geneva Gay, *Culturally Responsive Teaching: Theory, Research, and Practice* (New York: Teachers College Press, 2000), 8-9.

[4] "Performance Descriptors Social-Emotional Learning Grades 6-12," Illinois State Board of Education, http://www.isbe.state.il.us/ils/social_emotional/pdf/descriptors_6-12.pdf. See Appendix, page 343, for more information.

[5] "SEL & Academics," Collaborative for Academic, Social, and Emotional Learning (CASEL), http://casel.org/why-it-matters/benefits-of-sel/sel-academics/.

[6] James A. Banks, "Multicultural Education: Historical Development, Dimensions, and Practice," in *Handbook of Research on Multicultural Education*, ed. J. A. Banks and C. A. M. Banks (New York: Macmillan, 1995), 3-24.

[7] Eric Schaps, Victor Battistich, and Daniel Solomon, "Community in School as Key to Student Growth: Findings from the Child Development Project," in *Building Academic Success on Social and Emotional Learning: What does the research say?* ed. J. Zins, R. Weissberg, M. Wang, and H. Walberg (New York: Teachers College Press, 2004), 189-205.

[8] Seth A. Agbo, "Enhancing Success in American Indian Students: Participatory Research at Akwesasne as Part of the Development of a Culturally Relevant Curriculum," *Journal of American Indian Education* 40, no. 1 (2001): 41.

[9] Gloria Ladson-Billings, "Toward a Theory of Culturally Relevant Pedagogy," *American Educational Research Journal* 32, no. 3 (Autumn 1995): 465-491.

[10] Nancy S. Tobler and Howard H. Stratton, "Effectiveness of School-Based Drug Prevention Programs: A Meta-Analysis of the Research," *Journal of Primary Prevention* 18, no.1 (September 1997): 71-128.

[11] J. David Hawkins, Brian H. Smith, and Richard F. Catalano, "Social Development and Social and Emotional Learning," in *Building Academic Success on Social and Emotional Learning: What does the research say?* ed. J. Zins, R. Weissberg, M. Wang, and H. Walberg (New York: Teachers College Press, 2004), 135-150.

[12] M. J. Elias, "Strategies to Infuse social and emotional Learning into Academics," in *Building Academic Success on Social and Emotional Learning: What Does the Research Say?* ed. J.E. Zins, R.P. Weissberg, M.C. Wang, and H. J. Walbert (New York: Teachers College Press, 2004).

[13] Albert Bandura, *Self-efficacy: The Exercise of Control* (New York: W.H. Freeman, 1997).

[14] Richard Ryan and Edward Deci, "Self-determination Theory and the Facilitation of Intrinsic Motivation, Social Development, and Well-being," *American Psychologist* 55, no. 1 (2000): 68-78.

[15] Ladson-Billings, "Toward a Theory of Culturally Relevant Pedagogy," 473.

[16] Gloria Ladson-Billings, "But That's Just Good Teaching! The Case for Culturally Relevant Teaching," *Theory into Practice* 34, no. 3 (Summer 1995): 162.

[17] "SEL & Academics."

[18] Christy M. Byrd and Tabbye Chavous, "Racial Identity, School Racial Climate, and School Intrinsic Motivation Among African American Youth: The Importance of Person–Context Congruence," *Journal of Research on Adolescence* 21, no. 4 (December 2011): 849-860.

[19] R. Dreikurs, F.C. Peepers, and B.B. Grunwald, *Maintaining Sanity in the Classroom: Classroom Management Techniques* (New York: Taylor and Francis, 1998).; Barbara Rogoff, *Apprenticeship in Thinking: Cognitive Development in Social Context* (Oxford, England: Oxford University Press, 1990).

[20] Terrance Kwame-Ross, Linda Crawford, and Erin Klug, "Developmental Designs: A Description of the Approach and Implementation in Schools," *Middle Grades Research Journal* 6, no. 3 (Fall 2011): 147.

[21] John U. Ogbu, *Black American Students in an Affluent Suburb: A Study of Academic Disengagement* (Mahwah, NJ: Lawrence Erlbaum Associates, 2008), 193.

[22] Anthony S. Bryk and Barbara Schneider, *Trust in Schools: A Core Resource for Improvement*, (Chicago: University of Chicago, 2002).

[23] "SEL & Academics."

[24] "Fostering School Connectedness: Improving Student Health and Academic Achievement," Centers for Disease Control and Prevention, July 2009, 1-2, http://www.cdc.gov/healthyyouth/AdolescentHealth/pdf/connectedness_teachers.pdf.

[25] C. L. A. Weiss, D. L. Cunningham, C.P. Lewis, and M.G. Clark, *Enhancing Student Connectedness to Schools*, (Baltimore, MD: Center for School Mental Health Analysis and Action, Department of Psychiatry, University of Maryland School of Medicine, December 2005).

[26] Gay, *Culturally Responsive Teaching: Theory, Research, and Practice*, 44.

[27] Maxine Greene, "Diversity and Inclusion: Toward a Curriculum for Human Beings," *Teachers College Record* 95, no. 2 (Winter 1993): 218.

[28] Arlette Ingram Willis, "Reading the World of School Literacy: Contextualizing the Experience of a Young African American Male," *Harvard Educational Review* 65, no. 1 (Spring, 1995): 37.

[29] Gwendolyn Cartledge and JoAnne Fellows, Milburn *Cultural Diversity and Social Skills Instruction: Understanding Ethnic and Gender Differences* (Champaign, IL: Research Press, 1996), 14.

[30] Banks, "Multicultural Education: Historical Development, Dimensions, and Practice," 3-24.

31 Grant Wiggins and Jay McTighe, *Understanding by Design,* 2nd ed. (Alexandria, VA: ASCD, 2005), 303.

32 James A. Banks, *Educating Citizens in a Multicultural Society*, 2nd ed. (New York: Teachers College Press, 2007), 69-70.

33 Ibid., 84-85.

34 Linda Crawford, *The Advisory Book: Building a Community of Learners Grades 5-9*, 2nd ed. (Minneapolis: The Origins Program, 2012).

35 Linda Crawford and Christopher Hagedorn, *Classroom Discipline: Guiding Adolescents to Responsible Independence* (Minneapolis: The Origins Program, 2010).

How to Lead Face to Face Advisories

This book provides 127 advisory meetings focused on culture. They take participants from getting to know one another all the way to frank and challenging conversations about our differences. The conversations happen face to face, in circles, where all are included and equal. They are designed as advisory meetings, but they could be adapted for use in content-area classes. Most of them are designed for a group of between ten and thirty students.

The conversations teach skills fundamental to bridging cultural differences: flexible thinking, self-awareness, empathy, and optimism. These skills help students get to know and understand each other, and they also help students understand people outside their classrooms, their neighborhoods, their country, even outside their own time and place in history.

TWO DEVELOPMENTAL DESIGNS ADVISORY FORMATS

Circle of Power and Respect Advisory Format

The Circle of Power and Respect (CPR) format for advisories is ideal for creating inclusive communities.

Daily news

A short, friendly note welcomes students and gives them a preview of the day's meeting's focus. The daily news often poses a question to answer or think about. It may direct them to do something before the meeting begins. It helps them shift into thinking gear as they transition from home to school.

In each daily news message, a word is underlined. It may be related to the focus of the meeting, or it may be a word likely to be new to some students. A volunteer can define it for the group, or you can simply give the definition. Once the word is clearly defined, you can challenge students to use the word during the meeting (and cheer when someone does).

Greeting

Everyone in the circle is greeted by name by at least one other person, and everyone greets someone by name. Students learn the conventions of formal and informal greetings, greetings in languages other than English, and how to respectfully greet someone they hardly know or they don't particularly like.

Mrs. H, I like when we do the greeting, because that's the only time one of the kids says my name in school. (Sixth grade student)

Share

In *Face to Face* advisories, teacher and students share about their lives, usually in response to a question related to cultures. Sharing is a time to talk about issues of the day and to voice opinions on topics relevant to students' lives. For adolescents, relevance sparks discussion of challenging topics like bias, discrimination, justice, and acceptance. We want their authentic engagement and participation; the sharing component engages students' minds and hearts, encouraging expression of differences and simultaneously drawing the group together. Deborah Meier has written that we need to encourage students to "explore and act upon the fundamental intellectual and social issues of their times."[1]

In sharing, we find our commonalities as well as our differences—in music, activities, humor, life experiences, goals, families. (Seventh-eighth grade social studies teacher)

Activity

Students connect through play and activities that allow them to voice their opinions and discover commonalities. Many games make them think hard and fast. According to one experienced teacher of adolescents, "It's in the nonsensical parts of life that we get to know people." Play can be an equalizer: a student who is not succeeding academically may be the one who solves a problem or makes a mental connection in the context of a stimulating activity or cooperative game. At the end of the activity, students often reflect on the content and/or the process so that they can improve the experience for next time and to integrate the meaning into their lives. Whole group format is the default for the reflection.

Activity Plus (A+) Advisory Format

In the A+ format, as in CPR, the teacher writes a daily news message, and everyone in the group is greeted and greets someone. This is followed by participation in an activity. *Face to Face Advisories* activities are designed to by turns connect everyone, prompt thinking, problem-solve, create, and have fun together. The A+ format does not include a share component, thus allowing more time for the activity. Near the end of the A+ meeting, students reflect on what they have experienced, and on the implications of what they have learned or thought or heard, for them personally, for the school community, and/or for society. Unless the discussion format is specified, decide which would be best for your advisory: partners, small groups, or whole groups.

CPR and A+ advisory meetings connect students to school and to each other and the adult staff. School must seem relevant to adolescents before they will make an effort to do what schools demand. "A homeroom or advisory at the start of the day, when properly structured to meet adolescent needs, can promote social development, assist students in their academic programs, facilitate positive involvement among teachers, administrators, and students, provide adult advocacy, and a positive climate in the school community."[2]

In either format, students and their teachers learn about each other and grow closer. In a safe, inclusive atmosphere, mutual acceptance and enjoyment grow, even when the group discusses challenging subjects like racism and heterosexism. (For definitions of culturally-referenced words in *Face to Face Advisories*, see a glossary, pages 346-347.)

For a detailed discussion of the *Developmental Designs* CPR and A+ advisory meeting structures, see *The Advisory Book* (Crawford, 2012).

USING THE ADVISORY DESCRIPTIONS

The description of every meeting in *Face to Face Advisories* uses the following format:

Goal: Identification of the growth we intend in each advisory. Other gains are possible, but if the meeting is successful, it brings growth toward the goal.

Meeting components: For CPR meetings, the components are daily news, greeting, share, and activity; A+ components are daily news, greeting, activity, and reflection.

Tips: Tips are flagged thus: ⟴. They follow many component descriptions and are meant to help you head off problems and make the experience orderly, inclusive, and enjoyable for everyone.

Keep in Mind: "Keep in Mind" segments provide background information to make an advisory experience deeper and more meaningful. They discuss aspects of the education process that are especially relevant to considerations of cultural differences, and they provide references for further reading. They also discuss key issues in culturally responsive teaching, as well as the three mindsets important for teaching: the Growth, Action, and Objective mindsets.

Ask Yourself: Each advisory description ends with a reflection question for the leader to ponder to enhance his/her engagement.

Preparation

Read all the way through the description of the advisory, from goal to teacher reflection, before the meeting. Investigate the advisory topic further if you wish, and reflect on your views and experiences related to the topic.

USING ADVISORY TO CREATE AN INCLUSIVE COMMUNITY

Honest and fruitful conversations about culture, bias, and discrimination require a context of connection and safety. Everyone knows that she/he is included and safe. Establishing such an environment is crucial to building an inclusive school culture. It requires effort, intentionality, and patience from both teachers and students.

Students Get to Know the Teacher and Each Other in Advisory

In advisory meetings, teachers can strengthen their relationships with students by occasionally sharing about themselves. Trust grows when we know and understand each other, especially when there is a power imbalance, as between teacher and student. Sometimes an advisory description suggests that a teacher share on a topic, and students can then ask appropriate follow-up questions. Participating in discussions makes teachers more accessible, just as occasionally joining in a game somewhat eases the power differentials, without compromising discipline. After all, we are in this investigation of cultures together.

Once when I was having a hard time getting a group of eighth graders to participate in a CPR meeting, I told them about my new puppy and the trouble I was having training him to walk on a leash. I asked for help, and I got it! Some had advice for me, some told about training their dogs, and we talked about training different kinds of dogs. Finally we had to cut it off because we had run out of time.

My students know me. I feel that there are certain parts of my life that I can put out there for them to get to know me, for example my love of cars, and the dogsled racing I did when I was younger. I think them getting to know me is crucial. It opens the door for them to start sharing pieces of their lives that are totally outside of the classroom. I feel that the more transparent I can be with my students, the more they'll let me know them. When I taught in the neighborhood where I lived, when a student saw me at the grocery store, it opened up a whole new doorway of trust. We're in the same place outside of school! I have lunch with my students, one on one or in small groups. There's something casual about sharing a meal—it gets like a pizza party—lots of laughter. (Sixth grade teacher)

Playing helps us get to know one another

Play is our friend. Done well, it revives and refreshes, creates bonds, softens discord, and helps us move past pain. We can structure play to be inclusive and cooperative. Through playful interactions students and teachers can come to know each other better, culturally and personally.

In "Tip," a game my students love, the players have to jump in the air at the very moment that they throw or catch the ball. Tip takes real concentration, attention, and of course, coordination. It is competitive since it's based on elimination, but everyone seems happy playing it, whether they are in or out of the game at the moment. They encourage each other, cheer, and there are no hard feelings about the game—ever. They are so happy to be active together! And after the students play Tip for five minutes, they are able to focus back on their school work. (Seventh-eighth grade teacher)

Group play is a bonding force in a school community, and many *Face to Face* advisories include play. It is often related to the advisory topic, but sometimes it's simply a tension-breaker and equalizer. Lightening up and laughing together helps break down divisions and cliques and make school a friendlier, more inclusive place throughout the day. Fun helps unite us.

One group I had were able to responsibly call for a break in work when they felt the group needed it. We called it a "power of play moment." A student would stand and call out, "Middle School Break!" Whoever called out would then lead a little chant or exercise or hand jive for a couple of minutes. The students took responsibility for their own productivity, and improved everyone's concentration by calling the moment! (Middle level teacher)

Seating

All *Face to Face Advisories* meetings should be held in a circle. It is the only arrangement in which everyone can see and interact easily with everyone else. It helps equalize the power between students and adults and between students with less social power and those with more. Direct student seating sometimes, to get the cross-contact that makes for a healthy, inclusive community: *Today, please sit girl-boy-girl-boy. Sit next to someone you haven't spoken to yet today. Take a number from the basket and sit in the chair with that number.* Varying seating strategies allow students to have partner shares with many in the group, getting to know about many lives and perspectives. You can state the objective, inviting everyone to help foster the cohesion of the group by mixing things up. Invite students to invent new ways to scramble the seating.

Seating new students

When a new student joins the group, vary seating every day, so she or he gets to partner with a variety of people.

A story: students stand for inclusivity

A middle level social studies teacher in a school with 40% Latino and 60% European-background demographics, as well as 20% special-needs students, began the year by assigning seating through random means (name cards, number wheels, etc.). She assumed that once they were acquainted, students would on their own sit with anyone and everyone. After a month or so, she allowed them to choose their own seats in the circle, and the students went right back to sitting next to their old friends.

I told them what I was noticing. "I know you like to feel comfortable and be next to friends, but the result is divisions in our classroom. That's what happens most of the time in our world. How could we break down the cultural barriers at least in our own classroom?"

The students replied that no one had ever talked to them about this before, and they supposed that was because their parents and teachers just wanted them to be happy. They decided that what they really wanted was to try to make an inclusive classroom, so they created a seating grid that called for regular rotations and everyone had a chance to sit next to everyone else during the rest of the year. At the end of the year, I took a photograph of the group during their advisory meeting, and the photo revealed that they were, indeed, "all mixed up." It may be our natural tendency to want to sit next to the people we know the best, but if we have conversations about culture and about being collaborative workers, we can inspire students toward the greater purpose of inclusivity. (Middle level teacher)

Choice greetings

When students are invited to choose someone to greet (instead of turning to a neighbor), the danger exists that they will "shop around," looking at some people and *not* greeting them as they seek someone they feel like greeting. To avoid such favoritism, tell everyone before the greeting begins that they need to choose someone sitting across the circle. Encourage them to greet the first person they make eye contact with to reduce the possibility of being seen and rejected. In the individual advisory descriptions in this book, you'll find reminders about keeping choice greetings safe.

Varied ways to form partners

Forming partnerships for partner activities is also an opportunity to mix things up. For example, students can pick names or numbers out of a hat, or you can use a random factor like, *Partner with someone born in the same month as you,* or you can use a silly process like Dude.

Instructions for Dude

Calls out the following directions for the circle of students to follow. When you say *Ceiling!* everyone looks at the ceiling. Then you say, *Toes!* and everyone looks at their toes. Finally, say, *Eyes!* and everyone looks across the circle. The moment one makes eye contact with someone across the circle, the two point at each other and say, *Dude!* and sit down next to each other. Keep going until everyone has a partner.

Student Voice in Keeping Order

To make an environment safe for serious conversation, orderly and dependable expectations are essential. Every group has disagreements and problems at times, and sometimes a student may have a bad day. The group needs a protocol for when things go wrong. In the *Developmental Designs* approach, students create a Social Contract through participation in a democratic rule-making process. Here is how one school used the process to create their advisory rules at the beginning of the year:

"In the three homerooms, students formed pairs to think about rules we could use to help us achieve our goals. Each pair wrote three rules. Then the pairs united, shared their rules, and repeated the process, reducing the number of rules again to three. The consolidation continued: groups of 4 combined to make groups of 8, groups of 8 combined to make groups of 16, etc.—each time groups emerged with three rules. Finally, there were two large groups left, and the three rules from each of them were consolidated into one set. The homerooms did this by writing the last six rules on six thin strips of paper, posting them on the board, and consolidating them into a final set of three."[3]

Once the group makes its rules, they can be held to their own guidelines. It is much more effective to correct student behavior when the students make the rules in the first place. See also Community-building Advisories, Advisory 8 for a meeting focused on creating group norms or rules.

MIND YOUR MINDSETS

Our mindsets shape and color all of our participation and leadership. Three mindsets are crucial for success in *Face to Face Advisories* meetings:

- Growth mindset: you must believe that everyone in the group can become more aware, honest, tolerant, and skilled, regardless of where they are their starting

- Action mindset: you must name and confront bias every time you see or hear it, and guide others to do the same

- Objective mindset: you must not take disrespect and pushback so personally that you lose the capacity to see things from the other person's point of view.

Growth Mindset

A growth mindset gives us hope. It confirms that we are not owned by our biases; we can outgrow them, just as we can always grow in knowledge and skills. The goal of the "us versus them" (Perspective Three) advisories is to name our biases so we can begin freeing ourselves from them. To do this, we must transform opinionating into perspective-taking.

"If we are to achieve a richer culture, rich in contrasting values, we must recognize the whole gamut of human potentialities, and so weave a less arbitrary social fabric, one in which each diverse human gift will find a fitting place."[4]

An African-American girl in our school was always getting into trouble with teachers. She quarreled a lot with other kids, and ended up getting sent to the office or sent home because of her forceful won't-back-down attitude. She was mouthy and uppity with anyone who got in her way, and one day she actually mooned a teacher who was particularly critical of her! I set up a conflict resolution program in my classroom, and when she started to fight with someone, I had her use our conflict management technique, and the fights were resolved. She got really good at it and even became a facilitator in resolving other people's conflicts. I believed that she could handle it, and she did. She was proud of that. (Sixth grade teacher)

A growth mindset knows there can be harmony among people who differ, and we will find it.

Action Mindset

The teacher is the anchor for these discussions of inequity and prejudice. We keep the group together. If things get tense, we name the tension, investigate its causes, and, if appropriate, lighten things up with a few moments of play or an acknowledgment activity, so the solidarity of the group remains intact. We watch for, point out, and deal with discriminatory words and actions. We do not slack off, for if we did, an unconfronted put-down would undermine the safety and integrity of the whole community.

The action mindset calls us to action, despite discouragement, fatigue, or doubt.

A student was really struggling. He spent a lot of time doing homework in my office at my invitation. Then he started not coming to school, not working. I called him on his cell phone and said, "I have no intention of having you leave here without a diploma, and I want to help you. This is only the beginning of our talking. Next time I want your mother to be here." When we met, I told him, "I'm going to be calling your parents once a week." He made it to graduation by the skin of his teeth! You have to be courageous with kids, take their anger, stick with them. I stuck with him because I can't look a person in the face if I've not done everything I could do for them. I feel like I owe it to kids who didn't have what I had. I grew up privileged and have to give back. (High school principal)

Objective Mindset

It's likely, especially in the "us versus them" perspective (Perspective 3), that we will be offended at least once by something a student says or does. Rather than rushing to defend or correct, criticize, or show how wrong he is, you must respond to a statement of bias or out-and-out disrespect calmly. There is no use responding in kind, and that takes a cool head. To seek connections and alliances with people we perceive as different requires tolerance for ambiguity, and multiple ways of seeing something.

I met with a fifth grade boy in my office because once again he had been caught in a lie. Lying was a behavior I particularly disliked in kids. It acts like a wall between how things are and how they might be. If you can't get past the lie, you can't find a path for change in behavior. And my own family is really big on telling the truth no matter what, so I didn't look forward to this discussion. Somehow as we talked, I began to feel sorry for the boy. Finally I just asked him: "Why do you tell these lies all the time? They don't even get you what you want!" His usual upbeat look turned into sadness: "I don't know. I don't know. They just come out! It's like a bad habit!" Together we figured out a way he could start breaking the habit. (Principal, K-5 school)

TWO IMPORTANT DEFINITIONS

Culture

"Culture" in these meetings means the sum of all the influences that have shaped us in the past and continue to influence us all our lives, such as our ethnicity, class, religion, language, ability, age, sexual orientation, gender, and skin color. We choose this very broad definition so we are as inclusive as possible. One job of the facilitator of the conversations is to keep that fullness of meaning before the group, and not to let the meaning—or our goal—shrink. Any difference we exclude from our work could be important to the identity formation of someone in the group.

"Race"

To use "race" as if it designated a biological difference between one group of human beings and another is to ignore science:

The following is excerpted from the American Anthropological Association statement on "race" in 1998: "Evidence from the analyses of genetics (e.g., DNA) indicates that most physical variation, about 94%, lies within so-called 'racial' groups. In other words, conventional 'racial' groupings differ from one another in only about 6% of their genes. This means there is much greater variation within 'racial' groups than between them....The continued sharing of genetic materials across groups and over time has maintained all of humankind as a single species....Today scholars in many fields argue that 'race' as it is understood in the United States of America was a social mechanism invented during the 18th century to refer to those populations brought together in colonial America: the English and other European settlers, the conquered Indian peoples, and those peoples of Africa brought in to provide slave labor....As they were constructing US society, leaders among European-Americans fabricated the cultural/behavioral characteristics associated with each 'race,' linking superior traits with Europeans and negative and inferior ones to blacks and Indians. Numerous arbitrary and fictitious beliefs about the different peoples were institutionalized and deeply embedded in American thought....Ultimately 'race' as an ideology about human differences was subsequently spread to other areas of the world. It became a strategy for dividing, ranking, and controlling colonized people used by colonial powers everywhere."[5]

Biologically, "race" is a meaningless term. It is based primarily on skin color, but skin color is infinitely variable. Many African Americans, for example, have skin as light as many European Americans, but are considered, and consider themselves, black. Similarly, there are people who identify themselves as white but whose skin color prompts people to think of them as black. "Racial" labels have outsize implications and consequences in America. In this book, we use the term "race" to name a social construction related to skin color.

"Color-blindness"

Owning our history, it is disingenuous and counter-productive to pretend that "racial" differences don't exist. Many inequities today are rooted in "race." As we work to treat all students fairly, regardless of their cultural backgrounds, we must acknowledge current inequalities and the history of denial of freedom and opportunity to some based on their color. This is part of our country's legacy. And speaking honestly about our history might make a difference in how a disadvantaged student feels about school.

In *Face to Face Advisories,* we try to walk the line (and ask you as an advisory leader to walk it with us) between acknowledging the power of "race" as a life-shaping force and refusing to grant it legitimacy as a basis for categorizing human beings into separate biological categories. We often use "color" where others might use "race" to describe the visible target for discrimination. Skin color has been a basis for exclusion and persecution in America, and certain skin color that prompts store managers to watch certain people intensely, and police to stop and interrogate certain people, and neighborhoods to exclude them.

We must acknowledge the false basis of "racial" categories whenever necessary if we are to seem believable to students who live the reality of discrimination every day. We tend to perceive people who are different from us through what education reformer and scholar Lisa Delpit calls our "culturally clouded vision."[6] We make assumptions and generalizations, usually inaccurate, about cultures outside our experience. No American is blind to skin color, and we must be honest about the differences among us and the ways our culture treats "racial" differences. We must work consciously and continually to eliminate the prejudice and discrimination that have followed on the heels of "racial" labels, not simply pretend they do not exist.

Inviting conversations in school about issues surrounding the concept of "race," as well as issues regarding a host of other cultural differences, may make a significant difference in how students from disadvantaged groups perform. Students of color, recent immigrants, those who live in poverty, and many others are more likely, some perhaps for the first time in their lives, to take an interest in and connect with a school community that acknowledges and respects them for who *they* say they are.

USING GUESTS TO BROADEN CULTURAL CONTENT

In addition to the insights students share in advisory conversations, we can draw on their families and other guests to deepen our understanding. See the advisories that include inviting guests to talk with students about their cultures: Perspective One, Advisory 13; Perspective Three, Advisory 16; and Perspective Five, Advisories 5 and 13. The descriptions for advisory meetings with guests include detailed instructions for preparing both the guest and the students.

Audience Guidelines

In addition to guest events, students are audience from time to time for each other's reports and performances. But not all students have good audience skills. Rather than assume that they know how to be a good audience, we need to prepare them with guidelines and, perhaps, practice.

Good listening/watching skills

- Focus on the performers, not on yourself or audience members

- Listen actively and get ready to comment or ask questions about the performance. Even if you don't get to ask or comment, preparing helps you be an active listener

- Be ready to support with details any opinions you express

- Listen to other people's questions: you will get more out of the answers, and you can avoid repeating someone else's question

- Listen and watch for interesting, original, entertaining, enlightening, well-expressed aspects of the presentation, and be ready to comment on them

- Think about whether and how the performance could be improved. Be ready to offer respectful suggestions if they are invited. If a comment won't help the performer, say it another way, or don't say it.

Introduce these guidelines before the first talk or performance in your advisory meetings, whether the speaker/performer is a guest or a member of the advisory. Post them, and review them right before subsequent performances and visits.

QUESTIONS AND ANSWERS ABOUT LEADING MEETINGS

Q. Do I need to do each and every advisory meeting in order?

The meetings are organized in a purposeful, scaffolded sequence, beginning with getting acquainted (see Community-Building Advisories chapter), moving to learning about our differences, then to learning about our interdependence and our tendency to divide along the lines of our differences, then to realizing our possibilities for change and growth, and finally inviting everyone to take a stand for a just society based on equity for all.

If you need to have fewer than the complete set of meetings, keep the meetings in sequence. For example, you wouldn't want to talk with students about taking a stand for equity before you talk about our possibilities for growth.

To retain as much effectiveness as possible, plan a series of meetings throughout a Perspective rather than doing, say, simply the first ten advisories in a Perspective and then moving on to the next Perspective.

If you know your school's advisory groups can't do all the Perspectives in a year, you may decide on one of the following options.

Divide the Perspectives among grade levels. For example:
Sixth grade: Perspectives One and Two
Seventh grade: Perspective Three (and maybe Four)
Eighth grade: Perspective (maybe Four and) Five

Or the entire middle level may take three years to engage in all five Perspectives:
Year one: Perspectives One and Two
Year two: Perspective Three and Four
Year three: Perspective Five

Q. What if students seem low-energy or distracted and we're scheduled for a particularly heavy topic?

You can insert a community-building CPR or A+ meeting (see Community-Building Advisories chapter) or a meeting of your own design into the sequence at any time. This is important if students seem distracted or stressed, and a little fun together would help them have a better day. *The Advisory Book* (Crawford, 2012) includes many advisories on lighter themes and for building community, and an index for creating your own.

Finally, you can visit the *Developmental Designs* Web site (www.DevelopmentalDesigns. org) and gather greetings, shares, and activities from the many descriptions there.

You may decide to insert one or more community-building meetings so students can lead certain activities or a whole meeting. With guidance from you, students can lead a greeting or announce the share question or introduce an activity.

⮑ Students can get to the point where they can plan and lead an entire regular advisory meeting, but the cultural topics in *Face to Face Advisories* require adult guidance and judgment, and thus do not lend themselves to student leadership.

Q. Some of these conversations and activities are challenging. How can I tell if my students are ready to engage in them productively?

Observe how they interact during the community-building activities that precede the five Perspectives. Do not skip these, even if your group has been together for a long time. They renew connections, lift spirits, and reveal any problems that you need to address before moving into the Perspectives. For example, if a student consistently avoids participation or consistently gets into conflict with certain others, or if some dominate and others participate at a very low level, and you can use those meetings to gauge the readiness of the group.

Q. Some of the games involve students getting very close or touching. How can I handle this without creating discomfort for anyone?

Provide a quick training on respectful touching as it applies to the activity (many activities include guidelines). Be explicit about where and how it is acceptable to touch someone. Demonstrate, and have students practice if you feel it would help. You can have girls and boys do the activity separately. Allow students to opt out if they are too uncomfortable. Anyone who opts out of the activity should participate by being a supportive audience, encouraging the players and cheering them on. Be sure anyone who opts out is in no way disparaged or criticized.

Q. There are words in the advisory meetings that my students may not know. Where can I find student-friendly definitions to share with them?

The glossary on page 346 defines many terms used in conversations about culture. You can provide copies of the list to your students, and/or post it for quick reference.

Q. What should I do with the underlined words in the daily news for each meeting?

The underlined words are sometimes relevant to the day's conversation, but most are meant to stretch adolescent vocabularies, and perhaps bridge cultural differences. See page 17 for suggestions on using them during the meetings.

Q. I'm a high school teacher. Are these meetings appropriate for 15-to-18-year-olds?

The content of these meetings is definitely appropriate for older students and even for adults (you might try out a few of the meeting activities at a staff meeting). Although high school students may resist participating in games, if you can get them past the "I'm too mature for that kid stuff" attitude, they will probably relax and enjoy.

---

[1] Deborah Meier, *The Power of Their Ideas*, (Boston: Beacon Press, 1995), 170.

[2] Terrance Kwame-Ross, Linda Crawford, and Erin Klug, "Developmental Designs: A Description of the Approach and Implementation in Schools," *Middle Grades Research Journal 6*, no. 3 (Fall 2011): 148

[3] Linda Crawford, *The Advisory Book: Building a Community of Learners Grades 5-9*, 2nd ed. (Minneapolis: The Origins Program, 2012).

[4] Amy Laboin, "An Idealist's Practical Steps to Achieve Goals," *Developmental Designs: A Middle Level Newsletter*, (September 2010): 2-3.

[5] Margaret Mead, *Sex and Temperament in Three Primitive Societies* (New York: Harper Perennial, 2001), 300. (Originally published 1935)

[6] "American Anthropological Association Statement on 'Race' (May 17, 1998)," http://www.aaanet.org/stmts/racepp.htm.

[7] Lisa Delpit, introduction to *Other People's Children: Cultural Conflict in the Classroom* (New York: The New Press, 2006), xxiv.

[8] Crawford, *The Advisory Book*.

Fifteen Meetings to Build Trust and Connection

In order for honest and fruitful advisory conversations about culture, bias, and discrimination to occur, they need to happen in the context of a group that feels connected and secure, whatever their differences. The advisory group must occur for students as a place where everyone is included and *feels* included. To create such a context, we must pay attention to elements such as who sits next to whom and the degree to which everyone has a voice, participates, experiences a sense of autonomy, and feels known and accepted. No one will speak frankly unless the atmosphere is affirming and inclusive.

What can we do then to create a friendly, inclusive context for advisory conversations on the challenging topic of cultural differences? We can get to know one another across those differences. We can be sure that everyone is greeted every day. We can invite personal thoughts and stories from our lives outside of school. And we can play together. In play, we shift from our differences and focus on the challenge at hand. If there is silliness and laughter, lots of changing of partners, a variety of activities—so much the better. These important elements for inclusivity are established in these 15 meetings and then infused in all *Face to Face Advisories* meetings to keep community strong.

COMMUNITY-BUILDING ADVISORY 1 ▶ CPR

Greeting

Partner Introduction Greeting: Each person introduces his/her partner to the group, stating the partner's name and his/her answer to the daily news questions (*This is Roberto Mendez. He likes pizza and soccer.*) The group responds by saying, *Good Morning* (or *Hi* or *Hey*), *Roberto*.

➲ As students introduce their partners, record the information they provide with each student's name on a class list. See below for more about recording advisory group information.

> Good Morning, Advisory Group Members— welcome!
>
> Today is our first Circle of Power and Respect. I'm <u>anticipating</u> learning more about everyone. <u>Do Now</u>: Pull a name from the box. Interview that person, and be ready to tell the group answers to these questions:
>
> 1. Name
> 2. Food he/she enjoys
> 3. Activity he/she enjoys
>
> Take a seat in the circle. We'll begin our meeting at _____.

Share

Partner Interview Share: Provide partners with paper and pencil and two or three additional getting-to-know-you questions (see examples below). Partners interview each other and record the information under or beside their names. Specify a time limit for a share. Give a warning halfway through the share to ensure balanced sharing/listening. If there is time, one person from each partner group shares out.

➲ Record share responses on the list used for the greeting. Title the list "Our Favorite Foods, Activities, and Partner Interviews." You can also collect the papers and transfer the information to the list yourself. The group will compile this information and more to come into an Advisory Almanac (see Advisory 11). You will need six separate class lists in total. Store all the lists in an Advisory Almanac folder. Explain to students that they are gathering information about the group for a later project.

Interview question examples:

What is something you've never done that you would like to do?

What is your pet peeve (something that irritates you)?

Activity

Who Remembers? After everyone has shared information with the group during the greeting and the share, ask students to recall people's answers (e.g., *Who remembers what Jason has never done, but wants to do? Who remembers Sondra's pet peeve? Who in our group loves playing the piano?*).

COMMUNITY-BUILDING ADVISORY 2 ▶ CPR

Greeting

Clap Call and Response Greeting led by teacher: Teacher claps a rhythm and calls out the name of a student, *Hey, _____!* Whole group claps out the same rhythm, then the person named responds, *Hey, class!* (or *group* or *all* or *people* or *friends*). Repeat for each person in the class. After you lead this whole greeting at least once, when students are ready to lead and the group is ready to follow a student leader, you can invite students to lead in subsequent meetings.

> Greetings, Friends!
> We gathered some interesting <u>data</u> about ourselves yesterday, and today we'll learn more. Be thinking about an animal you have or would like to have for a pet.

Share

Whip Share: *Describe a pet you have, used to have, or would like to have.* Each student gives a brief response; responses go around the circle. Records responses on a class list for the almanac project in Advisory 11. Title the list "Our Pets."

➲ Remind students that you record each response, so they should watch you to pace their responses.

Activity

Call and Response Rhythms: Select a student to give the call (or do it yourself) by clapping or drumming a rhythm. Each individual takes a turn at responding to the call with an original rhythm. After each response, the leader repeats the individual's call, then everyone in the group repeats that rhythm. The leader then gives the call to another individual, who responds with an original rhythm of his own, and the process continues. Each person in the group gets a turn at responding to the leader's call with an original rhythm, which is then repeated by the group.

COMMUNITY-BUILDING ADVISORY 3 ▶ CPR

Greeting

Clap Call and Response Greeting: Teacher claps a rhythm and calls out the name of a student, *Hey, _____!* Whole group claps out the same rhythm and then the person named responds, *Hey, class!* (or *group* or *all* or *people* or *friends*). Repeat for everyone in the class.

> Good Morning, All! Today we'll continue with our Clap Call and Response greeting. Meanwhile, think about people you like and why you like them. <u>Do Now</u>: Put a check mark next to the <u>attribute</u> that is most important to you in a friend:
>
> Loyalty   Honesty   Kindness   Talent

Share

Whip Share: *What qualities are most important to you in a friend?* Each student gives a brief response; responses "whip" around the circle. Record responses on a class list for the almanac project in Advisory 11. Title this list "What We Value in Friends."

Activity

Talking Cards: *List the personality qualities you especially enjoy in people.* Students write their responses on index cards. No names—this exercise is anonymous. Collect the cards, read the responses, and tally them. Note how many different qualities the group enjoys and which ones were named by more than one person.

COMMUNITY-BUILDING ADVISORY 4 ▶ CPR

Greeting

Clap Call and Response Greeting led by teacher (or student): Leader claps a rhythm and calls out the name of a student, *Hey, _____!* Whole group claps the rhythm, then the person named responds, *Hey, class!* (or *group* or *all* or *people* or *friends*). Greet everyone in the circle this way.

> Hello, Music Lovers!
>
> Be thinking about your favorite kind of music, and get ready to share what music you think your mom would say is her favorite!

Share

Whip Share: *What kind of music do you like? What kind of music does your mom like?* Each student gives a brief response; responses "whip" around the circle. Record responses on a class list for the almanac project in Advisory 11. Title the list "Music We Like (and Our Moms Like!)."

Activity

When the Cold Wind Blows: Students sit in a circle. One student stands in the middle of the circle, and his chair is removed. He says, *When the cold wind blows, it blows for anyone who_____,* filling in the blank with a category such as *has a dog* or *is left-handed.* Everyone who fits that category rises and quickly finds a new place to sit, including the person in the middle. The one student who doesn't find a seat stands in the center of the circle and continues the game by saying, *When the cold wind blows, it blows for anyone who* _____, naming a new category. The teacher can call the first round.

⮑ To learn more about each other, use categories that relate to personal traits, interests, hobbies, and families, rather than, say, clothing or appearance. Give students some examples: *The cold wind blows for anyone who:*

- sometimes quarrels with siblings

- has attended two schools or more

- has a family pet

- is the youngest in your immediate family

- enjoys playing a team sport

- enjoys more than one kind of music

- has a hard time getting up in the morning

- likes to stay up late

- plays video games

- does babysitting at home or for others

- likes pizza

- likes turnips!

⮑ Before playing, model and practice safe chair-changing, including how to claim a chair by tagging it first, so students know how to move quickly and safely during the game.

COMMUNITY-BUILDING ADVISORY 5 ▶ CPR

Greeting

Clap Call and Response Greeting led by teacher or student: Leader claps a rhythm and calls out the name of a student, *Hey, _____!* Whole group claps out the same rhythm and then the person named responds, *Hey, class!* (or *group* or *all* or *people*, etc.). Repeat for each person in the circle.

> Greetings, Foodies!
>
> Our topic today is food—unusual foods and those we like a lot. <u>Do Now:</u> Write below a <u>victual</u> that your family eats that is unusual or that you especially enjoy. If the food is already named, add a check mark beside it, or think of a different one.

Share

Partner Share: Three foods in our dream meal. Note the favorite foods students have listed on the daily news chart. Then, on paper, partners list three foods they choose for their dream meal.

Activity

Spend the Dot: Display the papers (post or lay them on desks) so everyone can review them. Distribute markers to students. Individuals *dot* three of the dream meals that they like best. Collect the papers and count dots to determine the group's three favorite. Option: end activity with a pretzel for all (the talk about food will make everyone hungry!). Record the dream meals on a class list for the almanac project in Advisory 11. Title the list "Our Dream Meals."

COMMUNITY-BUILDING ADVISORY 6 ▶ CPR

Greeting

Name Exercise Greeting: Students spell their names, acting out the letters according to the following rules: For tall letters, such as t, l, and b, students stretch their arms up; for letters that are neither tall nor go below the line, such as e, a, and n, students hold their arms straight out; for letters that extend below the line, such as g, p, and y, students touch their toes. *Good morning. My name is Billy: B*(arms up), *i* (arms straight out); *l* (arms up); *l* (arms up); *y (touch toes).* Everyone: *Good morning, Billy.*

⮌ **Varition:** Time permitting, everyone spells out the person's name.

Share

Partner Share: *Discuss how this school year could be great for you. What goal do you have?* Specify a length of time to share. Issue a time warning halfway through the share to ensure balanced sharing/listening.

Activity

Huddle Up: Each time you read one of the following statements, students move about to find the group they fit into. When everyone is in a group, have the groups call out their category name, for example, *We like chocolate ice cream!* While waiting for the call-out time, groups can discuss their category (see topics below).

Huddle up with those who:

- *favor the same flavor of ice cream* (discuss what kind of cone you prefer)

- *have a birthday in the same month* (discuss what day)

- *enjoy playing or watching the same sport* (discuss what you like about it)

- *would like to visit the same state or country* (discuss what you would do there)

- *have achieved a goal* (discuss what goal)

COMMUNITY-BUILDING ADVISORY 7 ▶ A+

Greeting

Ball Toss Greeting: Select a student to begin, and give her a soft indoor ball, bean bag, or stuffed animal. She greets somebody verbally, then tosses that student the ball (model a safe, on-target, underhand toss). The recipient of the ball returns the greeting, greets someone else, then tosses him the ball. This continues until all have been greeted once and have received and tossed the ball. Students put their hands behind their backs to signal that they have been greeted. The last student greeted closes the loop by greeting and tossing the ball to the student who went first.

> Greetings, Friends!
> Today we'll revisit the cards we wrote on the qualities we enjoy in people, and we'll use the <u>Affinity</u> Process to decide which qualities are most important to us as a group.

➲ If time allows for additional rounds, challenge them to exactly duplicate the sequence of the first round, or add one more ball, then another, and have several going at one time.

Activity

Affinity Process: Students will discuss the qualities of people (the *qualities*, not the people!) they like (they wrote the qualities in Advisory 3, Talking Cards). They will look for qualities that everyone admires, or that many admire. Students mingle, talking with each other to find partners with whom they have responses in common (e.g., *I like people who make me laugh. Do you?*). Then the partners find another twosome and look for a characteristic they *all* share. Next, foursomes create affinity groups of eight who all admire the same quality, and so on, until all are in one large group with at least one thing in common that all enjoy in others.

➲ You may decide to stop the mingling/consolidating when it becomes cumbersome or when you're running short of time. One person from each group may report out what their group likes in others, and everyone can look for whole-group commonalities.

Reflection

Think about the qualities we have been naming. Which ones do you strive to develop in yourself?

COMMUNITY-BUILDING ADVISORY 8 ▶ A+

Greeting

Ball Toss Greeting: Select a student to begin and give her a ball (soft indoor ball, bean bag, or stuffed animal). She greets another student by name, then tosses that student the ball (model a safe, on-target, underhand toss). The recipient of the ball returns the greeting, greets someone else, then tosses him the ball. This continues until all students have been greeted once and have received and tossed the ball. Students put their hands behind their backs to signal that they have been greeted. The last student greeted closes the loop by greeting and tossing the ball to the student who went first.

> Welcome, Decision-makers!
> Today we will figure out some <u>norms</u> that will help us be the kind of people we want for friends. <u>Do Now</u>: Below, write one rule you think we should have for our group.

➲ For additional rounds, try to exactly duplicate the sequence of the first round or add more balls and have several going at one time.

Activity

Group Norms: Groups of four to six brainstorm guidelines for how our group should behave in order to be like the kind of friend we most want. (This process may require two meetings.) Sample norms: mutual respect; presume positive intentions; speak from your own experience; talk about yourself, not others. From the list developed with contributions from each group, use a consensus process to choose three guidelines that will support the safety and wellbeing of everyone in the group.

The consensus process involves discussing the list of suggested norms, allowing all views to be aired. If there is disagreement, the group makes modifications until all can agree on a list of three rules. In the *Developmental Designs* approach, this process is called creating the Social Contract (see page 22). The final three norms will be placed in the almanac.

➲ If necessary, take two advisory meetings to settle on three norms that everyone can support. They will be community guidelines for the entire year and are well worth the time it takes to go through the consensus process carefully.

Reflection

Exit Cards: *Which one of the norms we set will be easiest for you to follow? Which will be hard?* Students each write answers to the two questions on a card, which they hand in as they leave the room. Tally the answers and report the results at the next advisory meeting.

COMMUNITY-BUILDING ADVISORY 9 ▶ CPR

Greeting

Introduction Greeting: Have one person introduce every person in the circle, or have each person introduce the person to his/her right: *Good morning, everyone. This is _____.* The whole group responds in unison: *Good morning, _____.*

Share

Partner Share: *What might be challenges in following the rules we have made for ourselves? What can we do to help everyone stick to them?* Specify a time limit for a share. Give a warning halfway through the share to ensure balanced sharing/listening.

> *Good Morning, Friends!*
> I have tallied your Exit Cards from our last meeting. Here is the list of our guidelines for ourselves in the order of what most people considered the hardest to follow:
> 1)_____
> 2)_____
> 3)_____
> We'll talk today about how to help ourselves follow our rules.

Activity

Silent Line-up in Alphabetical Order: Students line up in alphabetical order (choose first name or last name) silently, so they must communicate without speaking—good practice in cooperation!

COMMUNITY-BUILDING ADVISORY 10 ▶ CPR

Greeting

I Sit in the Grass: Students sit in a circle in which there is one empty chair. To start, the student to the right of the empty chair says, *I sit,* and moves one place to the left, occupying the empty chair. The student to the right of the newly vacated chair says, *in the grass,* and also moves one place to the left, occupying the empty chair. The student to the right of that newly vacated chair also moves one place to the left and says, *with my friend _____,* naming someone across the circle. These two students then exchange a simple greeting (*Good morning, _____*). The one who was named responds with, *Good Morning, _____,* rises, and moves to the chair vacated by the student who named him. In doing so, his chair becomes empty, and the student to the right of it starts the process again, by occupying it and saying, *I sit.* This continues until all students have been called a friend and have been greeted.

> *Welcome!*
> Three things I like about Uncle Bernie are that he's a hard worker and generous and loves music. Think about someone you like and what it is you like about him or her. Get ready to share with a partner.

⊃ Substitute for "Uncle Bernie" a relationship, name, and qualities of someone you personally admire.

Share

Partner Share: *Describe a favorite person in your life. What about him or her do you especially enjoy?* Specify a length of time to share. Issue a time warning halfway through the share to ensure balanced sharing/listening. Volunteers share out. Record responses for the almanac project in Advisory 11. Title the list "Our Favorite People."

Activity

What's in a Name? Form groups of four; each group has a piece of paper and a pencil. Choose a topic (see examples below). Players write their names (first and last; middle optional) at the top of their group's paper. Groups then brainstorm words that both fit the selected topic and begin with letters that can be found in their names. When they are finished, each group stands up and names its best three words. Students can also be acknowledged for having the most words, the longest word, or the most words with more than three letters.

Topic examples:

List as many words as you can that are associated with weather.

List as many periodic-table elements as you can.

List as many different kinds of mammals (or birds or insects) as you can.

COMMUNITY-BUILDING ADVISORY 11 ▶ A+

Greeting

Ball Toss Greeting: Select a student to begin and give her a ball (soft indoor ball, bean bag, or stuffed animal). She greets another student, then tosses that student the ball (model a safe, on-target, underhand toss). The recipient of the ball returns the greeting, greets someone else, then tosses him the ball. This continues until all students have been greeted once and have received and tossed the ball. Students put their hands behind their backs to signal that they have greeted. The last student greets the first.

> Good Morning, Researchers!
>
> Today is the day we'll start putting together all the information we've been learning about each other. We'll create an almanac for our advisory, a record of who we are and some of the things we care about.
>
> Do Now: Below, write some topics we have not yet explored about ourselves. For example, we haven't found out about the books and movies we like best, or our hobbies.

↻ For additional rounds, try to exactly duplicate the sequence of the first round or add more balls and have several going at one time.

Activity

Advisory Almanac: Students collect addition information about the group and assemble this and the already recorded information into reports. Begin by brainstorming a list of questions (you'll need about half the number of questions as people in the group). Partners sign up next to a question on the brainstormed list. They begin asking other students their question and recording the answers. After polling the entire group, partners represent their results on paper with words, numbers, and/or visuals such as graphs and charts.

Almanac question examples:

- What are the genders and ages of your siblings?
- How many cousins do you have?
- Where were you born (city/state)?
- What is a place you would like to visit?
- What month and day is your birthday?
- What is a color you especially like?
- What is a sport you enjoy watching or playing?
- What is something you would like to get good at?
- Do you have a hobby? What is it?
- What school subject is easiest for you? Hardest? What is your favorite?
- What is something you have accomplished?
- Have you ever had an embarrassing moment? What was it?
- What's a mistake you have made?
- What is something that makes you happy?
- What is something that makes you mad?
- What qualities are important to you in a friend?
- Name a book that you enjoyed.
- Name a movie that you enjoyed.

➲ Partners who finish can create reports on the seven pieces of information already recorded from shares and activities:

- Our Favorite Foods, Activities, and Partner Introductions
- Our Pets
- Music We Like (and Our Moms Like!)
- What We Value in Friends
- Our Dream Meals
- Our Favorite People
- Our Rules

When all the information is gathered and compiled, the pages can be integrated. The resulting Advisory Almanac can be displayed on the walls or assembled into a book. The book can be placed in the classroom where students can look through it and it can be shown to visitors. The advisory group can also use their almanac to reflect at the end of the year on things that have changed.

COMMUNITY-BUILDING ADVISORY 12 ▶ A+

Greeting

Formal Greeting with group response: All wear nametags with first and last names. Each person greets the group by saying, *Good morning, everyone. My name is Mr. (or Ms.)* _____. The group in unison responds back: *Good morning, Mr.* _____. This process avoids the problem of students not knowing how to pronounce certain names.

> Hello, Students!
> What was your poll topic? List it below and initial your response.

➲ Smiles and giggles often result when adolescents try on formality. This is fine, but not sarcasm or mockery. If you detect any, direct the student to try it again with friendly respect (or to sit out, if it was intentional).

Activity

Advisory Almanac: Students continue to gather and assemble almanac information by creating and conducting mini-surveys and compiling data into reports.

Reflection

Why is it useful to take polls?

COMMUNITY-BUILDING ADVISORY 13 ▶ A+

Greeting

I Am Going to Paris (or choose another destination): Select a student to begin by saying, *I am going to Paris, and I will bring _____ with me* (names a person in the group). *Hi, _____ (the person he is inviting).* The next student names a new person,

then the previous student's person, so the list is cumulative. Play continues until all have had a turn and the last person has named everyone in the group in the order that they were named.

Examples:

Student 1: *I am going to Paris, and I will take Marvin. Good morning, Marvin.*
Student 2: *I am going to Paris, and I will take Marvin and Angel. Good morning, Marvin and Angel.*
Student 3: *I am going to Paris, and I will take Marvin, Angel, and Anthony. Good morning, Marvin, Angel, and Anthony.*
➲ Students can ask for help, which should be given quickly and with no hint of put-down. To make the greeting much easier and quicker, have each person name the person next to him or her, so as names are added, the greeters can just look around the circle to get the order of names correct. This takes both the choice and the challenge out of the greeting, but it is still fun to hear the list get longer and longer.

Activity

Planning Meeting on topic: *How should we celebrate our birthdays in advisory?* Follow this process:

1. Whip Share: *What is something you'd like to include in a birthday celebration?* Someone scribes the suggestions on a chart or board.

2. Consolidate the suggestions, and eliminate any that are impractical.

3. Allow students to briefly express support for an idea that they like.

4. Considering the time limitations of your advisory meeting, choose one or two suggestions from the list by consensus (general agreement of all, with those who would prefer another choice being willing to go along with the group). An alternative is to end with a list of ways to celebrate from which the birthday person could choose at the meeting before the birthday celebration.

Reflection

Some cultures do not celebrate birthdays, while many do so annually. Do you think it's important to celebrate birthdays? Why?

COMMUNITY-BUILDING ADVISORY 14 ▶ CPR

Greeting

Elephant Greeting: Students stand in a circle. Select one to be the first person to call out the name of a classmate. When a student's name is called, she becomes the elephant by dangling an arm in front of her face to represent the trunk. At the same time, the students to the left and right of her put their hands in front of *her* (not their own) ears, palms out, to represent the elephant's large ears. As soon as all three are in position, the student whose name was called quickly calls on another player to do the same, and the first group of three is finished with their elephant. This requires students to pay close attention at all times.

> Good Morning, <u>Celebrants</u>!
> What's your idea of a dream birthday? We'll share about that today.

Share

Partner Share: *What is one thing you would like to do to celebrate your birthday outside of school?* Share out around the circle. Each person names one way he or she would like to celebrate a birthday.

Activity

Simultaneous Clap: There are several "rounds" in this activity, and they are increasingly challenging.

1. In a standing circle, the starting person claps, then, moving to the right or left, each person claps in sequence around the circle, keeping a smooth rhythm and with no hesitations.

2. The starting person claps both hands with the person next to him (double high-five style). This clap is passed between pairs around the circle.

3. The starting two people turn to each other and attempt to clap their hands at the same moment (each claps her own hands). The next pair forms (one from the first pair and the next student) and attempts the clap, and so on around the circle.

4. As a closing, holding hands at the ready, everyone tries to clap at the same moment. This may take some practice and requires students to pay very close attention to each other.

➲ To avoid clapping that is too vigorous between players, practice gentle clapping before round one.

COMMUNITY-BUILDING ADVISORY 15 ▶ CPR

Greeting

Jig-A-Low Greeting: Ask for a student volunteer to be first responders in the following call and response chant. Going counter-clockwise around the circle, everyone is greeted.

All: *Jig-a-low, jig, jig, a-low* (say this twice)
Hey, _____ ! (name of volunteer)
Person named: *Hey, what?*
All: *Can you jig?*
Person named: *Jig what?*
All: *Jig-a-low?*
Person named: *I raise my hands up high* (raise hands over head), *my feet down low* (pointing to feet), *and this is how I jig-a-low* (make up a movement).
All: *His hands up high* (raise hands over head),*his feet down low* (pointing to own feet), *and this is how he jigs-a-low* (repeat movement).
All: *Jig-a-low, jig, jig, a-low* (say this twice) *Hey, _____ !* (name of next person in circle)

Continue chant until all students have been greeted.

➲ This greeting takes more time than most—especially if you have some in the group who make complicated moves!

> Dear Friends,
> Today I'll introduce you to the Jig-A-Low Greeting—get ready to share your good moves with us! We'll also see how well we already know each other, and we'll <u>simultaneously</u> learn more.

Share

Rare Birds Share: Give each student an index card. Ask students to write their names on the card and answer these questions:

List three things you like to do outside of school.

What is your pet peeve (something that annoys you)?

What is your philosophy of life?

Activity

Rare Birds: Collect and shuffle the cards. Then read the answers from one card aloud, not revealing whose card it is. The group has three guesses to determine who is the "rare bird" who gave those answers. The person who gave the answers adds a little detail about something he or she wrote on the card. Read and ask for guesses on as many cards as time permits; save the rest for other times.

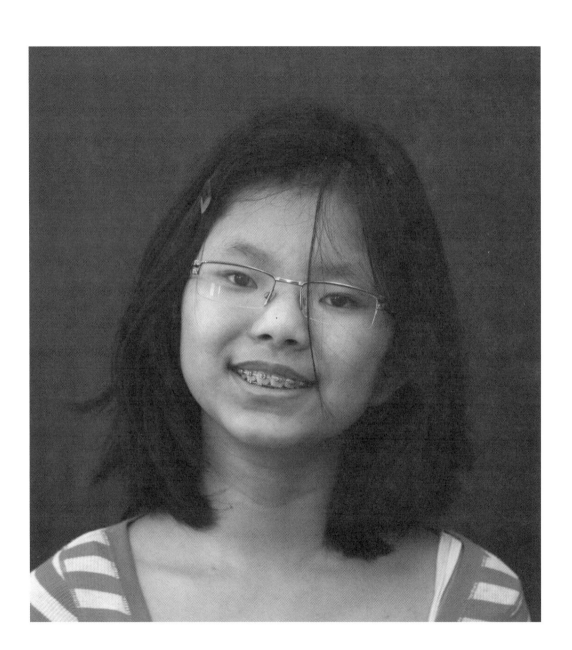

Identity and Diversity

In the youth novel *Bronx Masquerade*, by Nikki Grimes, Tyrone Bittings is a high school student who has come to believe that he has little chance for success in life:

"School ain't nothin' but a joke. My moms don't want to hear that, but if it weren't for Wesley and my other homeys, I wouldn't even be here, aiight? These white folk talking 'bout some future, telling me I need to be planning for some future—like I got one! And Raynard agreeing, like he's smart enough to know. From what I hear, that boy can't hardly read! Anyway, it's them white folk that get me with this *future* mess. Like Steve, all hopped up about working on Broadway and telling me I should think about getting with it too. Asked me if I ever thought about writing plays. "Fool! What kinda question is that?" I said. He threw his hands up and backed off a few steps."[1]

How did Tyrone become a person who thought the idea that he would plan for a future was ridiculous? How did any of us get to be who we are? That is the question we ask ourselves in Perspective One as we examine our lives—where, how, and with whom we live, and how all of it shapes us. We will examine complex issues: how our individual cultures affect us, our personalities and preferences, our relationships with others, the decisions we make.

Much of who we are is shaped by the circumstances into which we were born and the influences around us as we grow. Many of those influences persist into adulthood. Our diversity shows up powerfully in American public schools. The variety of languages, colors, ethnicities, religions, gender identities, abilities, and sexual orientations in our schools can give rise to misunderstanding and fear, or it can inspire us to explore our differences and similarities, our traditions and hopes, our diverse histories, and the ways our histories affect our lives and learning.

Exploration clarifies and strengthens students' ability to learn and educators' ability to teach the wide variety of learners in today's classrooms. Can it be done efficiently and effectively, even with enjoyment, in school schedules already pressed with federal and state requirements, standardized tests, and the developmental and behavioral challenges of adolescents?   The advisory period provides a great opportunity. In advisory, students come face to face with each other for fifteen or twenty minutes several times weekly. These can become the best few minutes of the week for making friends, strengthening the school community, and building understanding amid diversity.

The advisory meetings in Perspective One invite discussion about all aspects of culture.

Some aspects have greater impact than others: three that strongly influence students' education are their family and friends, their socio-economic class, and their ethnicity/color. Advisories 3, 4, and 6 are among the meetings that consider these influences in Perspective One.

Mindsets

The mental framework through which we view our students, their families, and our tasks as educators determines in large part the way we teach each day. Three teacher mindsets (first described on pages 22-24) are extremely useful in helping adolescents learn and grow. *Face to Face Advisories* also develop these productive mindsets in students.

Growth mindset

Growth includes change, and often requires us to shift our point of view. A teacher or student with a growth mindset can cultivate the skill of looking from several points of view. This is a good way to avoid getting stuck in stereotypes. In the advisory meetings designed for these conversations, we take the perspectives of people within a culture as well as people outside it. We listen to scholars who have studied cultures in comparison to other cultures, and we listen to first-hand accounts of people immersed in their cultures. We pay attention to stories of the powerless and the powerful. In other words, we expand our perspective and guard against oversimplification by presenting stories from multiple sources. This allows us to listen and think in an open-minded way, and perhaps see familiar things in new ways.

Action and objective mindsets

Working with each other across cultures requires leadership that is both energetic and diplomatic, rooted in commitment to honor everyone equally. Along the way, someone may say something that offends another. As leaders, we must notice and correct any slips toward biased thinking, explicit or implicit. This becomes a powerful model for students to internalize.

ADVISORY 1 ▶ A+

Advisory goal: Gain insight into our group—what we think, like, trust, and wish for as a group made up of unique individuals

Greeting

Ball Toss Greeting: Select a student to begin and give her a ball (soft indoor ball, bean bag, or stuffed animal). She greets another student, then tosses that student the ball (model a safe, on-target, underhanded toss). The recipient of the ball re-

> Hello, Advisory Members!
>
> Today we'll learn more about our group as a whole. Talking Cards will tell us, and they never <u>prevaricate</u>!

turns the greeting, greets someone else, then tosses him the ball. This continues until all students have been greeted once and have received and tossed the ball. The last student greeted greets and tosses the ball to the student who went first.

Activity

Talking Cards: Who are we? Students answer on index cards the questions below about themselves, one response per card (to save on resources, cut index cards in half for this activity). Students do *not* write their names on the cards, since the purpose of this activity is to see the range of answers in the group, not to learn about individual identities. But they do note the number of the question they are responding to on each card. Read each question, allow time for writing responses, collect and sort the cards by the question they address, and label each set with its question's number.

⮌ Students will complete the step of answering the questions in this activity and continue with the Talking Cards exercise in the next advisory meeting. Match the number of questions the students can successfully complete to your allotted advisory time. For example, in 20-minute advisories students will likely be able to answer all the questions; shorter advisories may allow for only some of the twelve questions.

Talking Card questions for Who are we?

Adapted from *100 Ways to Enhance Self-Concept in the Classroom*, by Jack Canfield & Harold C. Wells2

1. I'm at my best when ...

2. People I trust are ...

3. I don't like people who ...

4. The best thing that could happen to me is ...

5. When I don't like something I've done, I ...

6. When I like something I've done, I ...

7. I'm very happy that ...

8. I wish my parents knew ...

9. In general, I think school is ...

10. I would like to ...

11. I hope that someday ...

12. The thing I like best about this group is ...

⮑ Remember that the Talking Cards exercise is anonymous: it is meant not to reveal individual characteristics, but to reveal the variety of responses in the group. The responses can offer insight into the impact their cultures have had on students' lives.

Reflection

Reflection occurs in Advisory 2. See below for questions.

Keep in Mind

Definition of culture

In these conversations, we call the values, beliefs, attitudes, and practices—the sum effect of all the influences on us in the particular place, time, and environment in which we live—our culture (see page 24 for more about defining culture). Examining cultures provides insights into ourselves and each other, since our cultures strongly influence the choices we make and the direction of our lives.

Observing the answers students give to the Talking Cards *Who Are We* questions can reveal some of the ways they think both alike and differently, and students will begin to get a feeling for the variety of attitudes and values in the group. The activity is designed to begin a conversation about culture on a personal level, so students can talk about values and hopes and opinions in a non-judgmental, good-spirited way.

Ask yourself

What are your *answers to the Talking Cards questions?* Decide whether to participate in the activity by writing answers to the questions. Participating would show that you are with the group in this process.

ADVISORY 2 ▶ CPR

Advisory goal: Become familiar with a variety of languages and levels of formality in language, and gain insight into our group

⮑ If Spanish is the first language for many students in your advisory, you may want to choose a different language or remove the note about pronunciation. See page 349 for greeting language options.

Greeting

Language Greeting: All students greet with *Hola, _____,* either around the circle or in the All Group Greeting format. (All Group Greeting format: *Hola, everyone.* Group responds: *Hola, Daniel.*)

> Hola, Amigos!
> We can learn to say hello in several languages. Today we're using a <u>colloquial</u> Spanish greeting. The "H" is silent. We'll try out different greetings and make a Ways to Say Hello list as we go. <u>Do Now:</u> On the Ways to Say Hello sheet below, write a greeting you know in a language other than English. Think of ways to say "hello" that are used in informal English (for example, "howdy").

Share

Whip Share: *Share a greeting in English that does not include "hello" or "hi." These can be slang or colloquial words (for example,* Good day, S'up? What's happening? How do). *Repeats are OK.* Each student offers a brief response to the topic; responses quickly "whip" around the circle.

⮑ Record the greetings on the Ways to Say Hello list. You are creating a list that you can use for the rest of the year. Get as much variety as possible in the list by using not only different languages, but different levels of formality, so that some of the talk students use in their families and neighborhoods they can also use and hear in the classroom. Make two columns, one for more formal greetings and the other for less formal.

Activity

Talking Cards: *Who Are We?* (continued from Advisory 1) Divide students into the number of questions they responded to in Advisory 1. Distribute one set of response Talking Cards to each group. Groups sort them, grouping similar answers together, and tally the results. One member from each group reports the results to the whole group.

⮑ To guide successful whole-group reporting, suggest that students first indicate which question their cards address, then read directly what is written on cards that represent unique responses and paraphrase responses shared by a number of students, indicating how many gave roughly that response. (E.g., *Five students wrote that people they trust are people they know well or people they've spent a lot of time with.*)

Reflection

Were any of the questions difficult for you to answer?

Did any of the group's answers surprise you?

Do you think this group is typical of other groups of students in your school? In your town/ city? In the U.S.?

Keep in Mind

By using a variety of languages, including casual English used by students outside of school, we begin to remove the stigma attached to speaking in certain ways. Perceived as a flexible instrument that takes many forms and provides color and variety in life, language can connect instead of divide us. We must teach students how to use standard English so they can use it when necessary, but we also want our students to know that we respect their varied, often colorful ways of speaking a more vernacular English as well as other languages. Students are likely to feel more connected to school if they sometimes can relax into ways of communicating that are characteristic of their cultures. Throughout these advisory meetings, we sometimes play with language so that language itself becomes a topic of interest and enjoyment, not a code used by one group that alienates another.

Ask yourself

Are there informal words and phrases you use exclusively with friends and family?

ADVISORY 3 ▶ CPR

Advisory goals: Know one another culturally. Appreciate variety in language as a benefit of living amid a variety of cultures.

Greeting

Basic Greeting using Ways to Say Hello list (created in Advisory 2): Select a student to begin. She greets the student either to her left or right with one of the ways, for example, *Howdy, _____;* he responds with another of the ways, for example, *What's happenin', _____?* He turns to the next person and greets him, and the process is repeated around the circle.

> Ciao, Friends!
>
> Check out our Ways to Say Hello list, choose one, and greet the person(s) next to you. The share question today will be: What do you know about the meaning of your name and why it was chosen for you? We'll be looking for volunteers to share out.

Share

Partner Share: *What do you know about the meaning of your name and why your family chose it? Was it because they liked the sound of it? Were you named for someone? Does your name have special meaning?* Specify a length of time to share. Issue a time warning halfway through the share to ensure balanced sharing/listening. Afterward, volunteers share out to the whole group.

➲ Suggest that students who do not know about the significance of their given names ask about it at home. The information could be included in Identity Shares (see Advisory 5). To lessen any discomfort students may have about a lack of information about their names, assure all that this will be just one of many items that might comprise Identity Shares.

Activity

When the Cold Wind Blows: Students sit in a circle. One student stands in the middle of the circle, and his chair is removed. He says, *When the cold wind blows, it blows for anyone who_____*, filling in the blank with a category such as *has a dog* or *is left-handed.* Everyone who fits that category rises and quickly finds a new place to sit, including the person in the middle. The one student who doesn't find a seat stands in the center of the circle and continues the game by saying, *When the cold wind blows, it blows for anyone who _____*, naming a new category. The activity continues for several rounds.

➲ For today's game, in order to learn more about each other's lives, limit categories to ones that relate to interests, hobbies, and family, rather than allowing students to focus, say, on clothing or appearance. For example, *the cold wind blows for anyone who:*

- has more than two siblings
- has moved in the last year
- speaks more than one language
- is the oldest child in the family
- enjoys playing a sport
- enjoys music
- has a hard time getting up in the morning

↪ Model and practice safe chair-changing before playing, including how to claim a chair by tagging it first, so students know how to move quickly and safely during the game.

Keep in Mind

Our names help define us. To know my name is to begin to know me. This advisory meeting provides a taste of the kind of sharing about culture that helps the group get to know one another, learn about their cultural backgrounds, and get insights into what may have influenced who they have become.

Influence of family and friends

One of the greatest influences on us from the start is the people with whom we have close, frequent contact. Family members are the models we first imitate, and their imprint lasts a lifetime. In fact, our opinions and values may come mostly from our families, having little to do with autonomous choice. Here are some quotes from educators that reflect these influences.

My mother and father were Democrats; everyone in our family voted Democratic. When I was only four, my dad took me into the polling booth, pointed to the "D" for "Democratic," and told me to pull down all the levers on that side. I've been a Democrat ever since.

My dad was a labor organizer and fought for the rights of factory workers. I became a freedom rider in the civil rights struggles of the 60's.

My mom valued education, and even though we had little money, she made sure we all got good educations. I decided I wanted to be an educator.

Added to family influence is the cultural impact of our peers as we mature. Most adolescents talk and dress like their peers, watch and read the same things, use a shared peer language, and seek popularity among their peers.

When I was a kid and hung out with the cool kids from working-class Italian families, I felt I needed to deny my class, my father's wealth, so I would be accepted.

In her book *The Nurture Assumption*[3], Judith Harris asserts that our peers have greater influence on us than our families do. Even so, family influence carries great weight. Like it or not, we often find ourselves cooking and talking and opinionating in the same ways our mothers and fathers do or did.

Making it easier to share

We build community through play. Sharing and hearing about each other in the context of a game helps students relax and enjoy themselves. Playing an active game with vigor *and* safety builds the trust and self-control critical to cultural conversations.

Ask yourself

How was your name chosen for you? Consider sharing with your students.

ADVISORY 4 ▶ A+

Advisory goal: Understand the many cultural factors that shape our identities

Greeting

High Five Greeting: In sequence around the circle, students greet each other with a high five: *Hi, Ahmed.* (high five) Reply: *Hi, Kim.* (high five)

> Good Morning, Everyone!
>
> Today we'll continue looking at the elements in life that make us who we are, that shape our way of thinking and behaving. Think about what <u>influences</u> you.

Activity

What Shapes Our Identities? PowerPoint

(See www.originsonline.org/developmental-designs/what-shapes-our-identities)
The brief PowerPoint (15 slides) provides a series of images and captions that introduce aspects of life that contribute to shaping our identities. If you cannot show the PowerPoint to students, you can print its text and have students take turns reading it aloud.

Reflection

Distribute the Cultural Elements that Have Shaped Me form to each student, and direct them to describe in writing the elements that have affected their lives. Collect and save these forms as resources for the Identity Shares, which begin with a teacher Identity Share in Advisory 6.

Keep in Mind

Through the lens of cultural influences we can learn more about ourselves and others. There are many influences. The PowerPoint lists cultural elements such as family, neighborhood, color, ethnicity, language, school, natural environment, gender, religion, affluence, and social class. Social class influences learning in school particularly strongly.

More and more, America is a nation of extremes of wealth and poverty. Urban, suburban, and rural impoverished areas, where daily survival is a matter of coping with poverty, homelessness, pollution, and chronic hunger, stand in stark contrast to affluent neighborhoods. Many people who live in poverty are daily reminded of other people's affluence in their communities and in the media. They see safe homes, landscaping, cars and garages, clean parks with play equipment, easy access to plenty of food, but they live in crowded conditions, have to travel far to find any green space, and live on inadequate, low-quality food. The juxtaposition of wealth and poverty in America shapes the world views of both the haves and the have-nots. Schools can't fix the disparities, but healthy, honest social interactions can create a school climate that optimizes all students' chances for success.

When a boy from a rural lower-class home joined our small-town school made up of mostly middle-class, educated families, I observed him frequently alone on the playground or getting into fights when he first came, and by the end of his first year, still struggling both academically and socially. He wore his class in his clothes, his language, and his play and work habits. What was easy for the others took constant effort for him. It's a common story. As time passed, however, Dan picked up enough of the style of the middle-class children around him that he could get along pretty well with them. His vocabulary seemed to expand, as did his interest in some academic topics, and he learned to concentrate better. (Elementary school principal)

Poverty continues to be a primary determinant of student achievement in the United States.[4] "We've long known that children reared in low-income families start school well behind their more affluent counterparts and that, if anything, the gaps grow across the school years."[5]

Some say that mixing socio-economic groups is a key condition for children in poverty to succeed in school. Noted education writer Richard Kahlenberg points out that there is a large and growing body of evidence that "socioeconomic integration is one of the most important tools available for improving the academic achievement, and life chances, of students."[6] Historically, we have tried to bring children of different class backgrounds together in public schools. Despite the trend toward homogeneity in the return to neighborhood schools in some cities, and the establishment of some mono-cultural, high-poverty charter schools, many public schools are still places of mixed economic backgrounds.

Most teachers are white and middle-class, which adds class disparity to schools populated largely by students who live in poverty. Understanding across the wide gulf that divides haves from have-nots becomes crucial within a mix of people trying to accomplish the challenging tasks of teaching and learning.

Ask yourself

What effects have your family, friends, social class, ethnicity, and color had on you?

CULTURAL ELEMENTS THAT HAVE SHAPED ME

Cultural Element	Example	Example
Customs and traditions (family, neighborhood, country)		
Social organizations (neighborhood, community centers, schools, etc.)		
Language (formal and informal)		
Media (radio, TV, the Internet, the arts)		
Religion (in and outside of home)		
Government (local, state, national, international)		
Economics (personal, community, national)		

ADVISORY 5 ▶ CPR

Advisory goals: Create questions that will help you learn more about your culture. Discover things you have in common with your classmates

Greeting

Basic Greeting using Ways to Say Hello list: (See Advisory 2 for creating the list) Select a student to begin. She chooses a way to say hello and greets the student next to her in the circle, *Howdy, _____;* he chooses the same or a different way to say hello and responds, *Good morning, _____.* The greeting moves around the circle, each person choosing how to greet.

> *Greetings, Friends!*
>
> *Today we'll brainstorm questions you can ask family members about family traditions, customs, favorites, and history. What you learn from your family will help you do an Identity Share about some of the influences that made you the person you are.*

Share

Partner Share: *Brainstorm and write down at least two questions that you could ask a family member about relatives, family history, favorite food, stories, memories, etc. Your questions will help you gather information for an Identity Share in a future advisory.* Make a list of their questions as all partners share out with the group or, to save time, have partners write their questions on cards and organize them into a list later.

Sample questions for gathering family information for an Identity Share: You can mention a few of these examples to get partners started. You may add any of these to the student-generated list.

What countries or culture(s) did my ancestors come from?

When and how did our family members come to the United States? Were they indigenous?

Where was I born?

What is the origin of my name? Why was it given to me?

What language(s) do people in my family know and/or use?

What are my family's favorite foods? What foods are part of our culture?

Who in my family have graduated high school? College?

What jobs do people in my family do?

Why do we celebrate the holidays we do?

Is anyone in my family disabled physically or mentally?

What are some stories of people in my family overcoming difficulty?

How did we come to live where we do?

How does my family have fun together?

➲ **Variation:** You can give students a list of questions (see samples above), and use the share time to review and discuss them.

◌ Decide ahead of time how many meetings you want to devote to student Identity Shares, then ask for volunteer sharers to sign up for them. Advisories 14, 15, and 16 include Identity Shares; if you want, you can add meetings for the purpose of having more Identity Shares. You can plan meetings around the shares using the resources in *The Advisory Book*[7] or at DevelopmentalDesigns.org. Extending the Identity Shares may mean that you will not have time to engage in as many of the culture conversations as you would if you limit the sharing to fewer meetings.

Activity

Affinity Process: Students mingle, talking with each other to find partners with whom they have something in common. Then the partners find another twosome and discover a characteristic they all share. Next, foursomes create affinity groups of eight, and so on, until all are in one large group with at least one thing in common.

◌ Depending on the size of the group, you may decide to stop the mingling when it becomes cumbersome. You can then have groups report out, and everyone look for whole-group commonalities.

Keep in Mind

One of the first tasks in studying the great variety of cultures is deciding who gets to be heard. For example, there are academic experts on culture, there are the members of a culture, and there are those outside a culture who interact with its members. All have ideas, impressions, and/or information about the culture, and they may not agree. With diversity come many understandings, misunderstandings, interpretations, misinterpretations, perceptions, and misperceptions of cultures.

We get to define ourselves

Teachers and students are their own primary source of information about their own cultures. In these advisories, we listen to each other to get an authentic view of a sharer's culture—his or her own experience of it at this time. Multiple Identity Shares from members of a culture will present multiple points of view.

Teachers can lead and model this process of sharing about culture by describing themselves. We generally define ourselves according to what is important to us. But someone who struggles with part of his or her identity, or is especially proud of something, may mention that first. Some things may seem obvious, but we mention them because they are important. Then again, a person might define herself differently depending on who asks. Some people mention what is most important to their sense of self-worth.

I'm an Indian American, a Minnesotan, a teacher, a family member. My parents stressed that class doesn't matter. Color doesn't matter. I don't think of sexual orientation. My parents taught us to avoid labels, but when I was a kid, I acted white. I never wanted to see myself as different in culture from others. (Fifth grade teacher)

Avoid "othering"

As we explore our differences from multiple perspectives, we need to avoid making too much of them. Differences can be merely a matter of style—for example, the way a person walks, talks, dresses, eats, or greets. The differences may be personal, or they may be shared by a group. For example, some cultures have a tradition of flamboyance. The people like to be noticed, and they welcome attention. Some people may judge such behavior to be rude or too loud, while the expressive group may be irritated by shy people who don't say what's on their minds. After all, some people create and ride on the floats in the parade, tossing beads to the onlookers, and some prefer to watch, and try to catch the beads! It's a matter of style and preference, but when we judge a particular style or preference to be unattractive or inferior, we miss out on the parade of human diversity. We "other" people, and we lose both perspective and the possibility of relationship. "Thoughtful educators attend both to difference and to common ground across groups."[8] To avoid "othering" people who differ from us, we need to consistently acknowledge the similarities we share with them.

When you lead the advisory meetings described in this book, lead students toward awareness of and appreciation for both differences and similarities among people in their group and in other groups. Here are reminders for the group to help them avoid judging and to see both differences and similarities:

- Notice the thoughts and feelings you have as someone describes aspects of his or her culture. Be aware if you are judging certain ways of thinking and behaving.

- Look for similarities to your culture as you see and hear differences.

Ask yourself

Are there groups of people you think of as completely unlike you—other—because you are not mindful of the similarities?

ADVISORY 6 ▶ CPR

Advisory goal: Learn how to share about your identity by describing the influences from your culture that have shaped you

Greeting

Basic Greeting using Ways to Say Hello list: (See Advisory 2 for creating the list) Select a student to begin. She chooses a greeting and greets the student next to her in the circle; he chooses the same or a different way to respond. The greeting moves around the circle in this fashion.

> Bienvenidos, Students!
>
> Today I will do an Identity Share and describe ways that my culture has influenced me and helped shape my identity. On other days, I hope some of you will also be <u>amenable</u> to doing an Identity Shares so we can learn about some ways that your culture has influenced your life.

Share

Identity Share by teacher: *Ways that my culture has shaped my identity.* Model this share format by going first. Familiarize yourself with the Identity Share Guidelines and use them to design your share. Explain that students will have a chance to develop and do an Identity Share in the near future.

Identity Share Guidelines

Choose from the following list to share what you want people to know about your culture and how you feel about it.

- You may bring one or two objects that represent aspect(s) of your life and culture.

- How have the following influenced you?

  family traditions and characteristics (family members--siblings, cousins, etc.; favorite activities; holidays; customs; religion; foods you eat; languages spoken; attitude toward education. Are your parents strict? What are some family rules?)

  physical environment and neighborhood

  color/ethnicity

  appearance

  media/advertising

  gender

  school

  law and government

  economics (e.g., how much money your family has)

- Describe the origins of your name and why it was chosen for you.

- If your ancestors weren't indigenous (native) to America, from what countries did they come?

- What work do adults in your family do at home, in the community, or in paid jobs?

- What responsibilities do you have in your family?

- What is one way your family has contributed to or supported you?

- What other aspects of your life have influenced who you are?

Before you share, establish audience guidelines: *What does supportive listening and participation look, sound, and feel like?* See page 26 for suggestions. The audience then asks questions or makes relevant comments, allowing you to fill out your story by responding. Post the Identity Share Guidelines from which the audience can draw questions about topics the share hasn't already covered. Encourage students to ask open-ended questions (e.g., *How do you feel about having to take care of your little sister? In what ways does advertising affect how you dress? What does your mom say about how you dress and wear your hair?*).

Students can develop their own Identity Shares over the next week or so. Student shares begin in Advisory 14. Return their Cultural Elements that Have Shaped Me forms from Advisory 4 and keep the Identity Share Guidelines posted. These two resources will guide the students.

Activity

Shuffle 'em Up: Students write their names on large note cards. When you say, *shuffle 'em up,* students switch cards with one or more other players, then hold the new one in front of them like a nametag. Select a student to stand in the middle of the circle. S/he rearranges the cards in students' hands as quickly as possible so that everyone is once again holding his or her own name card. If there is time, when all students again have their own names, you may say again, *shuffle 'em up!*

➲ If students do not know each other's names well, each student can hold up his/her own name card and say the name out loud before the first round of Shuffle 'em Up. This will familiarize everyone with the names and correct pronunciations and avoid embarrassment.

Keep in Mind

Lead with an action mindset

You can model an action mindset (see description on page 23) and ease student discomfort regarding sharing about culturally-shaped identities by going first and pushing beyond your own comfort zone:

In my advisory, I often share about my own culture, which swiftly opens the door for students to share about their own cultures. It sometimes begins with me sharing about a cultural tradition or an incident shaped by culture. Then a student would say, "You think your brother had more rights than you for being a boy? Let me tell you about when my family...." And the conversation begins. (Middle level teacher)

I was telling a group of high school students about my culture's strong stand for peace in the world, and my personal fears about war. A student asked me if I thought another war was likely, and I said,

"Yes, it's hard to imagine that countries won't fight each other in the future." The student challenged me: "If you believe a war is going to come anyway, why do you keep working for peace?" He had caught me short, and after a pause, I said, "I guess I'm the kind of person who won't give up without a struggle." There was a long moment of silence in the room. I never forgot his question—or my answer. (Peace educator)

To create a space safe enough for students to stretch themselves to share about their own identities, get to know everyone's name, play cooperative games, and tell and read stories from different cultures.

Action mindset prompts honest identity sharing

The share component of CPR, in which students talk about their lives, is an opportunity to exchange stories. In the Identity Shares and beyond, students and the teacher can take turns describing parts of their lives and responding to the group.

An Identity Share presents an opportunity for teachers of color or those born in another country or into poverty to bring to the dominant school culture their stories and descriptions of how their past has shaped them. This will provide points of connection for students with similar backgrounds, enlighten those who differ, and set the tone for honest, open sharing about the way it was and is for you. Use your judgment about what and how much to share.

An Identity Share also presents an opportunity for European-American teachers to open up the topic of their experience of white privilege. Clashes can occur within a group when those in power do not acknowledge their power. For example, European Americans often lack awareness and recognition of white privilege—advantages white people have in the U.S. Unacknowledged, such privilege perpetuates inequity.[9]

White parents need to have discussions with their children, same as black parents. White parents need to talk with their kids about privilege and what it means for black and white alike to live in a white-dominated society. (Principal, K-8 charter school)

When I interviewed minority students during a review of a K-12 independent school that sought attendance by students of color, I heard comments like, "We still feel like outsiders. It's so easy for white kids—they don't even notice how easy it is." (Principal)

ADVISORY 7 ▶ CPR

Advisory goal: Learn about the various countries from which we came to America. Recognize a stereotype when you hear one.

Greeting

Language Greeting: Choose a language (see page 349 for list) or have students choose a greeting from your Ways to Say Hello list. All students greet in this language, either around the circle or in the All Group Greeting format. (All Group format: One student says *"Guten tag (or another form of "hello"), everyone."* Group responds: *Guten tag, Carla.*

⊃ Model and practice the greeting with the group to facilitate pronunciation. If a student speaks the language of the greeting, have him/her model it.

Share

Ethnic origins of our group: Read the words on the cards slowly and carefully. Students listen quietly and learn about the variety of ethnic identities in the group.

Activity

Discussion of Literature: *Let the Great World Spin*, by Colum McCann: Read aloud the following from McCann's probing exploration of experiences of "race," then guide a discussion.

> Buenos Dias, Amigos!
>
> This is a more formal Spanish greeting than "hola." Let's learn about some of the ethnic backgrounds in our group. Did you know that some <u>anthropologists hypothesize</u> that if you go back far enough, we are all <u>descendants</u> of people who lived in Africa?! <u>Do Now:</u> Write a word to describe a culture from which you are descended. No names are necessary.

⊃ Cards or sticky notes would work to provide privacy for this task, or you can have students write directly on the message or on a paper provided for this purpose.

⊃ Some students in your group may not know much about their ethnic heritage. Some may not be clear about their biological parentage. Take the pressure off by indicating that they can list the ethnicity of a primary adult with whom they live even if he or she is not a blood relation, since that adult would be an important influence

Gloria grew up in southern Missouri during the Great Depression, the only girl in a family of five brothers in a "falling apart" small house on the "colored side" of town. She went to college in Syracuse, New York, her family sending her off with a sign painted in gold ink, "Come home soon, Gloria."

"When I left Missouri, I was seventeen years old, and I made my way to Syracuse, where I survived on an academic scholarship. I fared pretty well, even if I say so myself. I had gifts for putting together some fine written sentences, and I could juggle a good slice of American history, and so—like a few young colored women my age—we were invited to elegant rooms, places with wooden panels and flickering candles and fine crystal glasses ....

"Late in the evenings I played the piano stiffly, but it was as if they wanted jazz to leap from my fingers. This was not the Negro they expected....

"We were ushered to the door by the dean of one school or another. I could tell the parties only really began after the door closed and we were gone.

"Sure I ached for the backroads of my hometown in Missouri, but leaving behind a scholarship would've been a defeat for my folks, who had no idea what it was like for me....I told them how much I loved my history classes, which was true. I told them I loved walking the woods, true too. I told them that I always had clean linen in my dorm room, true as well.

"I gave them all the truth and none of the honesty." [10]

Reflection

African Americans invented jazz over 100 years ago. Do you think that Gloria was correct in believing that the others at the party expected her to play jazz? Why would they want that? Why would she think that?

Gloria had the sense that the party changed ("really began") after the two African-American women left. Do you think she was correct in guessing that?

What did she mean by, "I gave them all the truth and none of the honesty"?

Would you be willing to step out of your familiar culture, if necessary, to go to college?

What challenges might you face?

➲ Decide before the meeting which reflection questions to focus on in the discussion, in case you do not have time for all of them.

Keep in Mind

One view of ethnic ancestry demonstrates Africa as a common beginning for all humans. Familiarize yourself with the following anthropologists' theory of the origins of humans in Africa. Decide whether it would provide supportive, interesting information for students in the context of this meeting's discussion of ancestry.

Recent African origins hypothesis: The hypothesis is that all modern people are descended from one single population of archaic *Homo sapiens* who migrated out of Africa roughly 100,000 years ago, replacing other archaic forms (for example, Neanderthals) due to their superior cultural capabilities. This is called the Eve or the Out of Africa hypothesis.

Though the recent African-origins hypothesis is the mainstream position, not every scholar supports it. Among those with opposing views are Chinese and Australian paleoanthropologists, who generally favor a multiregional hypothesis, in part because it fits better with the fossil discoveries from Asia and Australia.[11]

Implications of "race" in this book

To understand that "race" lacks biological basis but carries strong cultural weight, be sure to read pages 24-25 in *How to Lead Face to Face Advisories.*

Avoid stereotypes about ancestry

We usually define ourselves more accurately than anyone else can define us. Far too often, others' descriptions of people turn out to include negative stereotypes: whole groups can be labeled as aggressive, stingy, lazy, etc. Negative generalizations about whole cultures are unlikely to be true, and hurt people and damage society. A non-religious friend related to me a conversation he had with a religious colleague. The colleague said, "Since you don't practice a religion, I cannot really trust that you will do the right thing, because you have no standard for right and wrong." We write people off when we define them merely on our own terms, judging theirs as invalid.

Through our "culturally clouded vision,"[12] as Lisa Delpit calls it, it's easy and convenient to make assumptions and generalizations about cultures outside of our experience, and challenging to see clearly people who are different from us.

Literature can provide insights into cultures

We can read about cultures in literature, as well as draw from historical, anthropological, sociological, and current-events resources. Literature provides exposure to a wider variety of cultures than we usually come across in our daily lives. It can challenge and broaden us to think about differences from other perspectives—those of fictional characters—with minimal distortion from our own "culturally clouded vision."

That cloud often generates pre-judgments and assumptions that diminish a person. This advisory helps us see and hear those misjudgments in Colum McCann's novel. The African-American college student is misperceived, based on assumptions about African-American culture. You can discuss with students the dangers of assumptions. Perspective Three further discusses the tendency to make assumptions about other people's cultures. This story, offered during the time students are working on Identity Shares, provides some beginning understandings.

Ask yourself

Have you ever felt misunderstood because of someone's misperception of your culture? (Remember that our definition of culture includes gender, ability, age, appearance, sexual orientation, etc.)

ADVISORY 8 ▶ A+

Advisory goal: Become familiar with the aspects of our cultural lives that shape us, and their varying importance to people

Greeting

Greet Three Greeting: Pairs of students make eye contact, then greet each other using a greeting of their choice, and repeat this process two more times with other students. All groups meet and greet while milling about in the circle.

> Good Day to All!
> Today we'll take another look at the "What Shapes Us?" PowerPoint and play Spend the Dot to see which factors have <u>predominantly</u> influenced us.

➲ Model and practice how to mill about in the circle, looking for others to greet. The goal is to do this efficiently (gather with the first two people you encounter) and politely (with the same degree of friendliness for everyone).

Activity

Spend the Dot: What Shapes Us? review PowerPoint: Label separate note cards with the influencing factors listed in What Shapes Us? Post the cards where students can reach them (walls, desks, etc.). Students "spend the dots" by making a dot with a marker on the cards that name the three factors that have had the greatest impact on their lives.

The influencing factors listed in What Shapes Us:

Family

Neighborhood

Color, ethnicity, appearance

Religion

Economic and social class

Gender

Language

Environment

School

Media

Advertising

Food

Law and government

Reflection

What influences have had the most impact on us as a group (have the most dots)?
How might the results vary if our group members were more similar in one of the factors?
(Choose one or two factors that might give you some interesting variations from your actual results: What if students were more similar in color? socio-economic group? ethnicity? ability level? gender?)

➲ You can call students' attention to elements that were rated by the majority as less important, and together consider situations that would add more weight to the importance of the element. For example, if gender gets a number of dots equal to about half the class, check to see if girls dotted it, but boys didn't, and if so, you could discuss why girls might consider gender more important in shaping their lives than boys seem to.

Keep in Mind

Maintaining a balanced perspective

Comparing influences on us of various elements of culture broadens our understanding of how culture affects us. To keep ourselves clear and flexible as we learn about each other's cultures, we must guard against simplifications and generalizations that can distort our understanding and reduce the complex nuances of cultures to stereotypes. A normative, reductionist point of view distorts what we see. Avoiding a narrow point of view is crucial to the success of these conversations. There is no such thing as cultural neutrality.[13] Consciously or not, we stand in our own culture when we look at another, and that colors what we see, or think we see, or think about what we see.

During a study of China, a group of American fifth graders took a collective stand in opposition to the widespread practice of eating dog meat. Even though the teacher had carefully prepared them for this study by helping them see that cultures are shaped in large part by their circumstances, and even though they were all meat eaters, the children began to make critical generalizations about the "unkindness" of Chinese people, which had to be named and countered.

Because no one is culturally neutral, we need preparation, mental agility, and honest self-scrutiny to see each other's cultures clearly. Discussions about culture raise awareness of the lenses through which we habitually observe others and which can reduce us to generalizations and stereotypes. For example, a European-American student may list color or "race" as one of the less important factors that shape us, whereas an African-American student might rate it as very or most important. The white student may be less conscious of a factor that has not seemed important in determining his life. He is mistaken. White privilege has a big impact on every choice he makes and how the world responds to his choices. Pointing this out our lack of cultural neutrality as you discuss the results of the Spend the Dot exercise will correct some of the distortion caused by our filtered perspectives.

Avoid rushing to judgment

Although it may seem obvious, it is important to note that being similar in one way does not mean sameness in all ways, and being different in one way does not mean difference in all ways. Differences of style sometimes get confused with differences in beliefs and values. Sometimes skin colors are similar, but cultures differ. Africans and African Americans may share skin color and other appearances but perceive themselves as significantly different from each other. And European Americans who have made a great effort to reduce racism in their attitudes and behavior may resent being lumped in with other European Americans who have made no such effort.

Looking at our cultures through a variety of lenses, then, will help us gain a balanced understanding.

Ask yourself
How have various cultural elements influenced me?

ADVISORY 9 ▶ CPR

Advisory goal: Learn more about ourselves and each other. Learn about authentic voice in writing.

Greeting

Fist-Tap Greeting: Select a student to begin. Around the circle, students greet with *Good morning, _____*, adding a gentle fist bump. When time is short, you may choose to make this a silent greeting, or use the Fist-Tap Greeting as a quick simultaneous greeting. Model and practice fist-tapping before beginning: make a fist, then gently tap partner's fist as *Good Morning, _____* is exchanged.

> *Good Morning, Friends!*
> *Today we will hear "Where I'm From" poems. This poetry form gives us a way of telling about our cultural backgrounds that is both* <u>explicit</u> *and colorful. We'll write our own "Where I'm From" poems.*

Share

Where I'm From poem reading: Read aloud at least one *Where I'm From* poem from those below.

➲ Read the poem for inspiration, and to introduce the activity. If you wish to have a student read one of the poems out loud, choose a student who can read with expression and with a voice that projects well. In this case, it is more important that students get the feel and hear the poems clearly than it is to give students a chance to read aloud.

Activity

Write a Where I'm From poem: This is a free-verse poem, the model for which was created by George Ella Lyon.[14] Post a list of possible categories you can use to write a "Where I'm From" poem: foods; sights, sounds, and smells; special moments; activities and experiences; feelings; pets; names; family sayings and language(s); nicknames; and more. Students make a list of descriptions of these elements in their lives. You could construct a form with these categories for students to fill out. When the list or form is complete, they use the descriptions to create a *Where I'm From* poem. They will have time to finish their poems in the next advisory meeting.

➲ See George Ella Lyon's Web site[15] for more details about ways to teach students to create *Where I'm From* poems.

➲ It's important to begin by making the list first, and then use the *Where I'm From* format. Tell students they will have time to hear each other's poems, so they know there will be an audience for what they write. Stress the importance of authenticity.

Where I'm From

I am from family.
I am from traditions of lutefisk and lefse and
St. Olaf College.
I am from generations of teachers
And love of books and learning.
I am from parents who love and worry and hope.

I am from a house full of brothers.
From racing to keep up and be strong and independent.
I am from long family dinners.
I am from camping trips and sitting by the fire.
I am from Starlight Moonlight in the darkness of a summer night.

I am from church on Sundays
And praying before dinner.
I am from friends.
I am from memories.
I am from joy.
I am from love.

I am from my past.
I am from my future.
I am from building new traditions.
I am from making new memories.
I am from hopes and dreams that I pass on to my children.

—Ann Ericson, high school science teacher

Where I'm From

I come from spotless floors
From where everything is clean.
I come from thousands of memories.
I come from a big caring family.
I am from a family where we all eat soul food
From fried chicken to greens and beans.
From the ghetto where everyone is loud and crazy.

I come from Tangie and Peter.
From bad eyes and glasses.
I come from my mom being my mom and father.
I come from welfare and
From my mom doing her best to raise three children at 21.
I come from a hard life, but still being spoiled.

I come from where my dad isn't sh*t.
I come from where I just wish him to be hit.
I come from where he never tried,
All he did was tell me lies.
And it hurts me deep inside.
I come from where I'm trying to survive this stupid teenage life.

I come from where my and my mom barely gets along.
I come from my mom's past being so dark where all she has is anger.
Her life was full of danger.

I come from where my family never keeps secrets.
Where everyone doesn't know how to stop talking.
I come from where everyone loves each other but shows hate.
From where no one can get along because everyone thinks they know!
  —Jasmine, tenth grade student

Keep in Mind

By telling their own stories in this open-verse form, students can create a medley of impressions that will help them give others a sense of who they are, how they live, and what is important to them. Students use "I come from…" or "I'm from…." or both to create a glimpse into their lives that rings with authenticity, a self-definition that comes from them.

Labels assigned by others

In addition to all the other influences on our sense of self, others' labels for us can become part of the culture that shapes us. For example, others might assume you are something you are not, and that label can powerfully influence your position in society and your self-perception. In America, if your skin is brown or black, you'll likely be labeled African American, regardless of the mix of ethnicities you might actually be. You may be an African immigrant, and consider yourself Ghanaian or Nigerian, but you are likely to get lumped into the "black" category, right along with African Americans, some Native Americans, East Indians, South Americans, South Asians, Pacific Islanders, and countless mixed-"race" people.

Labels—people with disabilities are unintelligent; females are physically weak; poor people are not intelligent; gay men are effeminate, and lesbians are mannish—can frustrate students' efforts to self-identify. Perhaps they can push back, but an adolescent in the process of identity formation may internalize a feeling of being what others think he is. The label itself, accurate or not, begins to shape him.

I was East Indian in heritage and the only non-white student in the school, and immediately they put me in a Special Education classification. The librarian offered me African-American posters. I didn't want to fit anybody's idea of who I was, so I just shut down. (Fifth-sixth grade teacher)

From *Bronx Masquerade:* "Jump Shot. What kind of name is that? Not mine, but try telling that to the brothers at school. That's all they ever call me.

You'd think it was written somewhere. Tall guys must be jocks. No. Make that tall *people*, 'cause Diondra's got the same problem. Everybody expects her to shoot hoops."[16]

Bureaucracy supports labeling

Bureaucratic forms, including school forms, often require us to label ourselves simplistically and inaccurately. "Hispanic" on such forms usually means a wide range of Spanish-speaking cultures—Mexico, Puerto Rico, Guatemala, Spain, Argentina, Cuba, and more. "Asian" can include widely disparate cultures such as China, Korea, Japan, Thailand, Vietnam, Indonesia, and more. The members of those ethnic groups identify with their specific cultures, and they are keenly aware of the differences among them. Nevertheless, they are required to use the label unless they claim "Other" and take the time to write in an authentic label for themselves. Really, nearly all of us are "Other!"

Influence of disadvantage and prejudice on adolescent identity formation

Disadvantage and prejudice can become embedded in culture and thereby become a cultural influence. Advisories in Perspective Three focus on the cost of prejudice, but students can begin now to consider how these negatives may have influenced them and others. Adolescents who are part of an ethnic group that is disparaged and/or disadvantaged in society can react to such prejudice in their identity-building. They may identify as alienated from the dominant culture and purposely behave in ways that further separate them from it. They might refuse to conform to behavior standards, or to make any effort to learn, especially when the content of the curriculum is devoid of any elements of the student's own culture.

An African-American friend told me once that I was "acting white," and trying to avoid being myself. That prompted me to learn more about my heritage, which is East Indian, and to think more carefully. I had been getting an idea of who I should be from the media, and was trying not to be myself. My experience in school also made me really quiet and withdrawn. (Fifth-sixth grade teacher)

Damage to identity formation occurs when adolescents see themselves as lacking value because of their cultural identity. Internalized discrimination leads them to believe negative stereotypes others hold about their group. If youths from immigrant or "racial" minorities, for example, fail "to talk about what happened, why it happened, and what the consequences of almost 400 years of racism are,"[17] they are unlikely to have a self-image of a successful person in school or in life.

Ask yourself

Where am I from? Write a "Where I'm From" poem, then share it with your students.

⮡ Teacher participation, especially when there is risk-taking involved, supports student participation. A rule of thumb: Don't ask students to do activities that you are not willing to do.

ADVISORY 10 ▶ CPR

Advisory goals: Learn more about ourselves and each other. Know how to be a supportive audience for original work.

Greeting

One-Minute Mingle Greeting: Each person greets as many students by name as possible in one minute. Model how to accept and return a greeting, maintaining eye contact, before moving to the next person.

> G'day, Mates!
> We'll finish our "Where I'm From" poems today, and begin hearing some of them in our <u>poetry slam</u>. Be thinking about what good listeners do. After each reading we'll acknowledge the poet in the old-fashioned coffeehouse way—finger snaps!
> <u>Do Now</u>: Bring your poem to our meeting.

Share

Where I'm From Poetry Slam: Be the first reader. Before you begin, establish the poetry audience guideline of quiet listening: there is no commenting or questioning of the poets, and no talking or whispering while they are reading. Add to the cabaret or coffeehouse feeling by introducing a new way to acknowledge a reader: finger snapping (instead of clapping) after the reading provides quiet but enthusiastic support.

Activity

Where I'm From Poems (continued): Students finish their poems, practice reading them, and, if there's time, read them aloud. (Poetry slam continues in the next advisory.)

Keep in Mind

Think critically and with feeling

Since our cultures have shaped us to view the world in certain ways, we risk seeing it *only* those ways, and getting stuck in one point of view. There is an opportunity here to discuss and practice shifting one's perspective. Poetry allows us to go beyond lists of influences on us. When we include some of the color in our lives with rhythmic language and colorful images—that is, in poetry—there is a sensory and emotional quality to the sharing:

I am from a family
As big as Texas.
From the good times they turn bad.

> —Tenth grade student

We must not dry out the school experience by taking the emotion out of it. When our conversations occur in an atmosphere of trust and connection, we can be genuine and expressive with one another. The Where I'm From poems allow students to give each other verbal "snapshots" of their lives. It joins big moments to small ones, providing a more intimate view of student lives than they are likely to reveal in formal oral presentations.

Ask yourself

Did you learn something about yourself by writing your own Where I'm From poem?

ADVISORY 11 ▶ A+

Advisory goal: Become aware of the variety of cultures in your group. Develop attentive-listener skills

Greeting

High Five Greeting: students exchange a high five as they verbally greet each other: *Hi, Kate.* Reply: *Hi, Mohammed.*

> *Pay attention, Poets!*
>
> *That's the way we can honor each other's stories: by paying careful attention as we read to each other these poems about our lives.*

Activity

Where I'm From Poetry Slam: Ask students to reiterate the job of a poetry audience: quiet, attentive listening, finger snaps for acknowledgment. Then students read their poems to the group. The share in the next advisory provides more time for reading poems.

⮑ If a student is reluctant to read his or her poem during the slam, you might offer to read it for him. Make sure you bring out the best in the poem: that you can read the handwriting without stumbling, and you give it the expressiveness that makes it come alive. Reading the poem well will make the author proud, and may encourage him or her to read next time.

Keep in Mind

Everyone benefits from the poetry readings. Let students see your eagerness to hear them, and your confidence that their words are important and interesting.

Some students may feel they lack sufficient English skills to express themselves, or may be embarrassed to share personal matters, or may not feel safe to talk about certain situations at home. Do not force someone who really does not want to read his or her poem to the group. There are fifteen community-building advisories in this book to help you build a friendly, safe, inclusive community before starting Perspective One advisories. Give students time to grow in their comfort and trust in the group, and hope they will be willing to share next time.

Ask yourself

What have you done in the past to quiet your nerves when you had to do something publicly? Your students might be interested to hear your tips, and if you share them, they will realize that most people are nervous when they perform publicly.

ADVISORY 12 ▶ CPR

Advisory goals: Build community and foster appreciation for its diversity. Develop oral and written performance capacities

Greeting

One-Minute Mingle Greeting: Each person greets as many students by name as possible in one minute. Before beginning, model how to efficiently and politely mingle and greet, maintaining eye contact, saying a greeting, and perhaps shaking hands, before moving on.

Felicitations, Friends!

Keep those poems coming! They are really vivid and great fun to hear. Remember that we will be hosting a guest at our advisory meeting tomorrow or the next day, depending on when we complete our poetry slam.

Share

Where I'm From Poetry Slam (continued): If after the share time there are still students who haven't read yet, use the Additional Poetry Slam Advisory below to complete the Slam.

Activity

Where I'm From poem display or book: Make public copies of poems for display or to reproduce into a class book. If you choose not to do either, you can play a round of Simultaneous Clap:

There are several "rounds" in this activity, and they are increasingly challenging.

1. In a standing circle, the starting person claps, then, moving to the right or left, each person claps in sequence around the circle, keeping a smooth rhythm and with no hesitations.

2. The starting person claps both hands with the person next to him (double high-five style). This clap is passed between pairs around the circle.

3. The starting two people turn to each other and attempt to clap their hands at the same moment (each claps her own hands). The next pair forms (one from the first pair and the next student) and attempts the clap, and so on around the circle.

4. As a closing, holding hands at the ready, everyone tries to clap at the same moment. This may take some practice and requires students to pay very close attention to each other.

ADDITIONAL POETRY SLAM ADVISORY (IF NEEDED)

Advisory goal: Build community

Greeting

Movie Star Greeting: Introduce yourself to everyone using your middle name as your first name and your pet's name or the name of the street you travel on as your last name. For example, Harold James Starling of Bushberry Lane whose dog is Lucky becomes James Bushberry or James Lucky. The audience listens, and then frames the student by pretending to look through a viewfinder in the manner of a movie director or cinematographer, and says, *Oooooo, yeaahhhhh!* in an exaggerated way.

> *How's it going?*
>
> *Thanks to everyone for a great poetry slam! We've shared our truths with each other; now let's make stuff up! We'll play a bit with our identities today in a game called What's Your Name? Remember, we will be hosting a guest at our next meeting.*

Share

Where I'm From Poetry Slam for any poems not already read

Activity

What's Your Job? All sit in a circle. A student is selected to leave the room; her chair is removed.

She'll return in a moment and begin to ask each person in the circle, *What's your job?* While she's out of the room, one student is selected to respond, *I'm a student*—the truthful answer. The rest choose pretend careers. When the student returns and begins to ask others what their jobs are, all respond with their pretend jobs, but when the selected student responds, *I'm a student*, everyone gets up and moves to a new place in the circle. The student in the middle attempts to take a seat, too. The student left standing leaves the room, a new student is selected to be "a student", everyone else chooses a new pretend career, and the game continues. Before beginning, model and practice how to safely exchange seats and move in traffic.

⮑ For any chair-changing game, take a minute or two to review the guidelines about speed, body contact, and resolving the issue of two people at the same chair at the same time.

Keep in Mind

One of the best ways adolescents can get to know and feel comfortable with one another is through play. In this advisory, we play with our identities, saying *hello* disguised as movie stars and answering questions about our jobs or locations or names with made-up identities. You can mention that even though we are not telling the truth about our lives, we are still getting to know one another better.

Ask yourself

When you dress up for an occasion or do something unusual, do you enjoy the feeling of a change of identity? If so, you could share that with your students.

ADVISORY 13 ▶ CPR

Advisory goal: Develop the skills of getting to know someone new to you

Greeting

Language Greeting: Choose a language for the greeting (see page 349 for list). All students greet in this language, either around the circle or in the All Group Greeting format. (All Group format: *Salaam, everyone.* Group responds: *Salaam, Ava.*)

➲ Model and practice correct pronunciation ahead of time.

> Jambo, Friends!
>
> Please welcome our guest, Mr./Ms._____. (S)he has <u>magnanimously</u> agreed to do an Identity Share with us. Be ready to ask good questions like those you asked when I did my Identity Share. Consider volunteering to begin the student Identity Shares (tomorrow).

Share

Guest Identity Share: Ways that my culture has shaped my identity. Post and use the Identity Share Guidelines, see Advisory 6.

Suggested guests: To develop understanding of how culture shapes us, and to provide another example of an Identity Share, invite a guest. Anybody who is willing to be a guest can do so, but guests who have backgrounds different from the students' can broaden their understanding. Guests who are willing to talk about the influences in their lives, particularly the influences in their youth, will provide additional points of view. Older adolescents, college students, and young workers can garner student attention with stories of the environments and people who may still have a strong influence on them. Young people who have been in trouble and have learned from it may bear a particularly effective message for your students. We can invite to an advisory meeting older teens who are succeeding in school and/or in work, or young people who are still struggling but determined to succeed, so adversity can be seen as one of many influences that can shape the future for adolescents.

Guest preparation: Tell the guest about the conversations you have been having in your advisory, and about the makeup of the student group. Give them the Identity Share Guidelines from Advisory 6 and the Cultural Elements that Have Shaped Me form from Advisory 4. Suggest that they use storytelling to create a vivid picture for students. Suggest that they bring an object or two to add interest.

Student preparation: Before the guest arrives, prepare students with a short description of the guest so they will have a context to begin with. Refer them to the audience guidelines (established in Advisory 6; see page 26 for guideline suggestions) posted list of questions when the time comes for questions and comments.

Guest share process: The guest shares experiences that shaped him or her, using the object(s) s/he brought and following the guidelines.

Activity

Audience response: Students ask questions and make respectful comments about what they have heard. They might make comparisons or describe contrasts with their own lives. They can ask the guest some of the Identity Share questions from the posted list or ask new ones.

Acknowledgment: Choose a couple of students ahead of time to prepare to thank the guest by acknowledging the contribution she or he has made. Then any others who wish to may add their individual thanks. The group can also acknowledge the guest with a cheer (see list of cheers on page 350). Follow up with a thank-you note written by a student on behalf of the group and mailed to the guest.

⮑ Ask for volunteers to start the student Identity Shares in the next advisory. The next three advisories are designated for Identity Shares.

Keep in Mind

Culture shapes us, but not inevitably and indelibly, as we see in stories of people like Franklin Roosevelt, who became President of the United States even though childhood polio left him unable to walk, or John Fountain, an African-American professor and journalist who early in his life became a father and dropped out of college18, or Oprah Winfrey, who after a childhood of poverty described herself not as a poor, deprived girl who made good, but as somebody who from an early age knew she was responsible for herself and was determined to succeed.19 All three had growth mindsets, a crucial characteristic for success. A growth mindset allows us to take a positive hand in shaping ourselves and our destiny.

Maintaining a climate of respect

As people (you, a guest, and students) share about their cultural identities, help the group understand that we must not assume that they think their way is better just because people believe or behave differently from us. Defensiveness and judging have no place in these discussions. It is the teacher's job to insist on open, non-judgmental listening and a "not personal" point of view, even if it means stopping the conversation, reviewing the protocols, redirecting a violator, or terminating the conversation. There may even be times when you need to step back from the conversation to refresh your own objectivity. Students can mature to the point where they realize that "different" does not mean "better" or "inferior," and they can listen respectfully to opinions that differ from their own.

These conversations can increase students' capacity to think and feel at the same time and avoid rash words or behavior. That's an accomplishment for adolescents, since their brains are still developing. Inviting guests who have a variety of cultural backgrounds provides a healthy challenge for your students.

Ask yourself

Who else might I invite to do an Identity Share with students?

ADVISORY 14 ▶ CPR

Advisory goals: Become more able to describe your culture and how it has shaped you. Learn about each other's cultures.

Greeting

Language Greeting: Choose a language (see page 349 for list) or have students choose a greeting from your Ways to Say Hello list. All students greet in this language, either around the circle or in the All Group Greeting format. (All Group format: *Namaste, everyone.* Group responds: *Namaste, William.*) Practice correct pronunciation ahead of time.

> Good Morning, Good Listeners!
>
> Today _____ and _____ will be doing the first student Identity Shares. Use your <u>attentive</u> listening skills, and be ready to ask interesting questions (our list of questions is posted to remind you of some good ones to ask).

Share

Identity Share (student volunteer): *Ways that my culture has shaped my identity.* As support, give the sharer the Identity Share Guidelines from Advisory 6. They can also use their Cultural Elements that Have Shaped Me form from Advisory 4 to help them remember things they might talk about.

To support the audience, post the audience guidelines and the Identity Share Guidelines. Remind them that the share will end with a brief acknowledgment of something learned or a cheer (see page 350). If the pace seems to lag, prompt additional questions by directing students to the Share Guidelines for any topics not yet discussed. Listen carefully to the questions asked of a sharer, and intervene if a question seems to make the sharer uncomfortable.

⮩ Watch over the conversation to make sure students present a balanced picture:

- noticing similarities and differences
- stories of victimization of one culture by another and celebrations of joyful, productive aspects of cultures
- the facts about cultures and the emotions people have about cultures, both negative and positive

You can help maintain balance in the conversation by interjecting a question. If the sharer's emphasis is on how different a culture is from others, ask about broadly shared characteristics (e.g. *Is there an age when a boy or girl is considered an adult? Is there a holiday when families gather and relax together?*). If the share emphasizes persecution, ask questions that might bring out sources of strength or hope (e.g. *Are leaders and others working for peace at this time?*). If facts are overemphasized, ask a question about feelings (e.g., *Do you like being a member of a large family? What are the advantages and disadvantages?*), and vice versa.

Acknowledge students who do Identity Shares. Students can do a cheer for the sharers, or students can offer comments about what they specifically appreciated in the shares. Comments should be specific and descriptive, not general praise such as "You were great." The social skill of giving a compliment requires thinking in order to be authentic. Speak specifically to what was interesting, admirable, or informative in the share. A thoughtful comment, rather than empty praise, can mean a lot to the sharer, especially coming from a peer.

Activity

Name 'em All: Volunteers try to correctly name everyone in the circle

⮌ If the volunteer gets stuck, students can give a clue about a person not mentioned yet, for example, the letter the name begins with or a word it rhymes with. This will show the person whose name has been forgotten that others do remember her name.

Keep in Mind

Students love to share family artifacts during CPR. They bring photographs of ancestors, keepsakes, flags, maracas, and trinkets. I model the share by bringing a "mystery artifact" from my culture. I pass it around the circle and answer questions without disclosing what it is. Once everyone has asked at least one question, I ask students to guess what the artifact is used for. I then tell them what it is. I usually bring a piragua maker, a hand tool to make shaved ice dessert. Later in the year I bring a block of ice and we make piraguas in the classroom. I have had students share traditional foods like sweet breads and other baked goods. (Middle level teacher)

Create a climate of equals

An objective-minded facilitator projects belief in the value of each person's story, including his or her own. If students are not forthcoming in talking about their own and others' cultures, if they seem reluctant to participate, or if they discount the idea of discussing cultures, ask yourself whether you have established a climate of equals, in which everyone's contribution is valued.

There is no hierarchy of cultures. Everyone is the expert about his own life. Students will speak for themselves without fear of judgment in a climate of friendliness and trust. Advisory is an opportunity for creating that climate, and CPR is a structure for making it happen. Some things to remember:

- No disrespect can go uncorrected. Correct even "small" disses, which loom large in the mind of the target.

- Play is the best vehicle for stimulating participation, and cooperative play is especially effective in building community. Relationship-building with students never ends. Take a student aside if your relationship with him is deteriorating, and listen hard to find out what went wrong. Then take appropriate action to rebuild the relationship.

The way we got to know each other was in advisory—the Circle of Power and Respect meeting. It builds a level of respect that makes everything possible. Also, being able to support kids who are struggling academically was a big pillar in building trust—knowing where they are and moving them forward built confidence. (Sixth grade teacher)

Ask yourself

What are some ways you can help students feel comfortable sharing with the group?

ADVISORY 15 ▶ CPR

Advisory goal: Learn about each other's cultures. Improve focus and listening skills.

Greeting

Language Greeting: Choose a language (see page 349 for list) or have students choose a greeting from your Ways to Say Hello list. All students greet in this language around the circle. You can list and model and practice the greeting possibilities ahead of time to facilitate correct pronunciation.

> Greetings, Group!
> We'll hear Identity Shares from _____ and _____ today. We'll play a chair-changing game called Rumplestiltskin. Make a check mark below if you know who he is. (Clue: he lives in a fairy tale.)

Share

Identity Share(s) (student volunteers continue)

⮩ Talk about cultures is most interesting when it includes not only how we do things but why, not only what we do but how we feel about it. Does Rachel enjoy lighting the candles for Hanukkah? How does Ramon feel about celebrating the Day of the Dead? Is it hard for Fatima to fast during Ramadan? Does Joe get frustrated taking care of his younger brother and sister? Encourage questions from the group that get at the affect as well as the facts. Some students may not be comfortable about sharing certain aspects of their lives, and they do not have to. The questions are meant to show respectful interest.

Activity

I Sit in the Grass: Students sit in a circle in which there is one empty chair. To start, the student to the right of the empty chair says, *I sit,* and moves one place to the left, occupying the empty chair. The student to the right of the newly vacated chair says, *in the grass,* and also moves one place to the left, occupying the empty chair. The student to the right of that newly vacated chair also moves one place to the left and says, *with my friend _____,* naming someone across the circle. The one who was named rises and moves to the chair vacated by the student who named him. In doing so, his chair becomes empty, and the student to the right of it starts the process again, by occupying it and saying, *I sit.* This continues until all students have been called a friend or until time is up.

⮩ Chair-changing games present the challenge of keeping order within a context that is set up to confuse and also involves moving around. In I Sit in the Grass, the challenge is not so much physical (because the changing occurs one person at a time), but social. When the person named is slow to rise (which he/she often is because it takes a moment to register that you are the one who must move), the group may remind the person to move, but must not make critical or sarcastic comments. It will help to mention this ahead of time.

⮑ Watch for exclusion. Make it clear that you must name someone across the circle, not near you, and that the goal is to get many people to move. Usually not everyone moves, or the game would take too long to play, and there are inevitably people who move more than once because of the random aspects of the game.

Keep in Mind

When things get sticky in advisory, when people are lagging in their participation and energy is low, you can turn the mood around with some play. These advisory meeting plans are adjustable, and when you think it's time to loosen things up, or bring students closer together, you can always insert a meeting or activity that is light and playful. *The Advisory Book* is a rich resource for greetings, shares, and activities. Check out DevelopmentalDesigns.org for descriptions and rules of many games and activities.

Ask yourself

How do you loosen up and relax? What cooperative games do you enjoy?

ADVISORY 16 ▶ CPR

Advisory goals: Learn about each other's cultures. Develop the social skill of acknowledgment of others.

Greeting

Language Greeting: Choose a language (see page 349 for list) or have students choose a greeting from your Ways to Say Hello list. All students greet in this language around the circle.

Share

Identity Share(s) (student volunteers continue)

Activity

Zip Zap: Choose a student to be *It*. The other students learn the name of their zip (the person on their right) and the name of their zap (the person on their left). *It* approaches any student, points, and says, *Zip?* (or *Zap?*) and counts to five. The person must say the name of the neighbor on her right (if *Zip* was said, or left if *Zap*) before the count of five. If the person is successful, she is safe, and *It* remains *It*. If the person fails, she becomes *It*. *It* may point to someone and say, *Zip zap!* Then all students must find a new seat. *It* tries to take a seat, too. The student left without a seat is the new *It*.

Keep in Mind

Balance stories of victims and the victorious

Some students may have stories of struggle in their homes, in their neighborhoods, or in their countries of origin. When they share stories of trouble, hardship, or fear, encourage them to also think of and share times when they or others overcame difficulties. For example, in response to several violent deaths of young people in their neighborhood, a group of students in Minneapolis created a documentary film about their lives in the context of Dr. Martin Luther King Jr.'s work. It honors their late friends, criticizes the perpetrators, and cries out for justice. Young people living in the midst of poverty, violence, and racism took a stand, perhaps preparing to become leaders. Part One can be seen on the *Developmental Designs* YouTube channel. Here is an excerpt:

"We are tired of the everyday struggle, we are tired of the violence, the shootings, burying our sisters and our brothers, we are tired of living in poverty, and having to hold our heads up high knowing that our struggle is great. We ...have decided to create [a] documentary film to illustrate the real issues that affect our everyday lives in hope to raise awareness of the issues of war, poverty and racism, and how we are directly affected by these three evils."[20]

Ask yourself
When have you overcome a difficulty or taken a stand?

ADVISORY 17 ▶ A+

Advisory goal: Increase student awareness of self-identity

Greeting

Language Greeting: Choose a language (see page 349 for list) or have students choose a greeting from your Ways to Say Hello list. All students greet in this language, either around the circle or in the All Group Greeting format. (All Group

> Good Morning, World Citizens!
>
> Today we'll work with some questions about living in a world of all sorts of people. I'll ask questions, and you answer with integrity.

format: Boozhoo, *everyone*. Group responds: *Boozhoo, Nate*.) You can model and practice the greeting possibilities ahead of time to facilitate correct pronunciation.

Activity

Self-interview on Getting Along in a Multicultural World: Distribute the Self-interview Questions to students. Read them aloud, and be sure students understand them before anyone does the self-interview.

Responses may be written or oral and recorded. A schedule for students to record can be set up for one student at a time to come in before school, or to make his or her recording during an advisory meeting.

Collect and save responses to compare with the same interview conducted toward the end of the year (see Advisory 24 in Perspective Five).

⮑ It is important that the self-interview process is private. To get students to think/ speak/write about themselves as honestly as possible, point out that this is a process *for* them and will be viewed only *by* them, unless they choose otherwise. Have students put their completed written interviews into a sealed envelope, or store their recordings, until the end of the year, when they take the self-interview a second time. They will compare their two sets of responses, and you can have an interesting discussion about changes they notice in the way they see themselves and their world.

Reflection

Were there questions you found hard to answer?

Do you think adults would benefit from doing this self-interview?

SELF-INTERVIEW QUESTIONS

1. Do I associate with and have friends who are different from me in color, gender, religion, ability, language, ethnicity, appearance, sexual orientation, and/or age? Answer for each category.

2. What are some facts I know about cultures other than my own and about people who seem different from me?

3. How have my family and neighborhood affected the way I think, talk, and behave?

4. Are there groups or kinds of people I don't trust and don't want to associate with? Who are they? Why do I distrust and avoid them?

5. Do I feel that most students who know me like and trust me?

5. What connections do I feel with people who are different from me, for example, in color, religion, gender, or wealth? What connection do I feel with people in other countries? Do I agree or disagree with the statement that all humans are closely connected? Explain your answer.

6. Do I agree with the statement that prejudice hurts everyone, everywhere on the planet? Why or why not?

7. Am I open to the idea that I am changing all the time and there are lots of possibilities for me? Do I agree that having fun together and working to help the world can change this country for the better? Explain the answer.

8. Am I willing to make a commitment to try to make the world a more fair and caring place for all?

Keep in Mind

Students' responses to the questions in the self-interview give us a glimpse of how they view the world and how they see themselves: who has influenced them, whom they trust, how open they are to the possibilities of changing and growing. Here are the words of some students in their initial self-interviews:

- *I associate with friends who are different from me because it wouldn't be fun to just have friends that look or dress like me. It would be a little fun, but after a while it would get annoying.*

- *My family and neighborhood have not affected the way I think, talk, and behave.*

- *Some people I don't trust are people who are ethnicity rude, and people who only want their own race and who think they are the Alpha race. I avoid them.*

- *Honestly, the world will never change. We think that we're changing the world for the better but we do good things because we have to. Humans are greedy. Even though you think you're doing things good, you're doing it for your own benefit.*

- *There are a lot of possibilities out there that I want to change.*

- *I would personally be willing to make a commitment to try to make the world a more fair and caring place for everyone to live in, because if I do that I would feel much better about myself. Also I would be proud of myself for accomplishing something.*

Self-labeling

These responses show that the students speaking have already developed a sense of who they are. To an important extent, we get to define ourselves as we see ourselves. We put together an idea of who we are, and thus form our identity and our sense of other people's identities. Cultural influences push us to see ourselves in certain ways: a person may identify as Jewish, even though she doesn't practice Judaism, because her parents and extended family are Jewish. Skin color figures very importantly in identity; people of color tend to be very conscious of their color, in part because the cultural history of our country is scarred by racism, and in part because of the historically normative status of whiteness. Here is a sampling of adult responses to the question, "Who are you?"

I'm a human, an African-American father, an artist, advocate, a person of love and spirit.

I'm a mother, spouse, lifelong learner, community activist, a person who wants to influence the world, a woman of color.

I'm a Minnesotan with Scandinavian and Scottish background, a man, a father, an urban, middle class, music-loving teacher.

I'm a Unitarian-Universalist liberal, creative young gay male, Caucasian, and Swedish American.

I'm an Indian American, a Minnesotan, a teacher, a family member.

Ultimately, it is the right and the responsibility of every individual to lay claim to who she or he is, and to go beyond mere labeling to forge a self-identify that provides a guiding star for life. bell hooks, an African-American intellectual, poet, and activist, self-identified this way:

"If I were really asked to define myself, I wouldn't start with race; I wouldn't start with blackness; I wouldn't start with gender; I wouldn't start with feminism. I would start with stripping down to what fundamentally informs my life, which is that I'm a seeker on the path. I think of feminism, and I think of anti-racist struggles as part of it. But where I stand spiritually is, steadfastly, on a path about love."[21]

Increased awareness of the cultural forces acting on us can facilitate objectivity, and can decrease the tendency to automatically and reactively create our identities.

Identity foreclosure: Deciding too soon who you are

Do our students think of themselves as finalized, finished, written in stone? Psychologist Erik Erikson warns of adolescent "identity foreclosure," the premature identity decisions youth often make about themselves. Such decisions close down possibilities for them at a time when exploration is crucial to their full development.[22]

I can relate to kids who get excluded. I have been excluded from many different things for no specific reason. There is nothing unique about me, so people often think they are above me. (Seventh grade boy)

The challenge for our students and for us, the adults who guide them, is to make sure they see the great variety of cultures and of life choices that exist in the world, so their minds remain open and flexible long enough to see options for themselves and to mature into the most life-giving identity possible. It is crucially important that adolescent identity include productive mindsets such as belief in personal growth, understanding that we have power over our own lives, and realizing that effort can get us the life we want rather than the life we think we must settle for. See Advisory 21, focused on the growth mindset in Perspective Four.

Cultural position and power: deciding where we fit

Because identities are accorded various degrees of power and status in American society, each of us must come to terms not only with our own cultural identification but also with how a person of our identity is positioned and interacts with others of different identities. You may be very clear, for example, that you are Christian, but how do you perceive and relate to and interact with Jews and Muslims and atheists? You may be clear that you are African American, but how do you see yourself in the context of a society dominated by European Americans?

Most likely, we keep sifting through conversations and events to update our understanding of ourselves and others. Very young, we begin a sorting process, watching for cues: Who is telling the truth? Who is kind or cruel? Who has power over me? Who cares about me? By the time children get to school, they have developed ideas about who are likely to be allies for them.

Ask yourself
How do you answer the questions on the self-interview?

ADVISORY 18 ▶ CPR

Advisory goal: Identify the characteristics of a setting for optimal adolescent learning

Greeting

Language Greeting using American Sign Language: To sign "hello" in American Sign Language, smile, make eye contact, and make a friendly salute toward the person you are greeting. The first student starts by greeting the person on his/her right; that person returns the greeting, then greets the person on his/her right, and so on.

> Good Morning, Students!
>
> For sharing today, think about the <u>institution</u> of school and the effect it has had on you. Do you believe school is easier for some students, depending on their gender, color, size, appearance, ability, or socio-economic class? Check below on the <u>continuum</u>:
>
> No_____Yes

Share

Think Ink Pair Share: *Is school easier for some students, based on their gender, color, size, appearance, ability, or socio-economic class? Is school easier for girls than for boys? In what ways might school be different depending on how much money your family has?* Provide student with pencils and paper. Students quietly think about the questions for one or two minutes, and write down their thoughts. Then students form groups of two or three and share what they've written. Keep time, prompting groups to change sharers every two minutes to assure balanced participation. Volunteers share out their responses with the whole group.

Activity

Talking Cards: *What would help students make friends more easily at school and do well academically?*

Students write and then sort ideas and opinions so they are "heard" anonymously. The cards do the "talking."

1. Pass out two small note cards to each student (put extras in middle of circle)

2. Pose the question: *What would help students make friends more easily at school and do well academically?*

3. Students write responses on cards (one response per card). They write a suggestion and why they think it would help student do well socially and academically

4. Collect and shuffle cards

5. Ask for one volunteer to read the cards and one to record responses, grouping similar ones

6. Discuss the suggestions

⊃ In the Talking Cards activity, remind students that opinions are only as good as the evidence that supports them. Encourage students to give examples and data that will substantiate their suggestions for improvements to the school culture.

⊃ The discussion of how to make school a place where all students can do well both socially and academically may call for an additional meeting.

Keep in Mind

Adults in school spend a lot of time trying to create and maintain a program that successfully educates students both academically and socially. Asking students for input about how a school can best help them grow may provide insights into their needs.

Examples of student comments:

- Let students express themselves, be who they are
- Play music while students are working
- Go on more field trips
- Don't make rules that leave people out
- Be more open-minded
- Have more diversity in school
- Pay more attention to students
- Have more electives
- Make everyone feel welcome

(Students from K-12 school)

Ask yourself

When you were an adolescent, did you feel understood and supported by your teachers?

ADVISORY 19 ▶ CPR

Advisory goals: Be able to identify rhetorical manipulations used to influence thinking and behavior. Understand the media's power to manipulate thinking and behavior.

Greeting

Fist-Tap Greeting: Select a student to begin. Around the circle, students greet with *Good morning,* _____, adding a gentle fist bump. When time is short, you may choose to make this a silent greeting, or use the Fist-Tap Greeting as a quick simultaneous greeting. Model and practice fist-tapping before beginning: make a fist, then gently tap partner's fist as *Good Morning,*_____ is exchanged.

> Greetings, Eager Buyers!
>
> How much do the media and advertising try to <u>manipulate</u> you? Do you ever want things because you think they will make you better looking, more popular, or more important? How much do the ads we see and hear affect us? Today we're going to get the Gotcha's!

Share

Groups of four look over the Gotcha handout and think of examples of ads meant to manipulate them. Volunteers share out some examples. Advise students to pay close attention because, in the activity, their group will decide on a product they will try to sell to the rest of the group tomorrow, using as many gotcha's as they can.

⮑ Let students know that not only the media use "gotcha" techniques. Many people try to manipulate others into seeing things a certain way. During the sharing-out time, make sure the "gotcha" terms are understood. To save time and to clear up confusion, you can offer examples.

Activity

Gotcha! In the groups of four formed for the share, students decide on a product, real or imagined, that they will try to sell in the next advisory meeting by using one or more of the gotcha techniques. Students with the two shortest middle names are partners, and students with the two longest middle names are partners. Each pair decides on a product to sell. At the next advisory meeting, each pair will try to sell the other pair their product.

⮑ You can provide pictures showing products that appeal to adolescents from magazines, newspapers, or the Internet. You can also offer the option of bringing an object from home as their "product."

GOTCHA: GETTING SMART ABOUT MANIPULATION

Here are seven ways people try to trick others into believing something.

Card stacking

A very common technique is to tell only what the seller wants us to hear. They omit, downplay, or distort the fact(s) that would detract from the sales pitch (or show it up for a lie), so we will be attracted to their product. Gotcha!

Transfer or association

The idea here is for us to want a product because it is used by someone we believe in or admire. For example, seeing a favorite athlete wearing a certain brand of shoes, we may want the same shoes. The flag, puppies and kittens, luxurious homes and scenes, images of people having fun, and more are used to make us want products. Gotcha!

Testimonials

Testimonials and celebrity endorsements sell products, too. Advertisers pay them a lot of money to say positive things about the products. And even if they really do like the product, that doesn't mean we will, but we like to think we are somewhat like the celebrities. Gotcha!

Bandwagon

Everybody else loves this product, thinks this way, believes in this idea or person, so you should, too. If you don't, you aren't as pretty or handsome or smart or ... gotcha!

Plain folks

This technique says that regular, ordinary people like us like the seller's idea or product, and millions are buying it, so you should, too. Gotcha!

Sweeping generalizations

Sellers make broad generalizations about the importance or value of their idea or product. The generalizations appeal to emotions such as patriotism, family, freedom, wanting to be attractive, etc. People with bright white teeth are more popular; drivers of sports cars have more freedom than the rest of us. Gotcha!

Name calling

The advertiser can resort to negatives and describe the alternative to their product or idea as ugly, dishonest, or stupid (politicians often advertise this way). Truth, half-truths, and outright lies can be employed to make the point. Gotcha!

ADVISORY 20 ▶ A+

Advisory goals: Be able to identify rhetorical manipulations used to influence thinking and behavior. Understand the media's power to manipulate thinking and behavior

Greeting

One-Minute Mingle Greeting: Each person greets as many students by name as possible in one minute. Model how to accept and return a greeting, maintaining eye contact, before moving on to the next person.

> Salutations, Salespeople!
>
> Today you will take the role of an advertiser and try to convince us to buy your product. You can use as many "gotchas" as you can think will help you be an effective _vendor_. Good luck!

Activity

Sales Pitch: Students divide into the same groups of four they had in the previous advisory meeting. The first pair of partners have 30 seconds (a common duration for TV commercials) to advertise their product to the other pair, using one or more gotchas. The audience partners decide whether they would buy or not, and then identify the gotcha(s) they detected in the pitch.

Pairs switch role, and the second tries to sell the first their product.

⮑ Use a timer during the sales pitches so groups do not exceed the 30-second time limit. At the first signal, the first set of partners makes their pitch. At the second signal (30 seconds later) they must stop. Then allow several minutes for the audience partners to either buy or refuse to buy and then name the gotchas they observed. When groups seem ready, signal the beginning of the second sales pitch, and give another signal after 30 seconds.

Reflection (in groups of four)

How aware were you during the sales pitches that you were being manipulated with gotchas?

Do you feel better prepared to catch gotchas in advertising?

Volunteers share out.

Keep in Mind

Adolescents' susceptibility to media can lead to destructive judgments of themselves and others.

Young adolescents are self-conscious. They don't want people to think of them as odd, so they are often blatantly critical of and don't want to associate with students who do not fit the media norm (e.g., gays, lesbians, girls who don't fit the stereotype of "pretty," etc.). They are insecure and looking for an identity. They reject options that will have them be seen as a "nerd" or fat or gay. They are still likely to copy the behavior of their families, but the media also are a strong influence. I believe the media has pushed them toward sexism, racism, age-ism, homophobia. I never hear them questioning the media portrayals. (Youth worker)

Ask yourself

What media portrayals appear to you as attractive? How influenced are you by media?

ADVISORY 21 ▶ CPR

Advisory goal: Raise consciousness about the effects of the media on us

Greeting

Inside-Outside Circle Greeting: Form a double circle, one inside the other. As the inside circle rotates slowly, members of the inside circle greet people in the outside circle with a handshake and *Good morning, _____.*Each person greeted responds with *Good morning, _____* . Everyone greets everyone.

> Hail, Persuasive People!
>
> Now we'll check out your powers of persuasion again as you try to convince us to do some <u>unconventional</u> things. Get ready to play Media Mania!

➲ Make sure everyone in the inside circle has a partner in the outside circle. If you have an odd number of students, you can even things out by participating. In this meeting, the circles are used for both the greeting and share.

➲ This is a high-energy, fast-moving greeting, Even so, each greeting must include names. The need to do it right and do it fast makes for fun.

Share

Inside-Outside Circle Share: Gathered in the same circles as for the greeting, students face each other and greet by saying *Hi, _____.* They take turns answering the first question below. After each movement of the inside circle, everyone has a new partner. The new partners always begin by greeting one another, then they respond to the question. There are four questions, so there will be four rounds.

Ask a different question each time the inside circle rotates:

How much do the media shape and influence you?

Do some types of media seem to have more influence than others?

Have you ever bought something based only on what an advertisement told you about it?

How much does popular fashion (including sports clothing) influence what you wear?

Activity

Media Mania: Form five small groups, and assign each group one of the advertising projects below. The groups' job is to create a 30-second advertisement to convince people that they will be more attractive if they:

- make their eyebrows grow continually
- paint their noses different colors
- wear huge shoulder pads
- wear many layers of clothes
- wear a bustle (men and women)

Teams have two minutes to create ads, and then the ads are presented to the whole group. Tell them they'll have to work fast!

Keep in Mind

The media's influence on our values can be powerful. It can affect adolescent self-esteem dramatically.

The girls in our school were victims of advertising. They acted out what they saw depicted and behaved as the teenagers they were being marketed to be. The ones who matched the pictures best excluded the other girls to feel superior. (Fifth-sixth grade teacher)

The media can also prompt anti-social and risky behavior: "The portrayal of violence, sex, and drugs/alcohol in the media has been known to adversely affect the behavior of children and adolescents. There is a strong association between perceptions of media messages and observed behavior, especially with children."[23]

Ask yourself

Can you think of fashions, entertainment, arts, political points of view, etc., that attracted you after the media publicized and/or promoted them?

ADVISORY 22 ▶ A+

Advisory goals: Know the various factors that shape our identities. Understand the difference between unsubstantiated opinions and opinions supported by evidence.

Greeting

Basic Greeting: Select a student to begin. She greets the student next to her in the circle, *Good morning, _____;* he responds, *Good morning, _____,* turns to the person next to him and greets him, and the process is repeated around the circle. The audience's job is to watch each greeting politely and quietly.

> Jambo, Everyone!
>
> We'll try out the game Four Corners today to <u>ascertain</u> where each of us stands on a question about influences in life. Three big influences are family, friends, and media; which do you think is most powerful? Be prepared to answer and to support your opinion during the game. _____ will share with us today about influences in her life.

Activity

Four Corner Thinking: Designate the four corners of the room as 1 (highest influence), 2 (high influence), 3 (moderate influence), and 4 (low influence). Students move to the corner that represents their position on each statement the leader reads.

Statements: *Rate the following from 1 to 4 (1=highest) for how strongly they influence the lives of Americans:*

Friends' attitudes and beliefs

Color of skin

Gender

Sexual orientation

How much money you have

Religion

⮌ There may be enough time in the Four Corners game to ask after each question (or a couple of questions) for volunteers to share about why they went to the corner they did. You can allow students to change their minds and change their corners. You can ask someone who changed corners to share about why they did so. There aren't right or wrong choices; what's important is that students have reasons for why they made the choices they did. We are strengthening thinking and discernment skills adolescents need to sort out biased opinions from opinions substantiated by evidence.

Reflection

How many people had second thoughts about the corner they chose for some of the statements?

What is the value of second thoughts?

Keep in Mind

Asked to say how much influence something has on them, students think about how they came to be the persons they are, and how the influence of color, gender, class, sexual orientation, and so on, affects them currently. They have not completed their self-shaping. Their cultures are still affecting them, and will do so for all their lives. In Perspective Four we will examine how much in flux we and everything else in life are all the time. This opens up the possibility of growth: *I am still subject to influence. I can still grow and change. In fact, I am growing and changing at this very moment!* This is the attitude we need to cultivate to engage students in learning.

In Perspective One, focused in large part on how culture shapes us, we have avoided any hint of fatalism. Our cultures have a great deal to do with forming us, but we have a lot to say about the end result. Habits of bias need to be seen and named for what they are and the damage they do. Hopelessness may be a habit that a young person can identify and change. Thinking critically and shifting perspective when necessary, even temporarily, allows us to view life freshly, seeing differently what we thought was defective or dangerous or permanent.

Ask yourself

In what ways are you still growing and changing?

ADVISORY 23 ▶ A+

Advisory goal: Understand the challenge of communication across cultural differences.

➲ In the basket, put small pieces of paper, one for each student, lettered A through E. Students will form groups based on the letter they chose, all the "A's" together, etc.

Greeting

Greet Three Greeting: Pairs of students make eye contact from across the circle, move and greet each other using a greeting of their choice, and repeat this process two more times. All students greet simultaneously. Model and practice how to do this.

> Ahn neong, Everyone!
> That's Korean for "Hello." We'll have a quick greeting today, and then we'll form five groups for a simulation activity. Do Now: Pick a letter from the basket and bring it to the meeting.

➲ This is another "mix them up" kind of greeting. After students greet, have them return to seats next to the last person they greeted. This is especially important if you notice that the group needs more circulating and partner variety.

Activity

Culture Shock Simulation Activity: This exercise helps us become more aware of how we experience and respond to people who behave differently from us. You'll need bags of some kind of token, like marbles or stones. Students form five groups, A through E, based on the letter they drew. Each group behaves and communicates differently. Give written "cultural" behaviors to each group according to the instructions below. Groups are not to know about the behavior guidelines of other groups.

"Cultural" behaviors for each group

Group A: Use no eye contact when speaking to others, but when you are not talking or listening to someone talking to you, you can make eye contact.

Group B: You touch anyone with whom you are conversing. If more than one person is listening, the speaker touches all of them.

Group C: Wait seven ("one one thousand, two one thousand, three one thousand…") seconds before you respond to any question or statement from anyone, whether from your own or another group.

Group D: You each carry with you a bag of tokens. Move about, asking people, *Would you like a* _____? If they say yes, hand them one (no more). If they say no, move on. Don't converse with anyone who refuses a token, and don't let anyone reach into your token bag.

Group E: Don't take anything offered to you by anyone, and don't say, *No,* at any time, even in answer to a question.

Process: Give the groups time to practice their assigned ways of behaving (three minutes). Have the groups mingle and discuss the following question: *Do you think our country is getting closer to Dr. Martin Luther King's dream of a world of equality and justice for all?* (five to eight minutes)

⊃ This exercise challenges players to communicate with people who are different from them. Its purpose is to raise awareness of the challenges of communication in school and in everyday life.

⊃ Tell students at the beginning that this activity requires each character to stick with his or her behavior guidelines. If you see a student dropping away from his character's culture, remind him to stay with it.

Reflection

During the post-activity discussion, focus on the confusion and mistakes when we try to interact with cultures whose ways we do not understand. It's easy to see why we make mistakes and hurt each other's feelings! Partners discuss (three minutes):

How did you feel about the people you talked with?

How did they respond to you?

What does this tell us about how we react when we interact with people who behave differently from us?

⊃ During the partner reflection, tell students when one minute has elapsed, and that they should either change who speaks or move to the next question.

Keep in Mind

Crossing the cultural divides: mind your mindsets

Interacting with people whose cultures are very different from our own is a challenge. In the classroom, as in life, "we do not really see through our eyes or hear through our ears, but through our beliefs."[24] Once we become aware of our habitual, culturally-driven ways of being, we can take a stand to guide our students—*all* of our students, no matter how different from us they may be—toward success. Such a stand requires those three all-important mindsets.

Growth mindset

When we examine how we see the world and then seek new perspectives, we discover fresh ways of seeing, and a sense of growth and possibility for our students.

I was in my first year of teaching high school. I had three senior English classes, one college prep and two "regular." I used the same curriculum, the same literature, and the same lessons for all three senior classes, helping the less adept as well as the more accomplished keep moving along. A boy in one of my regular senior English classes said during the first month of school, "You're making a mistake. I found out you're teaching us the same stuff you're teaching the smart kids. You don't understand. We're the dumb ones." I replied, "It's true that I'm using the same curriculum for all of you—and you're all doing just fine with it!" (High school English teacher)

We can also let students know that we realize what a leap it is for many of them to go from their home cultures to the school culture. When the two ways of being collide, we can help bridge the gap with understanding and empathy, even when we believe the student needs serious correction. In those moments, we call upon our objectivity.

Objective mindset

Scholar Lisa Delpit describes her high school experience: "Although I grew up in a segregated Southern community, secure as a young child that the rich tapestry of our African-American lives was not merely beautiful but the *only* sensible way of functioning in the world, that tapestry unraveled quickly. When I enrolled in a newly integrated high school in the 1960's, suddenly many of the 'sensible' ways of doing things no longer seemed acceptable. My fellow black classmates and I had to cope not only with the overt racism that preceded our arrival, but with the subtle racism, infinitely more insidious, that developed when aspects of our culture—language, interactional styles, belief systems—became targets for remediation at best, and evidence for our inability to learn at worst."[25]

We can let our understanding of the profound effect of home culture influence our responses when it and school culture fall out of sync, and a student disrupts. A priceless benefit of this non-judgmental way of seeing students is that it helps us avoid taking student behavior personally, even when it seems intended that way. Instead, we allow our understanding of cultural differences to enlighten our response. We are more and more able to think and feel at the same time, and take effective action.

Action mindset

This isn't to say that rule-breakers are off the hook—the move is off the "hook" of personal upset and onto the "hook" of accountability to the community. In school communities in which students participate in making, interpreting, understanding, practicing, and reflecting on the rules, the rule-breaker is held accountable.

The teacher speaks for the learning community that has been disrupted, whose Social Contract has been broken. Bringing to bear your objective mindset, knowing some of the influences of his personal culture that may be pulling him in another direction, you urge him in the name of the community and its Social Contract to return to a positive relationship with the school community. This takes a lot of effort from both of you, but if both of you can do it, it is freeing. Both you and your student get to loosen the grip of your individual cultures enough to stand together, instead of opposite each other.

After on-the-spot redirection, call on your knowledge of cultural and developmental influences that may be at play. This is when your past work to build relationship with the student can pay off in his willingness to be more patient—to try to think and feel at the same time—and in your ability to speak meaningfully to him. Teach him what he needs to know and remember *in moments like this* so he can navigate successfully through life, even with people very different from him—people, for example, like his teachers!

Ask yourself

What can I do to maintain the growth, objective, and action mindsets I need to teach with the greatest positive impact on my students?

ADVISORY 24 ▶ A+

Advisory goal: Build community by getting to know one another

⮑ In the box, put three or four cards for each food, enough for each student to draw one card. For the activity, all the "apples" will be a group, all the "pizzas," etc.

Greeting

Language Greeting: Choose a language (see page 349 for list) or have students choose a greeting from your Ways to Say Hello list. All students greet in this language, either around the circle or in the All Group Greeting format. (All Group format: One student says *Shalom, everyone.* Group responds: *Shalom, Julia.*) Model and practice the greeting ahead of time to facilitate correct pronunciation.

> Bula, Everyone!
>
> That's "hello" in the Fiji Islands. We're going on a treasure hunt today, and all the "treasures" can be found within your small group. <u>Do Now:</u> Pick a group name from the box and find your fellow group members (all the group names are <u>edibles</u>!). Then join me in the circle.

Activity

Group Treasure Hunt: Organize into random teams of three to four people each. Share point system, below, with the whole group—write on a board or distribute printed copies to each group. Teams add up the points they have for each item on the list to see which team is the high scorer.

- One point for each person living in our homes
- One point for each button on our clothes
- One point for each team member who was born outside of this state
- One point for each team member who takes care of a younger family member at least once a week
- Points for hair color per person:

      Blond = 1 point

      Brown = 2 points

      Black = 3 points

      Red = 4 points

- One point for each shoelace hole or hook on one shoe of each person in the group
- One point for each sport at least one team member has played in the last year (count total number of different sports named; any sport counts)
- Two points for each academic goal members of the team have (write down goals)
- Five points for any team member who heard or saw a put-down in the last week and defended the person who was put down (be ready to tell about the incident)
- Five points if everyone on the team can sing the first verse of the National Anthem (be ready to perform).

⤳ Here is the first verse of *The Star Spangled Banner* by Francis Scott Key, 1814:

Oh, say, can you see by the dawn's early light
What so proudly we hailed at the twilight's last gleaming,
Whose broad stripes and bright stars through the perilous fight
O'er the ramparts we watched were so gallantly streaming?
And the rocket's red glare, the bombs bursting in air,
Gave proof through the night that our flag was still there.
Oh, say, does that star-spangled banner yet wave
O'er the land of the free and the home of the brave?

⤳ The Group Treasure Hunt is likely to take two advisory meetings. The groups must list their computations and tally their final scores. When the groups report out, their results need to be verified (teacher may check computations at random, then the accuracy of the final tally). There need be no reward for the winning team; it's all in fun, and it's more fun to win!

Reflection

What are the advantages in this activity of having a variety of people in your group?

What value in real life do you see in knowing and working with a variety of people?

Keep in Mind

All cultures value some qualities more than others, and what is valued may seem arbitrary to people of other cultures. In the Group Treasure Hunt, we operate with arbitrary values. There is an advantage in the game to speaking a foreign language, being born in another state or country, having many people living in your house, taking care of siblings, and speaking up when you hear a put-down. Advantage is intentionally skewed toward groups like students from poverty, or students who immigrated to the U.S. and have a native language other than English. In contemporary American culture, these characteristics are often disadvantages, so the game turns the values of the dominant culture upside down for a few minutes ... all in fun!

Ask yourself

Do you have friends from a variety of cultures? What do you see as the advantage of this, whether it is part of your experience or not?

ADVISORY 25 ▶ CPR

Advisory goal: Growth in appreciation for the advantages of a diverse society

Greeting

Language Greeting: Choose a language (see page 349 for list) or have students choose a greeting from your Ways to Say Hello list. All students greet in this language, either around the circle or in the All Group Greeting format. (All Group format: One student says *Bonjour, everyone*. Group responds *Bonjour, Max*.)

> Ya-ta-hey, Treasure-finders!
> That's Navajo for "hello." After our greeting, meet with your group, complete your treasure hunt, and come back to the circle with your score.

⮑ Model and practice the greeting ahead of time to facilitate correct pronunciation.

Activity

Group Treasure Hunt: Finish and report out

Reflection

What are some treasures we could seek in another Group Treasure Hunt?

⮑ When you create a new list for a treasure hunt, be sure to include points for some qualities that make for good relationships across cultures, and for qualities that disadvantaged students are likely to have.

Keep in Mind

As we learn more about each other's customs, especially those involving important passages such as birth, puberty, marriage, aging, and death, we come to understand that we all live out variations on a theme: human survival. The more carefully we look, the more we see the humanity in those who seem different from us. From this anthropological point of view, it can seem that there is so little difference among us it is hardly worth mentioning!

Ask yourself

What do you do to build relationships with students who are struggling in school?

ADVISORY 26 ▶ A+

Advisory goal: Build community by acknowledging each other

Greeting

High Five Greeting: In sequence around the circle, students greet each other with a high five: *Hi, Sal* (high five). Reply: *Hi, Leo* (high five).

> Welcome!
>
> We've come to know each other better over the last few weeks. Today we can acknowledge what we know: that each of us is a unique individual shaped by culture, and that each of us is also a part of the human family.

Activity

Tap Someone Who Acknowledgment: Students bend their heads down and close their eyes. Silently tap four students, who become the first tappers. They open their eyes and stand up as quietly as possible; others keep their eyes closed and heads down. Choose from categories listed below or create your own. Say, *Tap someone who,* and complete the sentence with a category. Tappers move quietly around the room, gently tapping the shoulders of players they feel fit the category. Give ample time for tapping before saying a new category. Play can continue for several categories. Select new tappers after three categories.

➲ Tappers remain anonymous. Watch for people peeking when you select tappers (students should keep their heads down as well as their eyes closed), and have them sit out a round.

➲ In this first experience of Tap Someone Who, choose students to do the tapping who tend to be generous, so as many people as possible get tapped. The hope is that everyone is touched once or twice during the activity.

Acknowledgment categories: Tap someone who...

is a good listener
will find a cure for cancer
will invent something
is as good as ... (gold, a chocolate sundae, etc.)
with whom you would share a secret
is a good friend
you don't often work or hang out with but would like to get to know better
helped you recently
would make a good (leader, accountant, computer programmer, dancer, comedian, etc.)
has made you laugh
you'd like to have lunch with
you admire
you would take on an all-expenses-paid trip to... (Alaska, New York City, Hawaii, etc.)
has taught you something

Reflection

Exit Card: Students answer the following question on an index card and hand it to you as they leave:

What is something you have learned about yourself from our conversations about culture?

Keep in Mind

Authentic acknowledgment of one person by another builds community. Authentic acknowledgments are honest, and they describe with specifics exactly what someone admires in another person's work or behavior. It takes both thinking and caring to deliver a good acknowledgment. Tap Someone Who provides a group warm-up for the practice of individual acknowledgments. In a light way, it lets people know that they are noticed and respected.

Our success with students depends on our good relationships with them across whatever cultural barriers there may be.

I taught in a school where punishment was part of the culture, and I established discipline through a punishment—anyone who broke the rules had to stay after school. It was a survival issue. I was concerned about losing control, losing face, losing credibility. Tom was a student I thought was put in my life to punish me! He was impossible. Every day he was disruptive and silly. He wouldn't ever participate in a genuine way. I responded by making him stay after school and talk to me. In the process, I got to know him. I saw that he was a true clown with a humorous outlook on life—especially on himself. When we talked, we laughed and laughed together. It very much changed how I saw him and how he saw me in class. All this messing up and distracting everyone that he did I found I could now address quickly and effectively before it got out of hand. I understood him, I cared about him, and I talked to him showing that I cared about him. (Fifth-sixth grade language arts teacher)

Ask yourself

In what ways have you gained a better understanding of your students during the conversations in Perspective One?

---

[1] Nikki Grimes, *Bronx Masquerade* (New York: Penguin Group, 2002), 7.

[2] Jack Canfield and Harold C. Wells, *100 Ways to Enhance Self-Concept in the Classroom: A Handbook for Teachers and Parents* (Upper Saddle River, NJ: Prentice Hall, 1976).

[3] Judith Harris, *The Nurture Assumption* (New York: Simon & Schuster, 1998).

[4] Donald C. Orlich and Glenn Gifford, Test Scores, *Poverty and Ethnicity: The New American Dilemma* (Pullman: Washington State University, 2006).

[5] Rohan Mascarenhas, "Examining the Effects of Inequality on Educational Outcomes: An Interview with Greg Duncan and Richard Murnane, October 13, 2011," Russell Sage Foundation, http://www.russellsage.org/blog/r-mascarenhas/examining-effects-inequality-educational-outcomes-interview-greg-duncan-and-richa.

[6] Richard D. Kahlenberg, "From All Walks of Life: New Hope for School Integration," *American Educator* (Winter, 2012-2013): 4.

[7] Linda Crawford, *The Advisory Book*, 2nd ed. (Minneapolis: The Origins Program, 2012).

[8] Margaret Allison Gibson, "Approaches to Multicultural Education in the United States: Some Concepts and Assumptions," *Anthropology and Education* 15 (1984), 94-119, quoted in Steven Z. Athanases, "A Gay-Themed Lesson in an Ethnic Literature Curriculum: Tenth Graders' Responses to 'Dear Anita'," *Harvard Educational Review*, 66, no. 2 (Summer 1996): 253.

[9] Peggy McIntosh, *White Privilege and Male Privilege: A Personal Account of Coming to See Correspondences through Work in Women's Studies* (Wellesley: Wellesley College Center for Research on Women, 1988), 4.

[10] Colum McCann, *Let the Great World Spin* (New York: Random House, 2009), 302-303.

[11] William A. Haviland, Harald E. L. Prins, Iana Walrath, and Bunny McBride, *The Essence of Anthropology*, 2nd ed. (Belmont CA: Wadsworth Cengage Learning, Inc., 2010), 90-91.

[12] Lisa Delpit, introduction to *Other People's Children* (New York: New Press, 1995), xiii.

[13] Arlette Ingram Willis, "Reading the World of School Literacy: Contextualizing the Experience of a Young African American Male," in *Education for a Multicultural Society*, ed. K.P. Afolabi, C.Bocala, R.C. DiAquoi, J.M. Hayden, I.A. Liefshitz, and Soojin Susan Oh (Cambridge: Harvard Educational Review, 2011), 25-26.

[14] George Ella Lyon, *Where I'm From: Where Poems Come From* (Spring, TX: Absey and Co, 1999), 3.

[15] "Where I'm From," George Ella Lyon, http://www.georgeellalyon.com/where.html.

[16] Nikki Grimes, *Bronx Masquerade* (New York: Penguin Group, 2002), 29.

[17] Marc Elrich, "The Stereotype Within," Educational Leadership 51, no. 8 (May 1994): 112-15.

[18] John Fountain, *True Vine: A Young Black Man's Journey of Faith, Hope, and Clarity* (New York: PublicAffairs, 2003).

[19] "Oprah Winfrey," Academy of Achievement, http://www.achievement.org/autodoc/page/win-obio-1.

[20] "Keeping the Legacy Alive: North Minneapolis Youth Speak Up!" Developmental Designs YouTube channel, www.youtube/developmentaldesigns.org.

[21] bell hooks, "Agent of Change: An Interview with bell hooks," *Tricycle Magazine* (Fall 1992), http://www.tricycle.com/special-section/agent-change-an-interview-with-bell-hooks.

[22] E.H. Erikson, ed., "Youth: Fidelity and Diversity," in *Youth: Change and Challenge* (New York: Norton, 1961), 1-23.

[23] K. A. Earles, Randell Alexander, Melba Johnson, Joan Liverpool, and Melissa McGhee, "Media Influences on Children and Adolescents: Violence and Sex," *Journal of the National Medical Association*, 94, no. 9 (September 2002): 797.

[24] Lisa D. Delpit, "The Silenced Dialogue: Power and Pedagogy in Educating Other People's Children," in *Education for a Multicultural Society*, ed. Kolajo Paul Afolabi, Candice Bocala, Raygine C. DiAquoi, Julia M. Hayden, Irene A. Liefshitz, and Soojin Susan Oh (Cambridge: Harvard Educational Review, 2011), 142.

[25] Delpit, *Other People's Children*, 73.

Interdependence

For all our variety and diversity, people are far more similar than different from each other. Cultures differ dramatically, but, as we saw in Perspective One, cultures' common function is to foster group and individual survival. And as our cultures meet our needs for food, shelter, clothing, community, and so on, they provide the context in which we come to be the people we are.

When we encounter other cultures, we tend to focus on differences. But we need to realize our commonalities, too, even when they are not immediately obvious. They are the foundation for relationships, and relationships—especially the ones across apparent differences—are immensely valuable to us personally, as educators, and as residents of planet Earth. In the most fundamental ways, our well-being and our fate are intertwined. We must keep this in mind when we struggle with our differences.

ADVISORY 1 ▶ CPR

Advisory goal: Understand how much we affect one another because we are interdependent

Greeting

Cumulative Greeting: Each person greets everyone who has preceded him in the greeting. The first student greets the student next to her; that student returns the greeting, then greets the person next to him. This student returns the greeting, and also greets the first person. This cumulative process continues around the circle; the last greeter must respond to being greeted by greeting everyone in the circle.

> Good Morning, Community Members!
> We'll see today how much we _influence_ each other's lives. Be ready to tell us about someone who has changed your mood, your plans, your attitude, or what you know.

⮑ In the end, everyone in the group is greeted by everyone else and returns each greeting. Students can add variety and interest by using different greetings (Hi, Ciao, How now, etc.).

Share

Whip Share: _Name someone who has affected you today and someone you have affected. In each case, say what the effect was._ Give students examples (_My little brother woke me up by jumping on me and I got mad;_ or _I helped a girl who dropped her books pick them up and she thanked me;_ or _The bus driver didn't yell at us today and bum me out before I got to school_). Allow a minute to think, then each student offers a brief response to the topic; responses "whip" around the circle.

⮑ The point of this share and of the activity below is to stimulate awareness that we make a difference in each other's days. Knowing that can help us be more sensitive to the effect we may have on others, for example, when we give a greeting that is lukewarm instead of friendly. In advisory, since we start the day with each other, we can help each other have a good day.

Activity

Chain of Effects: Read the following aloud to students.

Living things depend on one another. In chaos theory, scientists refer to the sensitive dependence on initial conditions. In other words, an event in nature affects other parts of nature, sometimes in surprising ways. One hypothetical example is that slight movement of air currents in one place could initiate a chain of effects that results in a hurricane in a location far away.

A classic example of the chain of effects is setting up dominos in a line so that one domino pushes the one next to it down, and so on, until all the dominos have fallen over; thus, the domino theory. Similarly, each day we affect the people around us by our actions and our moods, and they affect us.

My Day, by Charles D.: Ask a student to read the following story aloud.

This morning my mom made a lunch for me, and before I could grab it, my dog got it and ate it—every bit, except one cookie that rolled under the counter where he couldn't reach it. My mom was furious. She had to give me lunch money, and she was short on cash. She was so mad she told us to make our own breakfasts, then she left the kitchen to get dressed for work. My little brother and I each grabbed a piece of toast and went to school.

I was hungry and crabby by second hour. When Mr. King asked for homework, I told him I didn't have it. He asked why and I said the dog ate it, along with my lunch! That made him mad, so he gave me detention and said I could use it to redo my homework. In detention, I finished last night's homework and still had time left to do tonight's homework, and that meant I was free for the evening. I was so glad I even hung up my jacket when I came home. My mom noticed and smiled but didn't say anything. I hung out with a couple of guys for a while, and played catch with my little brother before dinner. He was happy. We had brownies for dessert.

Reflection

What effect did the dog have on the people?

What effect did the mom have on the boys in the morning? In the evening?

What effect did Charles have on Mr. King?

What effect did Mr. King have on Charles?

What effect did Charles have on his mom? On his brother? On you?

Keep in Mind

We create the climate for each other

This advisory meeting is based on the understanding that we influence each other's environments continuously. In addition to factors such as air and water quality, food quantity and quality, traffic, and other influences on our physical lives, we affect each other as we pursue happiness.

In a play that students performed, a mother woke up crabby, and was short-tempered with the father, who scolded the boy, who acted up at school and made his teacher angry. The teacher went home and was crabby with her own child, who then misbehaved at the dinner table and irritated his father, who yelled at his wife, who went to bed upset. In other words, the students dramatized how our moods and behavior affect each other's lives.

Our social climate is profoundly altered by how people respond to us, even in brief exchanges. You say what you say partly because of how I listen to you—the degree of attention I pay to you, my responsiveness, whether I interrupt with a thought of my own or wait for you to finish yours, and so on. In turn, the way I listen to you is affected by the tone and manner in which you speak to me— how fast and loudly you speak, whether you pause for a response, whether you look at me while you talk, etc. It's a dynamic circle of influences. If our communication is damaged, so are our relationships. No one acts in isolation; each affects and depends on the other.

Create a growth climate

Strongly influenced by the people around them, students build their sense of worth largely from the responses they get from peers, parents, and teachers. Students' willingness to learn is influenced greatly by the degree to which their teachers believe they can learn.

In her study of motivation and performance, psychologist Carol Dweck discovered "... some teachers preached and practiced a growth mindset. They focused on the idea that all children could develop their skills, and in their classrooms a weird thing happened. It didn't matter whether students started the year in the high- or the low-ability group. Both groups ended the year way up high. It's a powerful experience to see these findings. The group differences had simply disappeared under the guidance of teachers who taught for improvement, for these teachers had found a way to read their 'low-ability' students."[1]

Educator Gloria Ladson Billings observed two successful language arts teachers who worked very differently: "On the surface, Ann Lewis and Julia Devereaux employ very different strategies to teach reading…. However, beneath the surface, at the personal ideological level, the differences between these instructional strategies lose meaning. Both teachers want their students to become literate. Both believe that their students are capable of high levels of literacy."[2]

Just by believing in them, teachers' effect on the young people they teach can be transformative. The growth of each student depends on keeping the possibility for growth alive. Avoid judging students (or colleagues, or anyone else), and you preserve room for life's possibilities.

Ask yourself

Of the encounters you have had so far today, what is one that empowered you? Did another one disempower or increase stress?

ADVISORY 2 ▶ CPR

Advisory goal: Understand symbiosis among organisms and the interdependency of people who are different from one another

Greeting

Chain Greeting: The first greeter links arms with the person next to her, saying *Good morning*), _____, and is greeted back. Both, arms linked, greet the next person in unison and add her to the chain; now there are three. The greeting continues in this way: the chain of greeters say the greeting in unison, then link a new person to the chain, until the whole circle is

> *Greetings, fellow earthlings!*
>
> *The challenge today is finding examples of* <u>symbiosis</u>*, and playing a passing game called Al Citron, an activity that succeeds only when we all work together. A definition of* <u>symbiosis</u>*: a close association between or among living things that is* <u>mutually beneficial</u>*.*

linked together. You can do the Chain Greeting with all students standing from the start, or they can stand up as they link and greet, so the circle begins with everyone seated and ends with everyone standing.

Share

Partner Share: Read the following quote from naturalist John Muir and the symbiosis definition and examples aloud. For a more lively reading, students can read the examples. After the reading, partners collaborate to apply the symbiosis principle by naming a way that humans are mutually dependent. Ask partners to complete the following sentence: *We all depend on people who...* (e.g., grow food, clean streets, drive trucks). Ask volunteers to share out to the whole group.

"When we try to pick out anything by itself, we find it hitched to everything else in the universe."[3] John Muir

Symbiosis

Definition: a close association between or among living things that is mutually beneficial

Bees and plants: Bees drink a flower's nectar; meanwhile, pollen gets stuck to their bodies. The bees fly to flowers on other plants and drink. Meanwhile, the pollen falls onto these flowers and fertilizes them, and seeds are formed that fall to the ground and become new plants.

Other animals and plants: Animals eat fruit (apples, berries, bananas, etc.), including the seeds, unless they are inedible. As they move from place to place, they digest the fruit, but not the seeds, which they pass intact out of their bodies onto the ground, and new plants grow from the seeds, often far away from the original plants. Thus, plants spread far enough away from each other so they don't have to compete too much for soil nutrients, and biodiversity is enhanced.

Sea anemones and hermit crabs: Sea anemones hitchhike on the backs of hermit crabs. As the crabs move along, the anemones pick up food with their tentacles. At the same time, the anemones protect the crabs by using their stinging tentacles to fend off predators.

Oxpeckers and zebras: African oxpecker birds travel on the backs of zebras, elephants, hippos, and other large animals, eating ticks off the animals and sucking blood out of the open tick wounds. The oxpeckers warn their hosts when a predator is nearby producing a hissing, screaming alarm.

Goby fish and snapping shrimp: Snapping shrimp, which are nearly blind, construct and maintain burrows in the seabed. Gobi fish stand guard at the entrance, wagging their tails against the shrimps' antennae or in the burrow entrance to warn the shrimp of danger. In return, the fish are protected from predators by using the burrow to hide during the day and sleep with the shrimp at night.

Activity

Al Citron (a team-building game): All sit in a circle (on the floor is easiest, but chairs can work). A small object is passed from person to person counterclockwise around the circle in rhythm with the chant below. At the underlined syllables, each person passes the object one person to the right. On the first *triki,* everyone feigns a passing motion, then takes the object back, and then on *tron* actually passes the object, and the song begins again. It's important to keep the rhythm steady.

Al citron de la fandango

Sango sango sabare

Sabare de la rondello

Con su triki triki tron.

➲ Most of these lyrics are nonsense, but the *fandango* is a Spanish dance; the *rondella* is a stringed musical instrument; and *citron* is Spanish for "lemon."

➲ If things get confused (people pass when they shouldn't, or miss a pass—this happens a lot!), keep going to the end of the song. After a laugh, you can start over.

Keep in Mind

Interdependent exchange of goods and services

"All life is interrelated," wrote Dr. Martin Luther King, Jr., in his 1963 Letter from Birmingham Jail. "We are caught in an inescapable network of mutuality, tied into a single garment of destiny. Whatever affects one directly, affects all indirectly."[4]

Dr. King delivered this message about our interrelatedness in his *Christmas Sermon for Peace* in 1967, "You get up in the morning and go to the bathroom and reach over for the sponge, and that's handed to you by a Pacific Islander. You reach for a bar of soap, and that's given to you at the hands of a Frenchman. And then you go into the kitchen to drink your coffee for the morning, and that's poured into your cup by a

South American. And maybe you want tea: that's poured into your cup by a Chinese person. Or maybe you're desirous of having cocoa for breakfast, and that's poured into your cup by a West African. And then you reach over for your toast, and that's given to you at the hands of an English-speaking farmer, not to mention the baker. And before you finish eating breakfast in the morning, you've depended on more than half of the world. This is the way our universe is structured, this is its interrelated quality. We are not going to have peace on earth until we recognize this basic fact of the interrelated structure of all reality.[5]

Every student of the life sciences learns about the interconnected cycles of life: clouds drop rain; animals and plants drink; plants transpire, and streams and oceans evaporate water back into the air; clouds form; and on it goes. How we interact with or interrupt the water cycle affects everyone's access to this critical resource. And this is true for every resource and for every living thing. Problems arise when people disagree about how to interact with our environment: farmers may wish to use fertilizers, herbicides, and insecticides to increase the yield. Consumers like the lower prices that accompany higher yields. But people who live downstream from the farmlands and make their living fishing or shrimping may have to cope with ever-enlarging dead zones caused by fertilizer runoff.

In this simplified scenario of tensions among interest groups, the farmers feel the fishers and shrimpers don't understand their situation; the people downstream blame the people upstream for the algae-choked water; and consumers are unhappy about the rising price of fish and shrimp. All are affected in matters of food and water, essentials of life, by all the others.

Should we ban or regulate fertilizers, even though workers in the fertilizer industry might lose their jobs? Could fishers and shrimpers make a living taking tourists on boat trips instead of fishing? Would that make fish and shrimp unavailable to consumers? Would it help if we all ate less? An infinite number of questions arise from our interdependence.

Ask yourself
In what ways do you depend on the families of the students you teach?

ADVISORY 3 ▶ CPR

Advisory goal: Experience and understand the ways people are interconnected

Greeting

Web Greeting: The first person greets someone across the circle and then tosses a ball of yarn to him or her while holding onto the end of the yarn. The person greeted then greets someone else across the circle, holding onto the yarn and tossing the ball. When everyone has been being greeted and received and tossed the yarn ball, a connected web is formed.

> Good morning, allies!
> Yesterday we read a quote from John Muir (1838-1914), who was <u>instrumental</u> in preserving American wilderness: "When we try to pick out anything by itself, we find it hitched to everything else in the universe." Today we'll make and check some hitches by literally connecting all of us together in a web and by searching for what we have in common.

➲ You can reverse the order in which you made the web to roll up the ball of yarn again. An alternative is to ask two students to rewind the yarn during the Partner Share.

Share

Partner Share: *What might be fun about living in a commune? What might be hard?*

Before asking students to share, read aloud a definition of a commune (the Oxford English Dictionary defines it as a group of people living together and sharing possessions and responsibilities). Specify a length of time to share. Issue a time warning halfway through the share to ensure balanced sharing/listening. Volunteers share out.

Activity

Common Ground: Players circle up and form groups of three, four, or five. Through conversation, groups discover commonalities among some or all members and list as many as they can in two or three minutes. Group members share a few of their commonalities with another group. New teams can be formed and another round played.

➲ **Variation:** Groups can note "uncommon commonalities," those that seem unusual.

Keep in Mind

The Fellowship for Intentional Community defines communes: "intentional communities or cooperative living. We use 'commune' only when referring to communities that share their income and resources completely, or nearly so."[6]

During the 1960's when so-called "hippie" communes were numerous, the term *commune* was familiar to many. Communes persist throughout the world. Among them, *kibbutzim* (the Hebrew word for communal groups) have been an important segment of the Israeli community and economy since the early 20th century.

Ask yourself

How do you and your colleagues depend on one another in your school community?

ADVISORY 4 ▶ CPR

Advisory goal: Become aware of the effects of our interdependence

Greeting

Baseball Greeting: Baseball players can hit singles, doubles, triples, and homeruns. Students use one of these four types of hits to greet someone. Stand in a circle and select a student to begin. If he declares a single, he greets the student next to him; those who declare a double will greet the student two chairs away, and so on. Students may "high five" students as they pass by. Once a student has been greeted, she sits down and will no longer exchange high fives or be greeted again (the first greeter remains standing until greeted again at the end). The greeting continues until everyone has been greeted, with the last greeter greeting the first.

> Bienvenidos, Equipo! (This is Spanish for "Welcome, Team!")
>
> Teammates depend on each other. As we continue to explore our interdependence, think about your experience on teams and about others you depend on. Do players on professional sports teams affect your life? Get ready to share your thoughts with the group.

Share

Partner Share: *Who is someone you depend on? In what way(s) do you depend on him or her?* Specify a length of time to share. Issue a time warning halfway through the share to ensure balanced sharing/listening. Volunteers share out if time permits.

Activity

Chain of Effects: The effects of our words and actions extend beyond our families, friends, and school. Maybe *everything* we say or do affects everyone else in some way, but often the connection is not immediately apparent.

Divide students into eight groups and give each group one of the questions below. The group discusses its question, and one person from each group reports out to the whole group a few ideas about who would be affected in each case. The person with the most letters in his or her full name is the reporter.

1. *What effect does a motorcyclist riding without wearing a helmet have on others?*

2. *What effect does a factory worker who makes very little money in a foreign country have on a factory worker in the U.S.?*

3. *What effect does a talk-show host have who speaks in a derogatory way about certain people?*

4. *What effect on people does a politician have who promises that if he is elected, everyone will have more money and be happier?*

5. *What effect do people who drive cars have on others?*

6. *What effect does it have when a person in a wheelchair participates in a marathon?*

7. *What effect does it have when a motorist drives over the speed limit?*

8. *How does a person who lives alone in the woods raising, gathering, and hunting for his own food affect others?*

Keep in Mind

The chain of effects is universal, even when we can't see it. Through lifestyles, values, political systems, the environment, communication, and many other ways, all are interconnected. Because we are connected, other people's choices can affect our everyday lives. The stakes for making and keeping peace are very high.

An example is the first item on our list in the Chain of Effects exercise. If a motorcyclist wearing no helmet crashes, chances are much greater that he will suffer a brain injury than if he had been wearing a helmet. So if he crashes, what if he is disabled and needs medical and social services for the rest of his life? What if he can't ever work again? Should motorcyclists be required by law to wear helmets? Should motorcyclists who do not wear helmets be excluded from public medical assistance? Should wearing a helmet be a matter of choice?

Closer to home is our classroom interconnectedness:

The message I give my students is that when we mess up, everyone in the class is affected. I ask, "Who's affected by what happened?" I teach connectedness by introducing students to action apologies, where you don't just say you're sorry, but you also show it with an act of kindness. And if someone is absent, I say that I miss him or her, and when they return, I catch them before they come into the classroom and tell them that. Sometimes it's a little bit of acting, but I want them to get the message that we all are connected. (Seventh-eighth grade language arts and social studies teacher)

Objective mindset

If you see yourself as a custodian of the web of life in your classroom, you are highly aware that nothing happens in a vacuum; everything is in context. If, as in the Developmental Designs approach, you empower and guide students to democratically establish the rules, you can honestly say, "I enforce rules not out of anger, but out of the need for order and equality in our community. It's not simply that I don't allow certain behavior in my classroom, but that we decided that in order for all of us to get along and do our work, each person has to respect every other person." Aware that humiliation sparks rebellion, we keep behavior corrections as low-key and private as possible, so it will be easier for students to avoid taking things personally and to reduce push-back.

Ask yourself

What is the effect on the rest of the group when I discipline a student?

ADVISORY 5 ▶ CPR

Advisory goals: Develop an inclusive view of language. Build community.

Greeting

Formal Greeting: One at a time, students greet the person to their right using that person's last name: *Good morning, Mr./ Ms. _____* with a polite handshake, and the person responds, *Good morning, Mr./ Ms. _____.*

> Dear Group,
>
> Sometimes we use formal speech and other times we relax into slang. It's important to know how and when to use each, because they have different effects on listeners. Today we'll play with our <u>formal</u> (given) names and <u>informal</u> (nick) names. Think of a nickname or baby name to share with us, and we'll play a name game.

↪ **Whole-group alternative:** Each person greets the group by saying, *Good morning, everyone. My name is Mr. (or Ms.) _____.* The group in unison responds back: Good morning, Mr. _____. This alternative avoids the problem of students not knowing how to pronounce certain names. You can begin with the unison formal greeting, and on another occasion try out the individual formal greeting.

↪ Smiles and giggles often result when adolescents try on formality. This is fine, but noto sarcasm or mockery. If you detect any, direct the student to try it again with friendly respect (or to sit out, if it was intentional).

Share

Whip Share: *What is your nickname?* Each student gives a brief response; responses "whip" around the circle.

Activity

Name Race (team-building activity): Students sit or stand in a circle. Start timing at the moment the first person says his name (see variations below) and see how quickly everyone in turn can say his or her name around the circle. Complete the circle of names as quickly as possible, then try to better your time.

↪ Go faster and faster. You can try to set your best time for first names only, then try a round with first and last names, or first, middle, and last names. You can add Mr. or Ms. to be extra formal, or you can go the opposite direction around the circle and use nicknames. A stopwatch is useful. As you have fun with the Name Race, the students' names become more familiar and the community more connected.

Keep in Mind

When we are aware of our connectedness, sometimes we treat each other differently. Nicknames signal closeness and acceptance. In this advisory, we are building closeness and mutual connection, and at the same time using language in various forms for various places and occasions.

One way we can help students feel more connected to school is by assuring them with our behavior and language that the way they speak in their family or neighborhood is

OK — it is simply a variation on the way we ask them to speak in school. Make sure there is no judgment embedded in that.

Much can be made in a positive, instructive way, without judgment, of the language differences that exist among and within cultures. Starting with a simple consideration of formal versus informal speech initiates the discussion in a non-judgmental way. It challenges us to tune our language to connect with others, even at moments of disagreement or conflict, to help bridge the distance between us.

When I discipline students, I do different things to maintain the relationship while I'm correcting them. I try to use relaxed, everyday language and make references to things I know about them or experiences we've had in the past. I'm successful with some of the hardest students because we know each other. (Behavior specialist)

Ask yourself

Do you know what your students prefer to be called?

ADVISORY 6 ▶ CPR

Advisory goals: Identify similarities in the midst of differences. Develop the skills of teamwork. Experience leadership and followership.

Greeting

Same and Different Greeting and Share: Partners greet each other with a High Five, Low Five, or Fist-tap. As always, each greeting and response includes the name of the person. Then they identify three ways they are different from each other and three things they have in common.

> Hello, Friends!
>
> Sometimes we're surprised when we discover that we share characteristics or preferences or experiences with a person from whom we think we are quite different. Today our task is to note as many similarities and differences as we can.

Share

Venn Diagram Partner Share: Similar and Different: Using a Venn diagram, partners record ways they are different and similar, naming as many commonalities as they can. Students draw two circles of about 6" diameter which overlap by about 3" at the center. They write one of their names above the circle on the left and the other above the one on the right. They bring up cultural and personal characteristics, such as "has five siblings," "likes spring rolls," "good at babysitting," and determine where in the Venn diagram the characteristic should be placed—in an area representing one of them, or the area in the middle, representing both. Volunteers share out to the whole group examples of characteristics the pairs found that they have in common.

➲ The first time students do this, the teacher may give teams a list of characteristics to consider, such as differences or similarities in ages, families, favorite foods, things you are good at, language, color, places you've been, and ambitions.

Activity

Shape Up: Students form teams of four, five, or six. Using five pieces of flat elastic nine feet long, teams recreate a geometric shape drawn on the board by the leader. All team members must have contact with the elastic at all times. At first, the shapes should be simple (triangle, square, pentagon); as the students succeed, the figures should become more challenging (circles, regular and irregular polygons). For the greatest difficulty, blindfold all but one team member, who gives instructions to the others.

➲ You'll probably have time for only a few shapes. Flat elastic about 3/8" wide works best. You can buy it at craft stores and fabric stores.

➲ This is an activity where leaders tend to emerge. The team can't complete the figure unless they are somewhat organized, and the one who steps up to direct the organizing emerges as a leader. If there is time after the activity, students can discuss who helped the group organize its efforts. It's also interesting to note who was willing to follow. No one can lead unless others are willing to follow. In fact, it is said that great leaders are made by great followers—another example of our connectedness.

Keep in Mind

Discovering similarities builds relationship, and discovering differences stimulates curiosity and interest in each other. Both enrich community. The goal is for students to see differences as interesting, not off-putting. Help them see that underneath obvious differences lie not-so-obvious but important similarities.

Ask yourself

Are you more drawn to people who seem different from you or similar to you? Why?

ADVISORY 7 ▶ A+

Advisory goal: Develop skills of working in a group for the good of all

Greeting

Shape Greeting: While greeting in pairs, one student makes half a shape with her hands; her partner completes the shape by making the other half. Only the *Good morning, _____* part is voiced; the shape part is done silently. For example, *Good morning, Marcus* (makes a v-shape with fingers). *Good morning, Nicole* (makes an upside down v-shape with his fingers and touches his fingertips to hers, completing a diamond shape).

> Good morning, Team!
> Today we'll test our ability to communicate with each other silently in a game called Cooperation. It's all about shapes, as is our greeting.

Activity

Cooperation (team-building game): The object of the game is to reassemble whole shapes from cut pieces. Ahead of time, design five three-piece rectangles on 8½" x 11" sturdy paper or tag board, each different from the others (see examples below). Copy each pattern onto four additional pieces of sturdy paper, for a total of five of each design. Sort the designs into one of each design in five piles. Cut the five designs in one pile along the lines you drew; you will have 15 pieces. Mix up the design pieces, group in five sets of three pieces from different puzzles, and bundle together by placing them in envelopes or with paper clips. Then place those five sets in a larger envelope; that will be Set 1 for Team 1. Repeat this process for Sets 2, 3, 4, and 5.

Divide the class into five teams. Teams complete the task with no interaction with other teams. Hand each team one of the larger envelope sets, and have them pass out the bundles of three pieces (one to individual team members or pairs depending on your group size). When you give the signal, each team begins working to assemble the five rectangles without talking or gesturing. Each individual or team pair must assemble a rectangle. Since the pieces are scrambled, participants may give pieces to others on their team, but they may not *take* or even *request* pieces (verbally or non-verbally). Also they may not put pieces in the center for others to pick up. They may only *give* them to another individual on the team. Team members may not take or swap pieces with anyone except their teammates, and *silence is maintained* until the task is completed. The first team that assembles all five of their rectangles wins.

Examples of rectangles:

   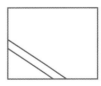

⮑ Once you have made a class set of the shapes (enough sets of five envelopes containing all five shapes cut apart, scrambled, and placed in envelopes), you are set to offer this activity each year. The same group may wish to try it more than once during the year, to see if they can beat their time.

⮑ You can make each team set of five rectangles a different color. This makes it easy to keep the sets together.

Reflection

What was the most difficult part of the activity for you?

What was easiest?

Keep in Mind

The greeting and activity of this advisory demand that students work together cooperatively, and leadership must emerge silently.

The payoff for the restrictions about how the team may communicate is that students are pushed to contribute to one another when they see a need. To win, teams must pay attention to each other's puzzles as well as to their own. Careful observation helps us see what's really happening around us, and helps us assess a situation before taking action. It slows down adolescent impetuosity enough to help them exercise judgment, a frontal-lobe brain activity that doesn't fully develop until their twenties. (See Perspective One, Advisory 25, page 102, for more on adolescent brain development.) The better our judgment, the more successfully we can sort facts from biased opinions.

Ask yourself

How might we play a quiet leadership role with our students, empowering them to succeed by their own efforts, with self-management replacing frequent direction from an adult?

ADVISORY 8 ▶ CPR

Advisory goal: Deepen understanding of what it means to be related to others

Greeting

Choice Greeting: The first greeter stands and crosses the circle to greet someone with *Good morning, _____.* The person rises and returns the greeting, then crosses the circle to greet someone similarly. This continues until all have been greeted. Those who have been greeted may clasp their hands as an indication to the greeter.

> Dosha, Friends!
>
> That's the way the Hidatsa, a Plains Indian tribe, say hello (it's pronounced "doh-shah"). Today we'll talk about a version of a family tree. In the Hidatsa way of thinking, many people who aren't related biologically or legally are nevertheless part of each other's families. We'll create an image of our families using that approach. Be thinking about what people mean when they talk about the "tree of life."

⮌ A Choice greeting is riskier than any other kind because we all want to be chosen, and being among the last to be chosen can feel like a "not popular" vote. On the other hand, in life we often greet people by choice, and practice in handling real life experiences is one of the benefits of CPR and A+ advisory meetings. Talk about the potential for discomfort in a choice greeting and restate your commitment that in this advisory group, the most important thing is for everyone to feel welcome and included.

Establish a policy of "no shopping," which rules out looking around for a while to see whom you wish to greet. Direct students to greet people seated across from them in the circle. This usually means that greeters simply walk across the circle toward one of a few people sitting directly across. It takes out some of the choice aspect, but it makes choice greetings socially safer. Choice greetings are also a nice way to mix up the seating, if the greeter and person greeted exchange seats in the process.

Share

Whip Share: *Who is an age mate (a person who is approximately your age) who is part of your family as we are defining it today?* Read the first paragraph of Hidatsa-style Family Tree (below) to explain the special meaning of "family" used in this share. Each student offers a brief response to the question; responses "whip" around the circle.

Activity

Hidatsa-style Family Tree: Hands Together Project (continues in next advisory): Define "family" for this project: *In this project we will represent all the people with whom we are connected in an important way, though not necessarily biologically or legally. In the Hidatsa tribe, a family tree includes not just blood relations but age mates (people roughly your age), neighbors, and close friends of the family.*

Hands together: Use the image of hands together to illustrate a Hidatsa-style family tree. Students place their hands in an interesting configuration on 8½" x 11" or larger paper (thumb-to-thumb, or interlocking fingers, or fingers pointing up on one hand, down on the other, etc.). Be sure there is room to write names on the fingers and on the palms. Partners trace around each other's hands in pencil.

Add names: Students write in the outlines of their hands the names of people or other living things who are important to them. On the board, make a list of possibilities to help students get started. They can include:

• people they have learned from

• people they have helped

• people who have been playmates or study partners

• people they have not met, but who have had an impact on them, such as politicians, authors, inventors, etc.

• pets

Students should plan ahead by listing the names before adding them to the drawing to be sure they have enough space for all of them

Materials: Students should use pencil for the initial drawing, and pencil is best for adding names, so mistakes can be easily corrected. When the image is complete, they can add color with colored pencils or other materials.

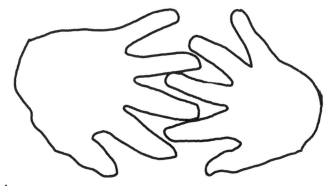

Keep in Mind

One of the advantages of connecting with other cultures is that we see things in new ways. Looking at people as part of your family who were born close to when you were born is a new way for most of us to think about family. The more students see that we understand and appreciate their ways of seeing the world, the more comfortable they will be in school, and engagement in or connection to school is closely associated with attendance and with success in learning.

"Researchers have found student engagement a robust predictor of student achievement and behavior in school, regardless of socioeconomic status. Students engaged in school are more likely to earn higher grades and test scores, and have lower drop-out rates. In contrast, students with low levels of engagement are at risk for a variety of long-term adverse consequences, including disruptive behavior in class, absenteeism, and dropping out of school."[7]

Ask yourself

What role do your age-mates play in your life as an adult? How does that compare to their importance to you in your adolescence?

ADVISORY 9 ▶ A+

Advisory goal: Broaden and deepen our understanding of family

Greeting

One-Minute Mingle Greeting: Each person greets as many people by name as possible in one minute. Before beginning, review how to efficiently complete a greeting. Model how to be greeted and return a greeting, maintaining eye contact, before moving on to the next person.

> Mitaku Oyasin! (Lakota, meaning "all my relations;" pronounced "mee-tah-koo-yay oy-yah-seen")
>
> We may be more a family than we ever thought. In the Hidatsa world view, if we hang out together, we're related.

Activity

Hidatsa-style Family Tree: (complete project begun in Advisory 9)

Reflection

In partners or triads, as students share their family trees, they answer the question: *Who is one person on your tree you especially enjoy spending time with?* Triads take more time (three to five minutes), but offer more audience and more variety. The group then writes a definition of family: One way to define family is: _____.

➲ You could post these definitions on the daily news for the next advisory, or make a poster with the definitions. Displaying the poster in the hallway with the question posed for passers-by to answer, graffiti-style: "What's your definition?" might attract some interesting responses and provide material for a future advisory conversation.

Keep in Mind

The U.S. Census Bureau defines family as "two or more people (one of whom is the householder) related by birth, marriage, or adoption, residing in the same housing unit."[8] A few dictionary definitions are:

- group of persons of common ancestry
- people or group of peoples regarded as deriving from a common stock
- group of people united by certain convictions or a common affiliation

By thinking of "family" as a somewhat flexible term, we can create a broad, inclusive sense of family to widen our perceptions about who belongs in our personal world, who is important to us, and whom we depend on. Such widened perception could reduce "outsider" feelings about being adopted or living in a foster situation, and other living situations. A broader net helps make discrimination and exclusion of "others" less likely.

Ask yourself

Whom do you consider to be part of your family?

ADVISORY 10 ▶ A+

Advisory goal: Build understanding of the importance of communication in living and working together

Greeting

Group Juggle Greeting: Students form a standing circle. The beginning student tosses a ball or beanbag to someone across from them and says, *Good morning, _____.* The person greeted throws the ball to and greets another, and so on, until all students are greeted.

⮑ Model and practice throwing the object underhand and gently.

Activity

Group Juggle (team-building game): Continue from the greeting. The beginning student tosses a soft ball or beanbag to someone, who throws it to another, and so on, until each student has received the ball once. The last student to receive the ball tosses it to the student who started. She may either stop or keep the ball in play by tossing it to the same person she tossed to the first time. The ball then moves across the circle, repeating the pattern from the first round.

⮑ **Variations:**

1. Record the time it takes to complete one round of the juggle.

2. When the group has mastered using one ball, add another, then another, and keep them all going in the same pattern.

3. Require that each person say the name of the person to whom he is tossing, and require the receiver to say "Got it!" This creates some confusion and adds to the challenge.

4. Ask students how to increase the challenge, and try some of their ideas. Any way you play it, Group Juggle builds teamwork and community.

Reflection

What teamwork strategies did we use that improved our time or our throwing and catching skills?

Keep in Mind

Enrich the discussion of interconnectedness with games and activities that focus on what we have in common and how we communicate and operate together. Here are some that keep the players focused on their connections. You can use them when you have extra time. You may even find it relevant to insert some into a class period. We have used some in *Face to Face Advisories.* See *The Advisory Book* or the *Developmental Designs* Web site for details of each activity.

Games that reinforce interconnectedness

Common Ground: Groups discover commonalities among them and list as many as they can within time limits. This game can be used to uncover commonalities among states or countries or historical or fictional figures.

Connections: Each person is given a noun, and each time a pair think of a connection between the persons, places, or things, they announce the connection to the group.

Cooperation: All players have pieces of rectangles, but they cannot complete them without trading pieces with one another. (See page 121 for a full description.)

Entourage: Individuals gather behind and support players who win at Rock, Paper, Scissors until eventually only one winner is left and the rest of the group has become an entourage connected to that person. This can be a tension breaker during long tests.

Huddle Up: Players gather in affinity groups on a variety of issues and preferences. This can be a way to show opinions about books, historical or fictional characters, or events in history.

I Sit in the Grass: A chair-changing game in which students call out the names of classmates to fill a continually shifting empty spot in the circle. This fast-paced game exercises students knowledge of each other's names.

Me Too: Players show their connection by standing up or snapping fingers and saying, *Me too* to statements they agree with made by successive players. (See page 165 for a full description.)

Shrinking World: Players gather in fewer and fewer circles of rope on the ground, making sure that everyone is completely inside the rope circle. (See page 143 for a full description.)

Simultaneous Clap: Everyone in the circle takes a turn at simultaneously clapping with a partner, then the entire group tries to clap at the same moment. This is a nice way to end the week with a class. (See page 75 for a full description.)

Yes!: A chair-changing game in students stand or sit in a circle and look each other's eyes. When students make eye contact, they both exclaim, "Yes," then change places. The game is timed to see how long it takes for everyone to make the "Yes" exchange at least once.

Ask yourself
How do you and your colleagues build team spirit and skills?

ADVISORY 11 ▶ CPR

Advisory goal: Build trust for others in the group

Greeting

Psychic Shake Greeting: Everyone silently picks a number from one to three. That is the number of times you will shake each hand that you shake in this activity (i.e., if you choose two, each time you shake hands you will do so twice, no more, no less). Students mingle in the circle and start shaking hands. If your number is two, you shake twice with each person. If the person you are greeting tries to shake a third time or resists shaking after one shake, you have not found a match, and you separate, and continue greeting others. If the person shakes exactly twice, you stay close together as you seek others who shake twice. The greeting has been completed when there are three clusters of people.

> Dear Students,
>
> This morning I will share with you about a person who is quite different from me for whom I have a lot of <u>trust</u>. I will invite your questions and comments after I share. We'll also try out an activity that requires us to have confidence in each other: Crossing the Great Divide!

Share

Venn Diagram Share: Differences and Trust: Teacher models the share. Prepare ahead of time a Venn diagram using yourself and a person you trust who differs from you culturally. Areas of differences include religion, urban/rural childhoods, language, age, ability, and ethnicity/color. Use the Venn diagram to show your commonalities and differences and ask for questions and comments afterward. (Students will prepare and share their own Venn diagrams, starting in Advisory 14.)

⮑ Have a student scribe the questions so the group can use them as a resource when students share their diagrams.

Activity

Crossing the Great Divide (trust-building activity): Two teams line up shoulder to shoulder, facing each other across the room or space. On a team line, the outside edges of each person's feet touch their neighbors'. The goal is for a team line to reach the middle before the other team without breaking contact with each other's feet. If anyone on a team breaks contact, the whole team begins again from the starting point. For a second round, challenge both teams to work together to get *everyone* to the center in the shortest amount of time. If time is short, skip the competition and go for the whole group accomplishing the task together.

⮑ This advisory is the first in a series of trust-building activities in Perspective Two meetings. The trust activities are designed to offset the tendency of adolescents to form cliques and ingroups, often based on cultural differences, in part from lack of trust of those who seem different from them culturally. (See page 186 in Perspective Three for a definition of "ingroup.")

⮑ State the goal of the activity, so everyone understands that they need to work together to reach the goal, which is for a team to cross a space together, everyone connected, everyone reaching the goal at the same moment.

Keep in Mind

In this meeting's Venn Diagram Share, the teacher describes a person as different but also a person with whom he or she has important things in common. Finding commonalities and trust in someone unlike you is a necessary skill of community-building and friendship. Our possibilities for friendship are greatly enlarged when we look for friends and offer trust in all directions, not just with others who share certain cultural traits with us. Young people need to be taught to trust *carefully and wisely* — not everyone, not all the time. The following story illustrates the importance of trust when interdependency runs so deep that survival depends on it.

Trust in a traditional Inuit village

Anthropologist Jean Briggs tells of her long stay in the 1960's in an Inuit village in the Central Arctic, during which a family invited her to share their food, their home, and their lives. One day when some *kaplunas*, white men, came and asked to borrow one of the two good canoes in the village, the Inuit readily assented. The men returned with the canoe badly broken and asked to borrow the other one. Briggs angrily told the visitors that it would be difficult to repair the broken canoe, and if they damaged the second one, the community would be left with no fishing boat. She said they would not loan the remaining canoe, but to her surprise, they did.

After the men left with the second canoe, she was shocked to find that no one would talk to her. They continued to feed her, but otherwise they avoided. Months later, when they began to talk with her again, she learned that the people had seen her angry behavior as a threat to the community, showing that the person was ungenerous, unpeaceful, and unpredictable. Their way of protecting the community from such behavior was to isolate Briggs. When enough time had passed and the anger didn't return, they renewed contact with her.

Briggs realized that the Inuit's survival in their extremely challenging environment depended on their coherence as a community; nobody could make it on their own. Since each depended on the other, disruption of the community's harmony was even more dangerous than losing the means to fish. Therefore, in their culture, people behaved pleasantly and got along no matter how intense the pressures.[9]

Because of their interdependency, the traditional Inuit had little tolerance for competition, quarrels, and domination of others. European American traditions of independence and competition can pull us in the opposite direction. A balance between the values of independence and interdependence could provide us both the energy and the harmony we desire.

Ask yourself

Considering life's dangers, what should we teach young people about trusting others?

ADVISORY 12 ▶ A+

Advisory goal: Build trust in the group

Greeting

High Five/Low Five Greeting: In sequence around the circle, students greet and high-five their neighbors. The neighbor returns the greeting, then passes it on. *Hi, Roberta* (high five). *Hi, Jake* (low five).

> *Good Morning, Trustworthy Students!*
> *We're going to challenge ourselves today with a series of activities that get incrementally harder as they go along. I know that together we can do them!*

Activity

Guide students through one of the following trust-building activities.

Touch This: Choose a large object in the classroom. Everybody places and keeps one hand on the object without touching anyone else. Once the first person touches the object, he must keep contact with it until everyone is touching the object at the same time without touching each other. The game progresses with everyone touching smaller and smaller objects. For example, first players touch a door, then a desk, then a chair, etc. Students often create interesting solutions for this challenging game such as using props as an extension of their bodies. As a variation, you can allow for a quick touch for short amount of time.

All Aboard: All students or a group of student volunteers stand on a board at one time. The size of the board and group number set the challenge level. The group must have all feet off the ground or floor for five seconds. Players can be held up with no feet touching the platform. Student reluctant to play directly can become coaches or strategists for the group.

⮑ Touch This requires close proximity, and All Aboard requires touching and even holding. These must be voluntary activities. At the beginning, remind everyone of school behavior rules (see also page 27 for guidance). Make it clear that students may opt out of the exercise at any time without explanation and without comment from anyone. An option that removes the possibility of cross-gender touching is to do the exercises in gender-specific groups. This will likely create a boys-versus-girls competition, but you can temper this by saying that the job of the group watching is to encourage the group performing to succeed.

Reflection

What helped the group succeed in the activities we did today? What role did trust for each other play?

Keep in Mind

Close proximity, which is required in this activity, is challenging to different degrees for different people. Trust is required. We build trust by repeatedly taking some degree of personal risk and experiencing positive outcomes. "Trust is a key ingredient in the formation and maintenance of healthy interpersonal relationships."[10]

Allow for feelings, but encourage thinking while you feel

As you discuss and test students' ability to trust one another, feelings may arise. When students are asked to focus on their connectedness and participate in activities that require close connection, they may respond with reluctance, confusion, resentment, surprise, embarrassment, or other feelings. Protect everyone with the agreed-upon ground rules (see page 22). Allow for lots of talking as students work through the challenges of close proximity. To encourage them, provide information or a story to widen their perspective. Help students think while they feel.

Personal story topics: Share a personal experience (someone else's if you can't think of one of your own) when you were reluctant to do something out of embarrassment or fear or memories of negative experiences in the past, but you pushed through the reluctance and were successful.

It was my group's turn to do the zip line. Each person had to grab onto an overhead bar and hold on for dear life as the bar was released and slid along a wire that stretched across a deep chasm between two cliffs. The only reason I got myself to do it was that the group kept cheering me on, promising they were with me and telling me I could do it. Thanks to their support, I did it! (Educator)

Ask yourself

In what situations do you feel a high degree of trust for others? What experience(s) has or have caused your trust level to drop?

ADVISORY 13 ▶ CPR

Advisory goal: Understand that trust can exist between people who feel culturally different from one another

Greeting

One-Minute Mingle Greeting: Each person greets as many students by name as possible in one minute. Before starting, review how to politely complete a greeting. If necessary, remind everyone to maintain eye contact during a greeting.

> Hello, Friends!
>
> Get ready to create your own <u>visual organizer</u> of a person you trust who comes from a culture different from yours.
> <u>Do Now:</u> Pick up a blank Venn diagram and think about the person you will describe.

Share

Venn Diagram Share: Differences and Trust: Students make Venn diagrams of people they trust who differ from them culturally. Display your Venn diagram from Advisory 11 as a model. Suggest areas of cultural difference to help students identify a person including differences in religion, urban/rural backgrounds, language, age, ability, and ethnicity/color. Students will share their diagrams with partners at the next meeting.

➲ As students work on their Venn diagrams, circulate and find out a little about the people they have chosen to describe. Remind them to do this exercise about someone they feel is very different from them culturally. Remind them of the Venn diagram you shared, and describe what you learned from stretching to find similarities.

Activity

Knots (trust-building activity): Students stand in a circle and link right hands with someone across from them. Then they link left hands with someone other than that person: the "knot" is complete. Students must untangle the knot without letting go of hands.

➲ Students can hold a strip of cloth in each hand and grab the cloth rather than hands (stretchy cloth makes the activity easier but less challenging). This reduces the closeness and touching required by the activity. Decide what degree of contact will work for your group. Boys and girls can form separate groups to play the game. This activity, like handshakes and high fives, can be a context for teaching about respectful touching.

Keep in Mind

We can grow aware of our mutual dependency by seeking out the similarities among us. For example, we can focus on people's abilities rather than their disabilities, and on each other's strengths rather than weaknesses.

I feel connected to people with developmental disabilities. Even though I don't have such a disability, we share the perception that it's great to be alive, and it's hard, too. (Teacher of people with developmental disabilities)

It is a daily challenge to look for points of connection with people who seem very different from us. We can look for skills and talents that may not be obvious, especially in students who push against the structures of school. We can learn from the stand that African history professor Asa Hilliard modeled: "I have never encountered any children in a group who are not geniuses. There is no mystery how to teach them. The first thing you do is treat them like human beings and the second thing you do is love them."

Kevin, a new student from Ghana, had a chip on his shoulder. He spoke English fluently, but kept talking about how he was different, even though all the students in my class were children of color, and several others were also African immigrants. Another student, Jordan, consistently got into a lot of trouble in school. I decided to pair him with Kevin to help Kevin get oriented. They actually became friends. Jordan was able to communicate with Kevin, and Kevin respected him. Jordan was pleased with his responsibility—it made him feel important. When Jordan saw how hard it was for Kevin, he began to act differently. It was an important experience for me, too. I realized that because I felt empathy for Jordan, and saw what these two different boys had in common, I was able to provide a project that helped both boys. (Fourth-fifth grade teacher)

Ask yourself

Thinking of a student who is hard to reach or consistently pushes back and breaks rules, what is a quality in him/her that you admire or enjoy?

ADVISORY 14 ▶ CPR

Advisory goals: Understand the complexity of events that affect the whole world; develop ability to address a problem from multiple points of view.

⮑ "Global Village" is an idea introduced by Marshall McCluhan in his book *Understanding Media.*[12] It refers to the greatly increased connectedness of the world's people through technology.

> Aloha, Friends! (a Hawaiian greeting that means "I am a part of all and all are a part of me")
>
> Today we will share our Venn diagrams about people who are different from us whom we trust. I hope you will be willing to share your diagram with the whole group in a future meeting. Talking about trust may help us solve a big problem as well, a problem shared by the Global Village.

Greeting

High Five Greeting: In sequence around the circle, students greet and high-five their neighbors. The neighbor returns the greeting. *Hi, Roberto* (high five). *Hi, Elizabeth* (high five), then passes it on.

Share

Venn Diagram Partner Share: Differences and Trust: Students share their Venn diagrams with partners. They should describe both the differences and the trust they have for the person. Specify a length of time to share. Issue a time warning halfway through the share to ensure balanced sharing/listening.

⮑ Post the list of questions asked when you modeled the first Venn Diagram Share (Advisory 11). Students can use them to inquire about their partners' diagrams.

⮑ Ask for student volunteers to share their diagrams with the whole group in a future meeting (Advisory 16 and 18).

Activity

Global Village Problem: Gulf Oil Spill: Begin by explaining the activity name. "Global Village" is a term originally used by author Marshall McLuhan in the mid-20th Century to describe how our planet has contracted into a village because of communication technology. The rapid movement of information brought social and political functions together by transforming communication. People who live far apart now know one another, communicate quickly, and affect one another's lives, just as residents of villages did in the past. New questions arise about poverty, discrimination, and the environment as the world becomes more conscious of its interconnectedness, and as people recognize their responsibilities to each other.

Read the facts about the spill aloud. Hand out stakeholder roles (see below) to pairs of students. If you have more stakeholders than pairs of students, you could give two stakeholders to some pairs. Students discuss the questions with their partners. Volunteers share out with the whole group as time allows.

Gulf Oil Spill, April 20, 2010—Facts

1. The BP oil spill was the biggest in American history, with between 17 and 39 million gallons spilled in the Gulf of Mexico.

2. The initial oil rig explosion killed 11 people and injured 17 others.

3. 16,000 miles of gulf coastline have been affected, including the coasts of Texas, Louisiana, Mississippi, Alabama, and Florida. In 2013, globs of oil still lie beneath the surface of the beaches.

4. Of the 400 miles of Louisiana coast, approximately 125 miles have been polluted by oil.

5. Over 1,000 animals (birds, turtles, mammals, and others) died, including many on the endangered species list. Of the animals affected by the spill that survived, experts attempted to clean about 6%, but biologists predicted they would die, too. NOAA reports that dolphins and whales continue to die at twice the normal rate.

6. The well was finally capped in July, 2010, but oil continued to wash up on shore and settle on the floor of the Gulf.

7. Over 30,000 people responded to help remove oil from the water, clean beaches, save animals, and help in other ways.[12]

Stakeholders

1. Family living along the Gulf Coast

2. Governors of Mississippi, Louisiana, Texas, Alabama, and Florida

3. B.P. Oil Co. president

4. Worker on an oil rig

5. Wife of worker on an oil rig

6. Fisherman

7. Truck driver

8. President of a national environmental organization

9. Leader of an oil-producing country in the Middle East

10. Manufacturer of solar- and wind-power technology

11. Mother of a family living in poverty

12. Investor in BP Oil Co. stock

13. President of an electric-car company in Japan

14. Farmer who raises corn in Iowa

15. 17-year-old student in New York City

16. Dolphin in the Gulf

Reflection

What might be each stakeholder's point of view about the following questions:

Who and what was most affected by the oil spill?

How we can prevent another spill?

What is the best way to deal fairly and safely with such a disaster?

⮑ You won't have enough time to hear from all the stakeholders in one meeting. Choose some that might have opposing points of view in order to represent different reactions and to illustrate the dynamic forces that can result when people have different, perhaps conflicting, interests. You may want to add a meeting to continue this conversation.

Keep in Mind

Learning to consider issues from multiple points of view teaches students how to think flexibly and equitably. We call on our perspective-taking skills to give their point of view fair consideration. In the case of an environmental disaster, the entire planet is affected. Understanding that we are interdependent helps us think about global issues from a global perspective.

Ask yourself
How did the Gulf oil spill affect you?

ADVISORY 15 ▶ A+

Advisory goal: Raise awareness that everyone in the world is affected by an uneven distribution of resources around the world

⮌ Before the advisory meeting begins, designate eight areas of the room to represent eight regions of the world, as listed in the population chart below. Distribute students' chairs into these areas in proportion to *wealth* distribution in those eight regions (e.g., put 34% of the chairs in the area designated for North America, and only 3% of the chairs in the area for China). See the distribution chart below for wealth percentages.

Greeting

Inside-Outside Greeting: Stand in a double circle (one inside the other). As the inside circle slowly rotates, members of the inside circle greet people in the outside circle with a handshake, *Good morning, _____.* The people in the outside circle person return the greeting. Many variations are possible; for example, high fives or low fives can replace handshakes.

> Welcome!
>
> Thanks to those who volunteered to share their Venn diagrams with the group. Talking about what we have in common helps us trust one another more. We'll need that trust as we experience how unbalanced a world we live in. <u>Do Now</u>: Gather in a standing double circle, the two circles facing each other, for an inside-outside greeting.

⮌ There are no chairs in the meeting area because all the chairs are distributed in the eight areas representing wealth distribution.

Activity

Competing for Resources around the World

1. Explain the areas of the room representing eight regions of the world. You will tell certain numbers of students to go to each area, based on the world's population distribution. For example, send 6% of the students to the area for North America (where there are more chairs than needed), and send 23% of the students to the area for China, where there are far fewer chairs.

2. Now ask everyone to sit down in their areas. There will be too few chairs for some groups and a surplus for others. Students reflect on what they notice about wealth inequalities. See reflection questions below.

⮌ An alternative, faster (chair-less) method is to divide students into eight groups according to population and then distribute fake money to illustrate wealth inequalities. Students can observe the greater money given to smaller groups and less money given to larger groups.

Percentage of world population and wealth: example with 25 students[13]

REGION	POPULATION	WEALTH	POP. CHAIRS	WEALTH CHAIRS
North America	6.1%	34.4%	1.5 (2)	8.6 (9)
Latin America & Caribbean	8.2%	4.3%	2 (2)	1.07 (1)
Europe	14.9%	29.6%	3.7 (4)	7.4 (7)
Africa	10.2%	1.0%	2.5 (0)	.25 (0)
China	22.8%	2.6%	5.7 (6)	.65 (1)
India	15.4%	.9%	3.8 (4)	2.25 (2)
Wealthy Asia-Pacific	5.0%	24.1%	1.2 (1)	6.02 (6)
Other Asia-Pacific	17.5%	3.0%	4.3 (4)	.75 (1)

Reflection

What do you notice about the way the world's population is distributed?

What do you notice about the way the world's wealth is distributed?

How might uneven distribution of wealth affect those who have more? Those who have less?

Keep in Mind

Consider a continuum of thinking about our interconnectedness: "big-planet" to "small-planet" thinking. On the big-planet thinking end, there seems to be plenty of room and plenty of resources without concern. Big-planet thinkers tend to feel that they have worked hard for what they have and want, so they are entitled to it. America is blessed with more acres per person than most developed countries; perhaps that's one reason why we have lots of big-planet thinkers.

On the other end of the spectrum, small-planet thinkers consider the burgeoning population worldwide, the shrinking amount of arable land, and diminishing natural resources and habitat, and allow those to influence their lifestyle choices. They tend to feel that most people work hard, but some get paid much more than others, and some were born in much richer countries than others. They consider their choices in relation to other people and the world.

During the discussion of the third reflection question, you might decide to comment on this tension between big- and small-planet thinking.

Ask yourself

Where do you place yourself on the small-planet-big-planet continuum?

ADVISORY 16 ▶ CPR

Advisory goal: Understand how community can influence performance

Greeting

High Five/Low Five Greeting: In sequence around the circle, students greet and high-five or low-five their neighbors. Neighbors return the greeting, then pass it on. *Hi, Celia* (high five). *Hi, Louis* (low five).

> Get ready to race, speedy ones!
> We're going to see how fast we can go when we have a team behind us for support. Also, two people will share about their trustworthy people today.

Share

Venn Diagram Share: Differences and Trust (continued): Volunteers share with the group their Venn diagrams of someone they trust. Draw from the list of people who volunteered to share during Advisory 14.

➲ A follow-up question: What else might the two people in this diagram have in common? Searching for our commonalities helps keep us positively connected.

Activity

Number Race: Divide the group into two or three teams. Create circles on the floor, outlined with yarn or string, one for each team. Place inside each circle paper plates or something similar numbered from one to ten and scatter them, number side up. At the start signal, teams send one member at a time into their circle to touch all ten numbers consecutively. Team members encourage and assist each other in finding the plates in the proper order (e.g., *Turn around! Number seven is behind you.*). Each team times the process and shares their results with the other teams, or tries to better their result if there's time to repeat the course.

➲ **Variation:** Experiment with the impact of group support on performance: time the course first without support and then with support. Compare the results and reflect: *How did it feel/impact your performance to do the course without and then with support?*

Keep in Mind

You can use this activity to demonstrate the effect the group can have on the performance of an individual. Encourage everyone to support each player as he or she runs the Number Race by cheering and maybe pointing to the next number. They can see how cheering and coaching can help a performer or competitor (on the other hand, if the player says the noise slows him down, teammates would stop cheering). In one experiment, "Verbal encouragement significantly increased performance compared to the control group by 39% and by 33.5% compared to the subject's own control trial." "Does verbal encouragement work? The effect of verbal encouragement on a muscular endurance task,"[14]

Ask yourself

What effect does it have on you when people encourage you?

ADVISORY 17 ▶ A+

Advisory goal: Develop sensitivity to the feelings of an outsider

Greeting

Choice Greeting: Students decide whom to greet. The first greeter stands and crosses the circle to greet someone: *Good morning (or sawa bona),* _____. The person rises and returns the greeting, then crosses the circle to greet someone. This continues until all have been greeted. Those who

> Sawa bona, Friends!
> That means "I see you" in Natal, South Africa. If I truly see you, I see that we are connected. Sometimes the connection is with people we don't even know, but we share some important commonality, as we'll see in the story we discuss today.

have been greeted may clasp their hands or cross their legs as an indication to the greeter. Remind students of the "no shopping" rule (see Advisory 8).

Activity

We Might As Well Be Strangers, by M.E. Kerr: Read aloud: *We Might As Well Be Strangers* describes a young Jewish woman coming out to her family about being a lesbian. She tells her grandmother that she is a lesbian, and her grandmother responds by sharing the story of her visit as a young girl to the non-Jewish family of a friend in Germany in the early 1930's. The maid refused to serve food to a person "of Jewish blood." Her grandmother says, "You don't have to tell me about prejudice. But Alison, I thank you for telling me about yourself. I'm proud that you told me first."[15]

Reflection

Do you agree that both Jews and gays could be considered outsiders?

What makes a person an outsider? Have you ever felt like one?

What connections do you feel with people who are different from you, but deal with some of the same problems you deal with?

➲ You can structure the reflection in several ways. You might begin with thinking and/or journaling time and/or a partner exchange on a question; that prepares students to contribute more actively to a complex or sensitive whole-group discussion.

Keep in Mind

There is much literature about our interdependence versus our separateness. In Robert Frost's poem *Mending Wall,* the speaker wonders why his neighbor wants to build a wall between them and he insists that it will make them better neighbors. He writes, "Something there is that doesn't love a wall."[16] The poem leads us to think about the price we pay for walling ourselves off from each other, and how we might make connections over those walls.

Ask yourself

Might someone on your school staff feel like an outsider? Do you ever feel that way?

ADVISORY 18 ▶ CPR

Advisory goal: Build community by building trust

Greeting

Choice Greeting: Students decide whom to greet. The first greeter stands and crosses the circle to greet someone: *Good morning, _____.* The person rises and returns the greeting, then crosses the circle to greet someone similarly. This continues until all have been greeted. Those who have been greeted may clasp their hands or cross legs as an indication to the greeter. Remind students of the "no shopping" rule (see Advisory 8).

> *Circle Up, Students!*
> *We're going to hear more shares about people we trust, then put our trust for each other to the test in an activity called Circle of Friends. I know we'll do it well!*

Share

Venn Diagram Share: Differences and Trust (continued): student volunteers share their Venn diagrams of a person they trust with the whole group.

Activity

Circle of Friends (trust-building activity): A group of at least ten students stands in a circle, each holding onto a rope with ends tied together into a circle, standing enough apart from one another so the rope is pulled taut. At the same moment, everyone leans back, letting the rope keep them from falling. Everyone is thus supporting everyone else. If anyone slacks on the rope, people will fall backward.

➲ At the start of the activity, make sure that everyone knows the goal: to lean back and let the rope support us as a group—something that no one could do alone.

➲ **Variations:** Have students start by sitting in a circle. If everyone holds onto the circle rope and pulls back at the same time, all can stand up. Or everyone can lock arms and stand up together, instead of using a rope.

Reflection

What did it take to make this work?

How are those qualities important in other work we do in school? At home? On a job?

Keep in Mind

Reflection after a group activity makes it more useful and memorable; many CPR activities are followed by reflection. Through thinking and talking, students can better understand what happened in the interaction, the meaning of what happened, and how to use it in the future. A shorthand version of questions asked in reflection:

What happened?

So what?

Now what?

Each of these questions demands a high level of thinking. Describing what happened accurately calls for careful observation and exactness in description. Responding meaningfully to "So what?" requires students to think about the importance and the implications of what happened. "Now what?" calls for creating a possibility for how what has happened can be applied to another project, or deciding what needs to happen next. Students articulate, analyze, and apply what they have learned.

Ask yourself

Has your staff done or considered doing trust-building activities together to strengthen connectedness? Would it be/has it been valuable?

ADVISORY 19 ▶ CPR

Advisory goal: Understand the effects of the world's increasing population and increasing communication

Greeting

Choice Greeting: Students decide whom to greet. The first greeter stands and crosses the circle to greet someone with *Good morning* or *sabaah el kheer, _____.* The person rises and returns the greeting, then crosses the circle to greet someone similarly. This continues until all have been greeted. Remind students of the "no shopping" rule (see Advisory 8).

> Sabaah el kheer! ("Good morning" in Arabic)
>
> The world is <u>metaphorically</u> shrinking as population increases and communication brings us closer and closer. Today we'll test our capacity to live in our shrinking world. Today is the last day to share your Venn diagram with the whole group.

Share

Venn Diagram Share: Differences and Trust (continued): Student volunteers share their Venn diagrams with the whole group about a person they trust.

Activity

Shrinking World (trust-building activity): Best done in an open space (outside or the gym—a wide hallway would do). Set up six or seven circles of rope. These circles represent the world. Students stand outside the circles. When the leader says, *Find a piece of the world to stand on*, everyone has ten seconds to get both feet in a circle. No foot can be touching outside a circle, but a person can have feet in two different circles, or a foot can be held in the air. After 10 seconds, the leader says "Freeze," and everyone does so. The leader inspects every player, and everyone who is safely in a circle gets to play the next round; others are out until the next game.

Everyone left moves out of the circles, and the leader removes a circle. When the leader says, *Find a piece of the world to stand on*, everyone again has ten seconds to get both feet in a circle. After 10 seconds, the leader says "Freeze," and everyone does so. The leader inspects every player, and everyone who is safely in a circle gets to play the next round; others are out until the next game.

The game continues, with the world continually shrinking. The purpose of the activity is for students to adapt as necessary to succeed, as we all must do in the real shrinking world.

➲ Cotton clothesline (not plastic or nylon) works well for this activity. Hula hoops are less effective unless you can find ones of different sizes to simulate the shrinking. Review with students at the start of the activity the guidelines for respectful touching and movement.

➲ As always, students who do not wish to participate may opt out. Give them the job of inspecting whether everyone is in a circle according to the rules at the end of each round.

Reflection

What strategies did you use to get everyone into the world?

In the game, the population shrinks to what the world can support; what strategies will help people in the real world deal with crowding?

Keep in Mind

Although the world is getting more crowded, we are also finding ways to better communicate with one another and get to know each other. Technology is changing our relationships, with those we see every day and with those far away.

Author Thomas Friedman in *The World Is Flat 3.0* writes: "Clearly, it is now possible for more people than ever to collaborate and compete in real time with more other people on more different kinds of work from more different corners of the planet and on a more equal footing than at any previous time in the history of the world—using computers, e-mail, networks, teleconferencing, and dynamic new software."[17]

Ask yourself

What strategies do you use to get along with others in confined spaces and crowded cities?

ADVISORY 20 ▶ CPR

Advisory goal: Understand the importance of trust among people who live and work together

Greeting

Choice Greeting: The first greeter stands and crosses the circle to greet someone with *Good morning (or jambo),* _____. The person rises and returns the greeting, then crosses the circle to greet someone similarly. This continues until all have been greeted. Remind students of the "no shopping" rule (see Advisory 8).

> Jambo, Everyone! (a friendly Swahili greeting)
>
> Let's take a spin today, in an activity called Driven to Trust that requires us to move along without seeing where we're going. We'll see how much we trust each other.

Share

Partner Share: *Who are the people you trust the most? Why do you trust them so much?* Specify a length of time to share. Issue a time warning halfway through the share to ensure balanced sharing/listening. One person from each partnership shares out reasons they gave for trusting. Write a list of reasons given for trust and read the list aloud at the end.

Activity

Driven to Trust: In same-gender pairs, one person is the car and the other the driver. The car has his/her eyes closed. The driver stands behind the car directing the car's movement around the room by placement of his hand on the car's back. The driver signals movement without words; he slides his hand from position to position to indicate:

- Forward: between shoulder blades

- Reverse: lower back

- Right: right shoulder

- Left: left shoulder

- Stop: hands off

- Emergency stop: both hands on shoulders

Partners drive around the room for two minutes, then the partners trade roles.

⮌ Model with a student how to play the game appropriately. State at the beginning the safety guidelines and expectations: drivers gently guide and avoid contact with any other car and driver, and car and driver communicate throughout the process so that the car does not feel threatened by any actions of the driver. Explain that trust all around is what makes this activity successful, including the trust you as the leader have that every student will follow directions (consequences for failing to follow the guidelines should include exclusion from the activity).

Keep in Mind

The car must trust the driver's directions, and the driver must be trustworthy or the car will refuse to move. Such is the importance of trust in our lives. Trust is extremely important in school, too — trust among teachers and students and their families and trust among the staff. A school with a climate of trust among adults is likely to be a school in which students succeed academically: "Schools reporting strong positive trust levels in 1994 were three times more likely to be categorized eventually as improving in reading and mathematics than those with very weak trust reports."[18]

Ask yourself

What would you say is the current level of trust in your school?

ADVISORY 21 ▶ CPR

Advisory goal: Understand how communities are strengthened by shared purposes and projects

Greeting

Handshake Greeting: Students say *Good morning, _____,* and shake hands. Review, as necessary, how a handshake should look and feel.

> Good Morning, Fellow Readers!
>
> Paul Fleischman, the author of the book we're going to discuss today, said, "Television, I'm afraid, has isolated us more than race, class, or ethnicity." Do you agree? Let's talk about it, and about Fleischman's book, *Seedfolks.*

Share

Partner Share: *Do you agree with Paul Fleischman that television separates us more than skin color or wealth or ethnic heritage? How might television have that effect on a community?* Specify a length of time to share. Issue a time warning halfway through the share to ensure balanced sharing/listening. Volunteers share out if time permits.

Activity

***Seedfolks*, a novel by Paul Fleischman:** Read aloud the following from Fleischman's engaging book exploring cross-cultural interaction in an urban neighborhood: Kim, a nine-year-old girl whose family emigrated from Viet Nam, now lives in an apartment in Cleveland, Ohio. Kim's family does not know their neighbors. One day, Kim plants a few lima bean seeds in the hard-packed soil littered with trash in a vacant lot near her building. Others, seeing Kim's little garden, get the idea to plant something themselves, and soon there are many garden plots in the vacant lot, tended by African Americans, Mexican Americans, Cambodian Americans, East Indian Americans, etc. All the gardeners tend to their own plots, and don't mix much. Sam, a 78-year-old white man, tells us:

"One Saturday, when the garden was fullest, I stood up a minute to straighten my back. And what did I see? With a few exceptions, the blacks on one side, the whites on another, the Central Americans and Asians toward the back. The garden was a copy of the neighborhood. I guess I shouldn't have been surprised. A duck gives birth to a duckling, not a moose. Each group kept to itself, spoke its own language, and grew its own special crops. One man even put up a pole and flew the Philippine flag above his plot."[19]

One day a Korean shopkeeper named Sae Young is attacked by a man who walks into her shop with a gun. He takes all her money, pushes Sae Young down, swearing at her and kicking her until her head hits the wall and she is knocked unconscious. After the robbery, she is "afraid of everyone, all the time." For two months, she doesn't leave her apartment. A neighbor brings her food, and she hires a Korean man to run the shop. One day Sae Young, still afraid, goes out and passes by the community garden. The next day she returns and starts a small garden.

It's very hot. Everyone is concerned about getting water to the plants. A young girl gets the idea to collect rainwater from the apartment building roofs into garbage cans. People chip in to buy big garbage cans.

The next day, Sae Young tells us, there was a thunderstorm that nearly filled the garbage cans: "Someone bring three old pots to scoop water out of cans. Hard to pour into narrow containers. I quick go to store. Buy three funnels to make much easier filling containers. I put one by each garbage can. That day I see man use my funnel. Then woman. Then many people. Feel very glad inside. Feel part of garden. Almost like family." [20]

Reflection

Describe some parts of the "chain of effects" that result in the community garden.

What influences worked for and against the community coming together?

If you had lived in this neighborhood in Cleveland, would you or your family have supported the garden? Would you have planted a garden there?

What causes separation in your community?

Kim didn't intentionally try to unite the community. The garden happened as a result of one small action that she took, and others joined in. What is an action you could take that might support people in your community?

➲ You can structure the reflection in several ways. You might begin with thinking and/or journaling time and/or a partner exchange on a question; that prepares students to contribute more actively to a whole-group discussion. Such techniques help them prepare for a good exchange, especially in *Face to Face Advisories* meetings, where the topics are often complex and sensitive.

Keep in Mind

Sometimes the differences among us dominate and separate us. We can bridge the gap with reminders of our commonalities. Awareness of all that we share helps our defense against difference lessen. It's easy to find similarities, because we are so much more alike than different. The tendency we have to notice differences is something we have in common!

Dr. King is our ally in this effort to connect to one another. After his Nobel Peace Prize acceptance speech, when he took a stand against three related evils —war, racism, and poverty—he was criticized by some because they felt he should stay focused on racism. But Dr. King recognized the connections among racism, poverty, and violence, and continued to point them out.

A good resource for this conversation is a documentary video made by black youths in Minneapolis, *Keeping the Legacy Alive: North Minneapolis Youth Speak Up!* An excerpt from the documentary can be accessed through the *Developmental Designs* YouTube channel.[21] The students who created the film want the kind of community that grew around the garden in Cleveland.

Ask yourself

How connected do you feel to the community around your school?

ADVISORY 22 ▶ A+

Advisory goal: Appreciate the value of compromise

Greeting

Silent Greeting: Students brainstorm silent greetings. Model and practice some of them, such as nodding, smiling, raising eyebrows, winking, etc. One at a time around the circle, students greet each other silently using one of the modeled silent greetings. When everyone has been greeted, you might discuss what it felt like to be greeted silently, and the power of non-verbal communication.

> Good Morning, All!
> We'll play a communication game today called ESP, Extra-sensory Perception. It shows us that people are so connected that we find ways to communicate with one another beyond talking and writing. It also underlines the importance of compromise.

➲ **Variation:** Students can look across the circle and connect with at least three of their classmates (e.g., make eye contact, nod, or wave). To ensure that everyone is greeted, students can clasp their hands together or cross their legs to indicate that they have been greeted.

Activity

ESP: Divide the whole group into at least three groups. Together, each group chooses an action and a sound—say, turning around once and clicking the tongue. The goal is to have everybody doing the same action and sound at the end. When you say "ESP," each group does their action and sound. Allow enough time for students to look around and notice who is doing what. Then ask groups to stop, gather again, and decide whether to stick with their movement and sound, or change to another group's. Each time you say "ESP," groups change their movement and sounds, hoping to match the other groups. It may take several rounds as groups compromise and do other groups' actions and sounds.

➲ ESP was first described by Dr. Joseph Banks Rhine (1895-1980), a professor of psychology at Duke University, Durham, South Carolina, to describe the apparent ability of some people to acquire information without the use of the known senses.

Reflection

Why did your group decide to change or not to change?

How did you decide what to change to?

Why did some people not want to change?

What helped you compromise?

What dangers to a group do you see in members only following individual ideas or goals?

What dangers to a group do you see in members compromising?

Keep in Mind

Compromise is an important skill when everyone depends on everyone else. Political theorist Amy Gutmann and author Dennis Thompson explain why it is a crucial element of a successful democracy:

"Almost no major change can happen without major compromises. Without compromise on health care and taxation or other major issues, the status quo prevails, even if it preserves a policy that serves everyone's interests poorly and even if it leads to a major crisis.[22]

"[Political] Campaigning in an uncompromising style—making unconditional promises and discrediting rivals—plays a moral as well as a practical role in democratic politics. It enables candidates to communicate where they passionately stand on important issues and to differentiate themselves from their opponents. It is a necessary element of an electoral system with competitive elections and is therefore a legitimate part of the democratic process. But so is governing. To govern, elected leaders who want to get anything done have to adopt a compromising mindset. Rather than standing tenaciously on principle, they have to make concessions. Rather than mistrusting and trying to defeat their opponents at every turn, they have to respect their opponents enough to collaborate on legislation."[23]

Ask yourself

How does your staff deal with differences of opinion? How do you resolve disagreements? Are you able to compromise to make important decisions?

ADVISORY 23 ▶ CPR

Advisory goal: Perceive the many ways that the people in the advisory group are connected to and dependent on each other in spite of sometimes feeling different and isolated

Greeting

Mimic Greeting: One at a time around the circle, students greet their neighbors in a way they choose, and neighbors mimic the greetings in return. Leaders can limit the words of the greeting (e.g., *Good morning, _____*), or allow students to choose both words and movement.

> Hola, Amigos! (Spanish for "Hello, Friends")
>
> Sometimes we feel connected to the people around us, and sometimes we don't. Today we're going to see how many connections between each other we can name. And we'll read a poem by a girl who began connecting with her friends by writing and reading an honest poem.

Share

Partner Share: *In what ways is everyone in this class connected to and dependent on everyone else? Write your answer(s) on an index card.* Specify a length of time to share and issue a time warning halfway through the share to ensure balanced sharing/listening. Volunteers share out with the group. Collect the cards at the end. You can use them to make a list which you can post to remind the group of their connections.

Examples of less obvious connections:

Moods can be "catching"

Styles of clothing, hair go in trends

We all use certain slang

One person disrupting the group can interrupt play or work for all

Jokes can make everyone laugh

We all create trash and garbage in school!

Activity

Bronx Masquerade, **by Nikki Grimes:** Read aloud the following.

The students in Mr. Ward's high school English class in a Bronx high school have taken a new interest in school and in each other as a result of the freedom to write their own poems and then perform them at a poetry slam called Open Mike every Friday.

Sheila Gamberoni, an Italian American, is one of only a handful of white students in the school. She so desperately wants to fit in and make friends that she tries to walk and talk like the African-American students. She even thinks of changing her name to better fit in. Wesley, a classmate, advises her:

"Oh, get a clue, girl! Everybody's different. It don't matter what your skin color is, or what name you call yourself. Everybody is different inside, anyway. We're all trying to fit in. Ain't nothing new about that."[24]

He suggests that if she really wants to fit in, she can do so, at least in Mr. Ward's class, by bringing in a poem and reading it at Open Mike Friday. Sheila decides to do it, and writes and reads aloud to the class her poem, *Private Puzzle*. In the poem, Sheila talks first about how she feels different from everyone else, and about her longing to fit in the puzzle of others around her. Through the encouragement of Wesley and the truth-telling of the poem, Sheila finally feels connected: "For a moment, the puzzle is done."[25]

Reflection

How do Wesley and the poetry Open Mike experience help Sheila feel more connected to the other students?

Have you ever felt separated from others because you were different in some way?

What keeps us from getting to know and accept one another?

Keep in Mind

Connecting by the way we learn together

The pattern in the share part of this meeting is one that is used frequently in these advisories. Partners respond to a question and share about their lives, opinions, and feelings. Then the group as a whole continues the discussion, as some individuals share with the group the conversation they have just had with their partners. Paired shares elevate learning by providing the opportunity for students to articulate their ideas to one another and to think together about issues. It is similar to other cooperative learning formats, for example the jigsaw, in which each member of the group is responsible for a piece of the learning and all benefit from each other.

Sharing ideas shows that we are often better together than apart. In jigsaws, each person is responsible for one part of the learning, so success for all requires the contribution of each. Psychologist Daniel Goleman writes, "To master the subject, the whole group must listen intently to what each has to say. If the others heckle them or tune out because they don't like them, they risk doing poorly....Students in jigsaw learning groups quickly let go of their negative stereotypes."[26] Goleman gives the example of Carlos, a fifth grader who transferred from a poor to an affluent school. In the class that used jigsaws for work groups, students who had made fun of him in other classes helped him so he could help them. "I began to love to learn," Carlos wrote [later], "and now I'm about to go to Harvard Law School."[27]

Set up small groups with accountability. Use jigsaw or partner shares or other interactive peer structures to ensure inclusivity, and save time for the groups to report back to the larger group or in writing. Set things up so each depends on the other, and from that interdependence, unity has a chance. Although in advisory jigsaws can take too long, we use other peer-to-peer interactions to build inclusivity.

Ask yourself

How can you help students in your advisory group feel more connected to school?

ADVISORY 24 ▶ CPR

Advisory goal: Be able to assess your own level of trust for others

Greeting

Handshake Greeting: Students say *Good morning, _____,* and shake hands. Review, as necessary, how a handshake should look and feel.

Share

Partner Share: *What are the qualities that help you trust someone?* Specify a length of time to share. Issue a time warning halfway through the share to ensure balanced sharing/listening. One person from each partnership shares out. Make a list of the qualities named.

Activity

Airport (trust-building activity): Divide advisory into two groups, reserving two students for special roles. The two groups create two straight lines facing each other, shoulder to shoulder, forming the "runway" space for the "airplane" between them. One of the two remaining students stands at the head of the runway; he is the control tower. The other student is blindfolded and stands at the other end, the "pilot" of the plane. The control tower's job is to guide the plane to the control tower safely, with no crashes (e.g. *Keep walking straight. That's good. Now take a step to your left. Good.* etc.). A crash occurs when the plane touches anyone standing along the runway. The runway people help the plane land safely by making low sounds to warn the pilot if s/he gets too close to the edge of the runway (i.e., is about to bump into someone). When a plane crashes, another person takes over being the pilot. When the pilot reaches the control tower safely, two other people take the roles of pilot and control tower. The goal is to land as many planes as possible.

Keep in Mind

The object of this game is to make the flight path as smooth as possible, not to create a ruckus physical experience. When the students work together well, the "plane" experiences trust and encouragement and there are no crashes. Judge the condition of your group and separate boys and girls to provide more safety, if necessary.

Ask yourself

What qualities do you look for in a person to begin to trust them? Have your criteria changed since childhood?

ADVISORY 25 ▶ A+

Advisory goal: To be able to trust and be trustworthy in a situation that has some risk

Greeting

Tower Greeting: Starting at waist level, partners alternate placing one hand on top of the other, moving them higher and higher until their arms form an arch between them. They look at each other under the arch and greet each other. Greeting continues around the circle.

Activity

Willow in the Wind (trust-building activity): A group of eight to ten people forms a tight circle with arms extended forward from shoulders, hands bent at wrist with palms out, fingers extended. One person stands in the middle of the circle, blindfolded, with arms crossed. The center person allows herself to sway in any direction, body stiff and knees locked, feet stationery. Members of the circle catch the person's shoulders or back with their outstretched hands, keeping their hands flat and fully open, and then gently direct the person toward someone else. The person in the middle is thus slowly and gently "passed" among the people in the circle, silently and gently. After a few passes, the person in the center removes the blindfold and shares about the experience. Then someone else can try being the center person, the "willow" moving in the "wind."

⮑ You can have separate girls' and boys' groups in order to further guard against inappropriate touching.

Reflection

Describe what it was like to trust your peers to catch you or whoever was in the center of the circle.

What was your trust level (a number between one and ten, ten being complete trust) at that time? What was it like to be trusted to take care of your classmate?

Keep in Mind

Willow in the Wind demands a high level of trust for your peers. It is the last of the trust activities in Perspective Two. There is not time for all students in the group to be in the center, but the others experience the feeling of being trusted and of depending on each other to catch their classmates.

Ask yourself

Can you imagine yourself being in the center of the circle and allowing yourself to trust your students enough to let yourself fall toward them?

[1] Carol Dweck, *Mindset: The New Psychology of Success* (New York: Random House, 2006), 66.

[2] Gloria Ladson-Billings, *The Dreamkeepers: Successful Teachers of African American Children* (San Francisco: Jossey-Bass, 1994), 116.

[3] John Muir, *My First Summer in the Sierra* (San Francisco: Sierra Club Books, 1988), 110.

[4] Martin Luther King, Jr., "Letter from a Birmingham Jail," African Studies Center, University of Pennsylvania, http://www.africa.upenn.edu/Articles_Gen/Letter_Birmingham.html. King, Jr. wrote this open letter written on April 16, 1963. The letter defends the strategy of nonviolent resistance to racism, arguing that people have a moral responsibility to break unjust laws.

[5] Martin Luther King, Jr., "A Christmas Sermon for Peace," The King Center, 2013, http://www.thekingcenter.org/archive/document/christmas-sermon.

[6] "Commune Directory: List of Communes," Fellowship for Intentional Community, http://directory.ic.org/records/communes.php.

[7] A.M. Klem and J.P. Connell, "Relationships matter: Linking teacher support to student engagement and achievement," Journal of School Health 74 (2004): 262-263.

[8] "Frequently Asked Questions," U.S. Census Bureau, http://www.census.gov/hhes/www/income/about/faqs.html.

[9] Jean L. Briggs, *Never in Anger: Portrait of an Eskimo Family* (Cambridge: Harvard University Press, 1970), 282-292.

[10] Ken J. Rotenberg, *Interpersonal Trust during Childhood and Adolescence* (New York: Cambridge University Press, 2010), 247.

[11] Marshall McCluhan, *Understanding Media: The Extensions of Man* (New York: McGraw Hill, 1964).

[12] "11 Facts about the BP Oil Spill," DoSomething.org, http://www.dosomething.org/tipsandtools/11-facts-about-bp-oil-spill.

[13] James B. Davies, Susanna Sandstrom, Anthony Shorrocks, and Edward N. Wolff, *World Distribution of Household Wealth* (Helsinki: UNU-WIDER, 2008), 8, table 2.

[14] Margaret J Bickers, "Does verbal encouragement work? The effect of verbal encouragement on a muscular endurance task," *Clinical Rehabilitation*, 7, no. 3 (August 1993): 196.

[15] M.E. Kerr, "We Might as Well All Be Strangers," *Am I Blue?: Coming Out from the Silence* (New York: HarperCollins, 1994), 23.

[16] Robert Frost, *The Poetry of Robert Frost: The Collected Poems, Complete and Unabridged* (New York: Owl Books, 1979), 33.

[17] Thomas Friedman, *The World is Flat 3.0: A Brief History of the 21st Century* (New York: Picador, 2007), 8.

[18] Anthony S. Bryk and Barbara L. Schneider, *Trust in Schools: A Core Resource for Improvement* (New York: American Sociological Association, 2002), 111.

[19] Paul Fleischman, *Seedfolks* (New York: JoAnna Cotler Books, 1997), 33-34.

[20] Ibid., 49-50.

[21] "Keeping the Legacy Alive: North Minneapolis Youth Speak Up!" *Developmental Designs* YouTube channel, www.youtube/developmentaldesigns.org.

22 Amy Gutmann and Dennis Thompson, *The Spirit of Compromise: Why Governing Demands It and Campaigning Undermines It* (Princeton: Princeton University Press, 2012), 30.

23 Ibid., 21-22.

24 Nikki Grimes, *Bronx Masquerade* (New York: Penguin Group, 2002), 134.

25 Ibid., 137-138.

26 Daniel Goleman, *Social Intelligence: The Revolutionary New Science of Human Relationships* (New York: Random House, 2006), 306.

27 Ibid., 307.

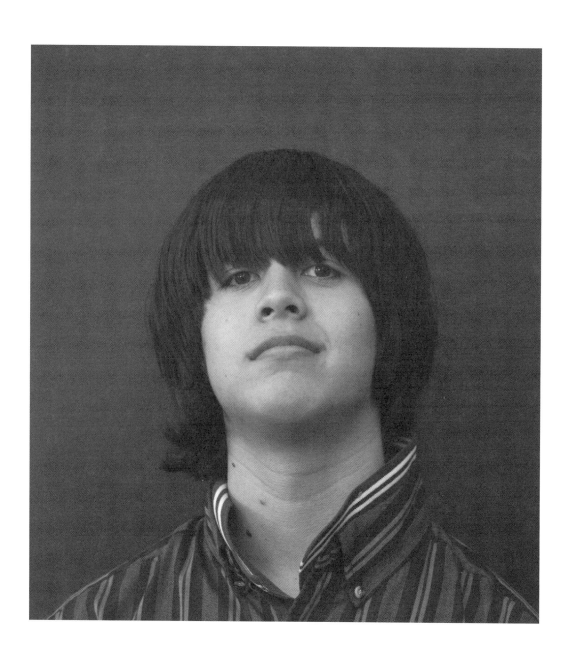

Us Versus Them

"Junior was an Interior Salish Indian living on the Spokane Reservation, but unlike all the other kids on the reservation, he went to school off the reservation in Reardon, a school with no other Indians attending. The comparison between his life at home (us) and his life at school (them) was dramatic.

"Let me tell you, we Indians were the worst of times and those Reardon kids were the best of times.

> "Those kids were magnificent.
>
> "They knew everything.
>
> "And they were beautiful.
>
> "They were beautiful and smart.
>
> "They were beautiful and smart and epic.
>
> "They were filled with hope.

"I don't know if hope is white. But I do know that hope for me is like some mythical creature....

"Man, I was scared of those Reardon kids, and maybe I was scared of hope, too, but Rowdy absolutely hated all of it."[1]

Junior saw clearly the differences between the kids on and off the reservation. In comparing them, he was doing something humans do well. Our capacity to distinguish one thing or person or idea from another is essential to our survival and to our ability to solve problems and to create. Consciousness inevitably involves noticing differences.

Difficulties arise when differences we notice about people cause us to fear them, or when they translate into discrimination. In school, we need to notice differences without judging them, and teach students to do so. To do this, we need to observe each other from more than one vantage point.

Bias and discrimination are everywhere, based on color, ethnicity, economic status, gender, age, disabilities, sexual orientation, religion, and more. In this chapter we examine the cost of individual bias, and the harm caused by institutional bias as it sweeps whole groups of people into secondary status and keeps them there. People in outgroups suffer the most, but we all pay a price. The advisories for this perspective illustrate for students the costs of prejudice in school, in their communities, and in the world.

Special advisory preparation: Advisory 21 uses a video, *Bullied: A Student, a School, and a Case that Made History*, a documentary produced by the Southern Poverty Law Center. The DVD is free, along with a teaching kit, at the Teaching Tolerance Web site.[2] Request it now, so you receive it by the time your group is ready for Advisory 21.

Words, words, words:

- See the glossary on page 346 for definitions of culturally-related words that are used in *Face to Face Advisories.*

- For each advisory meeting, a word in the daily news that may be unfamiliar to students is underlined. You can call their attention to it in a variety of ways. See *How to Lead Face to Face Advisories*, page 17, for suggestions.

Mind your Mindsets

To lead this set of conversations about bias and discrimination, we need to summon a growth mindset—belief that each person in the group can open her mind and confront her biases—and our commitment to act whenever necessary to maintain the safety of the environment. Students will take the risk of talking about a sensitive subject only if they feel safe to do so. It is likely that in the "us versus them" conversation, even the teacher will be offended by something someone says or the tone they use. Rather than rushing to defend or correct or criticize, respond to a statement of bias with calm tolerance. There is no use in escalating negativity, and that takes a cool head.

I remember the moment when my husband's grandmother, whom I enjoyed very much, was telling me a story and said, "And then I jewed him down." My stomach and heart sank together. Somehow I managed to stay anchored in my affection for this woman and said to her as neutrally as I could manage, "That expression is an insult to Jews." There was a long pause as she looked confused and then replied, "I've never made that connection. Oh, I'm so sorry!" And she was. The conversation left a little dent in me, and gave me some insight into small-town language, but no permanent damage was done to our precious friendship. (Educational consultant)

ADVISORY 1 ▶ CPR

Advisory goal: Understand the differences between competitive and cooperative play and the value of each

Greeting

Ball Toss Greeting: First person starts by greeting someone by name, *Good morning, Jake*, and tossing a soft ball or bean bag to him. Jake responds, *Good morning, Roberto*, catches the object, and greets another person, *Good morning, Monica*, then tosses it to her. She returns the greeting, and so on. Once someone has received and tossed the object, she puts her hands behind her back to signal that she has been greeted.

> Greetings, Group!
>
> Get ready for a fast-moving game of Silent Ball! Meanwhile, think about <u>competition</u> and whether and when it's good for people to compete.

➲ Before playing, model and practice tossing appropriately. The objective is to play quickly and smoothly, without dropping the object, and not taking time to choose someone to greet. Make sure students say the name clearly *before* tossing the object, alerting the recipient. Limit play to one round, everyone getting and giving a greeting once, so you have enough time to also play Silent Ball (the Activity). There are many variations on Ball Toss, including timing to see how fast the group can go.

Share

Partner Share: *Compare a cooperative game like Ball Toss with a competitive game. Do you prefer one type over the other? Give one reason why or why not (e.g., I prefer competitive sports because they help you get to be a better player, or I prefer cooperative games because I feel bad if I make the team lose).* Do not allow negative generalizations (e.g., *There's no point to cooperative games* or *Competition is dumb.*) Specify a time limit for a share. Give a warning halfway through the share to ensure balanced sharing/listening.

Activity

Individual Silent Ball (competitive game): Players stand silently in a circle. A non-bouncing object (a very soft ball or bean bag or stuffed animal) is thrown underhand back and forth across the circle. Players make sure to include everyone. If a player drops the ball, throws it out of control, or makes any noise other than catching and throwing (laughter counts), she must sit down. The last player standing is the winner.

➲ Model and practice how to throw the object underhand and in control. A "fair zone" between knees and shoulders may be helpful.

➲ There are variations on Silent Ball to make it less competitive, such as rotating players in and out (the first player out sits out; the next player who is out sits out and the first player goes back in), so there is never more than one player sitting out at a time. For this advisory, play Silent Ball as above, so students see the contrast between it and the cooperative Ball Toss greeting.

Keep in Mind

There is value in both cooperative and competitive games. The purpose of this advisory is to notice the differences between them, not to decide that one type is better. Most athletics are based on competition, and some students may have experienced only competitive play. This advisory meeting and the next one help students notice the differences between competitive and cooperative activities. They provide students experience of the pleasures and advantages of both.

Remind students that competition must be handled carefully, or it can lead to distrust, resentment, and other hard feelings for individuals, teams, large groups of people, or even countries.

Ask yourself

Do you enjoy competitive or cooperative games more, or both equally?

ADVISORY 2 ▶ CPR

Advisory goal: Appreciate the value of both competition and cooperation

Greeting

High Five Greeting: Moving in sequence around the circle, students greet each other with a high five. Dan says to Ari: *Hi, Ari* (high five). Ari returns the greeting: *Hi, Dan* (high five). Ari turns to Roxanne: *Hi, Roxanne* (high five). Roxanne returns the greeting: *Hi, Ari* (high five) and so on.

> Good Morning, Team Players!
> Today we'll think about cooperative and competitive play and the payoffs of each.

Share

Partner Share: *What was fun about each version of the ball tossing games we played last time: the Ball Toss Greeting and Silent Ball?* Specify a time limit for a share. Give a warning halfway through the share to ensure balanced sharing/listening.

Activity

Four Corner Thinking: Individualism and Community: Designate the four corners of the room: one is *strongly agree*, one is *somewhat agree*, one is *somewhat disagree*, and one is *strongly disagree*. Students move to the corner that represents their position on each statement the leader reads. After moving, give groups a minute or so to discuss why they chose the position they did, including, if possible, evidence to support their choice. You can then repeat the statement, giving students a chance to change their positions after hearing others' reasoning. You may choose to call on one or two students in each corner again to tell why they changed.

Warm-up opinion statements:

I enjoy French fries.

I enjoy other vegetables.

Individualism and community opinion statements:

I like to play competitive games.

I like to watch competitive games.

I like to play cooperative games.

I think communities benefit by playing competitive games.

I think communities benefit by playing cooperative games.

⤷ Time will dictate how often you can ask students to say why they chose the position they did.

At the end of the statements and choosing of corners, you may have time to read to the group the E.J. Dionne comment below and have them respond to it. A short paraphrase of the comment might be something like: Americans value both individualism and community and we know how to balance the two. After the reading and/or discussion, do one last round: *We need to balance competition and cooperation.*

Keep in Mind

What's better, competition or cooperation? Is it more important to be the best we can be as individuals, or work and play together successfully? Can we value and benefit from both?

A balance between individualism and community can help us be strong and successful as individuals, as a country, and as a world. According to political writer E.J. Dionne of the Washington Post, there are two values that Americans embrace: "our love of individualism and our reverence for community....*both* of these values animate the consciousness and consciences of nearly all Americans." They give us "our gift for managing our contradictions and balancing our competing impulses."[3]

Ask yourself

How have you used and/or experienced competitive and cooperative play to build community?

ADVISORY 3 ▶ CPR

Advisory goal: Understand that everyone notices differences among people

Greeting

Mall Greeting: As students mill around in the middle of the circle, call out, *Greet a passer-by!* Everyone <u>immediately</u> greets a person nearby. The idea is to keep the greeting pairs random, so there is no walking after the signal to greet. Then students mill about again until you call out, *Greet a passer-by!* Do two or more rounds. No one may greet the same person twice.

> *Good Morning, Friends!*
>
> *Today we'll pay attention to our similarities and differences. It's interesting that when we pay attention to our similarities, we can't help simultaneously noticing differences!* <u>Do Now</u>: *Sit next to someone with whom you share a characteristic such as hair color, birthday, or number of siblings.*

Share

Partner Share: *What sort of person do you like to spend time with?*

➲ Descriptors to get students started: *outgoing/social; has hobbies; plays sports; likes to read; likes to hang out; enjoys little kids; loves animals; silly; serious; etc.* Volunteers share out. To break the ice, you go first.

Activity

Me Too: A student begins by saying something that is true about himself, e.g. *I love to play basketball,* or *I have two brothers.* If this is true for others in the circle, they snap their fingers and say, *Me too!* The game goes around the circle until everybody has made a statement.

Keep in Mind

We discriminate among people and ideas carefully, and we want young people to learn to do so. But even wise, protective discrimination can bring us closer to bias and pre-judgment. As we saw in Perspective One, any sorting we do, no matter how necessary or innocent-seeming, is also a form of discrimination. If we're aware of that, we can prevent a slide in the direction of bias.

Games like Me Too and When the Cold Wind Blows (page 34) help students learn about each other, but they can cause moments of awkwardness when a student realizes he is the only one who seems to have a certain characteristic.

After When the Cold Wind Blows, we discussed how it felt to be the only person who stood up when a characteristic was called out. Students felt that there were categories that were OK to be unique in, such as "I play an instrument" or "I like the color red." But some felt uncomfortable being the only one who spoke a different language or had some other characteristic related to culture.... It sparked good discussion about being different when that difference had a history of exclusion or persecution. (Seventh/eighth grade science teacher)

Ask yourself

In what ways are the people on your staff similar to each other? In what ways do they differ?

ADVISORY 4 ▶ CPR

Advisory goal: Understand that certain cultural characteristics can raise or lower your status

Greeting

Reach Out Greeting: Students stand. When you state a category from the list below, everyone finds people who fit it, and greet them. Tell students that the idea is to greet as many people as possible before the category changes. You can gradually increase the degree to which students reach out:

> *Ohayou Gozaimasu! (Japanese for "Good morning")*
>
> *One of the things people do when they encounter each other is look for differences, even small ones. We might think: "Has he changed his hair?" "She speaks with an accent." Differences make life interesting, but also sometimes uncomfortable. Today we'll play with them a little bit.*

Greet people whose eyes are not the same color as yours.

Greet people who have the same middle initial as you.

Greet people of the opposite gender.

Greet people you haven't talked to yet today.

Greet people you don't know very well.

⮯ To minimize seeking certain people, keep this greeting moving along by calling out a new category before movement stops.

Share

Think Ink Pair Share: *There are many differences among us. At our school, are there some characteristics that tend to make people more or less popular? Write some down.* Students think quietly about the topic for a minute or two, write their thoughts on papers, and then share with their partners. Specify a time limit for a share. Give a warning halfway through the share to ensure balanced sharing/listening. Volunteers share out.

⮯ Thinking time is important, so students seriously consider how popularity works in your school. Students write their thoughts before sharing them. If there isn't time for students to share out with the whole group, or they are reluctant to do so, you can collect the ideas and read them anonymously at this meeting or the next one.

Activity

Something's Changed: Three students stand in the middle of the circle and slowly turn. Everyone observes them carefully, noting details such as clothing, hairstyles, accessories, etc. The three students then go out of sight and quickly change two or three things about their appearance: shift a watch or bracelet to the other wrist, take glasses off, untie a shoe, etc. They return to the middle and turn around slowly. Students try to see what has changed. One at a time, they guess.

⮯ Limit the number of guesses allowed per person based on the time available and on encouraging participation by everyone.

Keep in Mind

We need to pay attention to the bases on which we sort people. Although many characteristics about a person are not apparent immediately, when we first see someone, we tend to categorize them on the basis of immediately apparent, by definition superficial characteristics such as gender, age, weight, height, color, clothing, language/speech, etc.

Gender

One of the fundamental distinctions we perceive is gender. By third grade, eight- and nine-year-olds play almost exclusively with their own gender, and the separation continues even past the time when young people are dating. There are boy interests and girl interests, and the person who has interests in both may struggle to be accepted, or may attempt to hide one set of interests.

I feel excluded every time the boys and girls break apart from one another and go into gender-separated groups. The boys and girls don't seem to think they're better than the other group, but normally when I attempt to sit with a large group of boys, they say, "Aww, maan!" like they're trying to say they don't want me near them or something, just because I'm different! (Seventh grade girl)

On the other hand, some cultures are more comfortable with mixing genders than others, and the separation may be the choice of both genders or the request of a family.

The mother of an East Indian student expressed that her daughter did not feel comfortable working in pairs with boys or engaging in activities that involved close proximity to boys. (Middle level social studies teacher)

If you allow kids to sit on their own, they sort themselves by color and gender. And I hear generalizations about gender such as "Girls are always the good ones—they do things right." (Seventh-eighth grade language arts teacher)

Religion, politics, language, class

People have fought to the death over religion and politics as long as we have recorded our reasons for killing each other. And we use language by turns as a bond, a barrier, or a weapon. Until immigrants learn to speak English, they are not likely to gain much economic traction in America. At a workshop for educators, a skilled and inspiring facilitator who was a former principal and held a Ph.D. made some grammatical errors when he spoke. He had grown up in a poor, urban neighborhood, and was still working on some elements of formal American English. A participant complained that she didn't think much of her facilitator because he "couldn't speak correct" English. A few grammatical errors overwhelmed all the evidence that her facilitator was effective. See Advisory 10 for a discussion in the Keep in Mind of the cost to students when they are judged as generally deficient based on their use of language.

Class is a powerful, sometimes subtle basis for separation. In *Up From Slavery*, Booker T. Washington observed with amazement the courtesies afforded a few black men of his day. The discrimination normally exercised against blacks was suspended for a financially secure black gentleman of national reputation. Washington was welcomed by the captain, the staff, and passengers aboard a ship bound for Europe, and was "treated with the greatest kindness" where few others of his color would have been treated even civilly.[4]

"In 2010-11, 35 percent of undergraduates going to four-year state colleges or private nonprofit colleges received Pell grants. In general, the more selective the school, the lower that number was."[5]

In our school there is a gap between kids based on their different levels of language ability and different levels of class. Poverty divides the kids. (Seventh-eighth grade language arts teacher)

"Race"

We saw in the Introduction (page 24) that there is no biological basis for the concept of "race;" there is not enough genetic difference among people with various skin colors to make "racial" distinctions. However, the idea of "race" persists, and the associated variations in appearance, language, lifestyle, and shared history become the basis of "racial" discrimination.

Defining "race" is tricky. Skin pigmentation is a physical reality, therefore a legitimate physical distinction in the world. Only the socially constructed meanings associated with black or brown are artificial. (Educational organization director)

Everyone around me was an immigrant, my parents were immigrants, and so were my friends' parents. But I didn't identify that way and still don't. My exterior says African American. In my early years, the only choices on applications were Black or White. It still seems to boil down to White or non-White in this country. So I buy into being a person of color, African American, in solidarity with other dark-skinned people. (Seventh-eighth grade teacher)

Author Karen Manheim recalls: "At that time—hard as it may be to believe—I didn't think that anything was wrong with the fact that most of the students in the lowest tracks were African Americans who had come to my school from the inner city.... I assumed that because they were put in the lower tracks they weren't as 'smart.'"

All my perceptions of African-American students at this time were based on my assumptions about them, which came from what I had seen or heard in the media about life in the inner city and from the students' placement in these lower tracks....Back then I never considered the possibility that the tracking of these students, the curriculum and grading approaches used by teachers, and the teacher-student relationship could be contributing to the "underachievement" of these students."[6]

Ask yourself

What are some of the major differences among students in your school, culturally and in social and academic performance?

ADVISORY 5 ▶ CPR

Advisory goal: Recognize positive and negative responses to others who are different from us

Greeting

Huddle Up Greeting: As you make statements about personal interests, students respond by coming to the middle of the circle if it applies to them, greeting the others in the middle. After each huddle, students return to their seats. Those for whom the statement doesn't apply stay where they are, quietly waiting for the next statement. For example, *Huddle up if you enjoy watching football.* Everyone who likes to watch football comes to the middle of the circle and greets everyone else who shares this trait, while those who don't enjoy watching football remain seated.

> Hola, Compadres!
> Most of us have had moments when we felt like the odd person, the one who was different in some way. People seem to want to hang out with others who are like them. Today we'll get clear about different ways of responding to difference. Initial below if you have ever felt you were the "different" one in a group.

Call out categories of personal interests to demonstrate "soft" commonalities and differences in the group that are less likely to divide students from each other in a negative way, such as:

- *Huddle up if you like jazz*
- *Huddle up if you have a pet*
- *Huddle up if you like scary movies*
- *Huddle up if you like to sleep late*
- *Huddle up if you like to cook*
- *Huddle up if you like to talk on the phone*
- *Huddle up if you text*

↺ Make sure that everyone gets into the circle to greet at least once. The last two topics on the list above are aimed at getting everyone into the circle.

Share

Think Pair Share: *Tell about a time when you felt you were the only one (or one of few) in a group that was different in some way* (e.g., you were older or younger, or you were the "new kid," or you were the only person of your gender, color, culture, etc., in the group). Students think about the topic for a minute or two and then discuss their thoughts with their partner. Specify a time limit for a share. Give a warning halfway through the share to ensure balanced sharing/listening. Volunteers share out.

Activity

Responding to Differences Scenarios: Help students understand the continuum of possibilities for responding to differences. Explain that these scenarios are all examples of ways that we respond when we interact with people whom we perceive as different from us.

Assign one scenario to every three or four students. In each of the scenarios, whether the differences are described or not, students should assume that the people described are different from one another in color, ethnicity, language, sexual orientation, socio-economic class, ability, and/or religion. Using the categories defined in the Responding to Differences Continuum, give partners a few minutes to decide which category best matches the events in their scenario. Have partners share out with the whole group their scenario, the number they assigned it, and why. Thinking about the behaviors in each scenario will sharpen student appreciation for the nuances of behavior among people.

RESPONDING TO DIFFERENCES CONTINUUM

How do you respond to differences in the people you know?

1-EXCLUDE   2-AVOID   3-TOLERATE   4-ACCEPT   5-APPRECIATE

1. Exclude

You purposely keep this person out or deny him access to places, information, groups, and activities. For example, you do not let him join your game after school.

2. Avoid

You intentionally arrange things so you have as little contact as possible with this person. For example, if she is eating lunch at a certain table, you choose a different table, but you don't prevent her from sitting at your table if she chooses that.

3. Tolerate

You see the differences in this person as a negative, and although you don't go out of your way to avoid him, when he's around you might tease him about his differences or not talk to him. You say that people who are different in this way are OK, as long as they don't get in your way.

4. Accept

This person's difference doesn't bother you. You work with her sometimes and it's not a problem, but you don't seek her out for friendship.

5. Appreciate

You see the person's difference in a positive way and enjoy being around him. Sometimes you go out of your way to be with him.

RESPONDING TO DIFFERENCES SCENARIOS

Identify where the following scenarios fall on the Responding to Differences Continuum.

1. Alonzo and John are assigned to be lab partners. They don't hang out together at all outside of school. During lab work, they talk only when necessary. They get the work done, then wait silently for the period to end. When the bell rings, each goes to his friends and moves to the next class.

2. Mary finds out that Delores will be working on the dance decorations. To avoid her, she joins a different committee.

3. Robert asks Anthony, *Where'd you get those shoes, Anthony—the Goodwill?*

4. Jane often goes to Miriam's house after school. Miriam's mother and father are immigrants, and Jane enjoys listening to Miriam's mom tell stories about the old country. She enjoys the food Miriam's mom prepares, which is new to her.

5. Ed and Derek have been friends a long time. Sometimes Ed asks Derek for advice about what to do in certain situations when he feels social pressure. Derek encourages him to be himself and acknowledges his positives. Ed appreciates his friendship with Derek because he seems like the only person at school who understands him.

6. Francine is starting a new after-school group to raise money for the nearby community center. She invites other students to be involved, many of whom are people she hasn't hung out with at all outside of school. She understands that it will take many people with a variety of skills and working styles to launch this group, and she's willing to approach people she hardly knows.

7. Georgia intentionally does not invite Jessie or Ralph to her party.

8. David is Catholic and Martin is Jewish. They live in the same neighborhood and ride the same bus to school. They talk to each other almost daily about school and sports, and sometimes hang out together after school. They have never discussed their religious differences.

Keep in Mind

If I define myself as a white, educated, middle-class woman, I may unconsciously limit my social life contacts to people of a similar profile. I may not seek opportunities to engage with people of color, people who have received less formal education, or people who are poor. In this manner, my identity, shaped by my life so far, could end up shaping my life in the future.

Not many of us move freely between or among cultures. Sometimes we seek similarity right down to details: if you eat differently from the people around you or wear different clothes, you could be sorted for that; if you are a jock among intellectuals, you might not fit in, and vice versa. Sorting can become automatic, so that we do it for no other reason than habit.

A conflict was building on the playground between two groups of our fifth grade students. We called them together to discuss the issue, and as I watched and listened I noticed that to any onlooker, the two groups would be seen as practically identical to one another. Whether it was conscious or not, the only reason for the discrimination seemed to be that they were from different classrooms. Both groups were predominantly white, middle-class, mixed boys and girls, ten and eleven years old. Why couldn't they play with one another? (Principal, K-5 school)

Psychologist Scott Plous writes: "Social categories form an indispensable part of human thought, but because attributes such as race, sex, and age lie along a continuum, social labels are never more than approximations."[7]

"I seek, unsuccessfully, to establish boundaries between us and them, to find my way to a home I have never known."[8] Anthropology professor Signithia Fordham sees her heritage as a mix of colors, and questions the idea that people who *look* black *are* black, deciding that "our racialized identity has become a master status, superseding everything else about us."[9]

Black kids did better when their education was separate. In school integration, did we give something away of our humanity when we assimilated instead of integrating? Assimilating is just code-switching. Integrating is bridging between cultures. (Documentary maker and educational activist)

Skin color, ethnicity, religion, age, disability, sexual orientation, language, and more may be lived as self-defining and self-determining social clusters. Although they may help establish a sense of identity for adolescents, they also may contribute to a breakdown in "relational trust" among groups and individuals in schools. Researchers Bryk and Schneider defined relational trust as the interpersonal social exchanges that take place in the school community.[10] The divisions among us can generate a divisive school climate, a context in which achievement becomes less likely.

Relationships can crumble under "divide and conquer"

Oh yeah, you bet people have status in the African-American community if they are light-skinned. Your status with many of our people is determined by how light you are. We all know it. It even happens within families. (College teacher)

In their *Phi Delta Kappan* article, authors Tommie Lindsey, Jr., and Benjamin Mabie describe teaching a class of all African American boys, where it was apparent that subgroups were forming based on color, with darker- and lighter-skinned students clustering into separate subgroups. To break down the color hierarchy, the teachers read to the boys a speech said to have been delivered by the slave-master Willie Lynch in 1712. Lynch told his audience that slave-masters need to divide slaves according to their ages, sizes, and skin colors in order to weaken their solidarity and keep them down. It made a strong impression on the class that by unconsciously mimicking a slave-master, they were weakening their group. "By the end of the year, everyone was freely associating with everyone else. The class had become a safe environment in which every student equally participated, where there was no hierarchy and no exclusion."[11]

Ask yourself

What is the relational trust level within/across social categories among staff at your school?

ADVISORY 6 ▶ CPR

Advisory goals: Appreciate the value of heterogeneity. Understand the tendency toward homogeneity.

Greeting

Name Card Greeting: Give each student a note card to write his or her name on, then place them randomly face down in the middle of the circle. One at a time, each student selects a card, reads it, and greets the student indicated. Save the cards for reuse in a future Name Card Greeting.

Dear <u>Heterogeneous</u> Students,

Diversity is everywhere, so the ability to socialize and work with people who are different from us is an important personal strength. Is your main group of friends more homogeneous or more heterogeneous? Indicate on the continuum below:

<u>Homogeneous</u>   <u>Heterogeneous</u>

(I avoid mixed groups)   (I hang out with lots of different people)

Share

Simultaneous Share: *Use a show of fingers, one to five, to indicate how often you are an explorer: someone who likes to mingle with a variety of folks, many of whom seem different from you. Show one finger for rarely and five for most of the time.* Give a moment to think before students respond. Assure them that the number they show is just a rough indication of who they hang out with most of the time. On your count of three, all give their responses simultaneously.

Activity

Responding to Differences: My Relationships: Distribute resource on page 175 to students.

Keep in Mind

One time I was at my friends' house. We were all Latinos. And there was this one kid who wanted to hang out with us, but we just made fun of him because of the way he looked, dressed, and talked, and he left sad. That's one time I excluded. (Tenth grade student)

Helping students become aware of their excluding, avoiding, and merely tolerating behavior can help raise their consciousness and perhaps change exclusion to acceptance.

I did this [avoided someone] in lunch one time when there was this guy who was sitting at a table alone and I came and sat next to my friend and my friend felt bad and he called him over to sit with us. (Tenth grade student)

Avoiding avoidance

I purposely let students sit where they wish at first, and they always do so mostly along "racial" and class lines, although the more secure ones can accept all kids. Then I shape the partnering and mix the kids every day. The kids tend to gravitate back to gender and race, but after two years together, there is less and less of that discrimination. (Fifth grade teacher)

Exclusion as an element of cliques

There is a sense of safety and kinship in being part of a group. For example, students who identify with each other because of color, language, economic class, status in school, etc., often cluster together. Students with the greatest power and popularity may do so by choice, and some may even choose to move between groups. Those with little or no social capital, however, are likely to get a subtle or explicit message that they should stay in "their own" groups, and are not welcome to higher-status groups.

Looking from the inside out

Living in a sorted world, we often look at groups other than our own and size them up.

Tony, a fifth grader, described for me one day the pecking order of our student body. He said those at the bottom had no influence on others—they just went along whenever they were included. The next group hung out in little clusters and sometimes joined games, but they didn't organize the games and had to ask if they could join. The folks in the middle all mixed together, and took turns deciding things among themselves—they didn't have any power over the rest of the school. Then there were the ones on the top, the few with real power. The top three pretty much were the leaders, but one certain person had the final say. I asked Tony where he was located in this hierarchy, and he said he was at the bottom of the top group, and explained what it took to move up the hierarchy. "Why," I asked, "if you understand all this, aren't you on the top? Why don't you do what you have to do to get there?" "Too much work," he answered. (Principal K-5 school)

Our view of people may be quite different from how the insiders in a group describe themselves. When Joachim Krueger studied the personal beliefs of blacks and whites, he uncovered a widely held misperception: members of both groups underestimated how favorably they were viewed by the other. Krueger found that blacks and whites each thought, "We like them, but they don't like us," a belief that set the stage for misunderstanding, suspicion, and conflict.[12]

When my students did the self-interview [self-interviews are in Perspective One] and later shared them with each other, they discovered that almost everyone indicated that they felt others didn't necessarily like or trust them, but almost everyone also indicated that they liked and trusted pretty much everyone else. They realized the irony of this, laughed, and said, "Maybe we really do like each other!" It was a good moment. (Seventh-eighth grade language arts teacher)

Being aware of our human nature

As we have seen in Identity and Diversity, what are sometimes called our "constructed identities," are shaped by our "experience of class, race, gender or other socially defined identities."[13] It would be hopeless to try to do away with the interpretations and stories by which we sort ourselves into "us" and "them." They seem to be part of human nature. In fact, our imaginative thinking is part of what distinguishes us from other animals. So rather than attempt to escape this ancient human habit, we can choose to become editors as well as authors of our stories.

Ask yourself

Are the people you spend most of your social time with similar to you in color, class, ethnicity, religion, education, ability, etc.?

RESPONDING TO DIFFERENCES: MY RELATIONSHIPS

Think about the people you know, and describe someone for each of the categories below from the Responding to Difference Continuum. *This exercise is private and anonymous.* To protect privacy, students do not name the people they are describing. Return your completed paper to your teacher at the end of the meeting. This work is not to be shared with anyone else.

Example for category #2, Avoid

Example: She is a lesbian and everybody knows it. I don't hang out with her because when I do I get teased. I really don't care that she's a lesbian, but I don't want people thinking that I am.

1. Exclude

You purposely keep this person out or deny him/her access to places, information, groups, and activities. For example, you do not let him/her join your game after school/at recess.

Example:

2. Avoid

You intentionally arrange things so you have as little contact as possible with this person. For example, if she is eating lunch at a certain table, you choose a different table, but you don't prevent her from joining your table if she chooses to do that.

Example:

3. Tolerate

You see the differences in this person as negative, and although you don't go out of your way to avoid him, when he's around you might tease him or not talk much to him. You say that people who are different in this way are OK as long as they don't get in your way.

Example:

4. Accept

This person's difference doesn't bother you. You work with him/her in class sometimes and it's not a problem, but you don't seek her out for friendship.

Example:

5. Appreciate

You see the person's difference in a positive way and enjoy being around her/him. You seek out ways to be with her/him.

Example:

ADVISORY 7 ▶ CPR

Advisory goals: Recognize the dangers of ingroups and outgroups. Be able to identify biases.

Greeting

Partner Greeting: Partners choose how to greet each other. As always, the greeting must include the person's name, eye contact, and a friendly tone. If the choice presents too much risk for your group, use a Basic greeting (*Good morning, _____*).

> Bienvenidos!
>
> We all notice differences among people. The question we'll ponder together today is: When does noticing a difference become discrimination?

⟳ When a partner greeting precedes a partner share, the two flow together.

Share

Partner Share: *When is it OK to comment on differences among people, and when is it not?*

Activity

When Difference Becomes Discrimination: When a statement or behavior that recognizes differences between people becomes offensive, critical, or insulting, we have crossed the line between noticing differences and speaking or behaving in a biased, discriminatory way.

Read the following: There is a Sesame Street song that asks children to observe a group of things and identify which one is different and then states: *One of these things just doesn't belong....* The song is meant to encourage young children to notice differences between and among boats, birds, bugs, and more. But when a *person* is perceived as the one who is different, and on that basis "doesn't belong," then differences are used as a basis for discrimination. Sesame Street revised the song to ask neutrally: *Which one is different?*

Activity, part two

Divide the group into partners or triads, and give to each one of the following statements or situations in which differences are noted. The partners analyze their statement for possible prejudice and defamation, and get ready to share their thinking with the group. They read their statement aloud and comment on whether they think it is offensive or could be, and why.

1. At work, one person tells jokes about black people on welfare.
2. At family dinners my uncle tells jokes about drunken Irishmen, and everyone laughs.
3. My grandmother talks about "jewing people down" to a lower price.
4. My friends say "He's so gay!" whenever a guy hangs around talking with the girls.
5. I'm worried that my son will come home with a white girl.

6. My father tells stories that start, "This Mexican comes into a bar." He never says "This white guy comes into a bar."

7. Yesterday none of the Muslims showed up at school. They said it was a Muslim holiday. Well, St. Patrick's Day is a holiday, but I don't get to stay home!

8. I have a friend who walks with a limp, and my mother always calls her "that unfortunate girl." She still doesn't remember her name.

9. My friends and I always have lunch together, and so do the Spanish-speaking girls. We never sit at each other's table, but once one of Puerto Rican girls asked to sit at our table because their table was full. We let her, but no one talked to her.

10. The guys hang out together at the rec center. We shoot hoops and just talk. The girls are always hanging around us. It's really annoying that they can't take a hint that we don't want females around.

11. I'm trying out for the girls' basketball team, and two of the girls on the team are lesbians. My mom says she's afraid I'll end up like them.

12. She wears the same jeans practically every day, and only a couple of different tops! She probably sleeps in them!

Keep in Mind

Us *and* them becomes us *versus* them

It's easy to slip from noticing to discriminating, then to stereotyping the "other." And bias in favor of some almost naturally includes bias against others. As we choose similarity in our associations, we exclude difference, intentionally or unintentionally.

During recess, a quarrel developed among a group of fifth graders. They were excluding two children from a game. I intervened and discussed the matter with the excluders, requesting that they allow everyone to play. The leader of the excluders responded, "But this is recess! In class we have to all be together—why can't we choose to play with the people we want to on the playground? You grown-ups get to do that—you don't play with people you don't want to." (Fifth grade teacher)

Bias regarding class

In schools, children who are from economically depressed homes are often perceived as destined for failure. Sure enough, many do fail, but not all. The assumption that they will fail can operate as a self-fulfilling prophecy. But if someone believes in them, growth is far more likely.

In my school there were kids from wrecked homes and others who had prostitutes for mothers. These children tended to be lonely, defensive, and quiet, and they kept separate from others. One boy, the son of a prostitute, came to school dressed immaculately every day. He worked hard, but he had few friends, and he was teased viciously for his mother's line of work. His mother was deeply committed to him and never missed a parent-teacher conference. Years later, I ran into him and was delighted to see that he was prospering and happy. (Sixth grade teacher)

Bias regarding language and style

When the gap is great between a student and the school culture established by adults, a requirement for wholesale conformity can be damaging. If a student's cultural style is perceived as a shortcoming, they must adopt another way of being, at least in school. For example, call and response, familiar to African Americans from church sermons and public speeches, enhances the communal experience for audience members.[14] But spontaneous response to an adult is generally unacceptable in school; silent listening is required in most schools, and students who don't comply get into trouble. Southern University Professor Lisa Delpit asserts that this is a "gatekeeping point" students must pass to succeed in school: "[P]retending that gatekeeping points don't exist is to ensure that many students will not pass through them. One way or another, we keep students of color out of the club by ignoring their deficiencies until society rejects them for those deficiencies."[15]

Sometimes mere style differences are perceived as deficiencies. Students may be misidentified as needing special education services when in fact what they need is a teacher who can guide a wide range of behavior, including playful or loud interactions, toward learning.

Some teachers had trouble with African American students—more than any others. The African American kids were often demonstrative, outspoken, energetic. They had an exuberance that white teachers couldn't quell. A substitute once wrote a note saying, "I will never substitute for this woman again!" I found out that as soon as class began she told the kids to sit at their desks and be quiet. We always moved around freely in my class as we worked on projects, and kids were allowed to talk as they worked together. She had no idea how to let kids move around and talk. She wanted what they didn't want to give—silent compliance. Kids need to have enough freedom to find themselves. There are tremendous numbers of people who never get a chance to use their talents." (High school journalism teacher)

Students take a "refuse to learn" stand

In an environment they experience as alien, even hostile, some students consciously or unconsciously refuse to learn. The law removes the option to not attend, so they assert their autonomy by choosing to not learn whatever the school has to teach. Educator Herb Kohl discovered in his teaching in Harlem "the essential role that will and free choice play in learning, and it taught me the importance of considering people's stance toward learning in the larger context of the choices they make as they create lives and identities for themselves."[16]

Sometimes discrimination pervades a place, muffling everyone. Writer Alice Walker says "During childhood I wasn't aware that there was segregation or that it was designed to make me feel bad. White people just seemed very alien and strange to me. I knew that when they appeared everybody sort of stopped having fun, and waited until they left to become alive again. I think as a child you tend to notice that deadening effect of life, more than you would their color."[17]

Ask yourself
Everyone has biases. What are yours?

ADVISORY 8 ▶ CPR

Advisory goal: Understand the dangers of gossip. Be able to identify when language is derogatory or defamatory

Greeting

Grapevine Greeting (based on Telephone): One person begins by whispering to the person next to her, *Hi, _____* and then she says something friendly about someone in the class (teacher or student) in one

> Peace, Everyone!
>
> Here's an opinion poll for you to respond to. Put an "X" on the continuum to indicate how harmless or harmful you feel gossip is.
>
> Gossip is harmless_____Gossip is harmful

sentence (e.g., *Ms. Silva likes to watch soccer*). The person replies in a whisper, *Hi, _____*, and then greets the next person in the circle with the same greeting and the same sentence, repeating it the way he heard it. When the greeting has gone around the whole circle, the last person to convey the message does so out loud. Then the final version is compared with the original to see whether it has changed as it moved along the greeting grapevine. It usually has!

Share

Whip Share: Introduce the topic question: *Gossip is talking about other people when they are not present. Do you think gossip is usually harmful?* Each student offers a brief response that includes a reason or evidence for their answer; responses quickly "whip" around the circle. Some students may want to simply concur with what another said or add to it.

Activity

The Language of Us vs. Them: Read aloud the following definitions. To help you distinguish between *derogatory* and *defamatory*, read *Freedom of speech versus defamation*, below. Then apply the definitions to the scenario.

Gossip (n.): talk, often unsubstantiated rumors, about a person who is not present; talk that often comes from and passes on rumors about someone, usually about their personal, private affairs. *Synonyms:* tattle, rumor, chit chat.

Derogatory (adj.): disparaging, offensive, uncomplimentary language that tends to lessen the merit or reputation of a person or thing. *Synonyms:* belittling, critical, damaging, degrading, demeaning, detracting, disdainful, dishonoring, disparaging, fault-finding, humiliating, injurious, malicious, sarcastic, scornful, slanderous, spiteful, unfavorable, unflattering.

Defamatory (adj.): offensive, uncomplimentary language used about another person to harm their reputation with slander (spoken) or libel (written). *Synonyms:* abusive, defamatory, denigrating, derogatory, disparaging, injurious, insulting, maligning, opprobrious, vilifying.

Derogatory and *defamatory* have similar meanings, but *defamatory* is a stronger term and suggests that the demeaning language is so disparaging that it may be cause for legal action.

Antonyms of both *derogatory* and *defamatory*: approving, commending, complimentary, praising, acknowledging, appreciative, favorable, flattering.

Freedom of speech versus defamation: There is always a delicate balance between one person's right to freedom of speech and another's right to protect [his or her] good name. It is often difficult to know which personal remarks are proper and which run afoul of defamation law. The term "defamation" is an all-encompassing term that covers any statement that hurts someone's reputation. If the statement is made in writing and published, the defamation is called "libel." If the hurtful statement is spoken, the statement is "slander." The government can't imprison someone for making a defamatory statement since it is not a crime. Instead, defamation is considered to be a civil wrong, or a tort. A person that has suffered a defamatory statement may sue the person that made the statement under defamation law. Defamation law, for as long as it has been in existence in the United States, has had to walk a fine line between the right to freedom of speech and the right of a person to avoid defamation. On one hand, people should be free to talk about their experiences in a truthful manner without fear of a lawsuit if they say something mean, but true, about someone else. On the other hand, people have a right to not have false statements made that will damage their reputation. Discourse is essential to a free society, and the more open and honest the discourse, the better for society.[18]

Scenario

Read aloud the following scenario and reflection questions, or give printed copies to partners. Direct the partners to discuss the scenario and decide whether the statements are gossip, derogatory, and/or defamatory (they could be two or all three). Afterward, students share out their thoughts.

Martina tells Danielle that Anna got in trouble with her parents because she stayed out later than she was supposed to: *Now she can't go to the game on Friday because she's grounded. Her parents are such control freaks! And she wanted to see Justin play—I think she's got a crush on him, but I don't think she's his type anyway.*

What negative statements about others did Martina make?

Would you call those statements gossip?

Were they derogatory? Defamatory?

Keep in Mind

How much does intent determine whether a statement is harmful? We discuss student shortcomings as part of our effort to guide them to better behavior or more rigorous learning. When critical comments are made to a student or his family, they need to be accompanied by a clear statement of belief in the student's capacity to grow beyond the problematic behaviors. If unaccompanied by a committed growth mindset—if plans and possibilities for a better performance are absent from the conversation—critical statements could be mere complaint or even gossip.

"The experience of hope distinguishes a pedagogical life from a non-pedagogical one. It also makes clear that we can only hope for children we truly love, in a pedagogical sense. What hope gives us is this simple confirmation: 'I will not give up on you. I know you can make a life for yourself.'"[19]

Ask yourself
What protocols help teachers discuss students productively?

ADVISORY 9 ▶ CPR

Advisory goal: Appreciate people who are different from you

Greeting

Color-coded Greeting: Each student receives either a small blue or red piece of paper. Students do not choose the color. They make their color visible by either holding it up or taping or pinning it on in plain sight. The Basic Greeting (*Good morning, _____*) goes around the circle, but Reds may greet only Reds and Blues may greet only Blues. This means students bypass people of the other color.

⮑ At the end of the greeting, ask students how it felt to skip people and to be skipped during the greeting. Point out that the greeting is meant to provide a taste of exclusion.

Share

Rare Birds Share: *Write about ways you are different from most people you know.*

Students write down their differences. Collect the cards for use in the activity below.

⮑ Give some examples before students write their own: *I speak two languages; I'm double-jointed in my thumb; I've performed in a circus.*

Activity

Rare Birds: read the self-description from a card aloud. The group has three guesses to determine who is the "rare bird" who wrote it. The person who wrote it then tells a little more about what they shared on their card. Save the ones left over for other times.

Keep in Mind

Rare Birds is an opportunity to talk about the many-faceted nature of any person, and the fact that sometimes we are surprised to learn something about someone we thought we knew well. A community is strengthened by its differences. The stronger the sense of safety, the more likely students are to take risks in sharing.

Our community was strong and the kids supported one another. One day a student revealed in Rare Birds that both of his parents were in jail for drug violations. I was a little concerned about the response he might get, but the community rallied support for him. And another student wrote that he could hardly read when he first came to our school as an 8th grader. As far as I could see, nobody ever teased him about it afterwards. I sometimes used Rare Birds with a focus such as something about your family or about you as a student in our school. I learned a lot about my students that way. (Seventh-eighth grade language arts teacher)

Ask yourself

What ways do you use to get to know your students well?

ADVISORY 10 ▶ CPR

Advisory goal: Develop the skill of perspective-taking

Greeting

Guess My Feeling Greeting: Write names of emotions on index cards, one per card, and give one to each student. Using a Basic Greeting (*Good morning, Malika*), students greet each other one at a time around the circle, in voices that reflect the emotion: fear, pain, boredom, surprise, etc. Students may guess the emotion.

> sdneirF, gninroM dooG!
>
> Sometimes the facts or truth depends on our <u>perspective</u>. Can you read my <u>salutation</u>?

➲ Have students model a few of the emotions before the greetings begin.

Share

Partner Share: *What is something that you and your family see differently?* Specify a length of time to share and issue a time warning halfway through the share to ensure balanced sharing/listening.

➲ Provide a few examples to get students thinking: e.g., friends, food, doing homework, curfews, dating. You may model listening and asking socially inclusive questions (*Roland, what things do you and your family see differently?*)

Activity

Exercise on Visual Perspective: Sometimes differences of perception are literal. Even when we are looking at the same thing, we don't necessarily see the same thing. Give each group of three or four a copy of My Wife and My Mother-in-Law[20]. *Look at the picture for at least ten seconds, then share, one at a time, what you see. If you see different things, help one another see what each person sees.*

➲ Make enough copies of the picture so each group has one.

Reflection

Introduce the reflection: *If we see things differently at different times and differently from each other, it is difficult to say that only one version or one interpretation is the truth. What does this tell us about the opinions we have of each other?*

What does this tell us about our biases and prejudices?

⮑ For more images that can be perceived variously, see *The Best Optical Illusions Ever* on www.youtube.com.

Keep in Mind

Education helps people from different cultures learn to live together peacefully and productively. In our schools, we can look at our differences, affirm and enjoy them, and construct genuinely integrated communities. Cultivating the ability to see from more than one perspective is crucial; it helps bridge the distance between us and them.

Perceive the "other" in the context of culture

Our challenge is to relate to students from a variety of cultures in such a way that they feel connected to school. If we simply perceive and label deviations from a cultural norm as negative and undesirable, some students may never feel comfortable in school. They might adopt negative self-perceptions or other destructive behaviors, or feel alienated.

"The literature [on social skills] includes few comparative empirical investigations on the social behaviors of racial or ethnic minorities in schools....

"...The issue with culturally different students, as with all students, is not to view these differences [in social skills] as pathological but to assess the degree to which they tend to support or interfere with success in later life. Common practices in which culturally different behavior is stereotyped, and then overlooked or punished, are counterproductive."[21]

When a significant difference exists between the students' culture and the school's culture (defined by the adults), teachers can easily misread students' aptitudes, intent, or abilities as a result of the difference in styles of language use and interactional patterns. Secondly, when such cultural differences exist, teachers may utilize styles of instruction and/or discipline that are at odds with community norms. "Problems arising from culturally different interactional styles seem to disproportionately affect African-American boys, who, as a result of cultural influences, exhibit a high degree of physicality and desire for interaction. This can be expressed both positively and negatively, as hugging and other shows of affection or as hitting and other displays of displeasure. Either expression is likely to receive negative sanction in the classroom setting."[22]

Author Jawanza Kunjufu describes negative qualities often identified with special-education students and then offers positive interpretations of the same behavior. Sometimes it's a matter of interpretation, and the way you read a student may make all the difference in how you interact with him. The challenge for us as educators is to be able to see positive, creative possibilities in ways of being that at first don't seem to fit into school.

Characteristics Often Attributed to SPED Students (Who Are Disproportionately Also Black Boys)[23] From *Keeping Black Boys Out of Special Education*, Dr. Jawanza Kunjufu

NEGATIVE	POSITIVE
Hyperactive	Energetic
Impulsive	Spontaneous
Distractible	Creative
Daydreamer	Imaginative
Inattentive	Global thinker with a wide focus
Unpredictable	Flexible
Argumentative	Independent
Stubborn	Committed
Irritable	Sensitive
Aggressive	Assertive
Attention Deficit Disorder	Unique

In an urban school, African-American students came to an administrator troubled by tensions that had developed with Vietnamese-American students:

The African American students told me that the conflict between the two groups was because, for some reason, the Vietnamese students avoided them and wouldn't talk or hang out with them. "They don't like us." The administrator jumped on a table and, looking down on the youths, shouted: "Maybe they avoid you because they feel dominated by your style! Maybe this is what it feels like to them to have you towering over them and jumping around a lot and talking much louder than they talk to each other!" "Oh yeah," grinned the boys. "We get it! We get it!" (Charter high school administrator)

Left untangled, the mutual misreading of cultural signals damages the social fabric. In this case, both the Vietnamese-American and African-American students had an opportunity to raise their awareness of one another's cultural expressions and then adjust their behavior. And when there is a power differential, as there is between teachers and students, and culturally-driven behavior is misinterpreted and even punished by someone of a different culture, resentment and escalated reaction can result.

Misreading can take place when European-American, middle-class, female teachers correct and discipline African-American, male students for behavior that might be acceptable in African-American culture. Gwendolyn Cartledge and JoAnne Fellows Milburn describe a time when a first-year white teacher observed two African-American students engaging in what she believed was aggressive verbal exchanges. When she brought them to the principal's office, she learned that it was she who needed to adjust. The principal explained that she had misread African-American verbal sparring ("doin' the dozens," "capping," or "ribbing") as the beginning of a fight.[24]

Ask yourself
Have you struggled with a student, then changed your perspective so you saw the problem differently? What helped you or might help you do that?

ADVISORY 11 ▶ CPR

Advisory goal: Develop the skill of perspective-taking

Greeting

Language Greeting: *Shalom, _____ .* All students greet with this Hebrew word for *peace* around the circle.

Oodgay Orningmay!

Pig Latin is an exercise in <u>perspective-tak-ing</u>. Once you get the hang of moving the first letter of the word to the end, then adding "ay" or "lay," you can speak it. Today we'll keep working on noticing varied points of view on a topic or object.

Share

Partner Share: *What's your perspective: should athletic teams be mixed or single-gender?*

Activity

Point of View: An object (e.g., a wire whisk; a bicycle lock; a scarf—any object that lends itself to multiple interpretations—is passed around, and each student shares his point of view about what this object might be used for. You can't say anything that the object is *really* used for, and your interpretation must be appropriate for school.

⊃ If a student veers into inappropriateness, stop the action, take the object, have the student sit outside the circle for a while to center himself, and go on to the next person.

Keep in Mind

Outgroup homogeneity and ingroup bias

Outgroup and ingroup tendencies can be summed up this way: *I see plenty of variety within my group (the ingroup), but the other group (the outgroup) seems homogeneous—in certain ways, they all seem alike.* Research suggests that the pattern of forming preju-diced attitudes is not limited to a few pathological or misguided individuals. In his classic book *The Nature of Prejudice*, Gordon Allport wrote, "The human mind must think with the aid of categories.... Once formed, categories are the basis for normal prejudgment. We cannot possible avoid this process. Orderly living depends upon it.[25] Psychologists refer to this form of bias as the "outgroup homogeneity effect."[26]

In addition to being stereotyped by others, groups become the object of prejudice by default. Cultures around the world show a tendency of people to favor their own group, known as "ingroup bias." Psychologist Marilynn Brewer writes, "Ultimately, many forms of discrimination and bias may develop not because outgroups are hated, but because positive emotions such as admiration, sympathy, and trust are reserved for the ingroup."[27] Sometimes when students disrupt classes with behavior that is appropriate to their culture and their neighborhood, but not appropriate in school, we find them deficient not because there is something wrong with their culture but because we be-lieve our way is the best culture for learning.

Ask yourself

How can you help yourself see students freshly each day?

ADVISORY 12 ▶ CPR

Advisory goals: Develop the skill of perspective-taking. Understand how we tend to hold on to our belief systems and biases.

Greeting

Tower Greeting: Starting at waist level, partners take turns placing a hand on top of the other's, moving them higher and higher until their arms form an arch between them. They look at each other under the arch and greet each other. The greeting continues around the circle.

➲ Model the tower by going first with a student.

Share

Partner Share: *What are some characteristics you think of as typical of boys (if you are a girl) or girls (if you are a boy)?* Specify a length of time to share. Issue a time warning halfway through the share to ensure balanced sharing/listening. Volunteers share out if there is time.

➲ Note how generalizations about gender, like other generalizations about culture, are likely to have flaws. Invite ideas and examples that belie the generalizations.

Good Morning, All!

Get your thinking skills revved up! Today we're going to think about how we get from the world as it actually is to the world and people as they seem to us. The two are often not at all the same. Do we <u>consistently</u> see only what we expect to see? <u>Do Now</u>: Let's test this out: Write in the drawing of a school (below) one word that expresses how you see school. Let's find out if we all see it the same way.

Activity

Thinking Straight: Ladder of Inference: Share the Ladder of Inference with students as a projection or a handout. Give an example of your own experience of moving up the ladder into a belief or bias. Read the example in the exercise and point out that the ladder of inference refers to any established belief, about yourself, another person or group, or anything you interact with, that dictates your actions. In pairs, students try to come up with an example from their own lives.

➲ You can simulate the ladder by placing rods or sticks on the floor to represent the rungs of the ladder and having a student move up the ladder of inference from one rod to the next.

➲ Even if students skip a rung or two in their examples, the important thing is for them to understand that in life we tend to generalize our limited experience to assumptions and beliefs about that experience, and then we act on those beliefs.

LADDER OF INFERENCE

Each stage described below represents a step on the ladder toward establishing a belief and actions.

Bottom step–Experience and real data: We begin by gathering information from what we see and what we do. **Example:** At an amusement park when I was about ten years old, I drove a car in a simulation in which the road kept moving from side to side on the screen to make it hard to keep the car on the road.

Experience and selected data: We notice certain parts of what we see and do, and ignore others. **Example:** I drove off the road repeatedly.

Affixed meaning: We interpret what we experience. **Example:** I interpreted my driving off the road to be due to lack of skill and judgment.

Assumptions: We assume the truth of our interpretations. **Example:** I assumed that you either are or aren't a good driver

Conclusions: We come to conclusions based on our assumptions. **Example**: I decided I wasn't a good driver.

Beliefs: We develop beliefs based on our conclusions. After a while, our beliefs focus our attention on what confirms those beliefs. This is confirmation bias. **Example:** Every time I drive, I expect driving to be uncomfortable and risky.

Top step–Actions: We take action based on our beliefs. **Example:** I avoid driving.

Keep in Mind

We saw in Perspective One that culture influences us profoundly, including the development of our belief systems. This is how psychologists say it happens: we notice certain aspects of the world and fail to notice others, sometimes by accident, but mostly because the people and environment around us guide us to notice and interpret certain things and not others. Because humans are by nature meaning-makers, we ascribe meaning to what we notice, often unconsciously, and we build assumptions and draw conclusions based on that meaning. By adulthood, we have a whole system of beliefs that consist of all the conclusions we have drawn. This system of thinking is called the ladder of inference.[28]

The ladder of inference suggests that when the original interpretation of reality is biased toward or against certain kinds of behavior or appearance, the bias becomes part of our belief system, and the only way we can change it is to go back to the source—the meaning our culture gave to the behavior in the first place, and the conclusions we drew. For example, individuals who are biased against people of color cannot rid themselves of that bias until they look at the way their culture has shaped their encounters with people of color and how those encounters were (and still are) interpreted.

Ask yourself

What is a belief you have that might be based on experience in your youth?

ADVISORY 13 ▶ A+

Advisory goal: Understand that although we are shaped by our culture, we also have the power to change and grow in new ways with new insights

Greeting

Language Greeting: *O-si-yo, _____:* All students greet in Cherokee, either around the circle or in the All Group Greeting format. (All Group format: *O-si-yo, everyone.* Group responds: *O-si-yo, Carla.*)

> *O-si-yo!* (Cherokee for Hello)
>
> Sometimes we have a bias and don't realize it. That's called an <u>unconscious</u> bias. We seem to breathe in the way we see others as if it were in the air. Even when we realize that certain ways of seeing others are tied up in <u>stereotypical</u> thinking, it is hard to break from it. Today we'll talk about thinking straight in the presence of stereotypes.

Activity

***The Absolutely True Diary of a Part-Time Indian* by Sherman Alexie:** Read the following aloud to students:

Junior lives on the Spokane, Washington, Indian Reservation as a member of the Interior Salish tribe. His best friend was Rowdy, who had often saved Junior from getting beaten up. With encouragement from one of his teachers, Junior decides to go to a white school off the reservation, something that nobody ever did, and Rowdy, feeling deserted and betrayed, refuses to have anything to do with him. After Junior's grandmother, a woman much loved and respected by all the tribe, is killed in a hit-and-run incident, Rowdy comes around again to shoot hoops with Junior, just like old times. But it isn't like old times, because Junior has broken away, broken the stereotype of what Indians do. Rowdy and he have a conversation. Rowdy speaks first:

"'So anyway,' he said. 'I was reading this book about old-time Indians, about how we used to be nomadic.'

"'Yeah,' I said. [Junior is the "I" telling the story]

"'So I looked up nomadic in the dictionary, and it means people who move around, who keep moving, in search of food and water and grazing land.'

"'That sounds about right.'

"'Well, the thing is, I don't think Indians are nomadic anymore. Most Indians, anyway.'

"'No, we're not,' I said.

"'I'm not nomadic,' Rowdy said. 'Hardly anybody on this rez is nomadic. Except for you. You're the nomadic one.'

"'Whatever.'

"'No, I'm serious. I always knew you were going to leave. I always knew you were going to leave us behind and travel the world. I had this dream about you a few months ago. You were standing on the Great Wall of China. You looked happy. And I was happy for you.'

"Rowdy didn't cry. But I did."[29]

Reflection

What does it take to break away from ways of thinking about things that hold us back, for example, stereotypes about gender roles and people with disabilities and homosexuals?

Rowdy thought of Junior as strong. Do you agree? Explain.

What is a goal you have that you need to be strong to meet?

Keep in Mind

Unconscious stereotyping

We sometimes reduce ourselves and others to stereotypes without realizing it. We may pick up influences, preferences, biases, and attitudes of superiority from friends and/or family, our neighbors and classmates, and from media. "[E]vidence suggests that once a stereotype is activated, it can be reactivated by something as simple as a disagreement with someone in the stereotyped group, and if brought to mind frequently enough, can become chronically accessible…. Thus, even though media-based stereotypes may seem harmless when considered individually, their cumulative effect over time can be substantial."[30]

The teacher wondered, "What am I doing wrong? I'm not afraid to discipline these African American students. I am tough on them when I need to be, but the class is still bad." She finally saw that even though she wasn't actually afraid, she was coming across to the students as fearful and punishing the African American kids while overlooking the off-task, chatting, note-passing behavior of others. She saw that those others didn't walk around a lot, like the students she was disciplining, but they were still breaking the rules and everyone knew it. It wasn't fair, and that's why the kids keep saying, "You always choose African Americans to yell at. You are so prejudiced—it's always the same kids!" She saw that they were right. (Developmental Designs consultant, middle school)

Research into American stereotypes was initiated with a seminal study by Daniel Katz and Kenneth Braly in 1933, in which 100 Princeton University students (all were white men – Princeton began admitting men of color in 1935, women in the 1940's) were asked to indicate the traits they felt were characteristic of ten different social groups. The participants showed a high rate of agreement about the traits of certain color and ethnic groups, such as African Americans (described as superstitious by 84% and as lazy by 75%) and Jews (described as shrewd by 79%). Princeton's quota for Jewish admissions at the time was 200 per year.

Katz and Braly's research suggests that, in addition to the explicit stereotypes they measured, people unconsciously harbor biases.[31] Social psychologist Scott Plous observed that people sometimes discriminate after being exposed to stereotypes even though they don't consciously promote or endorse those stereotypes.[32]

Ask yourself

What do you/can you do when a student expresses a bias but seems unaware of doing so?

ADVISORY 14 ▶ A+

Advisory goal: Develop capacity to recognize bias in yourself

Greeting

Fist-Tap Greeting: Students greet each other using Basic Greeting format (each person greets his/her neighbor in the circle with *Good morning, _____*), adding a gentle fist bump. This may be a silent greeting, or use the Fist-Tap Greeting as a quick simultaneous greeting when time is short. Model and practice fist-tapping before beginning: make a fist, then gently tap partner's fist as *Hi* or *Hola* or *Ciao, _____* is exchanged.

> S'up?
> Sometimes the people we criticize are very much like us. Today we'll read about boys who focus on their differences.

Activity

I Apologize: **A poem by Sharon G. Flake**: The poem is written from the perspective of an African-American boy who lives in the suburbs. He is speaking to African American boys who live in urban neighborhoods and have fewer resources in life than he does. He accuses them of stereotyping him and his way of life, and at the same time describes them and their lifestyle with stereotypes. Read (or have students read) the poem aloud at least twice.

I Apologize

by Sharon G. Flake

For living in the suburbs,
For talking white,
For trying to be cooler than I am,
For locking my windows when my mom drives me into the city at night,
For choosing Harvard over Howard,
For not going to public school,
For taking Paige to the prom,
And for sitting up in church, singing hymns like life was ever hard for me.
I apologize
For that time I pretended not to see you cutting up,
Or the time I sat in the barber shop, scared that more than my hair was going to get cut.
I apologize
For looking like you, but not knowing exactly who you are.
But you can apologize too, you know.
I hear you laughing at the way I speak,
Pointing at the geek you say is me walking upon the street,
Asking why my family gotta act so white.
Stepping up to me because you think I can't fight.
I know what happens when I show up at a dance:
You and your boys sit back and don't give me a chance.

Laughter happens whenever you see me around,
Unless you need to borrow some money.
Then, well, of course me and you is down.
I don't always understand you.
You don't seem to get me at all.
I prefer golf,
You swear by basketball.
We are
City
And
Suburb,
A million miles apart.
Brothers
Still trying to understand and forgive one another.
So I apologize
For whatever.
And you?[33]

Reflection

Partners discuss reflection questions. Partners share out.

How are the speaker and the boys he is addressing similar? How are they different?

Why do you think the speaker feels that they are "a million miles apart"? What are the stereotypes they seem to have of each other?

Why do we tend to focus on our differences, sometimes even ignoring our similarities?

Can you cite an example in your life of people you believe have much in common, but perceive themselves as very different from each other?

↻ Students may not have time for all the reflection questions. You can either:

- give them the first one to discuss, ask for volunteers to share out, and then proceed with the next question, or
- give partners the questions, let them talk about as many of them as they can, and save enough time at the end to have volunteers share out.

Keep in Mind

Biases self-reinforce

After we create or adopt an idea about something or someone, we tend to keep reinforcing that idea, and eventually an idea becomes a bias. We lean toward or away from the person, prejudging him because of our bias:

When Mr. B. first was my teacher, I thought that he criticized the girls more than the boys. It seemed to us girls that he picked on us for little things. I thought he didn't like girls, even though after a while there weren't any times when he picked on us. But it was over a year later that I stopped thinking of him as against girls. He really didn't do anything against the girls all that time, but I kept thinking he favored the boys. (Eighth grade girl)

The term "confirmation bias" was coined by psychologist Peter Wason in 1960 to identify the drive in humans to confirm initial decisions and points of view.[34] The idea that people will seek or interpret information in ways that square with their existing beliefs dates back at least to the English philosopher Francis Bacon, who noted in 1620: "The human understanding when it has once adopted an opinion...draws all things else to support and agree with it."[35]

Bias toward our own culture may result in misreading students

Cultures clash when people behave the way their culture taught them to behave and then get a negative reaction from people from a different culture. This can be painful for both. For example, if a teacher is friendly and does not demand adherence to the rules at the same time, the interpretation by some African American (and other) students may be that this adult has no authority. "[T]he authoritative person gets to be a teacher because she is authoritative. ...teacher is the authority because she is the teacher."[36]

If the teacher is both friendly and firm, a "warm demander,"[37] whose academic and social demands on students are complemented with emotional support for them, cultural differences need not impede teaching and learning.

I had a Hmong girl in my advisory who didn't want to participate in any of the games, wouldn't share about herself, and spoke, when she did speak, in such a soft voice that we could hardly hear her. I would ask the other students, can you hear Jalia? Students would say no, but when she repeated the words, it was still in a tiny voice. So periodically I met with her and talked with her about school, reminded her that she needed to get a louder voice so everyone could hear her better, and kept pushing her to participate more. Slowly she began to join us in the activities. Periodically I would remind her in a quick conference to express herself, to get her voice up, to play with us. I never let up, but I never embarrassed her in front of the others either. Towards the end of the year, she found a different kind of "voice." She wrote a poem and won the school contest for poetry. She began to play the games regularly with us. And at the end of the year, she approached me to ask if she could teach the group a Hmong dance. And teach us she did, as not only a member of the group, but a leader as well! (Seventh-eighth grade teacher)

Ask yourself

When have you engaged with students as a "warm demander," insisting on certain behavior and maintaining a good relationship at the same time?

ADVISORY 15 ▶ CPR

Advisory goal: Develop capacity to recognize bias in yourself

Greeting

Reach Out Greeting: Students simultaneously greet one another with a handshake, using this greeting to expand their social world a bit. The directives below are arranged from least to most risky; choose the ones most appropriate for your group:

Greet someone with the same middle initial as yours.

Greet someone who was born more than ten miles from this school.

Greet someone of the opposite gender.

Greet someone you haven't talked to yet today.

Greet someone you haven't greeted in several days.

Greet someone you know a little but would like to know better.

> Good Morning, Friends!
>
> One of the trickiest things about discrimination is that the hardest place to detect it is in yourself and in the behavior of people close to you. Sociologists can help us be realistic about it by giving us data. Today we'll learn some facts about bias in the U.S.

Share

Whip Share with Follow-up: *Describe either a time when your words and deeds either matched up or a time when they did not.* Check for questions after you introduce the topic. Then each student gives a brief response; responses quickly "whip" around the circle.

Activity

Facts about discrimination: Share the following facts.

Although many countries have passed civil rights legislation over the past 50 years, discrimination continues to be a serious problem throughout the world—even in democratic countries that publicly affirm the ideal of equality. Here are a few documented examples of discrimination in the United States:

- According to a review of more than 100 studies by the U.S. Institute of Medicine, discrimination contributes to "racial" disparities in health care and to higher death rates among minorities from cancer, heart disease, diabetes, and H.I.V. infection.

- Hispanics and African Americans spend an average of over $3,000 more than European Americans to locate and buy the same house, often receive harsher criminal sentences than European Americans for the same offense, and are less likely to be hired than comparable European-American job applicants.

- Women earn an average of $.76 for every dollar men make, and face employment discrimination of such magnitude that monetary settlements have run into the hundreds of millions of dollars.

- A U.S. Justice Department study found that handicap-access provisions for disabled people were violated in 98% of the housing developments investigated .[38]

Exit Card: Ask students to respond to the following reflection in writing on a note card. Collect the cards as students leave.

Describe a time when you were biased or when someone showed bias against you.

If there is time, you can ask students to tell about a way that they or the other person might make up for the biased behavior or behave differently next time.

↻ Students will probably write more candidly on the cards if they are anonymous. You can follow up by reading some of the cards at the next advisory meeting. Acknowledge everyone for candidly describing their behavior.

Keep in Mind

Gathering support for our beliefs

We saw in Perspective One that we may be so invested in our culture that we exclude from our view of reality facts that conflict with our beliefs. For example, if we believe that we and the people around us are fair-minded, we tend to not notice when we or they treat others unfairly. We don't *intend* to ignore parts of reality, but we do so, usually unconsciously. We resist questioning what we believe, and what our ingroup accepts as true. This is a barrier to cultural proficiency.[39]

Bias is hard to identify at the individual level

Despite the prevalence of discrimination as supported by facts like those shared in this advisory, one of the greatest barriers to the removal of discrimination is the difficulty people have detecting it at the individual level. It is hard for people to recognize and admit their own biases. It is even hard for people to admit they have been discriminated against. Why?

- Individuals cannot serve as their own control group and test whether they would have received better treatment as a member of more privileged groups.

- Discrimination is easier to detect with aggregated evidence than single cases, because single cases are easy to explain away.

- Individuals may deny discrimination against themselves to avoid feeling that they actually *are* being mistreated by others or that they do not have control over their own situation.

For these and other reasons, women and minorities, for example, are more likely to perceive discrimination against their *group* than against themselves personally.[40]

Another way we hide from the truth of our biases, even when we are confronted with clear evidence of their falseness, is that we look for "sub-categories" to protect a generalization. For example, when introduced to a person who does not conform to someone's stereotype about his/her color, ethnicity, or religion, for example, a biased person may rationalize that this person is the exception that proves the rule. As a student at the University of Wisconsin, Madison, in the '60s, I was told more than once that I didn't "act Jewish," an insult posing as a compliment.

Ability biases in school

In school, we often sort students by what we perceive to be their abilities. Sometimes ability is gauged by past and/or current performance, sometimes simply by scores on standardized tests. The sorting can be helpful to a student if it is a signal for additional help in whatever the area of deficiency might be. But there are dangers, especially if groups are formed on a permanent or semi-permanent basis. Once applied, the sorting judgments can limit expectations of some students. In such cases are we establishing biases about the performance abilities of our students, and if so, will those biases become self-fulfilling prophecies?

In our school, there were the smart kids and the dumb kids. Groups were formed by "ability," numbered from one through seven. Everybody knew the kids the school had given up on. They were referred to as "the sevens." Everyone had low expectations of these students—it was said to be the kind thing to do to not ask much of them. (Former fifth-sixth grade teacher)

Ask yourself

Think of a student from whom, perhaps without realizing it, you expect a poor performance, either socially or academically. What might you be missing about this student that could change your expectations?

ADVISORY 16 ▶ CPR

Advisory goal: Learn about people's personal experience of bias.

Greeting

Basic Greeting: In sequence around the circle, each person greets his/her neighbor with *Good morning, _____.*

Share

Guest Share: *My experience with difference and discrimination.* (See Keep in Mind, below, for guest and student preparations.)

Guest shares his/her experience of being different from others and dealing with "us against them" attitudes from others. The guest may also talk about having his or her own "us against them" feelings, partly in reaction to bias and exclusion. Storytelling is the best vehicle for communicating experiences so that listeners can empathize and feel vicariously involved.

Listeners can ask questions and make respectful comments about their reactions to what they have heard and make comparisons or contrasts with their own lives. The guest may respond with question for the students, too.

Activity

Acknowledgment Chain for Guest: This is a group acknowledgment of one person. Each person writes on a strip of paper (approximately 1 x 6 inches) acknowledging the person for his contribution to the group. With tape or a stapler, the strips are joined together in a paper chain. Then the acknowledgment chain is presented to the person.

◌ **Partner Whip Acknowledgment alternative:** If time is short, you can use this alternative:

Partners decide together how they can acknowledge someone who has contributed to the group. A spokesperson from each pair gives the acknowledgment to the person.

Keep in Mind

Suggested guest protocol

Guest selection: To stimulate understanding of how differences turn into biases, invite guests who are more likely to have directly experienced bias or discrimination as a result of their identities or how they appear to others. Likely candidates would be people of color; people who are gay or lesbian, handicapped, elderly, immigrants, poor, non English-speaking, non-Christian—anyone who might frequently be the object of some form of bias or discrimination and is willing to share about that experience.

Guest preparation: Tell the guest about the conversations you have been having in your advisory, and about the makeup of the advisory group. Suggest that they use some storytelling to relate incidents in which they experienced being different from others and of feeling an "us against them" attitude in others and/or in themselves. Encourage them to talk not only about perpetrators, but also to describe their own feelings of separation, exclusion, and resentment of individuals and institutions as a result of what they experience in everyday life.

Student preparation: Prepare students before the guest arrives with a short biography of the guest so they have a context for what the guest may share. Brainstorm together possible questions to ask the guests, such as:

What was your earliest experience of feeling different from others?

Did you have friends who were significantly different from you?

What ways do you have of coping with being left out or excluded because of your difference?

Are you glad to be who you are, even though some people might give you trouble because of it?

Listening to each other's stories of exclusion

In addition to listening to guests talk about their experiences of bias, telling our own stories, and listening to each other's, is important, too. Future advisories are designed for student sharing about biases on both the giving and receiving ends. This may prompt stories of exclusion, teasing, and bullying, all possible outcomes of biases that may have begun as seemingly innocent "my friends/us and your friends/you." As we recall and describe our personal experiences of exclusion and listen to the stories of people around us, we become more powerfully aware of the costs of prejudice. Similarly, sharing personal stories in advisory builds positive relationships across the differences among students.

Ask yourself

What personal experience of bias can you share with your students?

ADVISORY 17 ▶ A+

Advisory goal: Develop the skill of looking at a person or an idea from multiple perspectives

Greeting

Reach Out Greeting: In response to the prompt, students greet others with a handshake, using this greeting as an opportunity to expand their social world a bit.

Greet people whose eyes are not the same color as yours.

Greet people who have the same middle initial as you.

Greet people of the opposite gender.

Greet people you haven't talked to yet today.

Greet people you don't know very well.

> Greetings, Friends!
> Many people characterize themselves or others as stubborn. Are you able to listen to a point of view that is different from yours and try on the other person's perspective? We'll see today!

Activity

Four Corner Thinking: Students stand in a line. Designate the four corners of the room as: *strongly agree, somewhat agree, somewhat disagree, strongly disagree.* Students move to the corner that represents their position as you read opinion statements. When they have settled in one corner or another, give them a moment to discuss why they have chosen their corner, including, if possible, evidence to support or illustrate their choice. Give everyone a chance to change their positions after hearing others' reasoning. You may choose to call on one or two students to tell why they changed.

Opinion statement examples:

School is a fun place to be.

Girls and boys are treated equally in our school.

Kids who get low grades are treated equally with kids who get high grades in our school.

We need a curfew for young adults.

Many people in our country are prejudiced.

Some kids get excluded in our school.

Adolescents watch too much media.

Students should be allowed to quit school whenever they want.

Being able to see from different perspectives pays off.

↺ Give students a chance to change their minds when you do Four Corner Thinking. We are cultivating open-mindedness, flexible thinking, and willingness to rethink an opinion.

Reflection

What influences you when you change your mind?

Are you able to listen to another perspective and adopt it if it seems reasonable? Give an example.

Keep in Mind

Practice perspective-taking

It may sound easy to look from more than one point of view. We try to keep an open mind, and we want what's best for our students. But it takes commitment and practice to become able to set aside what we already "know" and to really listen to and understand another way of seeing things.

To help us think from multiple perspectives, we can study ambiguous pictures and notice the variety of ways we interpret them. Advisories 10 and 11 include exercises that challenge us to look from more than one perspective.

For another example, consider this problem: *Mohamed has 100 more marbles than Brianna. The total number of marbles is 110. How many does Mohamed have? Don't settle for your first answer, even if it seems right. The task is to solve the problem correctly, not give the answer that* seems *right.*

How can you teach perspective-taking? In a social studies class, a teacher might follow an exercise like the marbles problem with a discussion of confirmation bias theory, pointing out how committed we are to our intuitive responses and habitual ways of thinking. In a literature class, students can discuss stories from various points of view, and in doing so, strengthen their capacity to see life from multiple vantage points.

We talked about switching perspectives all the time—when we read stories, when we discussed current events or life at school. A favorite book, for the boys especially, was S.E. Hinton's The Outsiders. The kids loved to hear about this family of three boys, ages 22, late teen, and early teen, who had a much tougher life than they did. We talked about the incidents from the different perspectives of the three boys. It was sometimes a stretch for the kids to switch from one perspective to another or bring in their own perspective. I might say something like, "They have to decide whether to go to the police—what would you do? If you were the older brother, what would you say to your younger brothers about getting into gangs? The boys got so involved in that book—they discussed with passion the different points of view. (Fifth-sixth grade language arts teacher)

Ask yourself

Can you think of a student about whom you changed your perspective once you got to know him or her?

ADVISORY 18 ▶ CPR

Advisory goal: Become aware of how we speak to and treat one another at school

Greeting

Fist Tap Greeting: Students greet using Basic Greeting format, adding a gentle fist bump. You may choose to make this a silent greeting, or use the Fist Tap Greeting as a quick simultaneous greeting when time is short. Model and practice fist-tapping before beginning: make a tight fist, then gently tap partner's fist as *Good morning,_____* is exchanged.

Share

Whip Share: Biased Speech. Ask the topic question: *Show fingers, one to five, to indicate how often you hear students put down others in our school on a typical day: one finger for rarely and five for many times a day.* Each student offers a brief response; responses quickly "whip" around the circle. Then distribute and discuss the Tracking Biased Speech survey form (below).

> Welcome, All!
>
> Today we're going to begin investigating our school culture and its language. On the continuum below, indicate with a check mark your estimate of how often we (adults and students) use biased language at school. Biased speech includes offensive or hurtful words that <u>demean</u> people.
>
> _____
>
> Never   Many times every day
>
> Pick up a copy of the Tracking Biased Speech form we will use to evaluate how much biased speech is going on in our school. In a few days we will <u>tally</u> our results.

↻ Results are tallied in Advisory 22.

↻ Give students some examples to help them understand what is meant by biased speech:

You're so lame! You're acting like a girl! That's so gay! There go the nerds. He's a Sped kid. Another dumb jock. You're a retard. Let's ask the Asian—he'll fix it. That looks really ghetto!

↻ Brainstorm: *How can you record an incident of biased speech if you don't have your form with you at the moment?*

Activity

Zoom: A player begins the activity by saying, *Zoom!* and turns her head quickly to her neighbor on either the right or the left. The neighbor passes the "zoom" to the next player and so on around the circle. The idea is to go fast. Challenge the players to go faster, and time how long it takes to zoom around the circle.

TRACKING BIASED SPEECH

Definition of biased speech: Prejudiced, offensive, hurtful words that demean or exclude people because of age, gender, religion, color, ethnicity, social class, sexual orientation, or physical or mental traits.

During one full school day, listen carefully to the conversations around you: things said by students and adults anywhere in the school, including by you. Tally derogatory remarks you hear in any of the categories listed. *Do this privately.* Don't comment on the biased remarks—just record with a tally mark that you heard them.

On the back of this page, write down a couple of the biased statements you overheard. Discuss how you felt before, during, and after doing the assignment. Also answer these questions: Was any of the biased speech your own? Was any of it language you sometimes use?

COLOR/ETHNICITY	WOMEN	RELIGION	SEXUAL ORIENTATION	PHYSICAL OR MENTAL ABILITY/APPEARANCE

Keep in Mind

Cost of discrimination in schools

When institutions fail to provide equal opportunity and equal protection to all, they create the context for discrimination. A school's recognition for athletes but not for intellectuals, acceptance of heterosexual relationships but not gay ones, lack of accommodation for immigrants or students who live in poverty, models and teaches that discrimination is acceptable. The price of such policies may include a student's future success or failure. There is a direct connection between a welcoming, culturally inclusive school environment and student success. Schools that allow bias, prejudice, and discrimination, all of which threaten the well-being of students, increase the likelihood of their failure. "[A]mong the major reasons cited for dropping out of school, several involve social and emotional factors: not getting along with teachers or peers (35% and 20.1% respectively), feeling left out (23.2%), and not feeling safe (12.1%)."[41] The degree to which the school culture and classroom climate affirm all students directly influences learning.

Stereotypes affect school performance

We discriminate by nurturing stereotypes about who is cool and who is not; who is smart and who is not; who is good looking and who is not, and so on. Stereotypes create anxiety and hamper performance on a variety of tasks.[42] For example, female math students taking a difficult test showed a drop in performance when they were told that the test revealed gender differences in math ability.[43] Another study found that when Asian women were reminded of the stereotype of Asians being good at math, their performance improved, but when they were reminded of the stereotype about girls' weakness in math, their performance declined.[44]

Cultural clashes make school difficult

Not knowing a group's cultural codes makes operating within the group difficult. The capacity to switch back and forth between your own cultural customs and those of another group supports success in the culture. Knowing the cultural code gives power.[45]

Two bright African-American boys attended our school. The mothers of both of them were single and poor. One mother carefully taught her son the code of conduct he should use in school with "people not like you." That boy had a positive experience in school, accepted by his teachers and peers alike. The other mother taught her son no codes other than that of his own culture. He did poorly in school. (Principal, K-8 charter school)

Cultural differences also make for different teaching styles. When the teacher is from the same culture as the majority of her students, they may well share the same expectations about how school should be. Lisa Delpit writes "[I]n many African-American communities, teachers are expected to show that they care about their students by controlling the class; exhibiting personal power; establishing meaningful interpersonal relationships; displaying emotion to garner student respect; demonstrating the belief that all students can learn; establishing a standard of achievement and 'pushing' students to achieve the standard; and holding the attention of students by incorporating African-American interactional styles in their teaching."[46]

Teachers from any cultural tradition may use a style different from that with which their students are familiar, and that style can easily be misread. "Good teaching is not thought of in the same way in all communities."[47] For example, students may also benefit from their teachers making it clear that there are many ways to hold and exercise authority, and that they *will* hold the line without fail—the students can count on it!

In sum, in a diverse society, occupational, ethnic, and other kinds of groups develop vocabularies and speech and behavior styles to facilitate communication, to help ensure the continuation of their privileges and traditions, to set themselves apart from everyone else, to symbolize ethnic and "racial" pride, and so on.[48] We need to realize that if we use language unfamiliar to the culture of the person to whom we are speaking, it may not communicate anything.

Ask yourself

Think of a student who is especially challenging for you to teach. *What is a quality he or she has that is especially difficult for you? What would it look like if this quality were used for positive purposes?* For example, a student who doesn't follow discussion protocols (is louder than acceptable, talks out of turn, wants to be heard on every topic)—if we can coach that student to use her behavior for learning, might it look like leadership? Then the question becomes: *How can I help her become a positive leader?*

ADVISORY 19 ▶ A+

Advisory goal: Understand the bases on which people accept and reject others and the costs of discrimination

Bonjour, Mes Amis! (French for "Hello, Friends")

Today we'll <u>contemplate</u> a novel called <u>The Road to Paris</u>. <u>Do Now</u>: Check below the bases upon which you choose your friends. Check as many as apply.

Looks | Personality | Actions | Recommendations by others | Popularity | Similar to you | Different from you

⮌ Monitor the daily-news area to make sure all students respond to the survey.

Greeting

Partner Greeting: A partner greeting can take any form (handshake, high five, a nod with *Hi, _____,* or *Hello, _____,* or *Good morning, _____,* etc.) Partner greetings are done in pairs, simultaneously, rather than sequentially around the circle. In this advisory, partners greet one another, listen to the description of the story, then discuss the reflection questions.

Activity

Us versus Them: The Road to Paris: Read the description of the story and the quotation.

Paris is a biracial girl with brown skin and blond hair. She and her brother run away from a cruel foster family where they never felt welcome and where Paris was locked in a closet and beaten as punishment for things someone else had done. When they turn to their grandmother for help, she turns them over to Social Services, where they are separated. Paris is sent to live with a family in upstate New York and her brother, the one person in the world she can rely on, is sent to a group home in New York City.

Her new family, the Lincolns, treat Paris kindly and lovingly include her in the family. She misses her brother terribly, but makes friends with Ashley Corbett, a white girl who lives down the street. They visit each other's houses frequently, but Paris has never met Ashley's father, who travels a lot. One day Paris rings the doorbell of Ashley's house and hears a man inside say, "What the hell is a little blonde-headed ["n" word] girl doing darkening the door of my house?" Ashley's mother pretends she doesn't know Paris and sends her away. Ashley sees the whole thing, but says and does nothing. After this experience, Paris never plays with Ashley again.

At home, Paris tells her foster mother what happened, and her eyes fill with tears. Mrs. Lincoln hugs Paris.

"I'm sorry you had to hear such words," she said, "but that's the way of the world, I'm afraid. There are hateful people in it, Paris, and some of them are white."

"I'll never have another white friend," Paris vowed.

"Don't say that," said Mrs. Lincoln. "You can't go through life judging people by the color of their skin."

"But that's what Ashley's father did!"

"Yes, honey. And he was wrong."

Paris couldn't argue with that. "Then what am I supposed to do?"

"Take each person as they come," said Mrs. Lincoln. "Judge them by their actions. Then decide whether

 to hold them close or push them away. That's what you do."[49]

Reflection

Partners discuss the reflection questions, then share out for a general discussion.

How does one person's bigotry (Ashley's father's) ruin a friendship between two other people (Ashley and Paris)?

If you were treated the way Paris was by a friend's parents, would you want to end the friendship immediately?

Paris' foster mother, Mrs. Lincoln, comforts her and argues against the idea that Paris would never have a white friend again. Do you agree with Mrs. Lincoln that even after someone of a different skin color disrespects you, "You can't go through life judging people by the color of their skin"? Explain.

Do you take each person you meet "as they come," and decide whether you want to be friends based only on the way they behave? Do you sometimes make pre-judgments about people?

How would you comfort someone who had been hurt the way Paris was?

Keep in Mind

The truth is hard but necessary to break patterns of bias

Adolescents need to learn about bias and its costs. Our emphasis needs to be on their possibilities for growth and accomplishment, but they will be better equipped to be effective in life if they have a realistic understanding of how society functions. As citizens of a democracy, they need to be aware of the harm people have done in the past (and still do) so they can avoid repeating them and help make the world better.

Different perspectives are necessary

Some students understand poverty and violence first-hand because they are everyday facts of their lives. They need to know that we know and care about how things are for them.[50] Disadvantaged youth who already know a thing or two about bias and its effects can learn to use that knowledge to change the world for the better. In Perspective Five, Advisory 17, students will learn about disadvantaged young people who navigate school structures successfully.

Students who do not have social disadvantages may be unaware of their difficulties and costs. We need to teach them the facts of life regarding prejudice and its consequences, inequality and conflict. Otherwise, they will be unprepared to help their society overcome these injustices. Underplaying or ignoring the cultural tensions among us, we risk repeating history's horrors. "Those who cannot remember the past are condemned to repeat it."[51]

In school, we can discuss the price we pay for individual and group acts of bias, to raise awareness and to prevent the behavior. At the same time, we must be aware of the effect such discussions may have on students: some may feel defensive or embarrassed, particularly if they have been taught to discriminate, or if they identify as victims; some may be shocked and/or discouraged, and others may feel affirmed in their beliefs. The teacher's job is to be aware of the variety of responses, and to temper the conversation so everyone stays present and engaged. Sometimes we point out possibilities for reform and renewal; other times, we may feel that the point hasn't sunk in yet, and we need more examples of the cost we pay to pierce the protective shield of complacency and/or ignorance.

Ask yourself

What cliques and alliances have you noticed that might exclude some members of your advisory group?

What can you do to build connections where they are currently weak?

ADVISORY 20 ▶ A+

Advisory goal: Understand that biased behavior sometimes takes the form of scapegoating

Greeting

Handshake Greeting: Students greet each other: *Ohayou gozaimasu, _____,* with a handshake. Review, as necessary, how you want handshakes to look and feel.

Activity

Four Corners: Japanese Americans during WWII: Designate the four corners of the room as: *strongly agree, somewhat agree, somewhat disagree, strongly disagree.* Have students read the background information aloud in round-robin style. Then ask students to move to the corner that represents their position on these questions:

The U.S. needed soldiers. About 300 Japanese-American men refused to pledge loyalty and fight for the U.S. until the government released the internees. In your opinion, were they justified in their protest?

> Ohayou Gozaimasu! (Japanese for "Good morning")
>
> Today we're going to look at the U.S. government's <u>internment</u> of Japanese Americans during World War II. Fear and prejudice took over in America when Japan attacked the United States, and <u>collateral</u> and perhaps unintended consequences resulted. We'll hear the story and the <u>aftermath</u>, and you will get an opportunity to express your own opinions.

⮑ This message contains three underlined words for vocabulary-building. Save an extra couple of minutes to discuss them.

Have volunteers from each corner explain their opinions. People may switch corners if they change their minds, and anyone who changes their mind may explain why.

Reflection

Group discussion: *What are ways that a U.S. citizen can legally protest a government action?*

Keep in Mind

Scapegoating on an individual level

Often we blame someone else for our problems: *He made me do it! She's a bad influence! He should have told me it's against the rules! Nobody likes her, so I didn't invite her.* On an individual level, we engage in a process of downward comparison to enhance our own self-worth. "Different from me" becomes "less than me" so I feel better about who I am.[53] Guilt may develop in the process of devaluing him, and the guilt prompts me to further demonize him.[54]

On a group level

When we blame whole groups of people, we "other" them. For example:

- Germans blamed Jews for their defeat in World War 1 and the ensuing economic crash. "The Holocaust did not start as a holocaust. It started with insensitivity of the German population toward scapegoating"[55]

- American business owners blame labor organizers and unions for their problems.

- Unions blame immigrants' willingness to work for low wages for their problems.

- The families of students who live in poverty are blamed for their children's failure to achieve in school.

- Teachers are blamed for students' low test scores.

Bias escalation

People who reject one outgroup tend to also reject others. A study of bias among college students by sociologist E.L. Hartley demonstrated that people who are prejudiced against certain groups are also intolerant of cultures they don't know. Identification with an ingroup, Hartley concluded, predicts a tendency to hold biases against any people not part of the ingroup.[56] Thus develop hate groups. Today, the Southern Poverty Law Center reports, there are extremists fostering hate all across America.[57]

Immunity to horror stands in the way of cultural sensitivity

Sadly, American children may be learning how to witness brutality, injustice, and tragedy and not react. Violence permeates television, movies, video games, and print media. Some experts warn that such elements in modern culture are pushing young people toward immunity to horror:

The typical American child will view more than 200,000 acts of violence, including more than 16,000 murders, before age 18. [Some] television programs display 812 violent acts per hour; children's programming, particularly cartoons, displays up to 20 violent acts hourly.

How does televised violence result in aggressive behavior? Some researchers have demonstrated that very young children will imitate aggressive acts on TV in their play with peers. Before age 4, children are unable to distinguish between fact and fantasy and may view violence as an ordinary occurrence.... Additionally, children who watch televised violence are desensitized to it. They may come to see violence as a fact of life and, over time, lose their ability to empathize with both the victim and the victimizer."[58]

Although most violence in the media is fictional, at any moment, real violence occurs, near and far, on large and small scales, perhaps ignored, perhaps commented on, perhaps not. This advisory is an opportunity to help students examine some of the roots of bias and the violence that can come with it.

Ask yourself

Have you ever felt that teachers were treated as scapegoats?

Are families ever treated as scapegoats for the poor performance of their children?

BACKGROUND INFORMATION:
JAPANESE AMERICAN EXPERIENCE IN WWII

Adapted from *Teaching Tolerance*, Southern Poverty Law Center[52]

On Sunday morning, December 7, 1941, Tsuyako [nicknamed "Sox"], her sister Lillian, and their mother, Yumi, were riding in the car near their home in San Francisco. A special bulletin on the radio announced that Japan had mounted a surprise attack on the U.S. naval base at Pearl Harbor, Hawaii. The girls translated the news for Yumi."This is terrible," Yumi said to them in Japanese. Because she was an Issei ("first generation" Japanese immigrant), she was not a U.S. citizen. Her native country was now the enemy.

Sox and Lillian knew that their lives were about to change. They were Americans, born on American soil. They listened to the same music, followed the same fashions, pledged allegiance to the same flag as everyone else. But over the next few weeks, anti-Japanese feelings rose up across the U.S., and shops posted signs telling Japanese customers to stay away.

In April, 1942, the U.S. government issued Civilian Exclusion Order Number 27, which declared that "all persons of Japanese ancestry, both alien and non-alien," would be "excluded" from the West Coast. Even Nisei (second generation)— those born in America to Japanese parents, like Sox and Lillian—were now considered suspicious. The order disrupted the lives of 112,000 people, two-thirds of whom were American citizens.

The government announced that all persons of Japanese ancestry, regardless of how long they had lived in America and regardless of whether they were American citizens, would be removed from their California, Oregon, and Washington homes and interned inland. The people were permitted to bring only the bare necessities, and were transported by bus to a racetrack. The building contained two back-to-back rows of 10 stalls each. Five adults - Sox and her three brothers and their mother - had a 9- by 20-foot enclosure to share. Manure littered the dirt floor. The walls were smeared with horsehair and dirt, and the walls reached only halfway to the roof. The nearest bathroom was a long walk away.

Police guards passed out cloth sacks for people to fill with hay for mattresses. Sox couldn't fall asleep. She couldn't stop wondering what any of them had done to deserve being penned up like animals. She couldn't believe this was happening in America.

At the end of the summer, they were moved to the desert area of Topaz, Utah. The housing was newly-built barracks. Sox thought this meant that at least they would not be killed. The new quarters measured 20 by 24 feet —a little roomier than the horse stall and a lot cleaner. A single naked light bulb hung from the ceiling. By stringing up sheets, families could create the illusion of privacy. The communal bathroom had six toilets and no doors.

The government policy was to not kill the interned Japanese, but they were shot to death if they got outside the fences. Everyone felt confined and stir-crazy. Barbed wire, police patrols, curfews, and watchtowers with armed guards constantly reminded them of their status. The temperatures were freezing in the winter and over 100 degrees in the summer.

Japanese soldiers join American forces

As the war in Europe and the Pacific intensified, the government realized that many potentially able soldiers were sitting idle in the camps. In early 1943, President Roosevelt wrote to the Secretary of War and contradicted his earlier Executive Order: "Americanism is not, and never was, a matter of race or ancestry. Every loyal American citizen should be given the opportunity to serve this country in the ranks of our armed forces." More than 30,000 Japanese Americans joined the armed forces, but about 300 refused to serve until their families were allowed to return home. These men were sent to jail for draft resistance.

Finally, in 1944, the U.S. government announced that the people would be released and the camp closed. In 1947, after the war was over, the men who were imprisoned for refusing to serve unless their families were released were officially pardoned, and, very slowly, the government began to repay people for their destroyed or confiscated property. In 1976, President Gerald Ford officially revoked the order of internment and formally apologized to Japanese Americans. In 1988, the Civil Liberties Act of 1988 paid $20,000 to each surviving internee.

ADVISORY 21 ▶ CPR

Advisory goal: Be aware of the damage bullying does to everyone in the school

Greeting

Handshake Greeting: Students greet *Good morning, _____,* with a handshake. Review, as necessary, how you want handshakes to look and feel.

Share

Partner Share: *What is a comment someone made to you quite a while ago, positive, negative, or neutral, that you have never forgotten?* Specify a length of time to share and issue a time warning halfway through the share to ensure balanced sharing/listening. Volunteers share out.

⮐ As students share out, note the characteristics of the comments we tend to remember and discuss them with students. Examples: *"I still remember my cousin saying that I was really stupid because I couldn't divide yet."* (generalization) *"I remember when a girlfriend told another friend that my hair always looks like I just woke up, and it went around as a big joke."* (teasing) *"Once a teacher said that I was an eager learner."* (praise)

> Hello to All!
>
> We often remember long afterward things that people say and do. People who have been bullied never forget it. The definition of bullying we will use in this advisory is: repeated, aggressive behavior against a person who has to defend himself or herself from someone who has more power than he/she does. Intimidation, rumors, gossip, and media can all be used to bully someone.
>
> Heads up: At our next meeting we'll compile the surveys we've been doing on our Tracking Biased Speech forms. Remember to bring your tallies to advisory. You have one more day to tally. If you need another tally sheet, ask me for one.

Activity

Watch *Bullied: A Student, a School and a Case that Made History*. *Bullied,* produced by the Southern Poverty Law Center, is available for free along with a teaching kit for the asking at the Teaching Tolerance Web site.[59] If you don't acquire the documentary, use the quotes below to tell the story.

Quotes from the documentary

Bullied: A Student, a School and a Case that Made History tells the true story of Jamie Nabozny, a student who endured persecution from anti-gay students, stood up to his tormentors, and filed a federal lawsuit against his school district. The suit led to a landmark federal court decision holding that school officials could be held accountable for not stopping the harassment and abuse of gay students. In *Bullied,* Jamie tells the story of the persecution he endured every day. The following are quotes from the film. Jamie is speaking.

I just know that it hurt a lot to hear those words on a daily basis—people calling me queer, fag, homo …saying really disgusting things about … sex …

When I was walking down the hallway I'd have things thrown at me … I'd be kicked, tripped, spit on, kicked.

One day when Jamie's science teacher stepped out of the classroom, anti-gay students attacked Jamie in the room.

And the two boys started harassing me. And they had started touching my legs and telling me, you know, that "you like it" and stuff, and I kept pushing them away. And then eventually I tried to get away from them and they pushed me to the ground. One of them got on top of me and were just continuing to—to touch me and being vulgar, I guess.

Reflection

After hearing the quotes, students discuss with a partner and then share out with the whole group:

Does bullying about sexual orientation happen in our school?

How does bullying affect all students, not just the ones who are bullied?

How is repeated teasing and jokes that target certain groups a form of bullying?

How much gossiping goes on in our school? What harm does it do?

Some schools have established a Gay-Straight Alliance (GSA) made up of both gay and straight students. GSA's offer programs, trainings, and resources to make their schools safe for all students, including LGBT youths. *How might a gay-straight alliance help our school?*

If your group seems to need or want more time to discuss these questions, you can extend the discussion into the next advisory. For quick meeting planning, use the suggested activities, greetings, and share formats in *The Advisory Book* (Crawford 2012) or at www.developmentaldesigns.org.

Keep in Mind

Adolescent social isolation

A feeling of aloneness and repeated exclusion can be extremely damaging to adolescents. Loneliness and perceived unpopularity are devastating for young people who are locked inside their own sense of low self-worth, and who may be perceived by others as "different" and/or loners. They struggle with an internal conversation of being the wrong color, or the wrong size, personality, ethnicity, speaking the wrong language, etc. In the adolescent search for identity, perceiving one's differences from others can bring social isolation. And since a safe, inclusive climate is directly correlated to academic success, such isolation is a ticket to failure.

I get excluded more than I exclude.

Sometimes I get left out of games and other stuff. I'm just like you, so please treat me like you want to be treated.

I've been excluded from many different things for no specific reason.

My anger rises because I don't like people that think they are better than everybody...but I try not to let it bug me.

(Seventh and eighth graders)

Bullying

If exclusion becomes overt, aggressive, or repeated, feelings of being different and unpopular or second-rate intensify. Several youth suicides have resulted from persecution of gay and lesbian students, and students with disabilities and students who are unpopular frequently suffer cruel treatment from other students.

Two weeks before Christmas, one of my 10-year-old twins came home from school, wrapped a cord around his neck, and attempted to hang himself. His sister found him, and from there was a whirlwind of four weeks of intense inpatient and outpatient therapy for my son as well as the rest of us. He had been bullied for months on the bus and in school and decided the only way to stop the bullying was to end his life. This was the first indication for me that anything was wrong with him. After therapy he was still depressed and apprehensive to return to school, but had to due to state regulations and because of the insurance companies denying payment for further treatment. So my son returned to school where the bullying continued and again two weeks later cut his wrist. As parents, it is hard to believe that a 10-year-old would have the mind capacity to make a plan and follow through with it. There has to be more that can be done for our children. (Parent of middle school student, from PACER's National Bullying Prevention Center)[60]

Definition of Bullying

Bullying is repeated, aggressive behavior that involves a power imbalance such that the target is forced to defend himself or herself against someone who has an advantage in strength or numbers or social acceptance. Bullying methods include direct intimidation, rumor and gossip, and use of media. Most bullying is based on perceived differences between the victim and the perpetrator(s). Students are bullied because of color, style, size, appearance, ability, interests, sexual orientation, or anything that makes them less socially admired. It is a short trip from bias to bullying:

Suicide is the third leading cause of death among young people, resulting in about 4,400 deaths per year, according to the Centers for Disease Control and Prevention. For every suicide of a young person, there are at least 100 suicide attempts. Over 14 percent of high school students have considered suicide, and almost 7 percent have attempted it.

Bullying victims are between 2 and 9 times more likely to consider suicide than non-victims, according to studies by Yale University; 10- to 14-year-old girls may be at even higher risk for suicide.

According to statistics reported by ABC News, nearly 30 percent of students are either bullies or victims of bullying, and every day, 160,000 students stay home from school out of fear of bullying.

It is impossible to imagine a youth who is a target of bullying getting anything positive from school. Capacity to perform withers under persistent harassment.

Ask yourself

What would you say is the highest cost of bullying for the victim? For the onlookers? For the bully?

ADVISORY 22 ▶ CPR

Advisory goal: Awareness of the amount and nature of biased speech in our school

> *Good Morning, Sociologists!*
>
> *Today we'll compile the results of our surveys. Below is a chart about biased speech with the same headings as your Tracking Biased Speech tally sheets. Do Now: Record your data on this master chart, and we'll see the results we got as a group. Make a tally mark for every comment you have heard under each category.*
>
> | Color/Ethnicity | Women | Religion | Sexual Orientation | Physical/Mental Ability |
> |---|---|---|---|---|
> | | | | | |

↪ Have them organize their tally marks in clusters of five. If some do not know how to use tally marks, teach them.

Greeting

Partner Greeting: Handshake with *Good morning, _____*. Partner greetings are done in pairs, simultaneously, rather than sequentially around the circle in the usual style.

↪ This greeting format is useful when time is short or the risk level needs to be lowered.

Share

Partner Share: Partners discuss results of their surveys on the frequency of biased speech, and any specific examples they recorded. Follow with a whole-group tally and discussion of the data on the master chart.

Volunteers share out any examples they collected. Brainstorm: *What might we say in response to biased speech that might shut it down or at least reduce its frequency?*

↪ **Possible responses to biased speech:**

I don't think that's funny.

That's the kind of language that really hurts people.

I'm surprised to hear you talk like that—I don't think of you as a person who is so prejudiced.

These phrases allow you to speak up against bias in a simple, straightforward manner. Sometimes they may open a dialogue. Other times, they simply allow you to challenge bias and take a vocal stand against it. And they could draw a snide comment from the person being addressed.

↪ If many students did not collect data, you can tally whatever results you have, take one more day to tally, and compile the results the next day.

↪ Keep your own tally. Add your results to the chart, and share language you heard in school.

Activity

Yes! Students stand or sit in a circle and look around at each other's eyes. When eye contact is made, both players say, *Yes!* Then they switch seats, high-fiving as they walk across the circle.

Keep in Mind

Some phrases are spoken in jest, with no intention to hurt someone (or are said to be "just kidding"), but they can nonetheless do damage. You can raise consciousness and begin the cleanup by identifying and demanding that students stop using the language. Then biased speech can be identified and interrupted by all who take a stand for everyone's safety and inclusion in the school community.

Ask yourself

Do you intervene when you hear biased speech?

ADVISORY 23 ▶ CPR

Advisory goal: Understand that all forms of bias and oppression, individual and institutional, are deeply damaging

Greeting

All Group Greeting: each person greets the group and the group returns the greeting: *Good morning, everyone! Good morning, _____!*

Good Morning, Friends!

Some people have described a "pecking order of oppression" in which some forms of discrimination are worse than others, but Henry Louis Gates, a writer and educator, says that we should avoid thinking that way. What do you think? Be ready to share with a partner.

Share

Partner Share: *Is bigotry aimed at some groups more damaging than bigotry aimed at others? For example, is discrimination because of color, religion, or socioeconomic class worse than discrimination because of disability or sexual orientation?* Specify a length of time to share and issue a time warning halfway through the share to ensure balanced sharing/listening. Volunteers share out.

➲ Provide students with a list of many of the targets for discrimination, such as color, ethnicity, religion, socio-economic class, ability, sexual orientation, language, gender, and age. There is no "right" answer. The point is to discuss the many targets of discrimination and bias.

Activity

Choral Reading of *Caged Bird* by Maya Angelou: Read the poem aloud. Then have the group read the poem once or twice in unison.

Caged Bird (stanzas 4 and 5)

by Maya Angelou

The free bird thinks of another breeze
and the trade winds soft through the sighing trees
and the fat worms waiting on a dawn bright lawn
and he names the sky his own

But a caged bird stands on the grave of dreams
his shadow shouts on a nightmare scream
his wings are clipped and his feet are tied
so he opens his throat to sing.[61]

Reflection

Written reflection in journal or on Exit Card (each student answers one of the following questions on an index card and hands it to you as they leave):

When do you feel like the caged bird and when do you feel free?

Are there ways you could have a sense of freedom even in "caged" situations?

Keep in Mind

Institutionalized discrimination

Sometimes bias, blame, and discrimination are promoted by people with political, religious, or other power. Discrimination can be encoded into law, promoted as a matter of faith, or rewarded by parents, teachers, and other authority figures. Then scapegoating and discrimination become institutionalized, and do even greater damage.

Institutionalized discrimination is often denied by those not adversely affected by it. It occurs against many groups, including people of color, believers in minority religions, people in poverty, women, people who are disabled, and anyone who is not heterosexual. It is supported by fixed culturally-shaped perceptions, us-versus-them antagonisms, and reluctance to acknowledge our interdependence and to share resources.

Cost of institutionalized discrimination based on color and ethnicity

Institutionalized racism is an institution's practices and procedures that have a disproportionately negative effect on people of color. Examples are *redlining*, in which banks avoid giving loans to people who live in certain areas; *steering*, in which real-estate agents guide minority clients away from certain neighborhoods and toward others; *de facto* segregated schools; and racial profiling by law enforcers and the general public. For a dramatic example of racial profiling by ordinary citizens as they watch a staged "bike theft," see an *ABC What Would You Do video.* [62]

"In fact, a disproportionate number of ethnic minorities have no insurance, are unemployed or are employed in jobs that do not provide health care insurance, are disqualified for government assistance programs, or fail to participate because of administrative barriers."[63] Sometimes institutional discrimination is blatant, as in the South before the 1964 Civil Rights Act ensured greater equality for blacks. Black children learned young that they were considered less than white people:

My grandfather was Hispanic (Cuban) with light skin, and his grandchildren were dark-skinned. One day we took the bus downtown with him. We climbed on the bus and sat on the first seats, right by the driver. The driver turned to us and said, "You can't sit there." Grandfather pretended he didn't understand English. "Comprende?" said the driver. I asked him why the driver said that to us and he told me, "Because your skin is dark." That was the beginning of a whole different consciousness about color for me." (Seventh-eighth grade teacher)

The early American economy was built partly with the labor of Africans dragged away from their homes and families, shipped across the ocean in horrible conditions, then sold to the highest bidder. We live with the legacy of slavery: damage to the descendants of the victims, and to our national consciousness. Widespread poverty, high school dropout rates, poor health, and high rates of crime and imprisonment plague African Americans today; some say these are also part of slavery's legacy, while others cite other causes. "For while it may be true that the most debilitating impediments to advancement among the underclass derive from patterns of behavior that are self-limiting, it is also true that our history has dealt poor blacks a very bad hand."[64]

Cost of institutionalized discrimination based on socioeconomic class

U.S. schools today remain highly segregated by socioeconomic class, notes Richard Kahlenberg of the Brookings Institution.[65] Contrary to what some believe, this remains true in urban, suburban, small-town, and rural areas.

Segregation of neighborhoods and suburbs by class and color supports segregation in schools, and vice versa. In urban areas, busing schemes intended to integrate schools have mostly failed. And a Civil Rights Project nation-wide report indicates that although charter schools were originally intended to increase equity in education, they continue the practice, intentionally or not, of stratifying students by class.[66]

Smaller towns are equally divided by class and color: "We are finding that it is common practice for governments of small and medium-sized towns to use their powers of annexation, zoning, provision of infrastructure and public services, long-term planning, and maximization of tax base to exclude minority and low-income communities from full participation in the town's benefits and governance."[67]

What is the cost of segregation by socio-economic status? "Numerous studies have shown that low income students generally perform better in middle class schools. Investing more heavily in socioeconomically and racially integrated charter schools would provide low income students with the documented benefits of peer to peer contact with a more diverse group of students, along with other resources related to school quality that, at least in the traditional public school context, are associated with increased school diversity."[68]

Poverty and poor health

Poverty—especially rural poverty—is statistically related to poor health, partially due to prejudiced attitudes toward poverty. Thomas Fuller-Rowell and his co-authors found that when being on food stamps or welfare was stigmatized, "there were clear differences in physical health, as measured by blood pressure, stress hormones, and body mass index...and those physical consequences of poverty were partially explained by discrimination."[69] The American health care system favors those with full-time jobs and benefits. Many people without such jobs cannot afford adequate health insurance for themselves and/or their children.

"As a society, we have chosen to use government programs to protect seniors from poverty. What the U.S. does for seniors is clearly good; so why do we not also protect children from the life-altering effects of poverty?"[70]

Cost of institutionalized discrimination against sexual orientation

I have been harassed by police for being a lesbian, and I've been harassed and called awful names by religious zealots. (Fifth-sixth grade teacher)

Institutional and personal hostility toward lesbians and gay men has been a fact of life in the United States. According to the U.S. Department of Justice's Hate Crimes Statistics reports, gay men and lesbians have consistently been the third most frequent target of hate violence over the past decade. Of the 6,628 hate crime incidents reported in 2010, nearly all (6,624) involved a single bias, and 47.3 percent of those incidents were motivated by race; 20 percent by religion; 19.3 by sexual orientation; 12.8 percent by an ethnicity/national origin bias; and 0.6 by physical or mental disability.[71]

Homosexuality remains stigmatized through institutional policies. Although decades of struggle have brought greater equity for homosexuals, and in June, 2013 the Supreme Court ruled that married same-sex couples were entitled to federal benefits, as of late 2013, no federal law existed to protect LGBT individuals from employment discrimination, and there were no laws in 29 states to explicitly prohibit discrimination based on sexual orientation. In fact, many states have anti-gay laws written into their constitutions. "As a result, LGBT people face serious discrimination in employment, including being fired, being denied a promotion and experiencing harassment on the job."[72]

Ask yourself

Are there biases and forms of discrimination that are built into life in your school?

ADVISORY 24 ▶ CPR

Advisory goal: Know the facts about inequalities between American men and women today and in the past

Greeting

Partner Greeting: Any greeting done in pairs, simultaneously, rather than around the circle.

> Greetings, Men and Women!
> Today we'll look at some sad facts about the status of women in the United States and think about what might be done to alleviate the inequality. We all pay a price for living in a sexist society.

Share

Partner Share: Status of Women in the U.S. Read aloud the statistics below or distribute them to students and have them read off the list, one person per bullet. Then discuss: *What ideas do you have for increasing women's rights?* Specify a length of time to share, and issue a time warning halfway through the share to ensure balanced sharing/listening.

STATUS OF WOMEN IN THE U.S

Although the Twentieth-century feminist movement brought advances, there is still a big gender gap in America.

As women age, the wage gap increases. For working women between the ages of 25 and 29, the annual wage gap is $1,702

- In the last five years before retirement, the annual wage gap is $14,352.

- Over a 40-year working career, the average woman loses $431,000 to the wage gap.

- In 2010, women who worked full time, year round, earned 77 percent of what men earned

- In all ethnic groups, women earn less than men in comparable jobs

- College-educated women earn five percent less the first year out of school than their male peers; ten years later, they earn 12 percent less

- Women are more likely to work in low-wage jobs such as retail sales, childcare, waitressing, and cleaning

Single women are even more adversely affected by the wage gap than married women. Single women earn only 78.8 percent of what married women earn, and only 57 cents for every dollar that married men earn.[73]

Activity

Simultaneous Clap: There are several rounds to this activity, and they become increasingly challenging.

> **1st round:** with everyone standing circle, the first person claps, then the person next to him claps, then the person next to her, and so on around the circle, keeping a smooth, steady rhythm and with no hesitations.

> **2nd round**: the first person claps with both hands the two hands of the person next to him, who does the same with the next person, and so on around the circle.

> **3rd round:** the first person claps his own hands at the same time as the person next to him claps her hands. She turns to the third person and they do the same, and so on around the circle with every pair trying each time to clap at the very same moment.

> **4th round**: holding hands at the ready, everyone tries to clap at exactly the same moment. This may take some practice —it requires students to pay very close attention to each other.

Keep in Mind

Cost of gender discrimination

Women's secondary status was long deemed "human nature," self-evident. The lower status of women was so generally accepted by society that the feminist wave of the late 20th century was met by a wave of anti-feminism, featuring leaders like Phyllis Schlafly, who wrote, "Feminism is doomed to failure because it is based on an attempt to repeal and restructure human nature."[74]

Ask yourself

What gender biases do you perceive in the field of education?

ADVISORY 25 ▶ A+

Advisory goal: Become aware of your own and others' personal experience with exclusion. Know the meanings of the many words associated with bias and exclusion

Greeting

Choice Greeting: The first greeter stands and crosses the circle to greet someone: *Good morning, _____.* The person rises and returns the greeting, then crosses the circle to greet someone similarly. This continues until all have been greeted. Those who have been greeted may fold their arms as an indication to the greeter.

↻ Reminder: If you've noticed patterns or habits in the way students sit in the circle, you can use the Choice Greeting to mix things up by directing students to take the seat of the person they greet.

> Good Morning, Friends!
>
> It's another good day for truth-telling!
>
> <u>Do Now</u>: Pick up a Four-Square paper and begin thinking about the exclusion experiences in your life. Label the four squares as follows:
>
> - Upper left: I've been excluded or bullied.
> - Upper right: I've excluded or bullied others.
> - Lower left: I've seen others be excluded or bullied and have done nothing to stop it.
> - Lower right: I saw others be excluded or bullied and intervened to help them.

Share

Think-Ink Four Square on Exclusion: Provide each student with a blank paper. Direct them as follows: *This exercise begins with thinking and writing about your experiences with exclusion—times when you or others have been left out, discriminated against, pre-judged, or have experienced bias. Fold your paper in half and then in quarters so when you open it up the paper is divided into four squares. Label the squares:*

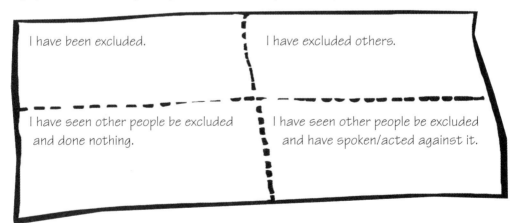

In each square, write a description of an experience you have had related to the category. Share with a partner one of the experiences you have described in your Four-Square diagram.

After partners share, volunteers may share out.

Activity

Carousel: Definition of Terms: Post or lay out on desks seven large pieces of paper, each with one of the following headings written across the top: Stereotype; Bias; Bigotry; Prejudice; Discrimination; Intolerance; Narrow-mindedness.

Divide students into seven groups and assign each group one of the headings. Groups start at their assigned chart, and spend five minutes writing on it words, phrases, examples that help define and describe that word. Then, on signal, the groups move to the next chart and the next, for one minute each, adding to and/or challenging whatever the original group for that chart already wrote. After their last chart, groups return to their original charts and read out all that they and others have written.

Definitions of Terms

Although the idea is to give students as much chance as possible to write what they already know about their terms before getting the official definitions, offer support whenever you think it's necessary, so the process doesn't stall.

Stereotype is an exaggerated belief or image, or a distortion of the truth about a person or group—a generalization that allows for little or no individual differences or social variation. Stereotypes are based on images in mass media, or reputations passed on by parents, peers, and other members of society. Stereotypes can be positive or negative.

Bias is a tendency to hold a certain opinion or *prejudice*, rather than to think open-mindedly.

Bigotry is the entrenched habit and practice of *discrimination* against certain people.

Prejudice is an opinion, prejudgment, or attitude about a group or its individual members. A prejudice can be positive, but in our usage refers to a negative attitude. Prejudices are often accompanied and supported by ignorance, fear, and/or hatred. Prejudices are formed by a complex psychological process that begins with attachment to a close circle of acquaintances or an ingroup such as a family. Prejudice is often aimed at outgroups.

Discrimination is behavior that treats people unequally because of their group membership. Discriminatory behavior ranging from slights to hate crimes often begins with negative *stereotypes* and *prejudices*.

Intolerance is an unwillingness or refusal to accept people who are different from you.

Narrow-mindedness is a limited and often intolerant attitude toward people or ideas different from your own.

Isms are *prejudices* against people for a variety of reasons: racism, heterosexism, classism, sexism, ableism, ageism.

Bullying is unwanted, aggressive behavior toward someone weaker or in some way vulnerable and with less power, often because of his or her difference from others.

Reflection

What is one example of one of these terms that you have personally experienced?

⮑ The carousel activity may require a second meeting to complete the carousel and to reflect on personal experience with the terms.

Keep in Mind

Advisory meeting to help provide balance to the conversation

To balance the examples of large-scale bias, prejudice, and discrimination, make sure you also focus on how we discriminate at a personal level. The effects of bias and discrimination are always personal, acknowledged or not. In American education, those effects can be seen in each youth who fails to find purpose in school. The statistics tell us the story of their disengagement from the democratic institution that was established to help them succeed in life. Personal stories tell us the results when students do not perceive school as a place where teachers care about them.

In school some teachers assumed that I wouldn't finish my education, that I was destined to be a teenage mom. But my parents insisted: "You're going to go to college." (College educator, Minneapolis, Minnesota)

If teachers don't care, they make you not care. (Middle level youth, Minneapolis, Minnesota)

On the other hand, we need examples of how we rise to our best selves—those times and those teachers who care and struggle to make a positive difference in the lives of their students:

NCLB [the No Child Left Behind law] has placed enormous stress on teachers. [Student test scores are] how teachers will be evaluated. Rubrics today are so narrow, there is no room for projects that really appeal to different kids.... [High schools often have] 45-minute periods so that the standards can be met. But you can't get to know the kids [in 45-minute periods]. Many teachers are insecure. They don't have the personal skills to succeed at teaching. ...I had a seventh grade girl stand up and call me a racist. I was so shocked and hurt....I gave a student a D on a writing assignment. He stood up and called me some nasty names. I think we've trained [teachers] to check their emotions at the door at school. [But] I sometimes would talk with students and their families and a tear would run down my face. The students would say, "It's OK—it's going to be OK."

I've learned more from the students than I've taught them. (High school principal)

When we see discrimination in action, hear discriminatory language, or catch ourselves in biased acts or attitudes, we must name it and stop it. Discrimination unnamed and unaddressed is a cancer, a silent killer. We must speak the truth about our biases regarding ethnicity, class, gender, sexual orientation, religion, etc. The challenge is to own our biases and not allow them to own us.

Ask yourself

What are the elements in your life that make it less likely that you will get to know people who are very different from you?

ADVISORY 26 ▶ CPR

Advisory goal: Become aware of your own and others' personal experience with exclusion

Greeting

Partner Greeting: Remind students that they can use any greeting, but must maintain eye contact, say their partner's name, and be friendly.

> *Peace, Partners!*
>
> *Today we will share our Four-Square charts with a partner. Be thinking about which one of the four squares you are willing to share with your partner. I'll go first. I appreciate your respectful <u>candor</u>!*

Share

Think Ink Four Square Partner Share: *Pick one of your responses in your Four-Square chart and tell your partner about it.* Specify a length of time to share, and issue a time warning halfway through the share to ensure balanced sharing/listening.

⮌ Share one of your responses with the whole group before the Partner Shares begin in order to model for students.

Activity

Five Standing: This is a game of intuition. Students sit in a circle. The goal of the activity is to have five people stand simultaneously—no more, no fewer. Signal play to begin. No talking or nonverbal communicating is allowed; students must try to sense the moment to rise, with four others, to win the game. Each time one or more student(s) rise(s) to a full stand, play stops so they can be counted. Play can continue for a specific amount of time or until group has been successful one (or more, if you have time) of times.

Keep in Mind

Self-awareness, not guilt or defense, is essential for growth. In conversations about difference and hurting each other because of difference, we must keep a cool head and engage in the honest, compassionate self-examination which is an essential first step.

Ask yourself

To uncover your biases about people, ask: *Toward whom do I tend to gravitate? Whom do I tend to avoid?* Look for patterns in the list of people you tend to avoid or have no contact with at all. Ask yourself why, and look for stereotypes and biases in your reasons.

1 Sherman Alexie, *An Absolutely True Diary of a Part-Time Indian* (New York: Little, Brown and Co., 2009), 50-51.

2 Teaching Tolerance, "Bullied: A Student, a School, and a Case that Made History," http://www.tolerance.org/kit/bullied-student-school-and-case-made-history.

3 E.J. Dionne, *Our Divided Political Heart: The Battle for the American Idea in an Age of Discontent* (New York: Bloomsbury, 2012), 4.

4 Booker T. Washington, *Up From Slavery* (New York: Dover Publications, 1995), 134.

5 Richard Pérez-Peña, "Income-Based Diversity Lags at Some Universities" *New York Times* May 30, 2013, http://www.nytimes.com/2013/05/31/education/college-slots-for-poorer-students-still-limited.html?pagewanted=all&_r=0.

6 Jennifer E. Obidah and Karen Manheim Teel, *Because of the Kids: Facing Racial and Cultural Differences in Schools* (New York: Teachers College Press, 2001), 25-26.

7 Scott Plous, ed., "The Psychology of Prejudice, Stereotyping, and Discrimination: an Overview," in *Understanding Prejudice and Discrimination*, (New York: McGraw Hill, 2003), 7.

8 Signithia Fordham, "Passin' for Black: Race, Identity, and Bone Memory in Postracial America," in *Education for a Multicultural Society*, ed. Kolajo Paul Afolabi, Candice Bocala, Raygine C. DiAquoi, Julia M. Hayden, Irene A. Liefshitz, and Soojin Susan Oh (Cambridge: Harvard Educational Review, 2011), 150.

9 Ibid., 151.

10 Anthony S. Bryk and Barbara Schneider, *Trust in Schools: A Core Resource for Improvement* (Chicago: University of Chicago, 2002).

11 Tommie Lindsey Jr. and Benjamin Mabie, "Life Skills Yield Strong Academic Performance," *Kappan* 93, no. 5 (February 2012): 35.

12 J. Krueger, "Personal beliefs and cultural stereotypes about racial characteristics," *Journal of Personality and Social Psychology* 71 (1996).

13 Kathleen Weiler, "Friere and a Feminist Pedagogy of Difference," *Harvard Educational Review* 61, no.4 (Winter 1991): 470.

14 Smithsonian Institution, "Say it Loud: African American Spoken Word," 2013, http://www.folkways.si.edu/explore_folkways/spoken_word.aspx.

15 Lisa Delpit, "The Silences Dialogue: Power and Pedagogy in Educating other People's Children," *Harvard Educational Review* 58, no. 3 (Fall 1988): 292.

16 Herb Kohl, *"I Won't Learn From You" and Other Thoughts on Creative Maladjustment* (New York: The New Press, 1994), 10.

17 Brian Lanker, Barbara Summers, and Maya Angelou (foreward), *I Dream a New World: Portraits of Black Women Who Changed America* (New York: Stewart, Tabori and Chang, 1989), 24.

18 Thomson Reuters, "Defamation Law: The Basics," *FindLaw,* http://injury.findlaw.com/torts-and-personal-injuries/defamation-law-the-basics.html.

19 Max van Manen, *The Tone of Teaching* (London, Ontario: Althouse Press, 2002), 81-82.

21 Ely William Hill, "My Wife and My Mother-in-Law," *Wikipedia*, http://en.wikipedia.org/wiki/

My_Wife_and_My_Mother-in-Law. "British cartoonist Ely William Hill (1887–1962) published the picture in *Puck*, an American humor magazine, on November 6, 1915, with the caption 'They are both in this picture — Find them.' However, the oldest known form of this image is an 1888 German postcard. In 1930 Edwin Boring introduced the figure to psychologists in a paper titled 'A new ambiguous figure', and it has since appeared in textbooks and experimental studies." This image is in public domain.

[21] Gwendolyn Cartledge and JoAnne Fellows Milburn, *Cultural Diversity and Social Skills Instruction: Understanding Ethnic and Gender Differences*, (Champaign, IL: Research Press, 1996), 32, 40.

[22] Lisa Delpit, *Other People's Children: Cultural Conflict in the Classroom* (New York: The New Press, 2006), 168-169.

[23] Thomas Armstrong, *The Myth of the A.D.D. Child* (New York: Penguin, 1995), 256, quoted in Dr. Jawanza Kunjufu, Keeping Black Boys Out of Special Education, (Sauk Village, IL: African American Images, 2005), 10.

[24] Gwendolyn Cartledge and JoAnne Fellows Milburn, *Cultural Diversity and Social Skills Instruction: Understanding Ethnic and Gender Differences* (Champaign: Research Press, 1996), 3.

[25] Gordon Allport, *The Nature of Prejudice* (Reading, MA: Addison-Wesley, 1954), 20.

[26] Plous, "The Psychology of Prejudice, Stereotyping, and Discrimination: An Overview," 10.

[27] M.B. Brewer, "The Psychology of Prejudice: Ingroup Love or Outgroup Hate?" *Journal of Social Issues* 55 (1999): 438.

[28] Peter Senge, *The Fifth Dimension: The Art and Practice of the Learning Organization* (New York: Doubleday/Currency, 1990). Find more discussion of the Ladder of Inference and bias confirmation in "Ladder of Inference: Short Circuiting Reality" by Gene Bellinger at http://www.systems thinking .org/loi/loihtm.

[29] Sherman Alexie, *The Absolutely True Diary of a Part-Time Indian* (Boston: Little, Brown and Co., 2007), 229-230.

[30] Plous, "The Psychology of Prejudice, Stereotyping, and Discrimination: An Overview," 27.

[31] Ibid., 21.

[32] Ibid., 3-48.

[33] Sharon G. Flake, *You Don't Even Know Me: Stories and Poems about Boys* (New York: Disney Book Group, 2010), 169-171. Reprinted with permission. See Copyright page for full rights information.

[34] Peter C. Wason, "On the failure to eliminate hypotheses in a conceptual task," *Quarterly Journal of Experimental Psychology* 12, no.3 (1960): 129–140.

[35] E.A. Burt, ed., *The English Philosophers from Bacon to Mill* (New York: Random House, 1939), 36.

[36] Delpit, "The Silences Dialogue: Power and Pedagogy in Educating other People's Children," 289.

[37] The term "warm demander" was first used by J. Kleinfeld in "Effective Teachers of Eskimo and Indian Students," *School Review* 83, no.2 (1975): 301-344. Among others, Geneva Gay also uses it in *Culturally Responsive Teaching: Theory, Research, and Practice* (New York: Teachers College Press, 2010), 56-57.

[38] Plous, "The Psychology of Prejudice, Stereotyping, and Discrimination: An Overview," 31-33.

[39] Franklin CampbellJones, Brenda CampbellJones, and Randall B. Lindsey, eds., *The Cultural*

Proficiency Journey: Moving Beyond Ethical Barriers Toward Profound School Change (Thousand Oaks, CA: Corwin, 2010).

[40] Plous, "The Psychology of Prejudice, Stereotyping, and Discrimination: An Overview," 33-34.

[41] National Center for Education Statistics, *Dropout rates in the United States 2000* (Washington, DC: U.S. Department of Education, Offices of Educational Research and Improvement, 2002), 1.

[42] C.M. Steele, "A threat in the air: How stereotypes shape intellectual identity and Performance," *American Psychologist* 52 (1997): 613-629.

[43] S. Spencer, C.M. Steele, and D. Quinn, "Stereotype Threat and Women's Math Performance," *Journal of Experimental Social Psychology* 35 (1999): 4-28.

[44] Margaret Shih, Todd. L. Pittinksy, and Nalini Ambady, "Stereotype Susceptibility: Identity Salience and Shifts in Quantitative Performance," *Psychological Science* 10, no. 1 (January 1999): 80-83.

[45] Delpit, *Other People's Children: Cultural Conflict in the Classroom*, 25.

[46] Ibid., 142.

[47] Ibid., 139.

[48] J. Peoples and G. Bailey, *Humanity: an Introduction to Cultural Anthropology*, 2nd ed. (St. Paul, MN: West Publishing, 1991), 60.

[49] Nikki Grimes, *The Road to Paris* (New York: Penguin, 2006), 133-135.

[50] Fordham, "Passin' For Black: Race, Identity, and Bone Memory in Postracial America," 145-170.

[51] George Santayana, "Reason in Common Sense," *The Life of Reason: Reason in Common Sense* (New York: Scribner's, 1905), 284.

[52] Teaching Tolerance, "Home Was a Horse Stall," www.tolerance.org/supplement/home-was-horse-stall.

[53] Thomas A. Wills, "Downward Comparison Principles in Social Psychology," *Psychological Bulletin* 90, no. 2 (September 1981): 245-271.

[54] Irwin Katz, David C. Class, and Sheldon Cohen, "Ambivalence, Guilt, and the Scapegoating of Minority Group Victims," *Journal of Experimental Social Psychology* 9, no. 5 (September 1973): 423-436.

[55] Rhoda G. Lewin, *Witness to the Holocaust: An Oral History* (Boston, Massachusetts: Twayne Publishers, 1990), 139.

[56] E.L. Hartley, *Problems in Prejudice* (New York: Kings Crown Press, 1946).

[57] Southern Poverty Law Center, "Hate Maps," 2012, http://www.splcenter.org/get-informed/hate-map.

[58] Eugene V. Beresin, "The Impact of Media Violence on Children and Adolescents: Opportunities for Clinical Interventions," *The American Academy of Child and Adolescent Psychiatry,* http://www.aacap.org/AACAP/Medical_Students_and_Residents/Mentorship_Matters/Develop-Mentor/The_Impact_of_Media_Violence_on_Children_and_Adolescents_Opportunities_for_Clinical_Interventions.aspx.

[59] Teaching Tolerance, "Bullied: A Student, a School and a Case That Made History," http://www.tolerance.org/kit/bullied-student-school-and-case-made-history.

[60] PACER's National Bullying Prevention Center, "I Am His Advocate," http://www.pacer.org/bullying/stories/. Story submitted by Kristin and posted 3/22/2013.

[61] Maya Angelou, *Shaker, Why Don't You Sing?* (New York: Random House, 1983), 16. Reprinted with permission. See Copyright page for complete rights permissions.

[62] Charnee Perez, "Lost Key or Bike Theft: What Would You Do?" *ABC News,* http://abcnews. go.com/WhatWouldYouDo/bike-theft/story?id=10556016. This link no longer includes the Bike Theft video. Please find the video on many YouTube channels such as www.youtube.com/ watch?v=ge7i60GuNRg.

[63] See U.S. Commission on Civil Rights I, supra note 2, at 98-103.

[64] Glenn C. Loury, "An American Tragedy: The Legacy of Slavery Lingers in Our Cities' Ghettos," *The Brookings Review* (June 1998): 38-42.

[65] Richard D. Kahlenberg, *All Together Now,* (Washington, D.C.: The Brookings Institution, 2001).

[66] E. Frankenberg, G. Siegel-Hawley, J. Wang, *Choice without Equity: Charter School Segregation and the Need for Civil Rights Standards* (Los Angeles, CA: The Civil Rights Project/Proyecto Derechos Civiles at UCLA, 2010).

[67] Cedar Grove Institute for Sustainable Communities, " Fighting Institutionalized Discrimination and Exclusion of Minorities," http://www.cedargroveinst.org/discrm.php.

[68] Richard D. Kahlenberg and Halley Potter, "Diverse Charter Schools: Can Racial and Socioeconomic Integration Promote Better Outcomes for Students?" *Poverty and Race Research Action Council* and *The Century Foundation,* (May 2012), 2-3.

[69] Robert Wood Johnson Foundation, "Class-Based Discrimination Harms Child Health: New evidence suggests discrimination is an important social determinant of health among White Americans," June 13, 2012, http://www.rwjf.org.

[70] American Academy of Pediatrics, "Poverty Threatens Health of U.S. Children," May 4, 2013, http://www.aap.org/en-us/about-the-aap/aap-press-room/pages/Poverty-Threatens-Health-of-US-Children.aspx.

[71] Federal Bureau of Investigation, "FBI Releases 2010 Hate Crime Statistics," November 14, 2011, http://www.fbi.gov/about-us/cjis/ucr/hate-crime/2010/summary.

[72] Human Rights Campaign, "Employee Non-Discrimination Act," http://www.hrc.org/laws-and-legislation/federal-legislation/employment-non-discrimination-act.

[73] Sarah Jane Glynn and Audrey Powers, "The Top 10 Facts About the Wage Gap," Center for American Progress, April 16, 2012, http://www.americanprogress.org/issues/2012/04/wage_gap_facts.html.

[74] Phyllis Schlafly, *Feminist Fantasies*, Dallas: Spence Publishing, 2003), 28.

Open to Change

"They must often change who would be constant in happiness." (Confucius, 551–479 BCE)

"Progress is impossible without change, and those who cannot change their minds cannot change anything." (George Bernard Shaw)

Our world is constantly changing. Perspective Four explores all this change as a source of possibility. We will consider the dynamic state of all living things, and we'll see that contrary thinking, playfulness, creativity, adaptability, and a growth mindset are tools for creating the openness necessary to bridge differences. The key is openness to growth in ourselves and in our adolescent students, many of whom are actively struggling with the question: Who am I?

Heraclitus said: "You cannot step in the same river twice." That's because both we and the river change constantly. From birth, our bodies have been constantly creating new cells as others die. We have been changed by experience again and again. In the time it takes to read this chapter, our brains will lose neurons, a little calculus will form on our teeth, our hair will grow a bit, and some will fall out. We will probably change our minds once or twice, and feelings and ideas will generate chemical changes in our bodies. We may think differently about something, transform a point of view.

We tend to resist challenges to our view of the world. Adherents to the bias reinforcement principle (see Perspective Three, Advisory 12), we tend to favor our old, familiar point of view rather than something new. The face-to-face meetings described in this book open the possibility of changing views hindered by preconceptions and biased generalizations. Now we can adjust our sails to catch the winds of change and growth.

Opportunity of Change in School

Imagine a culture for adolescents where nobody judged anyone, and everyone assumed that everyone was changing daily and couldn't be pegged. It would be a clique-free culture. There would be no bullying, no dirty looks, and no gossip. Everyone would be included. Students would *want* to come to a school where everyone counted, where they could engage in an array of learning activities and styles without fear of embarrassment.

We can help students learn about themselves and each other and create a more egalitarian, inclusive, tolerant community. We can do it with conversations and experiences that move us toward each other and make it clear that none of us is "cooked," finished, unchanging; we are all becoming.

To draw on the power of change, we can train ourselves to remain awake and alert to possibilities. This is part of the function of clowns and comedians, magicians and tricksters, storytellers and actors: they surprise us and keep us paying attention. Like our dreams, they remind us that things can be seen another way, and no one knows absolutely for sure the way things really are. Even though we are shaped daily by culture's powerful force, as long as we live, we're never finished with change.

Each time we reflect on our or a student's behavior, we have an opportunity to see things differently, to shift our perspective. We can resolve to perceive freshly, rather than see what we expect to see. A fresh perspective gives us fresh power. Remember: "Those who cannot change their minds cannot change anything."

With an attitude and perspective of freshness, we don't know exactly how a student will be from one day to the next. We don't inwardly groan when the student who was insolent yesterday arrives today, because we can't know for sure how s/he will behave today, and how we might help him or her grow. The fact that everything is in flux means that growth is always possible.

Challenge of Change

Some students may resist change because their lives are full of upheaval. Young people who live with the stresses of poverty or fighting parents, for example, have great uncertainty in their lives, and change can aggravate the stress. "Childhood stress can be caused by any situation that requires a person to adapt or change. The situation often produces anxiety. Stress may be caused by positive changes, such as starting a new activity, but it is most commonly linked with negative changes such as illness or death in the family."[1]

Fixed perceptions of ourselves and others can become self-fulfilling prophecies, so we end up living in the presumed safety of a predictable world, made up of already established (often unexamined) perceptions and opinions about people. We are somewhat:

Like the inchworm
We lean out into the air
To find the way, in vain,
And like that hilly hump,
For lack of solid place,
Turn again
To the branch
From first we came.[2]

The advisory meetings in Perspective Four take into account both the need for stability and the need for change. Through structured, intentional conversations, we practice flexible thinking and work toward more open minds.

ADVISORY 1 ▶ CPR

Advisory goal: Awareness of nature's constant flux

Greeting

High Five Greeting: In sequence around the circle, students greet each other with a high five. *Hi, Arnie.* (high five) Reply: *Hi, Fatima.* (high five)

Whip Share: *Weather changes all the time. What is your favorite kind of weather? Why do you like it?*

> Greetings!
>
> Have you noticed the changes that occur in nature every day? The sky, the weather, plants growing, flowering and dying, birds migrating…in nature, life changes constantly, and we are part of the natural world. Today we'll think about some of those changes.

↻ Be the first to answer the Whip Share question so students get the idea of connecting weather to other aspects of life—things you like to do, for your emotional state, awareness of others' safety.

Activity

Cooperative Board Relay—Changes in nature: Form teams of four to eight students. Designate a portion of the board for each team. Teams list as many examples as they can of changes that occur in the natural world. State the topic, and allow teams 30 seconds to discuss. At "go," players take turns going up to the board and writing examples. Each team sends one player at a time to write only one item.

Limit the time to three minutes or less. Once all players on a team have been to the board, the first person may go again. Players may look at other teams' lists and use those ideas. When time runs out, verify each item listed, and see which team listed the most. Then have each team pick one item from their list and tell how it could cause change in their lives.

Keep in Mind

We must embrace change for ourselves and our students lest we stand in the way of growth—not change for its own sake, but for keeping our thinking lively enough to avoid the ruts of bias. By this time in our face-to-face discussions, students are becoming able to see their stuck places and shake themselves loose. We've been working at making the community feel safe by getting to know each other personally and culturally, by examining the ways in which we are all shaped by our cultures and all connected, and by recognizing the price we pay for bias and discrimination.

Now they are invited to: flip ideas, events, thoughts and see from a humorous or contrary perspective; and engage in play to let go of fixed attitudes and have fun with others. By these means, sometimes we can break loose from exclusive thinking. Then we can relate more easily to a variety of people, because we have our own ways of thinking and doing, but at the same time, we are open-minded.

Ask yourself

How open to change are you?

ADVISORY 2 ▶ CPR

Advisory goals: Detect changes in yourself. Notice the ongoing nature of change.

Greeting

Choice Greeting: As the greeting goes around the circle, each person uses a different greeting from the one with which he was greeted. For example, Alex greets Brigid with *Good morning, Brigid* and a handshake, which Brigid returns; then Brigid turns to Clement and says, "*Bonjour, Clement,*" and salutes him, which Clement returns; then Clement turns to Davida and says, "*Good morning, Davida,*" and high-fives her, and so on around the circle.

> Good Morning, Everyone!
> Life never stands still; things are always changing. So are people, whether we like it or not! Tomorrow, bring in to share with us a picture of you as a baby or young child. It can be of you alone or with others.

⮑ If students don't have baby photos, they can bring in an object—a toy or a piece of clothing or a story about something they did or said as a very young child—something that shows that they were once very young, small, and inexperienced.

Share

Whip Share: *What is one way that you've changed since last year?* Each student offers a brief response to the topic; responses "whip" around the circle.

Activity

Something's Changed (Change One Thing): Partners face each other and have one minute to carefully observe each other's appearance. Then partners turn back-to-back. Each person makes one quick change in appearance (e.g., tucks in shirt, rolls up sleeves, switches a ring from one hand to the other). When both are ready, they turn around and face one another again. They have one minute for each person to detect and declare the change the other has made.

⮑ **Variation:** Groups of four play; each pair tries to detect changes in the other pair.

Reflection

Partners share about changes in their lives: What is a change you enjoyed and a change that you didn't enjoy in your life?

Keep in Mind

During the reflection following the activity, remind students that change/variety is something most people enjoy within limits: you may enjoy wearing different clothes every day or eating different foods, but you probably wouldn't want to change houses every day. Some things we want so much to change that we become change agents. Other things feel comfortable by their unchanging sameness day to day.

Ask yourself

What is something you like to change often? What is something you want to remain the same?

ADVISORY 3 ▶ CPR

Advisory goal: Become comfortable with change as preparation for growth that is life-enhancing

Greeting

Closed Eyes Greeting: Everyone closes his or her eyes, and the teacher chooses someone to begin. That person opens his eyes and says *Good morning, _____,* to someone in the circle. That person opens her eyes and returns the greeting, then greets someone whose eyes are still closed. The greetings continue until all have been greeted and have opened their eyes.

> Hello, Changers!
> Part of what keeps life interesting is that things keep changing. We change how we talk and act when we're with different people—we'll share about that today, and we'll try a new way to greet each other. Remember to bring a photo of yourself as a baby or young child, or a childhood object, for our next advisory meeting.

⮑ Some people are uncomfortable having their eyes closed while others have theirs open. To keep things relaxed and playful, if students open their eyes, give gentle reminders, but don't force the issue. As an alternative, students could cover and then uncover their eyes.

Share

Inside-Outside Share: *How do you behave with the following people: the adults in your family; your siblings; your friends; the opposite gender; younger kids?* Students form two groups and stand in concentric circles. Half are in the inside circle facing out, and half are in the outside circle facing in. Read the above question, ending with "adults in your family." Students respond to the question with the person facing them. After a minute, one of the circles moves one or more spots to the left or right, so everyone has a new partner. Read the above question, this time ending with "siblings." Continue in the same manner so students discuss all of the categories of people in the question.

⮑ Give an example (perhaps from your own life) to get students started thinking and talking about how they behave differently with different people. *I can be bossy sometimes, but I'm never bossy with my mother. I couldn't get away with it with her.* You could make a list of differences: the way you talk; the way you eat; which TV programs you watch with certain people, etc.

Activity

What Are You Doing? All stand in a circle. Select a student to begin. She mimes an activity, for example, playing the violin. The student to her left or right in the circle asks her, *Alisha, what are you doing?* The first student replies by naming an activity obviously other than the one she is miming: *I'm painting a picture.* Alisha sits down, while the one who asked the question mimes the activity (painting) that Alisha named. The next person says, *Benjamin, what are you doing?* and so on. This continues around the circle until all have had a turn.

⮑ Students should mime the activity to make it as easy to guess as possible. The joke in this activity is the cognitive dissonance between what the student is doing in mime and what the student says she is doing.

Keep in Mind

Most of us adapt our behavior to various circumstances and people. For adolescents, the ability to move from the informal mood of the neighborhood or home to the more formal one of school is crucial to success in both places. For students from socially disadvantaged homes, the skill can be a life-changer, facilitating a student's move up from poverty to life as an educated person with options in life.

Discuss language differences openly

Cultural clashes often occur around language. Such difficulties could be learning experiences if our approach to language were more curious and inclusive and less judgmental. We need to raise student consciousness about varieties of English and their effective uses. Lisa Delpit quotes an Alaskan Native teacher who gives her Native students practice in what she labels "Formal English," or standard English, and "Heritage English,"[3] the style of speaking in their village. They become fluent in two varieties of English.

Ask yourself

What changes in your language and/or demeanor do you make as you move between home and school?

Additional reading

To avoid the deficit model for students of color, Gloria Ladson-Billings suggests endorsement of both Black English and Standard English as options appropriate to different situations. For more reading on this topic, see *But that's just good teaching! The case for culturally relevant pedagogy*, by Ladson-Billings.[4]

ADVISORY 4 ▶ CPR

Advisory goal: Awareness of personal change and growth since early childhood

Greeting

One-Minute Mingle Greeting: All stand and mill about in the circle, greeting as many people as possible with *Good morning, _____*. Each greeting is accompanied by a handshake with good eye contact.

> Hola, Everyone!
>
> I hope you brought a photo of yourself when you were little, or a childhood object.
>
> <u>Do Now</u>: Put a sticky note on the back of your picture or object. Get a number from me, then write that number on the sticky note. We'll see if we can recognize each other by how we looked or what we played with when we were little.

Share

Individual Share Share of childhood memories: Teacher does first share. Show your picture and pass it around. Tell about a couple of things you did or said or thought when you were very young (these might be stories your elders have told you). Directly to you, students then ask questions or make comments about what you have shared.

Example: *Here's a picture of me on my first day of school. I lived in New York, and my mom walked me to school. I wore a new dress. I was worried about my mom leaving me there. I'm open for questions or related comments now.*

➲ The audience asks interesting, open-ended questions so the sharer can flesh out the story by answering the questions. Set a time limit for the share and discussion..

➲ Determine ahead of time the format in which questions or comments are to be stated. The format should vary: at times questions can be mandatory, going around the circle; sometimes raising hands and volunteering can be used. Whatever the format, encourage full participation.

Activity

How You've Changed! Partners guess the identity of classmates' childhood pictures and/or try to guess which object from childhood belongs to which classmate. After partners have a few minutes, call out a number; the partners who have that number say their guess, then the right person identifies himself or herself.

➲ Make sure every photo or object is guessed about.

Keep in Mind

It is difficult to identify a youth from a baby picture or a baby's object. The point of the activity is to have fun and to appreciate the huge transformation from babyhood to youth. Seeing the differences in how they were a few years ago and how they are now highlights the growing they have done. A growth mindset is the confidence that they are still growing and changing, and with effort they can achieve their goals.

Ask yourself

What is a way that you have grown in the last ten years?

ADVISORY 5 ▶ CPR

Advisory goal: Recognize both your need for autonomy and your need to relate to and fit in with friends

Greeting

I Say It So Greeting: First person says, *My name is _____; I say it so: _____!* After *I say it so*, he says his name in a special way—in a high or low voice, fast or slow, emphasis on a different syllable, dramatically, clapping hands, etc. Then everyone in the circle says, *Good morning, _____,* saying his name just as he did.

> Ciao, Children You Used to Be!
>
> _____ and _____ will share with us today about what he was like as a young child. Be thinking of questions you can ask that might give us insight into who he used to be. It's a tricky thing to keep track of each other, since we are all changing all the time. Our game today will make that clear!

⮌ Line up a couple students to share.

Share

Individual Share of childhood memories: A sharer passes around a baby picture or object and tells about one or two things they did or said or thought when they were very young. Audience members ask the sharer questions and/or comment about the object(s) or the story. If there is time, you can have more than one share.

Activity

Copy Cat: For one or two minutes, everybody watches and copies the actions of another person in the circle without revealing whom they are watching. When time is up, all reveal whom they were copying.

⮌ This activity causes constant change. Since each person must copy another, everyone must change what he began doing in order to copy the person he is watching, who also is changing in order to copy someone else, and so on.

Keep in Mind

Individuality and conformity are always in tension, especially intensely during adolescence, when both are essential developmental characteristics. The desire to be unique and original seems to conflict with the desire to fit in and have friends. In this advisory meeting, students greet and share about themselves as individuals, then, during the activity, struggle to conform to what someone else is doing. You can conclude this meeting by challenging students to keep the two in balance, especially while making important decisions.

A goal of these advisory conversations is to bring students to a place where what matters most is not with whom you play, but how much fun you all have together. To this end, many advisories focus on being open to change. We will introduce students to tricksters and other contrary thinkers, humor, and play for play's sake.

Ask yourself

What adaptations do you make to get along with friends and family?

ADVISORY 6 ▶ CPR

Advisory goal: Understand that verification is crucial to avoid distortion when information passes from one person to another.

Greeting

Let Me See Your Walk Greeting: The first person pantomimes an activity (a sport, hobby, chore, etc.) as he walks across the circle to another student. He greets her and asks to see her "walk." She returns his greeting, they exchange places, and she pantomimes an activity as she crosses the circle to another student. This is repeated until everyone has been greeted.

> Hello, Everyone!
>
> Facts and information can change a lot as they pass from one person to another. Even when we mean to say something exactly as we heard it, we often make small changes without realizing it.

Share

Individual Share of childhood memories (continued): A sharer passes around a baby or toddler picture or object and tells about one or two things they did or said or thought when very young. Audience members ask the sharer questions and/or comment about the object(s) or the story.

Activity

Telephone: Send two whispered sentences around the circle in opposite directions. When the sentences have gone all the way around, see how they have changed.

Reflection

Partner share: One partner answers the question: *How does Telephone demonstrate some of the dangers of gossiping?* The other partner answers the question: *Do similar distortions happen when rumors and gossip are spread on the Internet?* Volunteers share out.

➲ Help students make the connection between the distortion of words in the game and the distortion of facts and truth that occurs when rumors circulate and people gossip.

Keep in Mind

This advisory balances our positive embrace of change with our awareness of the dangers of altering information, especially about other people. Among adolescents, conversation among and about peers moves about constantly, sometimes via instant and far-reaching media, and distortion frequently occurs. Sometimes it's harmless; other times it's hurtful, even slanderous. Unverified, accidentally misstated, or intentionally false information can easily be taken as the truth by listeners and passed on, damaging reputations, the community, and lives.

Ask yourself

Have you or someone you are close to ever been the subject of a false rumor? What was the effect on you or them?

ADVISORY 7 ▶ CPR

Advisory goal: Develop the capacity to adjust language and behavior to contexts and circumstances

Greeting

Informal English Greeting: Brainstorm a list with students, or give them a list, of informal greetings in English, such as: *Hi, Hiya, Howdy, G'day, S'up? How do?, What's happening? How's it going?, What up, dawg?, Yo, Top of the morning.* You can refer to your Ways to Say Hello list from Perspective One (page 51). One at a time around the circle, each student chooses a greeting from the list and greets someone across the circle. The person returns the greeting the same way or with another informal greeting. Students can fold their hands in their laps to indicate that they've been greeted.

Hola, Amigos y Amigas!

Counting to eight is easy, unless you have to change to an unfamiliar language to do it! Today those of us who don't speak Spanish may become a bit <u>disoriented</u>.

↻ If many of your students speak Spanish, choose another, less familiar language. See the list of greetings in many languages, page 349.

Group reflection after greeting: *In what places, with what people, and under what circumstances is it appropriate to use informal greetings?* Discuss the need to decide what variety of English, formal or informal, we will use in a situation. See Keep in Mind below for ideas for the discussion.

Share

Individual Share on childhood memories (continued): A sharer passes around a baby or toddler picture or object and tells about one or two things they did or said or thought when very young. Audience members ask questions and/or comment about the object(s) or the story. Questions and comments are directed to the sharer. If there is time, you can have more than one share.

↻ If more students want to share their pictures and/or objects, you can identify and display them, perhaps with a note from each student about a memory. Or you can add additional advisories.

Activity

Bobo Ski Wottin Tottin: Students hold both hands at shoulder height, elbows bent. The left palm is up, and the right palm is down. Everyone's right hand hovers above (not touching) the neighbor's left hand. The words below are said or sung as the group passes a light hand slap clockwise from one person to the next in the rhythm of the song: the first person lifts her right hand and slaps (gently!) the right hand of the person on her left, then immediately returns her right hand to where it was. On the next beat, the person to her left (whose hand was just slapped) slaps the hand of the person on his left. The slap is thus passed around the circle clockwise in rhythm, until "eight" is said. The person whose hand is slapped on "eight" is out, and sits down, unless she can remove her hand before it is slapped. In this version, everyone counts in an unfamiliar language (number words below).

Bobo ski wottin tottin
Uh uh boom boom boom boom boom
Itty bitty wottin tottin
Bobo ski wottin tottin
Bobo ski wottin tottin
One two three four five six seven eight!

➲ This sounds more complicated than it is. It's fun!

Counting one to eight in different languages:

English guide	OJIBWAY	SPANISH	HINDI [phonetic]	ARABIC	SOMALI
one	bezhik	uno	[ayk]	wahed	kow
two	niizh	dos	[dough]	ithnan	laba
three	nswi	tres	[teen]	thalatha	saddex
four	niiwin	quatro	[char]	arba'a	afar
five	naanan	cinco	[bahtch]	khamsa	shan
six	ngodwaaswi	seis	[chay]	sitta	lix
seven	niizhwaaswi	siete	[saht]	sab'a	todobo
eight	nshwaaswi	ocho	[aht]	thamanya	siddeed

➲ If you have students in class who speak the language, they can enjoy helping their classmates with pronunciation. Being required to use an unfamiliar language can help students who are comfortable with formal English understand the challenge for those who are not.

Keep in Mind

Enjoying the varieties of language

Much could be made in a positive, instructional way of the constant change and variation that occur in language, the differences in language that exist among cultures, and the confusions and clashes that result from them. In advisory, we can acknowledge and enjoy the variety of speech patterns in the group, because they reflect the variety of backgrounds of the students.

You can play a little with the underlined word in each daily news message. Using the word's context, students can attempt to define the word, then check the dictionary to see how close they came. Once they know what the word means, they can try to use it appropriately during advisory. One advisory teacher honks a horn every time a student uses the underlined word of the day! Another makes it a game to see how many different times the group can fit the day's word into their conversations.

English vocabulary is ever expanding (Advisory 19 uses a list of the words Merriam-Webster added to their dictionary in 2011). In the context of such a rich language, we are all English language learners! Students new to English and those who speak with an accent can be affirmed as they practice American English in a context where everyone is working on it. Ideally, English is something to investigate, grow in for a lifetime, and play with—a bridge between and among cultures, rather than a wedge.

Code-switching

From a sociolinguistic point of view (an approach to linguistics that looks beyond formal interests, to the social and cultural functions and meanings of language use), code-switching is "the practice of selecting or altering linguistic elements so as to contextualize talk in interaction."[5] In other words, we switch our language in order to fit into a situation or group of people.

Some students are taught by their families and/or others to code-switch—to change their verbal and nonverbal language and social patterns in the context of another person and/or another culture. The young person becomes, in effect, multilingual and multicultural. Many students—and some educators—use code-switching as they move between their families or neighborhoods and school. It's a lot of work, but it builds resilience. It allows them to adapt without assimilating permanently into another culture and abandoning their own, and it's a way to reduce the distance between the home culture and the white, middle-class culture of most schools.

On the other hand, some students rebel from this accommodation and purposely emphasize their home and/or neighborhood way of speaking "for reasons of solidarity and intentional separation."[6] Sometimes, when certain language is stigmatized, students might use it even more, as an assertion of the validity of their culture.

After the greeting in this advisory, we can talk about how most of us adjust our language, some much more than others, and some with a lot at stake. Discussing the ways we speak and behave in various settings, students can see that we all do it to some degree.

Bridging

"Bridging" refers to the capacity to live successfully in more than one culture without self-suppression.[7] Bridging goes beyond code-switching (moving between the codes of cultures), and involves working to internally integrate two cultures, two ways of being. Bridging or code-switching may be used by any student whose home culture differs from the white, middle-class culture of most American educators and schools.

Whether I code-switch or bridge depends a lot on who I'm with—how well I know them and how well they know me. Being fully who I am as an African-American professional man is intentional. Sometimes, however, I bridge in a public situation where I don't know the people. Once on an airplane the stewardess told me I had to take my bag out of the overhead compartment and move it to another one further back, but she didn't say that to any other passenger. I moved the bag, sat down again, thought for a few minutes, and then called her over and asked her why she singled out my bag. I used polite, formal language, not my home/neighborhood informal language. But I left an edge in it, to let her know that I wasn't going to silently tolerate discrimination. The bin, she said, was reserved for first aid equipment they needed in that spot, and she apologized for failing to give me a reason in the first place. When she left, the passengers around me acknowledged me for the way I had handled it—assertive, but polite. That was my integrated self in action. (Educational administrator)

Additional resources

Code-Switching: Teaching Standard English in Urban Classrooms (Theory & Research Into Practice), Rebecca S. Wheeler and Rachel Swords.[8] The book addresses teaching students to recognize differences between formal and informal English so they can choose the language style to fit the time, place, audience, and effect they want to have.

Code Switch, Frontiers of Race, Culture, and Ethnicity, National Public Radio.[9] Created by a team of journalists investigating the overlapping themes of race, ethnicity, and culture, how they play out in our lives and communities, and how all of this is shifting.

Ask yourself

What adjustments do you make in your speech, behavior, and overall style in various circumstances?

ADVISORY 8 ▶ CPR

Advisory goal: Accept and adapt to the fact that people and situations change

Greeting

Funny Voices Greeting: The first person says, *My name is _____, and I want you to greet me in a _____ voice.* The class responds by saying, in the kind of voice requested, *Good morning, _____.*

➲ You can brainstorm some voice possibilities ahead of time: spooky, whisper, loud, soft, baby, tough guy, squeaky, slow, etc.

➲ Be the first to greet someone to model the Funny Voices greeting.

> Hi, All!
>
> Just when you think you know what's going on, things change! It can be that way in theater, too: just when you think you know what a character will do, something surprises you. Let's see if we can keep each other guessing in our theater game today, Park Bench.

Share

Partner Share: *Describe someone you changed your mind about, because he or she changed, or you did, or both.* Example: *I used to think my brother was really annoying, but now we have fun together. Maybe we both changed.*

Activity

Park Bench: Set two chairs next to each other to represent a park bench and select two student actors. Give them a card with a description of a real or imagined event. They have one minute to prepare; then they have a conversation about the event (who, when, where) without ever actually saying what happened. The audience guesses what the event was. The actors continue until the class names the event or gives up.

Example events:

What: a young goat and a cat become friends
Where: Iowa
When: over the last few weeks
Who: goat, cat, and boy who cared for them both

What: people make sandbags to prevent flooding
Where: Fargo, N.D.
When: over the weekend
Who: five teens from Minneapolis

Keep in Mind

Improvisation requires flexibility and openness to instant change. This is a life skill that often keeps (or gets) us out of difficulties and helps us stay open-minded toward each other. Albert Einstein says: "The measure of intelligence is the ability to change."

Ask yourself

What was a time when life forced you to improvise?

ADVISORY 9 ▶ CPR

Advisory goal: Develop the skill of adaptability

Greeting

Crazy Walk Greeting: Each student thinks of a silly way to move across the circle (crab walk, hip-hop walk, skip, hop, on their knees, etc.). The first person does her crazy walk across the circle and greets someone with a handshake, then returns to her seat. The person who was greeted does a crazy walk across the circle and greets someone, and so on, until everyone has been greeted. Students can fold their hands in their laps to indicate that they've been greeted.

> *Good Morning, Changeable Ones!*
>
> *A group of artists invented a game in which each person adds something to what has been created before, without knowing what it is. Things can get very interesting when we each do our own thing and we see what comes of all the variations. We'll try out the game today. It's called the Exquisite Corpse.*

Share

Partner Share: *What is an opinion you have changed in your life?* Model this share before students discuss the topic. For example: *I used to think girls' sports were just watered-down versions of boys' sports, but now I think girls can be tough competitors.* Give a time limit for a share and issue a time warning halfway through the share to ensure balanced sharing/listening. Volunteers share out.

Activity

Exquisite Corpse: Exquisite Corpse is a collaborative poetry game whose roots are in the Parisian Twentieth-century Surrealist Movement. Each person wrote a word on a sheet of paper, folded the paper to conceal the word, and passed it to the next person for his or her contribution.

Writing version of Exquisite Corpse

For the words to hang together with some meaning, set up a grammatical structure: *adjective, noun, verb, adjective, noun.*

- A noun is the name of a thing, e.g., *book, hammer, cake, lipstick*
- An adjective describes the noun, e.g., *big, tiny, beautiful, frightening, lavender, seven*
- A verb tells of an action, something being done, e.g., *sing, stumble, calculate, punish*

Example: *Sleepy beetles scream dramatic coffee.*

In groups of five, students write five words on separate pieces of paper: Student 1 writes an adjective, Student 2 a noun, and so on. Then the group looks at all five words and sets them in an order that allows them to create a sentence that contains all the words. Example: *Some sleepy beetles dramatically climbed into a coffee cup, drank the coffee, and ran away screaming!*

Drawing version of Exquisite Corpse

The game can be done with drawings rather than words. Students form groups of four, and each group folds a piece of paper accordion-style into four equal sections. Keeping the paper folded, the first person draws an image or a shape in the top section, leaving some lines at the bottom of the section for the next person to connect to. Then the first person folds the paper so that only the tips of the connecting lines are showing. The next person makes his or her drawing in the second section, connecting to the lines that show from the first drawing. The third person draws, then the fourth. The last person unfolds the paper and you see an image made up of all the parts that people have drawn.

If you want the image to look like a person or animal, you can say that the first person has to draw some kind of head, the next a torso and arms, the next the hands and legs, and the last person the feet.

Keep in Mind

The name "Exquisite Corpse" comes from a phrase that emerged from an early playing of the game, using words: "The exquisite corpse will drink the young wine."

Ask yourself

How adaptable are you when plans change at the last minute?

ADVISORY 10 ▶ A+

Advisory goal: Understand the relationship between the ability to remain open and flexible and the role of the trickster

Greeting

Elevator Greeting: Everyone stands close together facing the same direction, as if in a crowded elevator. Each person greets and is greeted by two or three of the people closest to him/her *(Good morning, _____)*, while everyone keeps their eyes fixed on an imaginary space above the imaginary elevator door, as if watching a floor indicator. Challenge students to make the greeting friendly even though they are not looking at one another.

> *Good Evening!*
>
> *That's the greeting a* <u>trickster</u> *might use in the morning. A trickster's job it is to keep people on their toes, ready for anything. Heyokas, the sacred tricksters of the Lakota tribe, have been described as "much bigger than their shadows." Heyokas sometimes ride backward on their horses and say goodbye when they first meet a person. Today we'll get acquainted with the trickster as he/she occurs in various cultures.*

⮑ It's not easy to communicate friendly acceptance while you are staring straight ahead, avoiding eye contact! The experience underlines the importance of eye contact in building relationship.

Activity

The Trickster: Tell the students a little about the trickster (see Keep in Mind below), then read the following story/poem to them. When a trickster gets interested, watch out! Here's the kind of thing he does:

Trickster Narrative

by Jacob Nibenegenesabe

Once I wished up a coat
wearing a man inside.
The man was sleeping
and when he woke
the coat was on him!

This was in summer, so many asked him
"Why do you have that coat on?"
"It has me in it!"
he would answer.
He tried to take it off
but I wished his memory shivering with cold
so it wouldn't want to remember
how to take a coat off.
That way it would stay warm.
I congratulated myself on thinking of that.

Then his friends came,
Put coats on,
And slowly showed him how they took coats off.
Even that didn't work.
Things were getting interesting.
Then his friends
Tried to confuse the coat
into thinking it was a man.
"Good morning," they said to it,
"Did you get
your share of fish?"
and other things too.
Some even invited the coat to gossip.
It got to be late summer
And someone said to the coat
"It is getting colder.
You better go out
And find a coat to wear."
The coat agreed!

Ha! I was too busy laughing to stop that dumb coat
From leaving the man it wore
inside.
I didn't care.
I went following the coat.
Things were getting interesting.[10]

Explain to students: The trickster wants life to remain lively—not necessarily right or true or even good, but in flux, unstuck, interesting. Why keep someone like that around? Perhaps because we have always needed people to point out to us the absurdity of thinking that we are in control, or that we always have the right answer or the right name for something, or even for ourselves. In Shakespeare's world there were jesters; in vaudeville there were slapstick comics who threw cream pies at each other. We need to laugh at life and at ourselves sometimes, and tricksters help us to do that.

Read the following quote from Black Elk: "You have noticed that the truth comes into this world with two faces. One is sad with suffering, and the other laughs; but it is the same face, laughing or weeping. When people are already in despair, maybe the laughing face is better for them; and when they feel too good and are too sure of being safe, maybe the weeping face is better for them to see."[11]

Reflection

What is something you think or do to help you lighten up or see the other side of things? (Go for a bike ride, talk to a friend, read comics, journal or write a poem, etc.)
Name some tricksters in our culture(s). (Comedians, magicians, etc.)
How could it help you to have a trickster for a friend?

⤷ Have students turn to partners to respond to the third question, then share out. If there is time, discuss both questions two and three with the whole group.

Keep in Mind

A great way to avoid being held captive by our habits, opinions, and judgments is to share a laugh. When you laugh with someone, it's hard to fear or resent them. At least temporarily, we can be free of thoughts and attitudes that divide us from one another.

Trickster as a model for open-mindedness

Educators and students benefit from contemplating the trickster, a mischievous character who populates stories and legends in many cultures. The trickster reminds us that things may not be what they seem. In many societies, getting stuck in one way of seeing the world is seen as a danger to the well-being of the community, and one or more persons are designated to be trickster(s). Their job is to invite—or practically force, if necessary—people to look at things differently.

The Lakota, a Plains tribe, have a tradition of "contraries" called *heyokas*. Their job is to be the opposite of everyone else: they might walk and talk backward, sleep during the day and raise a ruckus at night, go swimming in cold weather and sit by a fire in hot weather. The Black Elk quote above describes the heyoka reminding people that life isn't just one way, that our perceptions may be deceiving, and to cement them in our minds is counter to the principle of a world in flux.

Cultures around the world have tricksters with the same or similar functions. For example, Loki is a mischievous Norse trickster figure. He represents "the power of light and the power of words, which together reveal and persuade others of the truth...."[12]

Coyote is one of the most familiar of North American Native trickster figures. He is the wanderer, the transformer, the clown that saves us from ourselves. He moves among humans to show them the other side of things. When first given his name and his assignment in life, he is told, "I will give you a special power. You will be able to change yourself into anything. You will be able to talk to anything and hear anything talk except the water. If you die, you will come back to life. This will be your way. Changing Person do your work well!

"Coyote was glad. He went right out and began his work. This is the way it was with him. He went out to make things right."

Benefits of contrariness

Physicists, biologists, historians, and psychologists talk to us about the dynamic nature of our planet, our bodies and minds, and societies. Life is change, physically, emotionally, and socially. Nothing stays the same, ever—not even for a moment. This is the foundation of a growth mindset, one that perceives possibility everywhere, for everyone.

Ask yourself

How have you responded to student tricksters?

ADVISORY 11 ▶ CPR

Advisory goal: Learn to loosen your mind with silliness

Greeting

Mimic Greeting: One at a time around the circle, students greet their neighbors any way they choose. Greetings are returned in the same way they are given.

> Dear Dears,
> Among a trickster's <u>mischievous</u> skills is surprising or unsettling people with her silliness. Today's game will give you a chance to show that you know a trick or two!

⮑ Students may choose both the words and the manner in which they greet, or you can require certain words (e.g., *Good morning, _____*) and let them choose the voice and gesture. Allow for variety, creativeness, and silliness.

Share

Partner Share: *Tell about a time when you had fun being silly or when you laughed at yourself.*

Activity

Honey, Do You Love Me? Form two teams. A player from one team goes to a player on the other team and asks, *Honey, do you love me?* The player must respond, *Honey, I love you, but I just can't smile,* without smiling or laughing or he is "recruited" and moves to the other team. If the responder does not laugh, the initiator is recruited by the responder's team. The game ends when all players are on one team.

Keep in Mind

The trickster reminds us that change exercises our minds. Play is a source of invention and creativity: "Neuroscientists, developmental biologists, psychologists, social scientists, and researchers from every point of the scientific compass now know that play is a profound biological process. It has evolved over eons in many animal species to promote survival. It shapes the brain and makes animals smarter and more adaptable. In higher animals, it fosters empathy and makes possible complex social groups. For us, play lies at the core of creativity and innovation. Of all animal species, humans are the biggest players of all. We are built to play and built through play. When we play we are engaged in the purest expression of our individuality."[14] Play loosens our minds and our social interactions—it's a catalyst for bridging differences.

Playing with students builds community and practices social skills. Play gives us the chance to laugh together and builds a classroom and conducive to learning. (Middle level social studies teacher)

Devon had been kicked out of his last district with thirteen pages of "reasons why" following him. His work wasn't bad, but his mind seemed closed to making friends. In our school he wasn't treated punitively and was invited to play in recess and during classroom games. The first change I noticed was that he started to smile, and then one day during a P.E. basketball game when he and a girl grabbed for the ball at the same time, she fell down. I watched as he ignored the chance to score a shot and instead stopped to help her up! (Seventh-eighth grade teacher)

Ask yourself

How do you or might you bring humor into your teaching?

ADVISORY 12 ▶ CPR

Advisory goal: Loosen your imagination through silly play.

Greeting

Language Greeting: Choose a language for the greeting. All students greet in this language, either around the circle or in the All Group Greeting format. (All Group format: *Buenos dias, everyone.* Group responds: *Buenos dias, Carla.*) Leader can list and model and practice the greeting ahead

> *Ciao, Changers!*
>
> *The "contrary" is another name for the trickster. He is the one who loves opposites, saying "no" for "yes" and "up" for "down." Our game today will give us practice in being <u>contrary</u>.*

of time to facilitate correct pronunciation. Check your own Ways to Say Hello list (page 51) or the list of language variations for greetings on page 349.

Share

Whip Share: *Are you willing to say "No!" when you see someone giving someone else a hard time?* Each student offers a brief response to the topic so responses "whip" around the circle.

➲ This is an opportunity for students to publicly commit to speaking up when they see bullying or other mistreatment of one person by another. Some may say they will do so just to avoid embarrassment, but there is power in a public statement, and they might rise to their commitment the next time they see such a thing. This opportunity foreshadows Perspective Five, where students are asked to step up and take a stand against bias.

Activity

No, No, No: One student is chosen to start a story with a ridiculous remark such as, *Did you see that bus full of quacking giraffes?"* The next player says, *No, no, no,* and changes part of the story in an equally ridiculous way, for example, *No, no, no, that wasn't a bus of full of quacking giraffes! It was actually a boat full of roaring hamburgers!* The story continues to change as it goes around the circle and ends when everybody has had a turn.

➲ As always, you can model for students by going first (in this case, second). Ask a student before the meeting begins to be the story starter and open with a couple of sentences to get things going. Then you jump in with *No, no, no,* and introduce a different ridiculous element. Then other students add statements, beginning with *No, no, no!* If some students get completely stuck, they may pass and contribute later.

Keep in Mind

Humor and play are forms of self-expression that thrive in a lively and open environment. Their essence is variety, and they open us to a non-static way of living. If we could keep this open, lively spirit in our everyday encounters with each other, we might experience our differences as interesting, not threatening.

If you build a culture of play, relaxed lightness becomes a way of being. We do it in class when we have an extra moment, and then the kids play the games pick-up style spontaneously on the playground. Play in kids' lives outside of school is all organized and mostly competitive. We're missing the fun of spontaneous play. Middle school should be a place where kids can be wonderfully weird! It's the chaotic age. When you give them the openness to be themselves, they'll do it. You build a safe community during play by watching and listening carefully for moments when there is a put-down. If you speak up and address it as soon as someone rolls his eyes or says, "Awwww" when someone misses the ball, you build a space with secure boundaries. I think it's laughter that does it. Once you laugh with somebody, everything changes. You have to play games where you can be silly, lively, but safe. Middle level can be the most fantastic three years in their lives. Mixing cultures becomes an adventure. They find themselves and each other in the foolishness. (Middle level teacher)

Ask yourself

How do you introduce playfulness into learning?

ADVISORY 13 ▶ CPR

Advisory goal: Avoid getting stuck in certainty

Greeting

What Are You Doing? All stand in a circle, and a student is selected to begin. She mimes an activity, for example, playing the violin. The student to her left or right in the circle greets her, *Hello, _____, what are you doing?* The first student replies by returning the greeting, *Hello, _____,* and then naming any activity other than the one she is actually miming: *I'm painting a picture.* The first student returns to her seat, while the one who asked the question mimes the activity (painting) that was named. This continues around the circle until all have had a turn.

> *Good Morning, Friends!*
>
> *Did you know there is a name for literature that is full of <u>exaggerations</u>? It's called "tall tales." Paul Bunyan, Pecos Bill, and Br'er Rabbit are examples of American tall tales. Today we'll get into a contrary mood again and say the opposite of the truth.*

⮑ If necessary, remind everyone that only activities appropriate to school can be acted out in the greeting.

Share

Tall Tale Share: Each student shares something that is not true about him or her, starting with *One day I....* Proceed around the circle, each person telling a tall tale about an accomplishment or experience. To set an example, you go first: *On my fourteenth birthday, I ate fourteen hamburgers in a row, then I threw up, and I've been a vegetarian ever since!* or *I was born with two left feet, and they had to switch the one on my right leg around right away.*

⮑ This sharing activity might be hard to get started. Tell students that you are turning things upside down in this meeting. Usually sharing is when we tell about real things that have happened to us or others. In the Tall Tale Share, we playfully pretend and make up exaggerated stories about things we have done. Be the first person to share, and make it something so obviously "not you" that all your students will know for sure you would *not* have really done or seen such a thing.

Activity

Resisting the Certainty Principle: Draw each of these triangle signs on a separate piece of paper and hold them up for students to see, one at a time, for a few seconds. After you show each sign, ask students to write down what the sign said before you hold up the next one.

We tend to assume that we see what we expect to see—what makes sense to us. In this case, most will have written down "Paris in the spring," "Once in a lifetime," and "Bird in the hand." Have them look at the signs again.

Reflection

Begin by sharing with students a little about the dangers of the certainty principle (see below, Keep in Mind). Then discuss as a group:

Why did we tend to be certain that the signs said what we first thought they said?

What does that tell us about how accurately we observe the world?

➲ Students participate more fully if you begin with a partner share before a whole group discussion, so it's always useful to begin with partners. Students can also keep advisory notebooks, in which they write reflections before a whole-group discussion. Both techniques help "prime the pump" and increase participation.

Keep in Mind

Overcoming our resistance to seeing our mistakes

The certainty principle can get you into trouble! Being sure about things can give you confidence, but it can also predetermine your perceptions and cause mistakes. Being uncertain reminds us to check, double-check, and test ideas until we have plenty of evidence for them. Keep "wait and see" —suspended judgment—handy. It takes persistence to free ourselves in our thinking and behavior toward people who are quite different from us. These advisories guide students toward that awareness:

- They foster the development of productive cultural identities that are flexible and broadminded enough to include others who seem very different. (Perspective One)

- They call on us to tune up our language to include others, even at moments of disagreement or conflict, bridging the distance between us and them. (Perspective Two)

- They recognize the potential for rigid, unexamined thinking to feed bias. (Perspective Three)

- They encourage us to operate in an adaptive, changeable mode as much as possible, able and ready to adjust a point of view or shift our understanding when there is good cause to do so. (Perspective Four)

Even so, we catch ourselves digging in. In advisory meetings, as in academic classes and in life, when things get serious and/or difficult, students from time to time respond with resistance. Just when we need it most, opening up the ways we think about and perceive others becomes less likely. Maybe a joke, a game, a little silliness would loosen things up, deflect antagonism, and bring the group together again.

Ask yourself

What helps you get unstuck from an opinion or a habit?

ADVISORY 14 ▶ A+

Advisory goal: Develop analytical thinking skills to detect bias

Greeting

Meet and Greet Greeting: Divide students into groups of three or four to create Smart Thinking groups. Students then greet the people in their Smart Thinking group in any greeting format.

> Howdy, Partners!
>
> One of the ways you know that a person isn't <u>gullible</u> is that he asks a lot of questions. It's the best way to get at the truth or at least avoid flawed logic, biased thinking, and prejudice.

Activity

Smart Thinking: How to be a smart listener and speaker: Before the meeting, review and choose one of the arguments below, Funding for Mass Transit or Back of the Bus. In their Smart Thinking groups, students read aloud the selected argument and together answer the three reflection questions. One student reports out for the group.

FUNDING FOR MASS TRANSIT: SERVE DISADVANTAGED GROUPS

From *Streetsblog.org* post

"How much should passengers pay for mass transit? What with the financial woes of transit systems around the country, it's been a hot topic. Today on the Streetsblog Network, we're looking at the question from a couple of different angles.

"First, Yonah Freemark of The Transport Politic looks at the role of mass transit in promoting social equity, comparing policies in three U.S. cities (Chicago, Washington, and New York) and two European cities (Paris and London):

"[W]hile these three U.S. transit systems provide advantageous fares to children, the elderly, and the disabled, they largely ignore the needs of impoverished adults. On the other hand, London and Paris provide generous discounts for university students, people in poverty, and the unemployed. In addition, London provides free passes for veterans and their dependents, while Paris offers relief for families with large numbers of children. In both cities' cases, significant subsidies are provided to the transit operators by local and national governments to make up for lost revenue as a result of these discounts.

"It would be difficult to argue that transportation should be reserved for only those who can afford it, and therefore fare schemes that incorporate the needs of the poorest are necessary. Not only should we be pushing vigorously for *more* transit, but we should be asking for *cheaper* transit, at least for those without good-paying jobs....

"In this time of mass unemployment and reduced incomes all around, we must work to reduce fares for people who cannot always afford the mobility options transit offers."[15]

BACK OF THE BUS: MASS TRANSIT, RACE, AND INEQUALITY

From *TransportationNation*, an American Radioworks documentary

"Fifty-six-year-old Carolyn McMillan considers herself lucky. To get to work, she can drive to the Home Depot parking lot on Jonesboro road in Clayton County, Georgia, then take a bus to her clerical job in downtown Atlanta.

"'I'm just barely making it,' McMillan says. 'Because I have to put gas in the car. I'm just barely making it.' Not too long ago, McMillan could take a local bus before switching to the Atlanta system, MARTA. But Clayton County isn't part of MARTA, and last year, Clayton eliminated all bus service. Today it stretches south of Atlanta in an endless string of fried-chicken joints, tattoo parlors, check-cashing stores, and used-car lots.

"In the 1970s, when Clayton County voted not to become a part of MARTA, it was a mostly white, rural place. Now, as more affluent whites flock to downtown Atlanta, Clayton County is mostly black.

"'Transportation in Atlanta has always been mired in race and racism,' says Robert Bullard, director of the Environmental Justice Center at Clark Atlanta University. When Atlanta began building its commuter rail system in the 1970s, white communities like Clayton County wanted no part of it.

"'Public Transit was equated with black people and poor people and crime and poverty. And when the Metropolitan Atlanta Transportation Authority was created MARTA, it was a running joke that 'MARTA' – he spells it out – M-A-R-T-A – 'stood for moving Africans rapidly through Atlanta.'

"'It's transportation apartheid,' he says."[16]

Reflection: Draw your conclusions

Does the speaker connect what he says to other viewpoints, and what he has observed, and what is below the surface? Examples:

I can connect this to...

I want to add to...

When I looked more deeply...

I respectfully disagree with_____...

I agree with_____ on most of what he said, but I wonder....

Does the speaker provide evidence that is broad, reliable, and fits his interpretations and conclusions?

What support is there for your statement?

My evidence is...

On page__, it says...

Do you have any more evidence?

This survey shows....

The U.S. Census report says....

Does the speaker use good reasoning and avoid logical fallacies?

Could you clarify your statement? I'm not clear about ___

That's a logical fallacy because....

Here's my reasoning....

It doesn't make sense to me that ....

I will show with information from several sources what caused this.

Keep in Mind

Remind students that smart thinking starts with curiosity and willingness: *I'm not sure about this. I want to know more.* Smart thinking often starts with questions. Alice enjoyed Wonderland because, as she said, things kept getting "curiouser and curiouser." Don't forget our friend the trickster, who is happy when "things are getting interesting," when the obvious is disrupted, and we wonder.

This advisory helps students see that when ideas, facts, and opinions are presented, a thinking person asks questions, because ideas, facts, and opinions are only as good as the thinking and evidence behind them. Accepting a point of view without inquiring into it is a sign that you are gullible. A gullible person is easy to fool because, unlike a trickster, she isn't curious, doesn't ask questions, and doesn't *keep* asking until she understands and is convinced by the nature, amount, and source of the evidence and the logical reasoning of the speaker. A gullible person is susceptible to biased views because she does not question.

Ask yourself

When are you at your best as a smart thinker? Under what circumstances are you less smart in your thinking?

ADVISORY 15 ▶ A+

Advisory goals: Perceive the poor logic in logical fallacies. Learn to detect them in written and spoken language.

Greeting

Choice Greeting: *Greet someone you haven't talked to yet today.* Each person uses a greeting different from the one by which he was greeted. For example, Eve goes to Frank, whom she hasn't talked to yet today, and says, *Good morning, Frank*, with a handshake, which Frank returns; then Frank goes to Gerard, whom he hasn't talked to yet today, and says, *Bonjour, Gerard*, and salutes him, which Gerard returns; then Gerard goes to Hettie, whom he has not talked to yet, and says, *Good day, Hettie*, and high-fives her, and so on.

> Good Day, Everyone!
>
> It is a good day when we are <u>shrewd</u> enough to catch ourselves and others saying things that don't make sense. Put on your detective hats and get ready for the challenge of figuring out what's "off" when you hear or read arguments that don't hold water (that's an old expression meaning "don't make sense").

Activity

Logical Fallacies: Introduce the concept of logical fallacies: *Smart listeners and speakers avoid getting fooled. Watch out for logical fallacies: invalid, mistaken arguments. Sometimes they are intended to sound reasonable so they can deceive the listener, and sometimes they are unintentional. Remember the "Gotchas!"* (page 91)

Distribute the Logical Fallacies chart and "Reasons why football should/should not be a coed sport in middle and high schools" (below) to partners. Assign each set of partners at least one of the reasons. Partners describe in their own words what is wrong with the argument and try to determine which logical fallacy, if any, is represented in their argument. One of each of the partners shares out.

Reflection

Partner share: *Having caught the flaws in these arguments, what advice can we give others about being smart thinkers?* Give a time limit for sharing and issue a time warning halfway through the share to ensure balanced sharing/listening. Here some examples of advice:

Smart listeners and speakers: (examples)

- Connect what they say to other ideas
- Give evidence to support your opinions
- Use good reasoning

People who use logical fallacies a lot tend to: (examples)

- Keep on the surface and don't connect to other information
- Not supply reliable evidence
- Avoid or not understand logical thinking

Philosopher Roger Bacon (1220-1292) described four stumbling blocks to truth. Paraphrased they are:

1. Weak and unworthy authority (e.g., "A talk show host said....")

2. Longstanding custom   (e.g. "In my family we don't trust foreigners.")

3. The feeling of the ignorant crowd (e.g., "Our children should not have to go to school with openly gay people!")

4. Hiding our ignorance while faking knowledge (e.g., "Poor people are using up our country's resources with Medicaid and welfare.")

➲ This advisory may take more than one meeting. You can finish the logical fallacy exercise on the second day, then do the reflection.

Keep in Mind

In the reflection after today's activity, we identify what gets in our way when we try to think clearly. Roger Bacon said we have to think for ourselves, not just think and do what tradition or people around us or people in power tell us to think and do. We have to care enough about our fellow human beings to look for evidence—be willing to not know until we have reasoned our way to understanding. We must not be satisfied when we have only a partial picture, and we must not listen to others who pretend to know but lack clarity and evidence. There's no faking it: real understanding comes from the hard work of reasoning and caring.

Three of the logical fallacies named in this activity were also named in Perspective One when students discussed the way advertising tries to shape their thoughts and actions: sweeping generalization, name-calling, and bandwagon. You can remind students of that discussion. The next advisory meeting challenges them to put their fallacy-detection skills to use on the media.

Ask yourself
Do you ever use logical fallacies?

LOGICAL FALLACIES

Name of Logical Fallacy	Definition	Example
Sweeping Generalization	Making a broad statement based on insufficient evidence	Girls are sissies.
Name-calling	An attack on the person arguing against you	You said that because you are sexist.
Non Sequitur	The evidence may be true but it doesn't support the conclusion	Women make bad bosses. My uncle had a woman for a boss and she fired him.
False Choice	Only two alternatives are offered as an "either/or," and there are other possibilities	Who is better at athletics, girls or boys?
Red Herring	An irrelevant topic is brought up to take attention away from the issue being discussed.	I'm not voting for Henry. He wasn't born in this country.
Circular Reasoning	The evidence and the conclusion say the same thing, so you end up where you began.	The black kids will try out for football because black kids always try out for football.
False Analogy	Because two things are similar in one respect we can assume they are the same in another.	Andrea and Deanna live in the same neighborhood, so Andrea must have given the answers to Deanna.
Post Hoc, Ergo Propter Hoc	One event occurred after another, so the first event caused the second.	The special ed kids handed in their tests last, so they're the ones who cheated.
Straw Man	Pretending you are attacking the other person's position when you are attacking an idea that you brought up.	You shouldn't criticize me for coming to class late. Some kids play hooky, and that's against the law.
Slippery Slope	Proposing that a relatively small event will inevitably develop into a much larger and more problematic one.	If you let one student write an IOU for his lunch because he forgot money, everybody will want to do it.
Bandwagon	Speaker tries to get people to agree by pressure to conform to what others are doing.	More and more schools are requiring uniforms. We should, too.

Faked Precision	Making a claim with a mathematical precision that is faked or impossible to obtain or check out.	95% of students really *do* want to eat vegetables and fruits for lunch, but they aren't willing to admit it.
Appeal to Patriotism	Even though no proof is offered, opposition to an idea is said to prove a lack of care about or loyalty to the country.	We should have a school mascot because it's the American thing to do!

Reasons why football should not be a coed sport in middle and high schools

1. A girl was hurt playing football. Football is too dangerous for girls—they'll get hurt and shouldn't be allowed to play.

2. Lots of sports are played co-ed, like volleyball and tennis, so football should be, too.

3. Most schools have only boys on football teams. We should, too.

4. Girls can play rough sports like football, so co-ed football should be allowed.

5. The only people who are against girls in football are boys.

6. If you reject the idea of girls playing football, you are anti-girls.

7. If we say that every girl should be allowed to play on the football team, we're going to get a lot of bad football and kids will get really hurt.

8. Allowing girls to play football in school is like having women join the Boy Scouts.

9. Most girls really do want to play football, but they aren't willing to admit it.

10. A school I know let a girl on the football team and she quit after the first practice. Football isn't for girls.

11. We should allow girls on the football team because it is the right thing to do.

12. If we let girls play football, some people will be mad. If we don't let them play, some people will be mad. So we might as well let them play.

13. Once we let girls on the football team, girls will be using the boys' locker room and bathrooms, and then we've really got a problem.

14. Keeping girls out of football is a bad thing to do, so we should have girls play football.

15. Coed sports are the American way!

ADVISORY 16 ▶ CPR

Advisory goal: Recognize bias and logical fallacies in the media

Greeting

Ball Toss Greeting: Select a student to begin and give her a ball. She greets another student verbally and tosses that student the ball. The recipient of the ball returns the greeting, greets someone else, then tosses him the ball. This continues until all everyone has been greeted and has received and tossed the ball. The last student greeted closes the loop by greeting and tossing the ball to the student who went first.

> Media alert!
>
> We'll do more <u>sleuthing</u> today, this time in the media. Let's see if we can catch people in the media trying to persuade us using bias and logical fallacies. <u>Do Now:</u> How much bias is expressed in the media? Check your answer:
>
> A lot   Some   A little   None

➲ Which answer(s) did the majority of students give?

➲ Ask a student to model a safe, on-target, underhanded toss before you begin the Ball Toss Greeting.

Share

Think Pair Share: *Have you ever noticed media bias? Describe it.* Give students pencil and paper before the share to record their answers.

➲ Students may think back to Perspective One, Advisory 19, when they considered how media have influenced them. Today, they are trying to remember examples of bias they have seen and/or heard via media. If some students cannot think of an example, the Media Watch may be an eye opener for them.

Activity

Media Watch: Check the poll in the daily news to see which answer(s) most gave. Then give the following directions and chart to each student. Results will be shared in Advisory 22.

➲ Participate in Media Watch so you can discuss your results with students.

MEDIA WATCH

While you are watching TV or using other media:

1. Notice whether there is talk biased against people because of race, ethnicity, religion, gender, sexual orientation, or age. Listen for logical fallacies.

2. Under "Media," mark in which of the media you heard the bias or fallacy, then indicate which category the remark fits into: one of the culture categories or a logical fallacy.

3. Under "Comments," write notes about the item so you can describe it to us and explain why it was biased or illogical.

Example 1—"racially" biased remark: Golfer Sergio Garcia was asked a joking question about having dinner with his adversary Tiger Woods. Garcia said: "We will serve fried chicken." He later apologized for what he called a "silly remark," then added, "but in no way was the comment meant in a racist manner."

Example 2—logical fallacy: *Most women don't know anything about sports.* This is a sweeping generalization with no evidence.

Recording Chart

MEDIA	"RACE"/ ETHNICITY	RELIGION	GENDER	SEXUAL ORIENTATION	AGE	LOGICAL FALLACY
Ex. 1: TV	X					
Ex. 2: FaceBook						X
2.						
3.						
4.						
5.						

Comments

Example 1: Golfer Sergio Garcia was asked a joking question about having dinner with Tiger Woods. Garcia said: "We will serve fried chicken."

Example 2: *Most women don't know anything about sports.* (sweeping generalization with no evidence)

1.

2.

3.

4.

Keep in Mind

Media have tremendous power in setting cultural guidelines and in shaping political discourse. It is essential that news media, as well as other institutions, report fairly and accurately. The first step in challenging biased news coverage is documenting bias. FAIR (Fairness & Accuracy in Reporting), a national media watch group, has been offering well-documented criticism of media bias and censorship since 1986. They suggest ten questions to ask that help uncover media bias:

1. Who are the sources?
2. Is there diversity among the sources?
3. From whose point of view is the news reported?
4. Are there double standards?
5. Do stereotypes skew coverage?
6. What are the unchallenged assumptions?
7. Is the language loaded?
8. Is there a lack of context?
9. Do the headlines and stories match?
10. Are stories about important issues featured prominently?[17]

Ask yourself

What examples have you seen of biased or fallacious statements in the media?

ADVISORY 17 ▶ A+

Advisory goal: Understand the value of optimism

Greeting

Shuffle 'Em Up Greeting: Distribute a note card to each student. Students write their names on the cards. When you say, *Shuffle 'em up!* students switch cards with others three or four times, then sit down, hiding the card they are holding. When everyone is seated, tell students to stand again, find and retrieve their own name cards by finding, switching with, and greeting whoever is holding theirs, then sit down. When everyone has retrieved his or her name card and sat down, the greeting is complete.

> Hello, Change-makers!
>
> Today we'll take a look at two ways of being: optimistic (optimists expect good things to happen) and pessimistic (pessimists expect the worst). Since life is changing all the time, we know that good can turn bad, and what seems to be bad can turn out great. Today we'll try to transform one into the other as we play the Trickster with each other.

⊃ This is a very active greeting. Before beginning, discuss the appropriate way to circulate as you look for your card. Model how to hold the cards so they are easily visible, and review the criteria of a good greeting: eye contact, saying the person's name, a friendly manner. You may want to determine the words and gestures of the greeting ahead of time (e.g., high five and *Hi, _____.)*

As in any active process, students must use self-control. If they can't handle this fun and control themselves at the same time, stop the greeting: *We'll save Shuffle 'Em Up for another time when you can handle it.* (No scolding.) If only one or two students are out of control, direct them to sit out the greeting. At the end, be sure they get greeted.

Activity

Something Good about Something Bad: A student names something good in school, at home, or in life in general. The next person in the circle says, *Yes, but something bad about that is _____,* describing something bad about what the first person has stated. The next person says, *Yes, but something good about that is _____,* describing something good about what the second person stated. This continues around the circle as students alternately describe something bad about something good and something good about something bad. The "somethings" have to be plausible, not fantasy. The activity pushes students to think hard and imaginatively. The first person may begin either with something good or something bad.

Example: *I've got to go to my aunt's house on Saturday—what a bummer!*

Yes, but something good about that is your cousins might be there and you can hang out together.

Yes, but something bad about that is maybe your cousins will have friends over and ignore you.

⮒ If the good/bad cycle on one topic seems to peter out, you can end that cycle and have the next person in the circle start a new one. But it's fun to stick with the first one and see how many people can add something.

Reflection

Partners discuss:

Are you an optimist ("something good....") or a pessimist ("something bad....")?

Is one of these frames of mind more useful than the other?

⮒ Comment on the connection between optimism and a growth mindset (see below). Let students know they will explore the growth mindset in more depth in a coming advisory (Advisory 21).

Keep in Mind

<u>Optimists</u> (the word comes from the Latin word that means *best*) tend to expect good things to happen; <u>pessimists</u> (the word comes from the Latin word that means *worst*) are more aware of and tend to expect bad stuff. Optimism, the attitude that change is likely to be for the better if we work at it, is associated with a growth mindset.

Realism is the awareness that mistakes happen and things don't always turn out well.

Language like *Try again* and *I know you can do it* and *Mistakes and setbacks happen, but I can do this* keep alive the belief that productive work will yield positive results, even though there are setbacks along the way. With a mindset composed of a healthy mix of optimism and pessimism, we have the best chance of reaching our goals. "Something Good about Something Bad" demonstrates that life is a mix, and the way you look at it can determine the outcome. Advisory 21 looks in depth at the benefits of a growth mindset.

Ask yourself

In what ways does a growth mindset benefit your teaching and learning?

ADVISORY 18 ▶ A+

Advisory goal: Maintain an attitude about yourself that is open to possibility

Greeting

Cumulative Greeting: Each person greets everyone who has preceded him in the greeting. The first student greets the student next to her; that student greets her back, and greets whoever is next to her in the circle. This student greets her back, and also greets the first person. This cumulative process continues until the last greeter must respond to being greeted by greeting everyone in the circle.

> Good Morning, Friends!
> It's easy to misjudge people. When we see we were wrong, the thing to do is to step up and say so. Today we'll read about two guys who set things straight.

↻ Remember that a good greeting includes the name of the person, so the last person will name everyone in the room as he greets each one.

Activity

Rapping Freestyle from *Bronx Masquerade*, by Nikki Grimes: Read this paraphrase and excerpt aloud to students. Remind them that although today there are many good white rappers, in the early days of rap, almost all rap artists were black.

The students in Mr. Ward's high school English class in a Bronx, New York, high school write poems and then perform them at a poetry slam "Open Mike" hour every Friday. [Pause to explain that a poetry slam is an event where several people read aloud their poetry. "Open Mike" means that whoever wants to read can do so, within the time limits of the event.] Tyrone, Wesley "Bad Boy" Boone, and Sterling like to do "ciphers" (a joint poem recited by two or more rappers free-styling together, reciting extemporaneously, each feeding off what the other one says and the established rhythm). They could be battling, or simply playing off of each other.

One Friday, Tyrone stands up to perform a cipher with Wesley "Bad Boy" Boone and Sterling on guitar and is surprised when a white boy, Steve Ericson, asks to join him and his friend to perform the cipher. Tyrone just knows Steve is going to mess it up:

"The world ain't but one big surprise after another. Just look at Raynard. Or look at Steve. That white boy got more up his sleeve than anyone would guess. I ain't lying.

"Yesterday me, Wesley, and Sterling got up to do a cipher for Open Mike Friday and here come Steve, jumping up to join us. I laughed out loud. Didn't even try to hide it. I ain't never seen no white boy do no free-style poem. You know how hard that is? One person starts a poem, then the next guy has to step into the rhythm, pick up the poem where the first guy left off, and keep it going. Then, after a while, the third guy steps in, if there is a third guy, and he takes over, and then the fourth guy, and so on. You go round and round like that, long as you can keep it tight, or until somebody finishes off the poem, or you get tired. Whatever.

"Me and Wesley usually team up, going back and forth, with Sterling on guitar layin' down the beat. Sometimes we let Chankara jump in. She ain't half bad either, but then, she's a sister. What you expect? But Steve? Please. So of course I laughed.

"'Boy,' I said. 'Sit your white butt back down before you hurt yo'self.'

"'Give the guy some slack,' said Sterling. See why we call him Preacher?

"'Yeah brother,' said Steve.

"'You hear this white boy?' I said. I'm thinking he must like to take his life in his hands.

"Wesley studied Steve a minute. 'The question is, do you flow?' I figured that would be the end of it, 'cause I was sure Steve wouldn't even know what the brotha was talking about. How could he?

"'Yeah,' said Steve. 'I flow.'

".... I shook my head. I cut my eyes at Steve, betting this boy had never done a cipher in his life.

"'Just try to keep up,' I told him. 'Y'all ready?'

"Preacher set up the beat, and we took off.

"And guess what? That white boy can flow. Makes you kinda wonder 'bout his family tree, now, don't it?

"What else can that boy do that I don't know about?"[18]

Reflection

Give partners one question at a time, allowing a couple of minutes for them to discuss each question. After the discussion of each question, ask for volunteers to share out.

Sometimes we have fixed ideas about people. Tyrone was convinced that Steve couldn't perform well in the cipher. On what did he base his opinion?

Have you ever made a judgment about someone and then found out you were wrong? What was the situation? How did you handle it? Were you change your opinion?

What part did color and culture play in Tyrone's opinion? What stereotypes have you had (or do you have) about people from cultures different from yours?

Steve didn't live out the stereotype of his culture. Instead, he learned a skill associated with another culture. Have you ever learned a dance or game or worn clothes or liked music from a culture different from your own? How did you come to like it?

What was Tyrone's reaction after the boys performed? Did he change his opinion? Have you been able to revise any stereotypes you hold? Are you open to change?

If you won't have time for all five questions, choose a few beforehand to focus on.

Keep in Mind

Steve apparently had a self-identity that allowed him the flexibility to do things not generally associated with his color/ethnicity. That openness to ways of being and doing allowed him to try new things, to extend his talents, and to stretch the thinking of the people around him beyond stereotypes.

Productive use of identity

The productive use of identity is a way of knowing that we can bring into conversations with others, people like and unlike us. "We can create positive and meaningful identities that enable us to better understand and negotiate the social world... and in the process discover how it really works. They also make it possible for us to change the world and ourselves in valuable ways. This is what democratic and progressive social movements, such as the struggles for civil rights or the equality of women show very clearly."[19]

The danger in establishing a sense of ourselves is a locked-in identity that becomes a kind of prison. Then others might see us in that small compartment we have created for ourselves. Philosopher Michel Foucault rejected the idea of identity as assigning "a station in life, a recognizable identity, an individuality fixed once and for all...." Such a confining identity can only limit life, and Foucault said that any advantages from categorizing people would accrue only to the more powerful over the less powerful.[20]

Mental yoga

We have many options and possibilities, and a flexible sense of self allows us access to them. It can be unnerving to examine your self-concept if you have been settled in it for a long time; it's also difficult to do when you are still figuring out who you are and where you stand. Even so, staying flexible and open to growth is essential. When we attempt to wall ourselves off from change, not only do we fail to stop change, we also miss out on the good that comes with change.

Do our students think of themselves as finished projects, people who definitely *are* a certain way? It is especially important for adolescents to avoid the trap of what psychologist Erik Erikson called "identity foreclosure," fixing on an identity before one has lived enough to get to know oneself and one's possibilities. Such decisions close down possibilities for young people at a time when exploration is crucial to their development.[21]

Ask yourself

Have you closed down possibilities for yourself because you think of your own identity as settled and permanent?

ADVISORY 19 ▶ CPR

Advisory goal: Appreciate the vitality of language, a dynamic expression of the changing nature of culture

Greeting

Meet and Greet Greeting: Students stand, form groups of three, and greet each other. Groups invite anyone having difficulty finding a group to join them, even if it means having a group of four. The groups stay together for the Whip Share.

Dear Change Watchers,

Everything is changing all the time, including our language, which adopts <u>neologisms</u> *all the time. We're changing all the time, too. In fact, we'll all be a little different when we leave this room from when we arrived!*

➲ You may leave the form of the greeting up to students as they greet, or provide the form, or decide on one by consensus before beginning the greeting.

Share

Share in Meet and Greet groups: *Name one change that will have occurred to you by the time you leave this room—one apiece, no repeats.* Each student offers a brief response to the question (e.g., skin cells sloughed off; hair growth; aging; stomach emptier). You can invite students to share with the whole group a few of what they consider to be the most unusual or funny or dramatic changes mentioned in their small group.

➲ When groups share out some of their change ideas, make sure they identify whose idea each change was. Naming students who contribute something to a discussion acknowledges their contribution and encourages participation.

Activity

Our Changing Language: Students form partners. Give a card with a word and its definition to each pair of students. Students create a short dialogue using their word as it is defined. (Students may look up the origins of their word if they have time and have several up-to-date dictionaries.)

Presentation: Students perform their dialogues for the group and share their research if they have done any. To make the activity more playful, the presenters can "perform" the word and the audience can guess at its meaning based on its context in the dialogue. Students will already know some words, and others will be new to them.

Changing language definitions: Each year, Merriam-Webster publishes a list of the words it has recognized in American English that year. Following are 15 words that were accepted in 2011. The definitions following the words were composed from several sources, and the Merriam-Webster Online Dictionary definition follows, identified as MW. The first two words' origins are described to give an idea of the varied and imaginative ways language changes. The students who are assigned those words should share with the group how the words came into the language so students can see the twists and turns language takes.

- **bling** n. flashy jewelry worn to show wealth (from African American Vernacular Language—AAVL); first known use in 1999 by Weezy F. Baby (Lil Wayne) as a sound for gemstone sparkle.

- **bromance** n. Close platonic male friendship. MW: a close nonsexual friendship between men. This word derives from putting bro (slang for brother) together with part of romance, and was first used in 2004. Bro's origins have many explanations: derived from bros, an abbreviation for brothers, first used in 1838; from African American slang (AAVL); from skate-board culture; from the Afrikaans, broer, and others. Like many new words, various cultural influences combine to create a new word in English.

- **chillax** v. To calm down and relax. MW: to calm down

- **flash mob** n. Brief gathering for a common purpose, announced by e-mail or text. MW: a group of people summoned (as by e-mail or text message) to a designated location at a specified time to perform an indicated action before dispersing

- **frenemy** n. Friend with whom one has frequent conflict. MW: one who pretends to be a friend but is actually an enemy

- **green-collar** adj. Of or relating to workers in the environmentalist business sector. MW: of, relating to, or involving actions for protecting the natural environment

- **hypermiling** n. Altering a car to maximize its fuel economy. MW: the use of fuel-saving techniques (as lower speeds and frequent coasting) to maximize a vehicle's fuel mileage

- **locavore** n. One who primarily eats locally grown food. MW: one who eats foods grown locally whenever possible

- **meme** n. Image, video or phrase passed electronically on the Internet. MW: an idea, behavior, style, or usage that spreads from person to person within a culture

- **riff** v. To expound on a particular subject. MW: a rapid energetic often improvised verbal outpouring

- **rock** v. To do something in a confident, flamboyant way. MW: slang : to be extremely enjoyable, pleasing, or effective <her new car rocks>

- **staycation** n. Vacation spent at home. MW: a vacation spent at home or nearby

- threads n. (plural) clothing (AAVL)

- **viral** adj. Circulating rapidly on the Internet. MW: quickly and widely spread or popularized especially by person-to-person electronic communication

- **webisode** n. Episode or short film made for viewing online. MW: an episode especially of a TV show that may or may not have been telecast but can be viewed at a Web site

Reflection

Conclude the study of these new words by again pointing out the dynamic nature of culture, as we have already done in Advisory 7. Language is a dynamic, changing element of life, and every language has multiple forms: regional and cultural dialects; formal and informal forms; expanding vocabularies. We work to help students master formal, correct English; we do so in an atmosphere of acceptance and appreciation of the varieties of English.

Keep in Mind

Flexible use of language: background information that may be useful

Human language began about two hundred thousand years ago. There are between 6000 and 7000 languages in the world.[22] Language can be gestural, vocal, or visual; abstract or concrete, elaborate or abbreviated; emotional or cool, formal or intimate. Above all, language is social. We choose our words and tone and method of communication for our listener(s) and watch for response. The process is generative: we make it up as we go, designing the message as we deliver it.

English is an extraordinarily flexible language, adopting new words (neologisms) constantly. Many begin in slang; others are invented to describe a new object or process or custom.

Ask yourself

What are some words or abbreviations that have become memes among educators?

ADVISORY 20 ▶ A+

Advisory goal: Expand your view of yourself and others to be all that you and they might be, not just what you and they have been in the past

Greeting

Formal Greeting: Begin the greeting by having everyone state his or her last name: Mr. or Ms._____, around the circle. Then the individual greetings begin, again around the circle: *Good morning, Mr. Landry; Good morning, Ms. Costello*, with a handshake, as it would be in a business setting.

> Greetings, Friends!
>
> Even when we think we know someone, we miss the little changes he or she makes day by day. Watch out for the "stereotype slide," the tendency to see someone else as fixed and a certain way. Today we'll all choose <u>alter egos</u>, and we might be in for some surprises!

⮑ **Whole-group alternative:** Each person greets the group by saying, *Good morning, everyone. My name is Mr. (or Ms.) _____.* The group in unison responds back: *Good morning, Mr. _____.* This alternative avoids the problem of students not knowing how to pronounce certain names. You can begin with the unison formal greeting, and on another occasion use the individual formal greeting.

⮑ Maintain the line between nervous giggles and disrespectful laughter.

Activity

Secret Identity: Split the group into two teams, except for one student who becomes the announcer. Each team chooses a speaker. Every team member writes an "identity" or "alter ego" on a note card. The identity represents a part of themselves that may be quite different from their public face. The identity may be expressed by naming a famous person with whom the student identifies, or it could be a general designation such as "movie star" or "circus performer." Team members give the cards to the leader, who keeps the two team piles separated). The leader reads an identity from Team B. Team A decides together which member of Team B might have chosen this identity as his alter ego and tells their speaker who they think it is. The Team A speaker says the guess chosen by the team. If the guess is correct, the person identified moves from Team B to Team A. Then Team A gets another chance, and they continue to guess the identities of people on Team B until they guess incorrectly. When an incorrect guess is made, the leader reads an identity from Team A and Team B gets to guess. The game continues until all players are on one team or until you run out of time.

Reflection

Were you surprised by any of the alter egos? We tend to stereotype others, even our friends and family members, thinking we know them when there is lots we don't know. Share about a time when someone you thought you knew well surprised you.

Keep in Mind

Think critically and with feeling

In this advisory meeting (as in many of the meetings), we need balance between high-spirited playfulness and clear, careful thinking. Both must be expressed in respectful ways at all times, and it is our job to intervene if respect slips. Sometimes the intervention happens with the whole group. Other times it involves a private conversation. The goal is to encourage a sense of wellbeing, surprise, and excitement, along with respectful acceptance of everyone in the group, and willingness to see things from more than one point of view.

In the individual formal greeting, if a student has a hard time pronouncing someone's last name, have the person pronounce it clearly. If the greeter still can't say it correctly, have him practice it for the next time you do a formal greeting, and greet the student yourself, modeling the correct pronunciation. Explain that it is a sign of respect for someone to pronounce his or her name correctly and that everyone in the group needs to work on getting right everyone else's name. This is fundamental cultural respect.

In the activity, Secret Identity, we encourage students to try out different ways of being, to avoid pigeon-holing themselves or each other, so that everyone feels free to experience new ideas, new feelings, and new relationships. In a constantly changing world, there is always the possibility of change for the good. Yet sometimes as educators we flag in our belief that every child wants to be good, and can make changes to be a better person and a better student. Sometimes there is so much negative evidence! As we make room for the erratic ways that adolescents find their footing in life, keep in mind that they have the capacity to grow. All of them can learn successfully if we help them channel their exuberance, help them convert negativity to productivity, change old ways of remaining separate to new way of being together.

Ask yourself

Thinking about a student who has limited self-control or low motivation to learn, what do you wonder about that student?

What don't you know about this boy or girl?

ADVISORY 21 ► CPR

Advisory goal: Appreciate the benefits of a growth mindset

Greeting

P & J Greeting: Create pairs of note cards, each of which has a word which complements a word on another card. Give each student one card. Students mill about, each looking for the student who holds the index card that complements theirs. Students may say their words aloud, hold their cards aloft, and/or mime their words. When partners find each other, they greet each other and sit down.

> *Good Morning, Cognizant Ones!*
>
> *There's a big payoff for all this change we've been talking about. If everyone and everything keeps changing all the time, what does that tell us about ourselves?*
>
> *We'll talk about that after you find your P & J greeting partner. Pick a card from the pile and join us in the circle. Reminder: Bring in your Media Watch results next time!*

Pairs examples: salt/pepper; ketchup/mustard; wind/sailboat; milk/cookies

Share

Whip Share: *Encouragement based on belief that someone can get better and better at throwing, catching, or any other skill is essential for coaching in athletics, academics, and in working for a more peaceful world. If you were playing catch with a seven-year-old who couldn't throw or catch very well, what would you say to coach her or him?* Each student offers a brief response to the question so responses "whip" around the circle.

Activity

Mindset: Distribute the Mindset resource to students.

Reflection

A person with a strong growth mindset would answer: 1. Strongly disagree; 2. Strongly agree; 3. Strongly disagree; 4. Strongly agree. Considering your answers, would you say you have a fixed or a growth mindset? If fixed, how can you move toward growth?

Keep in Mind

Believing that we are all changing and capable of growth pays off. If we let go of our ideas of a "fixed" self and open up to the possibilities of our own growth and the growth of our students, we make room for healthy development.

My parents believed in me: "You will be successful!" My dad was an immigrant and he would work with me on homework and on my handwriting. From first grade on, I had to do 90 minutes of homework before I could play. That was the routine. They told me, "We can't help pay for your college, but you'll definitely go to college!" I believed them and I did it. (Seventh-eighth grade teacher)

The influence of culture is ongoing, and so are opportunities for change: when a door closes, a window opens. A growth view of human development sees all students in the process of becoming. It helps us shift from being absolutely sure about students to believing, hoping, working, and watching for change. British Prime Minister Harold

Wilson noted, "He who rejects change is the architect of decay. The only human institution which rejects progress is the cemetery."[23]

I had a student who had never experienced a demand for his personal best, so he didn't make an effort and was slow and sloppy in his work. He also would give digs to the other kids, for example if they had to take a break for a bit because of behavior. I was attracted to other misbehavers, but this boy was hard to get to know and like. I asked myself what would have to happen for him to be accountable. I decided to ask him a lot of questions that would help connect whatever topic we were on to what he knew, to his experience in life. I also realized that there was no one home after school, so I had him stay in my room to get his homework done. Spending that time with him in my room helped me like him more. (Sixth grade teacher)

Despite the limitations imposed by cultural and environmental influences, if we realize that something about our understanding might be faulty, or too limited, we can refrain from judgment. In the space that creates, there are possibilities for our students and for us.

One girl who would hardly speak at the beginning of the year was teaching us Vietnamese dances by the end of the year! (Fifth grade teacher)

I have had students who have challenged my repertoire of strategies and patience. I have seen students who have given up on themselves, and that is very scary to me. I once had a student who resisted doing any written work, but not due to a disability. He still participated verbally and was a CPR leader. He loved debates and read so he could argue his points. He was also a very talented artist. So I differentiated assignments for him so that he could first sketch his response, and then the drawings helped him record his answers in writing. Giving up is not an option. (Middle level social studies teacher)

I told my students I am dyslexic to show them that we are who we are, and that's the starting point. We grow from there. One year I decided to see if they could go outside on a nice day and work there, taking responsibility for their own productivity. It was a challenge for them to grow into, and it worked. They got so responsible we could work outside every nice day. Scattered throughout the playing field, they worked on math or social studies. They really worked. I could see them concentrating. It was a thrill for me. This is teaching—launching young people toward responsible adulthood. It was a thing of beauty. (Seventh-eighth grade teacher)

Tell stories of growth following setbacks

To keep open to the possibilities in life, students need to hear about people who have changed their lives for the better. Tell them about a time when things were going badly for you and you nearly gave up, or about students who have gone from failure to success, or famous people who failed at first, but never gave up.

See the Online College Web site list of famous people who failed at first. For example, Albert Einstein didn't look like a genius in his early years: "Einstein did not speak until he was four and did not read until he was seven, causing his teachers and parents to think he was mentally handicapped, slow and anti-social. Eventually, he was expelled from school and was refused admittance to the Zurich Polytechnic School. However, in the end, Einstein won the Nobel Prize and changed the face of modern physics."[24]

Additional reading
Mindset: The New Psychology of Success, Carol Dweck.[25]

Ask yourself

What is a way that you are growing?

MINDSET

Consider these two different ways of thinking:

Fixed mindset: Some people believe they have turned out, and they either have what it takes to succeed or they don't. They think everything is pretty much settled and fixed. They have a *fixed mindset.* When stuff happens, they know that they (or other people) are this or that kind of person, and the way things are is pretty much the way things will be. It's as if they are riding in a train, and they can only go where the tracks go.

Growth mindset: Some people think that when things are going smoothly, or changing fast, or when things seem to be stuck, we have choices. We might need help seeing the choices that are available to us, but we can work to make things better. These people have a *growth mindset.* When things go wrong, they think about what they can say or do to make things go more the way they want them to go. It's as if they are riding a bike, and they can pedal faster or slower, turn left or right, or get the tire fixed if they have a flat.

Which mindset do you have? Answer the following questions:

1. People are either born with talent and intelligence or they're not, and you can't change how talented or intelligent you are.

   Strongly agree   Agree   Disagree   Strongly disagree

2. No matter who you are, you can develop your talent and intelligence all your life.

   Strongly agree   Agree   Disagree   Strongly disagree

3. Failing at something proves you do not have the talent or intelligence to succeed in it.

   Strongly agree   Agree   Disagree   Strongly disagree

4. The most important factor in success is effort—how hard and persistently a person works at something.

   Strongly agree   Agree   Disagree   Strongly disagree

ADVISORY 22 ▶ A+

Advisory goal: Perceive media bias and illogic wherever it occurs

Greeting

High Five Greeting: In sequence around the circle, students greet each other with a high five. *Hi, Arnie.* (high five) Reply: *Hi, Roxanne.* (high five)

> Welcome, Media-watchers!
>
> Today we'll report on evidence we've gathered from the media—logical fallacies we've <u>detected</u>, and statements that seem to show bias. <u>Do Now:</u> Get out your tally results and add your tally to the chart.

Activity

Media Watch (results): In groups of three or four, students share with each other their results and examples of what biases or logical fallacies they have heard or seen in the media. Then small groups share out their results.

Reflection

Having watched for bias in the media and for logical fallacies, what is your impression about how widespread each is? Very widespread? Somewhat? A little? Not at all? What is your evidence?

↪ You can do the reflection as a share in small groups or ask for an Exit Card response. The latter will save time and will avoid having other people's opinions influence responses. Report the results to students in the next advisory meeting.

Keep in Mind

Americans' assessment of the accuracy and objectivity of news reporting is at its lowest level in more than two decades of Pew Research surveys, and our opinions of media bias and independence are very low. Just 29% of Americans say that news organizations generally get the facts straight, while 63% say news stories are often inaccurate.[26]

Ask yourself

Do you perceive much media bias? Where? How much?

ADVISORY 23 ▶ A+

Advisory goal: Know the degree and nature of the growth in human rights in the U.S. since the 19ᵗʰ Century

Greeting

Handshake Greeting: *Good morning, _____,* with a handshake. Review as necessary how you want handshakes to look and feel.

> Good Morning, Historians!
>
> Today we'll think about the way things used to be for certain groups of Americans: women, African Americans, Jews, immigrants, people who are gay or poor or handicapped or very young or old, and whether we are going in the right direction, and whether we're changing fast enough.

Activity

The Way It Used to Be: Group students into triads and distribute The Way It Used to Be. Triads review the resource and discuss the questions. One person from each triad (person with the longest name) reports out to the whole group one or two thoughts of the triad.

Reflection

Select volunteers from the whole group: *Who are the people who make changes in civil liberties happen in the United States?*

Keep in Mind

Cultural changes invite individual change

Culture changes, and we change. For example, people have changed dramatically in response to the automobile, radio and television, computers, and the Internet. Each of these technological innovations altered our culture, and people changed in order to take advantage of new opportunities and to cope with new challenges.

Major cultural shifts in our history include equality under the law for African Americans, Asian Americans, Native Americans, immigrants, children, people with disabilities, homosexuals, and women. These equity changes have been and continue to be fought over, demanded by some, resisted by others, but they are the law of the land. Slowly but surely, we change our ways of living and thinking. It's both unnerving and reassuring to know that our culture is constantly shifting.

Ask yourself

Does my teaching reflect excitement for my students' futures?

THE WAY IT USED TO BE

Human rights in the U.S., then and now

Then: 19th Century	Now: 21st Century
Slavery for people kidnapped from Africa or children born of people already enslaved	African Americans are officially free, but still struggle for fairness in voting laws enforcement, and other areas
Unfair wages, long, long hours, and terrible working conditions	Labor unions established basic working conditions, hours, and wages
No restrictions regarding how much or the kind of work children did	Only children 12 or older may work; hours are limited
Native Americans allotted only certain government-owned land to live on; many massacred	Tribal government and ownership of land; widespread extreme poverty
Only white men could vote	All men and women can vote, although some are systematically thwarted in certain states
Asians excluded from citizenship	People of all ethnicities can become citizens
Segregation by race	"Racial" segregation prohibited
Women prohibited from serving in the military; gays must stay in the closet	Women and gays have the right to serve in the military
No accommodation for people with disabilities	Persons with disabilities have equal access to public buildings and cannot be discriminated against
No government support for the elderly	Older people receive support from the federal government through Social Security, Medicare, and other programs

Reflection

Do you wish you had lived in 19th Century America? Why or why not?

What do you think caused the growth in civil rights and liberties over the years?

What further growth is needed in civil rights and liberties for all Americans?

ADVISORY 24 ▶ A+

Advisory goal: Learn the value and skill of seeing an issue from multiple points of view

⮑ Create letter/number tags ahead of time in sets of six using this model: A1, A2, A3, A4, A5, A6, B1, B2, B3, etc. Create as many tag sets as you need for all students. If students don't evenly divide into groups of six, spread the remaining students into already existing groups by making tags that read A7, B7, etc. See more instructions below.

> Welcome to the haberdashery!
> Today we have six different hats available for you! Pull a letter/number tag from the box to learn which group you'll be in and which hat you'll be wearing. In your group, you'll get your hat.

Greeting

Small Group Greeting: Students gather into their letter groups for the greeting. Each person greets the group, and the group greets back: *Good morning, everyone. I'm Irv.* All: *Good morning, Irv.*

Activity

Six Hats Exercise: The purpose of the Six Hats Exercise is to look at an issue from many points of view. The perspectives on the event switch as the different "hats" speak. At the end, the group analyzes the value of seeing things from more than one perspective.

Create groups using the tags students pulled (see daily news above). Each member of the group puts on one of the following "Six Hats" and speaks from that point of view during the discussion. (In groups of seven, two students can share a "hat.") The person with the Facilitator hat directs the process and does not have a particular point of view.

1. **Factual hat:** describe only the objective facts of the incident

2. **Emotional hat:** express how you feel about the incident (E.g., *I'm disgusted with the mayor and the council, and I don't believe them.*)

3. **Problems hat:** tell what is problematic about how people behave in the incident. (E.g., *Here's the problem: there's a breakdown in trust, because the mayor and council won't say who else was denied permission to march, and the GLBT group don't believe them.*)

4. **Sunny side hat:** tell what was positive about how people behaved in the incident. (E.g., *The gay group has been patient. They have followed the rules and procedures. And the mayor gave a good reason for turning them down, so everybody should feel OK.*)

5. **Solutions hat:** suggest ideas for how the incident could be resolved (E.g. *The gay group could be promised a spot in the parade the next year.*)

6. **Facilitator hat:** direct the process, calling on different hats to speak during the discussion: (E.g., *First, let's hear from the Factual Hat. Now we'll hear from the Emotional Hat. Tell us how you feel about this situation.*)

Incident: A city hosts an annual Halloween parade. A GLBT (Gay/Lesbian/Bisexual/Transgender) group, formed after the suicide of a gay high school student who was bullied at school, requested permission to march in the parade. The city council refused their request. The GLBT group protested, saying the council was discriminating against them, just as the high school had done when it tolerated the bullying. The city council said they were not discriminating. Their leader, the mayor, said there was no discrimination, and a number of other groups had also been refused admission. He said it was because the organizers wanted to limit the size of the parade so it wouldn't go on too long. When asked to name the other groups they had turned down, the organizers refused.

Reflection

The Facilitator for each group responds. Ask as many questions as you have time for:

How did switching points of view affect the discussion?

Do you think you can try on different points of view in your own mind when considering a complex issue?

Would it be useful to be able to switch "hats," or perspectives?

Keep in Mind

Being open requires safety

Being open to change makes it less likely that we will get stuck in stereotypes about people who are different from us. To guide students toward openness, we must maintain a questioning attitude regarding assumptions about others and about ourselves. A classroom culture of open-mindedness requires that everybody feel a sense of safety in the group. Without safety, student participation is greatly reduced: *I won't take the chance of being vulnerable unless I have confidence that my teacher and classmates respect me.*

We must create a safe climate in which people can be themselves. This takes a collaboratively constructed set of classroom norms (in the *Developmental Designs* approach, this is called a Social Contract; see page 22) and the teacher's enforcement of those norms by respectfully correcting rule-breakers. Playfulness helps students and teacher make and maintain connections, and high spirits are welcome but kept within bounds.

Students who have chaos in their lives may especially fear change. They need to see change as a source of hope and possibility. Growth is not possible without change. Talking with students about the big payoff in life of a growth mindset helps, but for a failing student, or a disruptive one, embracing change may be the crucial shift necessary for a turnaround. It is a daily challenge for teachers of adolescents to provide outlets for students' spirited energy while we guide them forward.

Malia, an angry, defiant girl with the Special Education designation "Emotional and Behavioral Disorder" came to our school. In conversations with her I asked, "Why are you doing these things? Why are you so angry? How can we help you?" That invited her to reflect a little, and she finally began to talk. It turned out that kids were calling her names. She was being bullied daily.

Her Special Education teacher and I worked with her every day for a while. We taught her how to manage her anger, to say "Stop!" and walk away. We also set up a conflict resolution process between her and the two sixth graders who had been the leaders of the name-calling. We had trained all of the students in the conflict resolution process, so we let Malia handle it herself. They did it! The boys were surprised but cooperated, and afterward I challenged them to step up as her protectors whenever she was hassled. They took on the responsibility and checked the bad stuff as soon as it started. Malia built the social skills she needed, and her behavior changed. She became focused. Her academic skills improved. Finally we were able to take her off the Special Education list, and she didn't have to leave the classroom because of her behavior for the rest of the year. (Fifth grade teacher)

Objective mindset

It's easier to refrain from judging a student if we ourselves feel secure. When our own needs are being met, we can be generous, and we can see that all our students have growth potential and can benefit from our guidance. When we're feeling strong and supported, we don't feel the need to blame them or their families or the school district or the legislature. *I can do this. I can be a guide for this child, even when she's offensive, even though I cannot understand right now where she's coming from. I don't have to take it personally.*

The world is in flux, and the troublesome students of today can be the achievers of tomorrow, especially with our help. With open minds, we can examine all the evidence regarding what is good for our students and what hurts them, and operate based on the evidence.

I gave a student a "D" on a writing assignment. He stood up in class and shouted a dirty expletive at me. I said pretty calmly, "You're going to have to leave now, and we'll talk about this." Later when we talked, I told him that I was a "fake target" for him. He listened, we talked, and over time we worked things out. Three years later, a young man was calling my name on the street. I looked around and saw it was that same student! He just wanted to say hello and went out of his way to do so—no grudges there! School is all about nurturing those relationships so kids can grow. (High school journalism teacher)

Ask yourself

Do you think you can switch your point of view when considering a student behavior or performance issue? How might the ability to switch be useful?

ADVISORY 25 ▶ CPR

Advisory goal: Develop flexible, open-minded thinking

Greeting

One-Minute Mingle Greeting: All stand in the circle and greet people with *Good morning,_____,* and a handshake. The greeting is returned, with a handshake. Students see how many people they can greet in one minute.

> *Good Morning, Friends!*
> *One mark of a strong person is that she or he is willing to change her or his mind when evidence supports that change. Keeping your mind muscle flexible keeps it strong!*

Share

Partner Share: *When you are thinking about an issue in real life, which of the six hats we wore yesterday are you usually most comfortable wearing?* Post a list of the Six Hats. Give a time limit for a share and issue a time warning halfway through the share to ensure balanced sharing/listening. Volunteers share out.

1. **Factual hat:** thinking mostly or only about the objective facts of an incident
2. **Emotional hat:** expressing how you feel about an incident
3. **Problems hat:** addressing what you think was problematic about how people behaved
4. **Sunny side hat:** focusing on what was positive about how people behaved
5. **Solutions hat:** suggesting how an incident could be resolved
6. **Facilitator hat:** acting as the person who keeps the conversation going, but doesn't express an opinion

Activity

Opinion Continuum: Designate the two ends of the continuum of opinion at two points far apart in the classroom with signs that say "Strongly Agree" and "Strongly Disagree."

Connect the two points with a line of string or chalk and mark a midway point. Explain to students that you are going to read statements to them, and their job is to move to a spot along the line or at one of the two signs that shows their opinion about the statement:

- If you strongly agree with the statement, go to the "Strongly Agree" sign.

- If you partially agree, but have reservations, go toward the agreement sign and stop close to it if the reservations are small, farther from it if they are serious.

- If you disagree, go to the "Strongly Disagree" sign or someplace between the middle and the strongly disagree sign, depending on the strength of your disagreement.

When the statements are read, students have fifteen seconds or so to place themselves along the opinion continuum. Then they talk with others about why they chose the spot they did. They listen to other people's reasons, and if they are persuaded in one direction or another, they move to a different place along the continuum line.

When students are settled, a spokesperson for each of the two end positions tells why s/he chose that position. After the statements of the end people, give students a moment to change their positions if they have changed their minds. One by one, volunteers can voice their opinions, and students can shift their positions if they change their minds. At the end, students can indicate which arguments that they heard were most compelling for them, whether or not they moved.

Statements:

1. Vegetables are the best foods to eat.

2. A person with an open, fair mind might change her position on an issue if the evidence seems to point that way.

➲ At this point, most students may be on the "strongly agree" end of the continuum. Allow a few minutes to talk about why it is important to change your mind about an issue when necessary. Invite students on the "disagree" side to state their opinions. The message of the continuum, like the message of Six Hats, is that we respect each other's opinions and we are willing to change our opinions if the evidence calls for it.

Keep in Mind

The purpose of many of the advisories in Perspective Four is to help students become comfortable with developing and maintaining a mind that is open to change when evidence leans in a different direction. Without this skill, we are likely to become stuck in a point of view, and in the belief that certain types of people *are* a certain way. This is the seed from which bias grows.

Ask yourself

Are there places where you find yourself stuck in an opinion and unable to pay attention to evidence to the contrary? Are there groups of people about whom your opinions are stuck, and you allow yourself to maintain a bias or prejudice?

---

[1] "Stress in childhood," U.S. National Library of Medicine, National Institutes of Health, http://www.nlm.nih.gov/medlineplus/ency/article/002059.htm.

[2] Linda Crawford, *To Hold Us Together: Seven Conversations for Multicultural Understanding* (Minneapolis: The Origins Program, 1990), 100.

[3] Lisa D. Delpit, "The Silenced Dialogue: Power and Pedagogy in Educating Other People's Children," *Harvard Educational Review* 53, no. 3 (August 1988): 293.

[4] Gloria Ladson-Billings, "But That's Just Good Teaching! The Case for Culturally Relevant Pedagogy," *Theory into Practice* 34, no. 3 (Summer 1995): 159-165.

[5] Chad Nilep, "Code Switching in Sociocultural Linguistics," *Colorado Research in Linguistics* 19 (2006): 1.

[6] Django Paris, "They're in My Culture, They Speak the Same Way: African American Language in Multiethnic High Schools," *Harvard Educational Review*, 79, no. 3 (Fall 2009): 432.

[7] W.E. Cross, L. Strauss, and P. Fhagen-Smith, "African American Identity Development Across the Life Span: Educational Implications" in *Racial and Ethnic Identity in School Practices* ed. R. Sheets and E. Hollins (Mahwah, NJ: Lawrence Erlbaum Associates, 1999).

[8] Rebecca S. Wheeler and Rachel Swords, *Code-Switching: Teaching Standard English in Urban Classrooms* (Urbana, IL: National Council of Teachers of English, 2006).

[9] Kat Chow, Luis Clemens, Gene Demby, Karen Grigsby Bates, Shereen M. Meraji, Matt Thompson, and Hansi Lo Wang, "Code Switch, Frontiers of Race, Culture, and Ethnicity," National Public Radio http://www.npr.org/blogs/codeswitch/.

[10] Jacob Nibenegenesabe, *The Wishing Bone Cycle: Narrative Poems from the Swampy Cree Indians,* ed. and trans. Howard A. Norman (Santa Barbara: Ross-Erikson, 1982), 33-34.

[11] John G Neihardt, *Black Elk Speaks: Being the Life Story of a Holy Man of the Oglala Sioux* (Albany: State University Press of New York, 2008), 149.

[12] Carl Bryan Homberg, "Loki the Norse Fool," *Fools and Jesters in Literature, Art, and History* ed. Vicki K. Janik (Westport, CT: Greenwood Press, 1998), 295.

[13] Barry Holstun Lopez, *Giving Birth to Thunder, Sleeping With His Daughter: Coyote Builds North America* (New York: Avon Books, 1977), 3.

[14] Stuart Brown and Christopher Vaughan, *Play: How It Shapes the Brain and Opens the Imagination* (New York: Penguin Group, 2009), 5.

[15] Sarah Goodyear, "Finding Effective Arguments for Funding Mass Transit," Streetsblog, May 12, 2009 http://www.streetsblog.org/2009/05/12/finding-effective-arguments-for-funding-mass-transit/.

[16] Andrea Bernstein and Nancy Solomon, with Laura Yuen and Casey Miner, "Back of the Bus: Mass Transit, race and inequality," TransportationNation by American RadioWorks, http://transportationnation.org/backofthebus/.

[17] "How To Detect Bias in News Media," Fairness and Accuracy in Reporting (FAIR), http://fair.org/take-action-now/media-activism-kit/how-to-detect-bias-in-news-media/.

[18] Nikki Grimes, *Bronx Masquerade* (New York: Penguin Group, 2002), 129.

[19] Linda Martin Alcoff, Satya P. Mohanty, Michael Hames-Garcia, Paula M.L. Moya, *Identity Politics Reconsidered* (New York: MacMillan, 2006), 6.

[20] Michel Foucault, *Discipline and Punishment* (New York: Random House, 1991), 291.

[21] Erik H. Erikson, ed., "Youth: Fidelity and Diversity," in *Youth: Change and Challenge* (New York: Norton, 1961), 1-23.

[22] Mark Liberman, "Languages of the World," http://www.ling.upenn.edu/courses/ling001/world_languages.html.

[23] Harold Wilson, speech to the Consultative Assembly of the Council of Europe 1967, *The New York Times,* January 24, 1967, 12.

[24] "50 Famously Successful People Who Failed At First," Online College.org, February 16 2010, http://www.onlinecollege.org/2010/02/16/50-famously-successful-people-who-failed-at-first/

[25] Carol Dweck, *Mindset, the New Psychology of Success* (New York: Random House, 2006).

[26] "Press Accuracy Ratings Hit Two-decade Low: Public Evaluations of the News Media 1985-2009," PewResearch Center for the People and the Press, September 13, 2009, http://www.people-press.org/2009/09/13/press-accuracy-rating-hits-two-decade-low/.

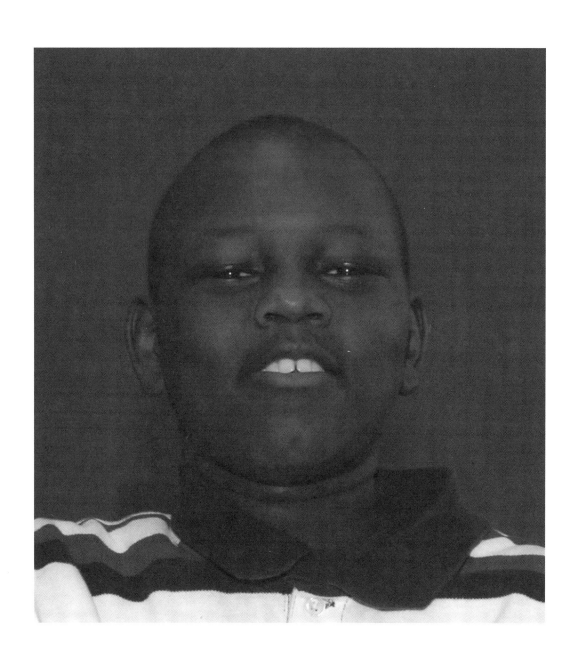

Taking a Stand

"Courage is what it takes to stand up and speak; courage is also what it takes to sit down and listen." (Winston Churchill)

Do we now have the courage to take a stand against bias and discrimination and *for* equity and inclusiveness? We saw in Perspective Two: Interdependence that we are we are interdependent and interconnected, even if we are unaware of or resist these connections. In Perspective Three: Us Versus Them, we saw that bias and discrimination are rampant, and what it costs us, others, and the world to keep people down.

We saw in Perspective Four: Open to Change the advantage we gain by accepting variety and change: we get unstuck from opinions that hamper our relationships and effectiveness in life and flex the muscle of perspective-taking. We may be wary of difference, but we can see the possibilities in ourselves and others.

Taking a stand against bias is risky. It can spark conflict, embarrassment, and/or rejection. But *not* taking a stand can leave one appearing to sanction prejudice. Saying or doing nothing can be passive acquiescence.

In an advisory community where students listen carefully and respectfully to one another, understanding and community take root. When students greet each other, play together and share stories about where they come from and where they hope to go in life, trust and safety begin to grow, and students can begin talking about more difficult things and take the risks required to bridge differences.

Taking a Stand in Advisory

Horace Mann, the "father of American public education," admonished graduates of Antioch College in 1859 to "be ashamed to die until you have won some victory for humanity."[1] In his lifelong work to bring public education to all of America, Mann helped people see the connections among poverty, ignorance, and mental illness, and their impact on society. He stressed that public institutions are essential for America to live up to its ideals, and public education is one of the most important of those institutions. He worked to convince people of the critical need for quality education for all. He wrote, "Education, then, beyond all devices of human origin, is the great equalizer of the conditions of men, – the balance-wheel of the social machinery."[2]

Today's schools have a lot of work to do to become "the great equalizers." Profiles of students who are Latino, African American, Native American, Alaskan Native, or living in poverty reveal that their ethnicities and socio-economic status are directly correlated to a reduced likelihood that they will succeed in school (see Appendix, page 345). An inclusive, culturally-responsive school experience can be the beginning of equity and success for adolescents.

A Vision for Community in Advisory

The meetings in *Face to Face Advisories* give adolescents daily experience of an advisory climate of respect, inclusiveness, discernment, and risk-taking. Such a supportive climate counterbalances divisiveness, bullying, chronic misbehavior, and academic failure. It is an atmosphere that makes school positive and rewarding for all students, regardless of their advantages and disadvantages.

An African American boy was considered gifted by the school, and they advanced him a grade, so he was the only sixth grader in my seventh-eighth grade advisory. The kids saw him as a sixth grader, so when I saw that he was good with words, I had him read my morning message aloud and try substituting other words for the ones I had used. I had to coach him on speaking loud enough for the students to hear him. Eventually he started writing his own morning messages, and I required all students to check with him first if they had any questions about the message. That helped him grow into the leader he became. (Seventh-eighth grade science teacher)

Sometimes great strides forward in learning come as the result of influences outside of school. Youth workers provide daily support for many adolescents who struggle with serious issues both at home and at school.

Kids in violent neighborhoods are often throwaways. They turn to violence and gangs and pick on each other in ways that are very destructive. Adults often don't help because they're trapped by their own limitations and biases. Morale deteriorates. This life prepares you or destroys you—you never know what will be the trigger point for a kid, what will help him disassociate from other youths and gain a larger perspective. Usually it's a strong adult. It all depends on having a resilient personality that gets toughened by experience, and it depends on luck to some extent. I worked with one high school senior who was an undocumented immigrant. She had given up and stopped working. I intervened, got dollars for her from a settlement, and she went to college. (Youth worker)

I was the coach of a boys' basketball team. They were young boys who had been expelled from school and were hanging out and playing ball. I told them they had to work in school to be on the team. I helped them value their education. Now some are fathers already, but out of the group, at least four of them went on to college. (Youth worker)

The work we do in advisory meetings to challenge bias can mirror conversations to counteract human cruelty on a larger scale. Holocaust survivor Elie Wiesel organized an extraordinary conference in Haifa in the summer of 1990 on the subject of hatred, attended by writers, scientists, and scholars who had all survived terrible experiences of human animosity. They pondered the causes of hatred and looked for hope despite the human tendency to turn personal hate into collective hate and murder. They had no final answers, but one after another, they agreed that the only thing that can stand up to the power of hate is people absolutely committed to freedom. Prime Minister Jan Scyce of Norway quoted Edmund Burke: "When bad men combine, the good must associate, else they will fall one by one."[3]

ADVISORY 1 ▶ A+

Advisory goal: Understand the courage and character needed to take a stand

Greeting

Cambodian Greeting: For a formal greeting, place palms together with thumbs close to your chest and say "*Chum reap suor*" (pronounced "choom reb suah") as you lean toward the person and lower your head slightly. For an informal greet-

> Welcome, Friends!
> Today we'll begin talking about what it takes to survive hard times, even <u>atrocities</u>, and develop the courage and determination to help others.

ing that could translate into something like "How's it going?" you can simply say "suk sa bye," pronounced "sook sah bye," with no hand gesture or bow.

➲ Do not permit disrespect. The gesture in the formal greeting is a small bow toward the person being greeted; it shows respect and friendliness. You can introduce the formal greeting by saying that you know everyone can do this respectfully. The informal greeting does not include the gesture. Choose the one your students can handle.

Activity

Arn Chorn-Pond, Cambodian genocide survivor, and Moments of Courage: Read the Arn Chorn Pond resource to students. After the partner reflection, introduce the Moments of Courage project.

Arn Chorn Pond

The Khmer Rouge was a political and military regime that controlled Cambodia with immense cruelty from 1975 to 1979. During its reign, more than 1.5 million Cambodian men, women, and children were murdered. Millions of Cambodians fled to refugee camps just over the border, in Thailand, where they lived in fear and hunger for years. Arn Chorn-Pond's family was murdered in a Khmer Rouge death camp when Arn was nine years old. Of the five hundred children in the camp, only sixty survived. The Khmer Rouge forced Arn to undress the children and hold their hands as they killed them. Arn finally escaped. He survived on his own in the jungle for a time, and then got to a refugee camp in Thailand. Eventually, he was adopted by an American couple, moved with them to New Hampshire, and graduated from high school there. But he was haunted by dreadful memories. The fact that he had survived when so many had died depressed him. In 1984, Arn co-founded Children of War, dedicating his life to ending the suffering of children who survived the Khmer Rouge nightmare. He has helped Cambodian youth in Cambodia and in the United States and has also worked to preserve Cambodian traditional music.[4]

Optional: Listen to Arn Chorn Pond on the Facing History and Ourselves Web site (ten minutes).

Reflection

Partners discuss as many of these questions as you have time for. Be sure to include #5: it is the beginning of a project in which the group gathers their thoughts, memories, and observations about moments of courage when people take a stand against prejudice and for justice.

1. How might the saying "What doesn't kill you strengthens you" apply to Arn's life? What qualities does Arn exhibit that probably helped him survive his ordeal?

2. Do you know someone who survived hard times and helped others? Have you?

3. If Arn had come to your school when he left Thailand, would you have gone out of your way to be his friend? Why or why not?

4. Describe any courageous acts you have witnessed, heard about, or done yourself, recently or in the past. Using an index card for each act, record three facts:

    • Who took the action? (Identify the person in some way: name, age, gender, or relationship to you

    • Where did you witness the event?

    • What happened?

    • What were your thoughts and feelings about it at the time?

    • Do you think you could do this yourself?

Moments of Courage Cards

While students read and interact with the daily news message for the next week or so, give them time to record on note cards moments of courage they experienced recently or remember from the past, in school or elsewhere. Collect these cards as students write them by having students drop them in a box next to the daily news.

⮑ **Before this advisory meeting,** write down on note cards moments of courage you have witnessed, heard about, or done yourself. Read your cards to students to help them understand the purpose and method of this project. Point out that small acts are important, too, like smiling at a stranger or sitting next to someone who's alone at lunch and starting a conversation.

Keep in Mind

It can be awkward and frightening to speak up against prejudice, bullying, or exclusion, or to call someone on a statement or act of bias, or to reach out to someone who seems different from you. This assignment calls on students to watch for and record any such moments they experience or observe or hear about, especially those that occur at school. An action need not be huge to require courage—for example, a moment when you could have kept quiet when you heard some gossip but spoke up against it, or when you could have ignored someone you don't know, but instead said hello.

You are an everyday hero

It's much easier to just watch out for ourselves, but educators watch out for others, too—a job that calls us to act courageously every day. Helping students learn, and helping them untangle a few strands in their often complicated, difficult lives, can bring satisfaction.

I never want a kid to feel the way I did when I was in school. (Fifth grade teacher)

I feel as if I live to make a difference in the world—to raise awareness about culture. I continue to educate myself, model behaviors I want to see, and know that I haven't figured it out and must keep on learning. (College educator)

In her book *What Keeps Teachers Going*, Sonia Nieto describes how teachers' commitment to their students is one of the biggest motivators for them: "Teachers who keep going in spite of everything know that teaching is more than a job. Junia Yearwood's [a Boston high school English teacher] thoughts about teaching probably reflect this idea best:

"'Maintaining my enjoyment and passion for teaching for over 20 years can be attributed to several reasons, two of which include the love and respect I have for my students and my personal need to remain intellectually alive. However, the principal reason why I continue to enter the classroom with energy and a sense of hope lies in how I view what I do. Teaching is not just my profession; it is my calling; it is my mission.'"[5]

We know a great deal about best practices, but they alone cannot address the frequently large gaps between a teacher's and a student's cultures. There are so many different styles and needs to consider and address, so many culturally-skewed opinions about each other, that only a strong commitment to serve and lead till students succeed can bring us over the finish line to success for all.

Ask yourself
Why did you become a teacher?

ADVISORY 2 ▶ A+

Advisory goal: Know about young people who have taken a stand for others

Greeting

Fist-Tap Greeting: Students greet each other around the circle silently or with *Good morning, (name)*, adding a gentle fist bump.

⮌ You can also use the Fist-Tap Greeting as a quick simultaneous partner greeting when time is short. Model and practice fist-tapping before beginning: make a fist, then gently tap partner's fist as *Good morning, _____* is exchanged.

> Attention, Everyone!
>
> Today we'll learn about ten young people who have been <u>designated</u> Giraffe Heroes, people who "stuck their necks out" to help others. <u>Do Now:</u> if you have a moment of courage to record, do so now on a note card and place it in the box. <u>Do Now:</u> Pick a number and sit next to the other person who has that number.

Activity

Giraffe Stories: Share the following with students: From students who speak up when someone is being bullied to young people who establish organizations to reduce the violence that cultural hatred breeds, there are young people who take action instead of walking away. The Giraffe Heroes Project honors risk-takers—ordinary people who "stuck their necks out" for what was right, in the U.S. and around the world.

Distribute stories: Divide the class into ten groups. Copy and cut apart the ten stories below, and give one story to each group. After deciding how they want to do it (in unison or one reader at a time, etc.) each group reads aloud their description of their "giraffe." If you need more giraffe stories, you can find them at www.giraffe.org.

⮌ **Optional performance extension:** You can make this a performance piece by adding some music or rhythm sounds between the readings. Use this advisory to prepare: practice reading expressively, add an introduction and a closing (perhaps invite the audience to step up and stick out their necks to reduce bias and discrimination), and/or add a musical/rhythm element. Your production could be performed for other advisories or at an assembly, or you could make a video. Use the optional meeting on page 299 to perform for an advisory.

GIRAFFE HEROES PROJECT STORIES

1. Sarah Cronk was a high school cheerleader when she decided to create a more inclusive cheerleading squad in her school. Her brother was excluded from many activities because he was on the autism spectrum, and this made her aware of the outsider status of students with disabilities. The Spartan Sparkles cheerleading team now includes ten disabled cheerleaders. Her goal is to start one hundred inclusive cheerleading squads through her organization, The Sparkle Effect.

2. Eric Love was a college student when he led protests against white supremacist rallies in Idaho and worked to make Martin Luther King Day a state holiday in Idaho. He also spoke publicly against homophobia at a rally and lost some support by doing so, but he continued his anti-bias stand.

3. Tammie Schnitzer, Sarah Anthony, Wayne Inman, Margaret Macdonald, Brian Schnitzer, and Keith Torney all responded to intimidation from anti-Semitic Aryan supremacists in Billings, Montana, by showing solidarity with Jewish families at Hanukah time. Like the Jewish families, they all put menorahs in their windows, despite the possibility that their homes, might become targets of the bigots.

4. Cheryl Perara, of Toronto, Canada, was inspired as a teenager to work to protect children being used as sex slaves in countries around the world. Cheryl founded OneChild, run by youth, working to stop commercial sexploitation of girls and boys.

5. Desiray Bartak wanted all kids who have been sexually abused to know they could stand up for themselves, so she went public about being abused by a relative. She convinced a high-profile attorney to bring a suit for damages against her abuser, and she won. Despite harassment from her classmates, Desiray continued to speak out and founded a support network for abused kids.

6. John DeMarco was 13 when he reported a neighbor for painting "racial" epithets on a home in his neighborhood—a home that a black family was considering buying. Neighbors objected to John's action, but he **persisted and testified** against the perpetrator, who was convicted.

7. Ernesto Villareal was a star high school football player who took a stand to stop racist taunts at football games. He risked his spot on the team by organizing Latino players to boycott football practice. The action stopped the name-calling.

8. Franklin McCabe III, a Navajo/Sioux teenager in Parker, AZ, used a music and light show he created in seventh grade to speak out against substance and alcohol abuse at Native American social events.

9. Roosevelt Johnson, a high school student in Selma, Alabama, founded a local chapter of 21st Century Leadership, an organization that enlists gang leaders in confronting racism. He also helped pressure slumlords to improve housing, established study groups, counseling, and voter registration drives.

10. Alberto Esparaze, took a stand to use his time and knowledge to help others. He created programs that help especially poor people and minorities in Arizona improve their lives.[6]

Reflection

If time is short, you may choose to select questions from the following list.

Why did they do it? What feelings or experiences might have caused each of these young people to want to help others in the ways they did?

What character and personality traits would help a teenager to take a stand and help reduce poverty, prejudice, and discrimination?

Do you know someone or know about someone who you feel is a "giraffe"?

Name one way, small or big, that you could stick your neck out and help reduce bias and bigotry.

How could our advisory share these giraffe stories with others to inspire them to stick out their necks against exclusion and bias? Do you think it would be worth our time?

➲ Before the reflection, remind students that change and growth are always possible, especially when someone commits to a project. (See Keep in Mind directly below for ideas to share with adolescents on this topic.)

Keep in Mind

There are plenty of resources about people who have acted heroically. It is important for adolescents to understand that these were not saints, geniuses, or people with special powers. They were ordinary people who lived by their values. In Perspective Five, students hear about and do research on people, including teenagers, who have taken a stand for a just and culturally-inclusive society. They learn about young people who made a commitment to work for justice and brought to their commitment the mindsets needed to make it happen.

Mindsets that empower us to take a stand

We need a *growth* mindset that keeps possibility present in the face of failure.

My uncles, grandparents, and father were all Sikhs in India. They were committed to serving, were mediators in disputes—peacemakers. My father taught me, "Be the first one to put your hand out." He taught me a code of conduct with people who were different from me, that I should treat lower caste people the same way as higher caste, that all were equal. I respected these men. I became a teacher because of them. Teaching is about passing along to the younger generation what really matters—making the world a better place. That's where I operate from: What can I do right now to help this child? Help the world? (Principal K-8 school)

We need an *action* mindset that keeps us vigorously helping students move from where they are to where they could be from the day they arrive until we pass them on to their next guide.

My colleague, Ms. A, and I both taught with a sense of investment and urgency. Two boys were acting out, had lots of suspensions. They were running me ragged. One day Mrs. A said to them, "You know Ms. L. loves you. No other teacher would go this far for you. At the rate you're going your future is either jail or you'll be dead. You need to take responsibility for your destiny." She spoke to them as a mother, a grandmother. "I'm not going to let you ruin your life. You cannot afford to do what you're doing." (Fifth grade teacher)

Teachers don't ask you what's wrong if you're quiet. My fifth grade teacher was my favorite—she helped me more when I was struggling. She talked to me. (Middle level student)

We need an *objective* mindset that preempts an angry retort and keeps us focused on the goal.

I say, "Let it go, and let's move on." I use this deflector whenever I see a conflict brewing. It is very important, and its implications are many: we need and value the student; we're in this together; we are responsible for our learning and our behavior; in order to move on we have to not get stuck in a minor conflict. (High school behavior specialist)

For a fuller discussion, review the mindsets descriptions in How to Lead Face to Face Advisories, pages 22-24.

Ask yourself
Which of the three mindsets is easiest for you to work on? Which is hardest?

OPTIONAL ADVISORY FOR GIRAFFE STORIES PERFORMANCES ▶ A+

Advisory goal: Become aware of people who take a stand

Greeting

High Five Greeting: In sequence around the circle, students greet each other with a high five. *Hi, Marta.* (high five) Reply: *Hi, Dan.* (high five)

> Good morning, Storytellers!
>
> Are you ready to spread the word about people who have had the courage to stick their necks out for others? Today we'll perform our readings for each other.

Activity

Giraffe Story performances: As time allows and as needed, prepare and practice. Remind students of the responsibilities of the audience; refer to posted guidelines, if available. See page 26 for audience guideline suggestions.

Keep in Mind

Although students can be inspired by reading and hearing stories about people who have taken a stand for equity, creating a performance has greater power: "The challenge of performance brings a sense of shared purpose, solidifies relationships within the learning community, and establishes motives for future community efforts and endeavors."[7]

Ask yourself
Do you know anyone who has stuck out his or her neck to take a stand against bias?

ADVISORY 3 ▶ CPR

Advisory goal: Understand the nature and purpose of codes of honor

Greeting

Handshake Greeting: Students stand. Going around the circle, students greet each other with *Good morning, _____* and a handshake. Review as necessary how handshakes should look and feel.

Share

Moments of Courage Share: Read aloud from the cards collected so far a few moments of courage. Acknowledge students for contributing to the project. Point out that acknowledging such acts is a way of speaking up.

It happened all the time, and I never had to cue them. Students thanked and acknowledged one another for things they shared in our advisory meeting, especially when the person sharing was someone awkward or introverted, Someone, could be a boy or girl, a close friend or not, might say, "Wow, you really did well today!" One boy was extremely introverted and acted as if he wanted to bolt for the door when called on to speak. He shared about something in his life one day, and another student said to him in a quiet, kindly way, "See, Sam, that wasn't too bad, was it?" One boy visited his brother while he was in jail, and shared about it on Monday morning. Three or four students acknowledged him for sharing something so hard, and said things like, "I hope you can visit him again soon." (Seventh-eighth grade teacher)

Activity

King Arthur and the Knights of the Round Table: Share the following information with students. The Lancelot story is better told than read, so if you can, relate it in your own words.

The Knights of the Round Table were carefully chosen by King Arthur and were said to be the best of the British military. The knights followed a code of honor and service. Here is a version of the code.

A Knight of the Round Table pledges:

- To never do outrage or murder
- Always to flee treason
- To by no means be cruel but to give mercy unto whoever asks for mercy
- To always assist ladies, gentlewomen, and widows
- Not to take up battles in wrongful quarrels for love or worldly goods[8]

Lancelot of the Cart synopsis: Following is a synopsis of a famous Round Table legend, "Lancelot of the Cart." The story is told in *Le Morte d'Arthur*[9] (The Death of Arthur):

Queen Guinevere was picking flowers in the woods behind Westminster Castle, with her ladies-in-waiting and page-boys and ten of the Queen's Knights. Sir Meliagrance, aware that Lancelot was not present to protect them, attacked with 160 men. To avoid her knights' being killed, Guinevere surrendered to Meliagrance, but sent a messenger with her ring to Lancelot with a plea to rescue her.

Gawain, who saw the abduction and rushed to follow Meliagrance and Guinevere, met up with Lancelot, and they continued together. Suddenly Lancelot's horse died. He stopped a cart that was passing by. The cart was for carrying lowly criminals, but Lancelot swallowed his pride and rode in the cart all the way to the gates of Meliagrance's castle. He was willing to suffer any shame to save the Queen. Gawain, on the other hand, followed the code of chivalry, refused to ride in the cart, and went another way. Lancelot arrived at the castle quickly enough to take Meliagrance by surprise. Meliagrance immediately surrendered, Guinevere was saved, and Sir Lancelot became known as 'Le Chevalier du Chariot,' the Knight of the Cart.

Reflection

On what basis did Lancelot make the choice to stain his reputation by riding in the cart? Was he following the code of the Knights of the Round Table?

What is the value of a code like Arthur's? How does the Arthurian code differ from your own?

With a partner, think of something you would include in a code of honor.

As partners share out, take notes to end up with something of a "code" that the group may adopt.

Keep in Mind

The Round Table was first mentioned in writing by Wace in his "Roman de Brut" (Story of the British by Wace of the Isle of Jersey, 1155 CE). The Knights of the Round Table were the highest Order of Chivalry in the Court of King Arthur, a British king of the 6th Century, and they met around a round table, which exists in England today. Although people today don't often talk about chivalry, many organizations have honor codes.

Codes of honor

"A cadet will not lie, cheat, steal, or tolerate those who do." (United States Military Academy)[10]

"I have neither given nor received unauthorized aid on this assignment." (Middlebury College)[11]

I will do my best to be honest and fair, friendly and helpful, considerate and caring, courageous and strong, and responsible for what I say and do, *and to* respect myself and others, respect authority, use resources wisely, make the world a better place, and be a sister to every Girl Scout. (The Girl Scout Law)[12]

Ask yourself

Do you and/or your family live by an honor code?

ADVISORY 4 ▶ A+

Advisory goal: Become informed about one way that a citizen of the U.S. can work for equity and against bias

Greeting

Handshake Greeting: Students greet each other around the circle with *Good morning, _____* and a handshake.

Activity

Guest shares about justice work against bias and discrimination

Guest possibilities: To inspire students to take a stand for justice and against bias and discrimination, look for a guest who has taken such a stand. This need not be his or her main career, but it could be. The guest may be someone who volunteers in work for justice, through an organization or independently. Consider people who work for affordable housing or for discrimination-fighting organizations such as the NAACP. Students need to know there are many ways to work for equity and social justice.

Guest preparation: Tell the guest about the conversations you have been having in advisory, and about the demographics of the group. Suggest that the guest tell a brief story about his/her work, and that he/she share his/her feelings about the work. Ask him/her if the students may ask questions after his/her talk—and he/she may want to ask the students a question, too. Whether the guest works for pay or is a volunteer, she should talk about the satisfaction she gets from her work. She can include the parts that are satisfying and sometimes fun as well as the discouraging parts and frustrating parts.

Student preparation: Prepare students with some context: who is he? What does he do? Where? Brainstorm some questions, such as: *When and how did you first stand up against bias? Why is your work important? Do people thank you? How much does it cost to do your work? Where do you get the money you need? Do you ever feel discouraged? Do other people work with you? Is it ever fun? What made you decide to work for this cause?*

Audience response: Students ask questions and make respectful comments about their reactions to what they have heard and make comparisons or contrasts with their own lives.

Guest acknowledgment: Choose a couple of students ahead of time to prepare to thank the guest by acknowledging the contribution she or he has made to the group. Any others who wish to can add their thanks. Follow up with a written thank you note to the guest.

> Good Morning, Friends!
>
> Please welcome our guest, _____.
> She works for equity and tolerance in her job as _____. She'll share with us some moments of courage that she has had or has <u>witnessed</u>. Be ready to ask questions that will help us better understand her work and why she chose it.
> <u>Do Now</u>: Record a moment of courage on a card and drop it in the box.

Reflection

What insight or information did you gain from our guest?

➲ You can ask this while the guest is still present or after she leaves.

Keep in Mind

Try to avoid inviting guest who might bring overt political or religious messages. Some examples of types of organizations from which a guest might come to speak about working for cultural equity are:

Civil rights

Immigration rights

Disability rights

Elder, family, children's right

Women's rights

Gay, lesbian, bisexual, transgender rights

Ask yourself

Have you overlooked an area of equity and justice concerns that a guest might address? (This might guide your choice of guest.)

ADVISORY 5 ▶ A+

Advisory goal: Understand the courage it takes to speak up for someone else

Greeting

Roll Call Greeting: Start a steady rhythmic clap that all students join. Once the rhythm is steady, students chant the following:

Roll call, check the beat,

Check, check, check the beat

Roll call, check the beat,

Check, check, checka begin!

> *Good Day, Everyone!*
> *Today we'll use the Roll Call Greeting. Get ready to check the beat! We'll also read about Chiune Sugihara, who took action for others even though it cost him personally.*
> *Do Now: Record a moment of courage on an index card and place it in the box.*

As the rhythmic clap continues, individual greetings begin. Select a student to greet first, who says:

My name is (name)!

Group response: *Check!*

Next, the student says: *They call me* (nickname)!

Group response: *Check!*

The student says: *I am a student!* (or something else, as long as it's positive)

Group response: *Check!*

The student says: *That's what I am!*

Group response: *That's what s/he is!*

The class resumes the chant: *Roll call, check the beat....* When the chant ends (*Check, check, checka begin!*), the student to the right of the first student says, *My name is_____!* The group responds: *Check!* and the greeting exchange continues until all have introduced themselves.

⮑ If this is your first Roll Call greeting, keep the rhythm very simple. As students become more familiar with it, they can vary the rhythm as well as the self-descriptions.

Activity

The Heroism of Chiune Sugihara: Read the following story aloud.

"[I]n 1940, a Japanese consulate official in Lithuania, Chiune Sugihara, guided by his Samurai values, signed more than 2,000 visas for Jews hoping to escape the Nazi invasion, despite his government's direct orders not to do so. Every morning when Sugihara got up and made the same decision to help, every time he signed a visa, he acted heroically and increased the likelihood of dire consequences for himself and his family. At the end of the war he was unceremoniously fired from the Japanese civil service.

"Accounts of Sugihara's life show us that his effort to save Jewish refugees was a dramatic finale to a long list of smaller efforts, each of which demonstrated a willingness to occasionally defy the strict social constraints of Japanese society in the early 20th century. For example, he did not follow his father's instructions to become a doctor, pursuing language study and civil service instead; his first wife was not Japanese; and in the 1930s, Sugihara resigned from a prestigious civil service position to protest the Japanese military's treatment of the Chinese during the occupation of Manchuria. These incidents suggest that Sugihara already possessed the internal strength and self-assurance necessary to be guided by his own moral compass in uncertain situations. We can speculate that Sugihara was more willing to assert his individual view than others around him who preferred to 'go along to get along.'

"Also, Sugihara was bound to two different codes: He was a sworn representative of the Japanese government, but he was raised in a rural Samurai family. Should he obey his government's order to not help Jews (and, by extension, comply with his culture's age-old more not to bring shame on his family by disobeying authority)? Or should he follow the Samurai adage that haunted him, "Even a hunter cannot kill a bird which flies to him for refuge"? When the Japanese government denied repeated requests he made for permission to assist the refugees, Sugihara may have realized that these two codes of behavior were in conflict and that he faced a bright-line ethical test.

"Interestingly, Sugihara did not act impulsively or spontaneously; instead, he carefully weighed the decision with his wife and family. In situations that auger for social hero-ism, the problem may create a "moral tickle" that the person cannot ignore—a sort of positive rumination, where we can't stop thinking about something because it does not sit right with us."[13]

Many Jews were saved by Sugihara's decision to allow them passage through Japan. One of these might have been Agathe Glaser, a twelve-year old girl, who traveled by train from Germany all the way to Japan, hoping to take a ship to America. At Japanese customs, officials held up her papers:

"For what seemed like hours but was perhaps only minutes, the officials sat bent over my passport, grinning in what I thought was embarrassment. Suddenly I knew—my visa had expired! That was why Fred had to get me out of Berlin first. That was why I had to leave without my brother. ….Then they called me. One of them wrote something in the passport, another stamped it and handed it back to me. They all smiled broadly and bowed. I was free to go…."[14]

Reflection

What two codes of behavior did Sugihara have to choose between? What choice did he make?

Why did he make that choice?

What choices would you have if you saw someone bullying someone?

Can you tell about a time when you made a choice based on your values and code of honor?

Describe an incident you know of when someone took heroic action based on his or her values.

Keep in Mind

Taking action

Through the Perspectives' advisories, you have been taking action for respect and appreciation of people's differences and against bias. By the time you arrive at this fifth perspective, which asks everyone to take a stand, you have demonstrated courage on a daily basis for quite a while! The same is true for your students, to the extent that they have participated fully and with open minds in the advisory conversations.

Here are two more avenues for action:

Read about the Righteous Among the Nations: During an advisory or a class period, introduce students to the stories of non-Jews in Nazi Germany and in occupied countries who risked their lives to save and protect Jews. If not for their courage, many more Jews would have been killed by the Nazis. Over 22,000 people performed these acts of human kindness because helping people in need is the right thing to do. They are honored as the "Righteous Among the Nations" at Yad Vashem, the world center for documentation, research, education, and commemoration of the Holocaust.[15]

Use film clips: There are many film clips that can deepen a discussion of the price we all pay for human cruelty. The University of Southern California Shoah Foundation Institute for Visual History and Education Web site offers a library of nearly 52,000 video clips.[16] You can watch a video clip of an interview with a rescuer and reflect on it in a future advisory meeting or during a class period, if appropriate to the curriculum. The mission of the Shoah Foundation is to overcome prejudice, intolerance, and bigotry and the suffering they cause through the educational use of the Institute's visual history testimonies.

Ask yourself

What was a time when you spoke up on behalf of someone who needed support?

ADVISORY 6 ▶ CPR

Advisory goal: Learn to respond to negativity with positivity

⮑ As students are gathering and reading the message or writing on cards, you can engage with individuals about moments of courage they can write about, especially if someone has not written a card yet.

Morning, All!

A 1968 song from Sly and the Family Stone called "Are You Ready" says: "Don't hate the black/Don't hate the white/If you get bit/Just hate the bite!" Find your beat, and get ready to make a rap or song or poem or cheer that tells people to accept others who are different from them. <u>Do Now</u>: Record a moment of courage on a note card and put it you-know-where.

Greeting

Partner Greeting: Partners greet each other in a way of their choosing. Of course, the greeting must include the person's name, eye contact, and a friendly tone.

⮑ Students keep their partners for the share and activity. You can have some fun setting up the partners. See page 22 for ideas.

Share

Partner Share: *Who are some rappers or singers you like? What do you like about them?* Give a time limit for a share and signal when partners should switch roles. Volunteers share out.

Activity

Speak Up: In partners, students create a four-line rap, song, poem, or cheer meant to inspire people to love, not hate.

⮑ Write a rap, song, poem, or cheer and share it with students to give them an additional example. You can also share examples of cheers (examples on page 350).

Keep in Mind

It's important to speak out against bias and for equity. One way we can do that is by using poetry or song, appealing to listeners both rationally and emotionally. The power of imaginative forms of communication is that they can move us to action not just because we *think* it's the right thing to do, but also because we *feel* committed to setting things right.

The protest song *We Shall Overcome* was derived from a gospel song and became an anthem of the civil rights movement. Protesters sang it marching and in jail, at sit-ins and concerts. Today it is sung and continues to inspire people worldwide.

Ask yourself

Has a song, poem, or rap ever shifted your thinking from negative to positive?

ADVISORY 7 ▶ A+

Advisory goal: Learn to respond to negativity with positivity

Greeting

One-Minute Mingle Greeting: Each person greets as many students by name as possible in one minute. Model how to be greeted and return a greeting, maintaining eye contact, before moving on to the next person.

Activity

Speak Up (continued): Allow a few minutes for students to prepare to perform their raps, songs, poems, and cheers. Partners perform for the group. Draw names at random if people are reluctant to go first. If more time is needed for the performances, add an advisory.

⮑ One way to shorten the time of the performances is to have partners perform in groups of six instead of for the whole group. This lowers the pressure, but it means you have to monitor several groups at the same time.

> Hey, Group!
> Today you'll finish your raps, songs, poems, and cheers and have some time to share them. To get things started, I'll perform first! Write below one way that an audience member can <u>reinforce</u> a performer. Put your initials next to your idea. Heads up! <u>Do Now</u>: Record a moment of courage on a note card and put it in the box. Tomorrow we'll hear some of the moments we've written down. Keep your eyes and ears open for a moment you can record.

⮑ See page 26 for audience guideline suggestions. Post the guidelines near the message as a reminder, and briefly review them.

Reflection

What is the advantage in using a song, poem, rap, or cheer to get a message across to others?

Keep in Mind

A growth mindset prompts people to live for the possibilities of the future. Skepticism about the likelihood of success need not stand in the way of commitment and action to make our school or our neighborhood a place where everyone is welcome. Since the world is constantly in flux, it is likely that we will at least partially succeed!

Whenever we talk about changing the world, someone is bound to be skeptical. Watch out for naysayers disguising as realists! Ask them to consider how it weakens us to let the past determine the future. Defeatism is based on fear of failure; hope is based on understanding that what we do can change who we are.

I want to be a student all my life and pass that on to young people. If you don't remain a learner, you foreclose yourself. My job is to get those foreclosure signs down! In middle schools kids begin to put up a know-it-all façade and I need to tell them that tough guys don't need to have a façade. They can say to themselves, "I don't need to know everything now." The process of discovery is what is important for them—and for me! (Middle school principal)

Ask yourself

What do you do to keep on the sunny side?

ADVISORY 8 ▶ CPR

Advisory goal: Imagine yourself intervening on behalf of the target in a situation of bias or discrimination.

Greeting

Let Me See Your Walk Greeting: A student is selected to begin. He pantomimes doing something he enjoys (e.g., playing ball, doing homework, eating) as he walks across the circle to another student. He greets her and asks to see her "walk." She returns his greeting, they exchange places, and she pantomimes a favorite activity as she crosses the circle to another student. This is repeated until all have been greeted.

Welcome, Walkers!

Today we'll see how many ways we can dream up to perambulate (that means walk!) across the circle and greet each other in the Let Me See Your Walk greeting. We'll also hear some of the Moments of Courage we have been collecting. Do Now: Record a moment of courage on a note card and drop it in the box. Last chance!

Example: Ted mimes swinging a baseball bat as he walks across the circle to Shalana. He says, *Good morning, Shalana, let me see your walk.* Shalana says, *Good morning, Ted, watch this!* and crosses the circle pretending to paint. She greets another student and the greeting continues.

Share

Partners Talk It Over Share: Present the focus quote below. Then partners discuss the focus question: *Has there ever been a time when you could have spoken out against bullying or exclusion, but didn't? Why not?* Volunteers share out.

Focus quote—read aloud: Pretending that acts of prejudice and discrimination are not your fault, going along with bad things that people in authority do because you are indifferent to what does not noticeably harm you, or because you are simply doing your duty, or you are afraid, is avoidance of responsibility. Pastor Martin Niemöller described the result of such avoidance:

"First they came for the socialists, and I did not speak out because I was not a socialist. Then they came for the trade unionists, and I did not speak out because I was not a trade unionist. Then they came for the Jews, and I did not speak out because I was not a Jew. Then they came for me, and there was no one left to speak for me." (Pastor Martin Niemöller, c. 1946)[17]

➲ Martin Niemöller (1892–1984) was a Lutheran pastor in Germany during the Nazi era. He was an early supporter of the Nazi regime, but was later imprisoned for his opposition to government control of the Lutheran Church. He survived, and afterward expressed regret for not having done enough for other Nazi victims before he was arrested.[18]

Activity

What Would You Do? Situations that call for courage: Read aloud from a few of the Moments of Courage cards. Courage is all around us in ordinary life. Noticing and acknowledging it is inspiring. Read more cards in future advisories.

What Would You Do?

In this activity, students think about how they could act courageously. Read the following scenario and question. Partners consider the scenario together and come up with responses. Volunteers share out.

➲ If several people want to speak, limit responses to one minute to allow all to be heard.

Scenario: There is gossip going around school about two boys who are best friends. People are saying they are gay. *What would you do if you heard the gossip?*

➲ A powerful alternative would be to consider a current issue in your school, or create a scenario inspired by one of the Moments of Courage described by students, withholding what the actual response was until students have said what they would do.

Keep in Mind

Action

Commitment requires action. In turn, action reinforces commitment, which then requires more action. Creating an inclusive advisory and building student skills in bridging cultural differences is the action this book calls for. Beyond this considerable task, teachers and students can brainstorm projects and actions students could take, or look for projects that the group could do together that would be steps toward a more inclusive school and society.

Ask yourself

Is there a situation of bias or prejudice in your school that you might address in this or a future advisory meeting?

ADVISORY 9 ▶ CPR

Advisory goal: Appreciate the importance of being responsive with one another

Greeting

Basic Greeting: In sequence around the circle, each person greets his/her neighbor with *Good morning, _____.*

Share

Readers Theater Share: Jesús Colón's sketch from *Little Things are Big*: Read aloud, or give to students to take turns reading portions. Then partners or group discuss the reflection questions.

> Hola, Friends!
>
> Jesús Colón was born in Puerto Rico, moved to New York when he was sixteen, and became one of the first Puerto Ricans to write and publish his writings in English. He said that sometimes daily little decisions we make in life are the most important. Do you agree? Place a check mark next to either Yes or No.
>
> Yes   No

LITTLE THINGS ARE BIG

Colón first wrote this sketch in 1957 as part of Puerto Rican in New York and Other Sketches *for a New York magazine, Mainstream.*

"I've been thinking; you know, sometimes one thing happens to change your life, how you look at things, how you look at yourself. I remember one particular event. It was when? 1955 or '56...a long time ago. Anyway, I had been working at night. I wrote for the newspaper and, you know, we had deadlines. It was late after midnight on the night before Memorial Day. I had to catch the train back to Brooklyn; the West Side IRT. This lady got on to the subway at 34th and Penn Station, a nice looking white lady in her early twenties. Somehow she managed to push herself in with a baby on her right arm and a big suitcase in her left hand. Two children, a boy and a girl about three and five years old, trailed after her.

"Anyway, at Nevins Street I saw her preparing to get off at the next station, Atlantic Avenue. That's where I was getting off, too. It was going to be a problem for her to get off; two small children, a baby in her arm, and a suitcase in her hand. And there I was also preparing to get off at Atlantic Avenue. I couldn't help but imagine the steep, long concrete stairs going down to the Long Island Rail Road and up to the street. Should I offer my help? Should I take care of the girl and the boy, take them by their hands until they reach the end of that steep long concrete stairs?

"Courtesy is important to us Puerto Ricans. And here I was, hours past midnight, and the white lady with the baby in her arm, a suitcase and two white children badly needing someone to help her.

"I remember thinking; I'm a Negro and a Puerto Rican. Suppose I approach this white lady in this deserted subway station late at night. What would she say? What would be the first reaction of this white American woman? Would she say: 'Yes, of course you may help me,' or would she think I was trying to get too familiar or would she think worse? What do I do if she screamed when I went to offer my help? I hesitated. And then I pushed by her like I saw nothing as if I were insensitive to her needs. I was like a rude animal walking on two legs just moving on, half running along the long the subway platform, leaving the children and the suitcase and the woman with the baby in her arms. I ran up the steps of that long concrete stairs in twos and when I reached the street, the cold air slapped my warm face.

"Perhaps the lady was not prejudiced after all. If you were not that prejudiced, I failed you, dear lady. If you were not that prejudiced I failed you; I failed you too, children. I failed myself. I buried my courtesy early on Memorial Day morning.

"So here is the promise I made to myself back then: if I am ever faced with an occasion like that again, I am going to offer my help regardless of how the offer is going to be received. Then I will have my courtesy with me again."[19]

Reflection

What do you think would have happened if Colón had offered to help?

Have you ever been conflicted about whether to speak up or step up? Describe.

What would you do if you were in a situation where it was risky to offer help?

Activity

Call and Response Rhythms:

1. "Call" to the students by patting your knees, clapping your hands, and/or snapping your fingers in a rhythmic pattern.

2. The student to your right responds with his own short rhythm.

3. Repeat your initial rhythm.

4. Everyone simultaneously repeats the first student's response.

Repeat Step 1: Call to the students again (use the same rhythm each time you call), and the next student responds with her rhythm, you repeat the call, and then the whole group responds with the second student's rhythm. Continue around the circle: each student listens to your call, responds with his own rhythm, you repeat your call, and everyone simultaneously repeats each student response.

Keep in Mind

Responsiveness helps us get along in a diverse world. It requires watching carefully for opportunities to help others. The Merriam-Webster definition of *responsive* is "quick to <u>respond</u> or react appropriately or sympathetically." Responsiveness helps us make music together, work together, play well, and make friends across our differences. We don't get it right every time, but the intention to be responsive to our fellow human beings can carry us a long way toward a mutually supportive diverse society.

Ask yourself

On teaching days when you don't feel very energetic, what strategies help keep you connected to and supportive of your students?

ADVISORY 10 ▶ CPR

Advisory goal: See the good in overcoming fear and discomfort to stand up for what you think is right

Greeting

High Five/Low Five Greeting: In sequence around the circle, students greet and high-five their neighbors. The neighbor greets and low fives them back. *Hi, Roberta* (high five). *Hi, Jake* (low five).

> Welcome, Dancers (that means everyone)! Get ready to move as we try Doin' the Rumba!

Share

Whip Share: *What is a time when you were embarrassed or afraid?* Each student offers a brief response; responses quickly "whip" around the circle.

➲ This is a risky share topic. Go first—share a small embarrassment or moment of fear that you overcame: *I was embarrassed when I forgot my lines in a play. I was afraid when I started swimming lessons. I was really scared the first day I came to school as a teacher rather than a student!*

Activity

Doing the Rumba: This activity calls for students to stick out their necks in a "dance" performance. Making ourselves vulnerable in public may help warm us up for taking risks to support each other.

With everyone standing in a circle, one student begins making dance gestures while saying, *This is the way to do the rumba.* Everyone repeats the action. The next person says, *No, this is the way to do the rumba,* and adds another action. The group adds the second move to the first, doing both moves. The third person says, *No, this is the way to do the rumba,* adding a third action. The group repeats all three actions in order, and the game progresses in this manner around the circle.

➲ Point out that even a simple move will add to the challenge as the gestures accumulate.

Keep in Mind

One reason bystanders don't interfere with bullying is that they don't want to call attention to themselves. That's tragic, because "When peers intervene, they are successful in stopping bullying about half the time."[20] If we can help students call up the courage to step in when peers are being bullied, we can significantly reduce the incidence of bullying in schools.

Ask yourself

Was there a time when someone needed help and you risked embarrassment or disapproval to assist him or her?

ADVISORY 11 ▶ CPR

Advisory goal: Appreciate the challenges of having a gay, lesbian, bisexual, or transgender sexual orientation

Greeting

Meet and Greet Greeting: *What is your favorite lunch? Why?* Students form groups of three, greet each other, then talk about the topic. To foster inclusion, encourage groups to invite into their cluster anyone who hasn't found a group.

⮌ Being clear that the groupings are flexible and directing students to invite in someone who hasn't found a group yet mirrors the inclusion message in Mix It Up Lunch Day.

> *Good Morning, Friends!*
>
> *Have you ever heard of "Mix-It-Up Lunch Day"? It's an annual event sponsored by an organization called Teaching Tolerance. The idea is for everyone to break their usual pattern and have lunch with someone they have never eaten with before. What could be the benefits if our school tried that? Think about it!*

Share

Partner Share: *Parents' Night* by Nancy Garden, from *Am I Blue?* Read the description aloud from Garden's moving story of a gay teen's coming-out experience with her parents. Then partners discuss reflection questions.

Parents' Night: Karen is a teenager who is a member of the Gay-Straight-Bisexual Alliance (GSBA) in her school, but she is not out to her family. Karen and her mother, a social worker, argue about her mother's refusal to take on clients who have AIDS. Her mother defends her position, and Karen criticizes her:

"I just happen to prefer working with normal people who need social services through no fault of their own.

"Then I really exploded. I could feel it coming, but there wasn't any way I could stop it. 'Fault of their own!' I yelled. 'Normal people! God, how unfair. What you're really saying is that if my gay brothers and sisters get AIDS, it's their fault and they deserve to get sick!'"[21]

Her words are followed by silence, as her family realizes that she has just told them that she is a lesbian. She apologizes for having yelled it out to them, and is met with anger by her father and tears by her mother. Both walk out of the room.

Karen stays with her GSBA group and continues with her plans to help with a booth they will set up at Parents Night. Two days later it is her birthday. Her father has given her a yellow rose on her birthday every year since she was born, but this year there is no rose.

When Parents Night comes, Karen nervously staffs the GSBA booth with her girlfriend, Roxy. After repairing their booth sign which had been defaced with the words "faggots and dykes," the girls get behind the booth and begin talking to people. Lots of people take AIDS literature, and a couple of visitors thank them for being there.

Finally, Karen's parents walk into the gym.

"Talk about cold sweats! I put as much of a smile on my face as I could and started to say, 'Hi. Thanks for coming.'

"Dad looked very embarrassed, and as nervous as I felt. He sort of scanned the gym as if he were checking for people he knew, and he gave Mom a desperate look. She nodded in a stiff kind of way, and Dad bent down awkwardly so his head was sort of half inside the booth, and he kissed me."[22]

Reflection

Why did Karen wait so long before coming out to her parents? Why do many young gays and lesbians fear coming out?

Why do you think her parents reacted the way they did?

If you learned that a close friend was part of a group about which you have biased feelings, would that change the way you act or the way you feel about people in the group? About the friend?

Activity

Mix It Up Lunch: Learn about and organize a Mix It Up Lunch Day at your school. A national campaign launched by Teaching Tolerance a decade ago, Mix It Up at Lunch Day encourages students to identify, question, and cross social boundaries.[23]

Keep in Mind

Studies have shown that interactions across group lines can help reduce prejudice. When students interact with those who are different from them, biases and misperceptions can decrease. Teaching Tolerance offers free online resources to help school groups and classroom teachers explore the issue of social boundaries. These activities can be used as ice-breakers during the planning process for Mix It Up at Lunch Day, to get the group geared up for the event, or they can be used as classroom activities by teacher allies seeking to support the Mix It Up effort.

I did Mix It Up at Lunch with the student council at my school. I had them create a ten-question getting-to-know-you survey that they had students take. Then they collected the surveys, and created a seating chart for mix-it-up day based on one commonality each pair had. Then at the event each partner had an initial conversation topic: I wonder what it is we had in common in our survey answers? It worked very well because the students generated everything. The year before, the staff tried to do one FOR the kids, and they hated it. (Seventh-eighth grade language arts teacher)

Ask yourself

Are students with a gay, lesbian, bisexual, or transgender orientation accepted by their peers and adults in your school?

ADVISORY 12 ▶ CPR

Advisory goal: Know about resources available to GLBT students in school

Greeting

Ball Toss Greeting: Select a student to be-gin and give her a soft, indoor ball or a bean bag, stuffed animal, etc. She greets a student across the circle, then tosses that student the ball (model a safe, on-target, underhand toss). The recipient of the ball returns the greeting, greets someone across the circle, and tosses him the ball. This continues until all have been greeted and have received and tossed the ball. Students can place their hands behind their backs to indicate that they've been greeted.

> Welcome, Everyone!
>
> Let's welcome our guest this morning, _____, who will tell us about Gay-Straight Alliances, why they are formed, and how they help create safe, <u>hospitable</u> schools.

Share

Guest Share: Invite a member of, or someone knowledgeable about, a Gay-Straight Al-liance (GSA) to share about GSA's and their purpose and effects in schools. If no guest is available, you can introduce GSA's to students using the activity below. Read more about GSA's at www.teachingtolerance.org.

Activity

Gay-Straight Alliance: discuss GSA's and their benefits and risks: Read the ten tips for starting a GSA. Discuss harassment of GLBT students and why GSA's are started in schools. Inform students that the most common targets of harassment in middle schools are lesbian, gay, bisexual, and transgender students, or students *perceived* to be gay. The Gay, Lesbian, Straight Education Network (GLSEN) climate surveys are effec-tive ways to determine the level of harassment problems in schools:

"The 2009 survey of 7,261 middle and high school students found that nearly 9 out of 10 LGBT students experienced harassment at school in the past year, and nearly two-thirds felt unsafe because of [the threat of harassment.] Nearly a third of LGBT students skipped at least one day of school in the past month because of safety con-cerns."[24] Many gay and straight students respond to this threatening environment by forming Gay-Straight Alliances.

10 Tips for Starting a Gay-Straight Alliance

1. **Follow guidelines.** Check your student handbook for rules for estab-lishing a club, such as getting permission from an administrator, finding an adviser, and/or writing a constitution.

2. **Find a faculty adviser,** a counselor, nurse, or other staff member who you think would be supportive.

3. **Inform administration immediately** of your plans, and ask for help in connecting with teachers, parents, and the school board. Let your ad-ministrator know that forming a GSA is protected under the Federal Equal Access Act.

4. **Inform guidance counselors and social workers** about the group. They may know students who would be interested in joining.

5. **Find a meeting place** that offers some privacy to encourage participation.

6. **Advertise.** Use the school bulletin, fliers, and/or word of mouth. If your fliers are defaced or torn down, don't be discouraged! Replace them. Posting fliers with words like "end homophobia" or "discuss sexual orientation" can help raise awareness and can make other students feel safer–even those who don't attend

7. **To increase attendance, serve food**

8. **Plan your meeting.** The agenda can include why people think the group is important and brainstorming about things your group would like to do.

9. **Establish ground rules** to ensure that group discussions are safe, confidential, and respectful. To increase comfort, you can adopt a rule that no assumptions or labels are to be used about a person's sexual orientation.

10. **Plan for the future.** Develop an action plan that includes goals and activities. Contact the GSA Network to connect with other GSA's in your area and to learn about ways to get involved.

These ideas were adapted from the GSA Network.[25]

Keep in Mind

The Teaching Tolerance Web site of the Southern Poverty Law Center offers a list of actions that teachers can take to make their classrooms feel safe for GLBT students.

From Teaching Tolerance: Tips for Teachers—Ally Yourself with LGBT Students

"Visible support and small acts of kindness go a long way in helping these youth feel safer and find harmony at school. Not only does fulfilling the role of ally let them know they are not alone, it models for other students that gay and transgender classmates are their peers, worthy of respect and acceptance. More often than not, bullies operate with the tacit approval of the school community.

"Here are six LGBT-friendly actions teachers and school staff can take to turn their classrooms and hallways into Safe Zones.

1. **Post a "Safe Zone" sign** in your classroom and office. It signals to LGBT youth that you've got their backs.

2. **Confront homophobic remarks**, including slights and slurs that you overhear. Many students use terms like "fag," "dyke," and "that's so gay" without thinking. Let them know in no uncertain terms that such speech is unacceptable.

3. **Seek opportunities** to incorporate the contributions of LGBT people in science, history, athletics and the arts into your curriculum.

4. **Don't assume any student is gay**—or not gay. If LGBT students do

confide in you, thank them for their trust. Follow the student's lead about what else you should do. Perhaps sharing this information is enough at this point. But if the student needs additional support, you can provide invaluable help by being versed in the LGBT-competent resources available in your school, district, and community.

5. **Organize or encourage** district administrators to arrange an in-service with a qualified youth advocate about how to create a safer school for LGBT students.

6. **If your school has a Gay-Straight Alliance**, volunteer to act as its faculty advisor, or contribute in other ways."[26]

Ask yourself

What biased speech have you called students on in the past?

ADVISORY 13 ▶ CPR

Advisory goal: Take a step toward active acceptance of others who are different from you

Greeting

Handshake Greeting: Students greeting with *Good morning,_____,* and a handshake around the circle.

> Sawubono, Friends!
>
> That's a Zulu (a southern African tribe) "hello." The response is "Ngkhona (pronounced 'n-kona')," "I am fine." Let's try it.

Share

Partner Share: *How often do you hang out with people who are different from you?* Give a time limit for a share and issue a time warning halfway through the share to ensure balanced sharing/listening in each pair.

Activity

Friends with a Difference Project: Distribute the following description to students and discuss it, including the steps. Students do not select their "friends" today; rather, they think about people who are significantly different from them. Participate in this project yourself with a colleague or someone outside of school so you can share with students your experience of a friend with a difference.

Like the "Mix It Up for Lunch" event, this project stretches us past our "usual." Mention to students that their Friend with a Difference could even be the same person with whom they had lunch, an extension of that first get together, if they and their lunch partner are different from one another in some significant ways. The point of Friends with a Difference, then, is to more thoroughly get to know the new person.

⮑ You begin the project in this meeting by discussing it. In Advisory 21, students will reflect together on their experiences with this project in a Talking Cards exercise.

Keep in Mind

Food for thought: a Zulu saying is "A person is a person because of other people."

In this discussion, the focus is on each person making a commitment to live harmoniously with others in a highly diverse society. At this point in our conversations, we have come to know one another culturally and personally, shared about our lives, talked about the challenges and benefits of living in a diverse society, and been as honest and discerning as possible so bias and discrimination do not slip by us undetected. We have shared some sad moments, and we have laughed and played together.

Now it's time for us to say what we are ready to do to make the world better. We can start by making a friend.

Ask yourself
Whom will you choose as a Friend with a Difference?

FRIENDS WITH A DIFFERENCE PROJECT

This project calls for everyone to step outside their usual group of friends and get to know someone who is different from the people they usually hang out with. The purpose is to stretch beyond the typical pattern of making friends almost exclusively with people who are similar to us. The project challenges us to live just a little in the space between your usual friends and all the people who seem "other."

Directions

Choose another student that you may know a little, but haven't talked with very much. The person can be different from you, for example, in color, socio-economic class, language, ethnicity, sexual orientation, gender, age, appearance, and/or ability.

Step 1: Find an opportunity to talk to the person, at least for a few minutes. Invite the person to have lunch together or sit together on the bus. If you feel comfortable doing it, meet in a coffee shop or for a walk. Talk about anything that interests the two of you. The following topics might be good places to start:

- What you enjoy doing
- Music
- Movies or TV shows
- Hobbies and/or pets
- Your families: parents, siblings, relatives in other states or countries

Plan a second get-together if both of you are willing.

Step 2: During one of these conversations, if it seems appropriate, you can bring up the difference you perceive between you: *I thought of you because you are in the wheelchair – I've never known somebody with a disability.* Or *I don't really have any white friends [or friends of color, or Latino friends], but I would like to.* Honesty is the best policy. You might feel uncomfortable, but when someone knows you are sincerely trying, they are likely to be patient.

Step 3: Reflect on your time together. You can do this together or separately.

How did it feel at first to purposely try to get to know someone different from you?

Did you also find some similarities, shared interests, points of view? Describe them.

What were the benefits of getting to know someone quite different from you?

Were there any problems? Describe them.

Will you continue the friendship with your friend with a difference? Why or why not?

Has having a friend with a difference changed the way you perceive other people in any way?

ADVISORY 14 ▶ A+

Advisory goal: Develop strategies for handling challenging situations

Greeting

Greet Three Greeting: Students make eye contact from across the circle, move and greet each other using a greeting of their choice, and repeat this process two more times. All greet simultaneously.

> Hi, Everyone!
>
> Get ready to do some <u>strategic</u> thinking together. We'll look at several situations and figure out how to handle them effectively.

➲ Model and practice how to do this gracefully. Remind students that they have to look around after the first greeting to find partners to greet two more times.

Activity

Carousel: What Would You Do? Post scenarios around the room on charts. Ask students to consider what they could and would do if they were dealing with each of the scenarios below involving bias, prejudice, exclusion, and discrimination. This activity will take more than one period. Aim for groups to have responded to half or more of the scenarios in this meeting.

Students in groups of two to four move from one scenario to the next. They read each scenario, discuss possible responses, decide on one or two, and write it or them on the chart. Each small group has a different colored marker, and each scenario should have at least one response from each group when the activity is completed.

➲ You can give students a time limit for each scenario and signal them when there is one minute remaining and then again when it is time to move to the next.

Scenarios: What would you do or say?

1. The cafeteria is crowded, and a student wearing a *hijab* (head covering) is looking for a place to sit. There is room for one more at your table. You've been hoping that a friend would join you.

2. A teacher is older than most. You overhear another student say, "She's too old to be teaching. They ought to get rid of her!"

3. One of the players on your basketball team is openly gay. Some players are going out for pizza after practice. You notice that he is still in the locker room by himself as the rest of you leave.

4. A group of boys is watching a girl walk by and they comment on her body: "That's curvilicious!"

5. Every day after practice, the white players leave together and the black players leave together.

6. You and a friend are walking along singing, with your arms around each other. Your friend drops her arms, laughs, and says, "People will think we're lesbians!"

7. An overweight girl tries out for cheerleading. She knows all the cheers and does them well, but she is not picked for the squad. All the cheerleaders are slim. None of the heavier people are chosen.

8. You are invited to join a student committee to plan Christmas decorations for a hallway.

9. Two Latino students who speak accented English always keep to themselves and stay out of conversations.

10. Several of your black girlfriends complain that black boys are dating white girls.

11. A boy puts his arm around a girl. She steps away from him, and the boy says, "Come on, babe, don't be cold," and reaches for her again.

12. A girl often comes to school wearing the same clothes she wore the day before. Two of your friends comment, "It's gross that she wears the same thing all the time!"

13. Your friend is clowning around, singing and pretending he's Michael Jackson. A boy walks by and says loudly, "That's so gay!"

Reflection

When all the groups have visited all the scenarios, read each scenario and its responses aloud and discuss them. The reflection will take place in the next advisory.

Keep in Mind

Student as everyday hero

Students are called to the same challenge as the adults in their school: to make an effort to accept others who are different from them, and to take a stand for mutual acceptance. Adolescence is a time of passion, and the same youths who take crazy risks and try out roles for themselves can become outraged over injustice. The emotions that show up in rule breaking one day can appear the next day in a manifesto for mutual acceptance:

Stand out! Shout up! It doesn't matter whether you have darker skin than me, or if I have different beliefs! (Seventh grade student)

I want to hang out around people who are different from me until they get it into their heads that they can't get rid of me and that they will just have to accept me! (Seventh grade student)

I'd get people who are different together. I would be a middle man and make friends with both kinds of people and letting them meet without telling them the other's "difference," and if they become friends, they might work something out for their two different groups. (Eighth grade student)

Ask yourself

Have you known a student hero?

ADVISORY 15 ▶ A+

Advisory goal: Develop strategies for handling challenging situations

Greeting

One-Minute Mingle Greeting: Each person greets as many students by name as possible in one minute. Model how to efficiently complete a greeting before starting. Give examples of how to be greeted and return a greeting, maintaining eye contact, before moving on to the next person.

> Good Morning, Everyone!
> Today we'll finish our carousel and make sure we hear all the responses to the sce-narios so we're ready to take action when a situation calls for it.

Activity

Carousel: What Would You Do? Complete the activity from Advisory 15.

Reflection

When each group has responded to each scenario, one or two students stand beside each chart and read the solutions aloud. The group then discusses the pros and cons of the responses. You can ask for thumbs up or down or sideways to indicate agreement, disagreement, or ambivalence about the responses, and note which responses elicit the most discussion. Don't count—just get the general sense of the group.

➲ Alternatively, you could do a Spend the Dot process: students have markers and make small dots next to the responses they think are good. Then they can give reasons for their choices, and the group can discuss. This may well extend into another advisory meeting.

Keep in Mind

Thinking about possible responses to situations gives practice in using good judgment. Adolescents have a limited capacity for the abstract thinking or cognitive analysis necessary for complex decision-making: "The sequential maturation of various brain systems is a central issue in understanding adolescence, since several brain systems that are critically important to autonomous adult life don't mature until upper adolescence."[27]

Ask yourself

What strategies do you use in situations that potentially or directly involve bias?

ADVISORY 16 ▶ CPR

Advisory goal: Develop strategies for coping with bias

Greeting

One-Minute Mingle Greeting: Each person greets as many students by name as possible in one minute. Model how to be greeted and return a greeting, maintaining eye contact, before moving on to the next person.

Share

Triad Share: *Describe your typical experience in stores. Discuss why you are or are not treated with full respect in a store. Brainstorm ways to handle profiling.* Give a time limit for a share and signal when it is time for the next share. Volunteers share out.

Hello, Shoppers!

Most of us buy things in stores from time to time. Indicate below whether you enjoy shopping and the degree of respect you get from salespeople most of the time. Use a scale from 1 to 10, 10 being the most respect. Teens in the story we discuss today describe being <u>profiled</u>, suspected of being potential shoplifters because of their appearance.

Name	Enjoy shopping? Yes or no	Degree of respect from salespeople?

Activity

Read the following story and discuss the reflection questions afterwards.

I hang out with a diverse group of kids and our best discussions are about what it's like for each of us to live as black or Hispanic or Asian or white. We're fine with each other, and we all accept peoples' differences pretty well—politics, color, sexual orientation. But we all experience the institutional racism and other biases that are out there.

Once I went to a high-end fashion store with a friend. We wanted to see what famous designers were putting out. Zach and I were just walking around the store looking at stuff. We noticed that two "loss prevention agents" who dress just like ordinary shoppers, were following us wherever we walked. And salespeople kept asking us over and over, "Can we help you?" And over and over we answered, "No, we're just browsing."

We knew what was going on. We were the only black people in the store and no one else was being followed. Finally we started walking in circles just to see what they would do, and then they walked in circles behind us—it was pretty funny. After a while we got bored and annoyed so we left. (High school student)

Reflection

What price did the two boys pay for being black teenagers shopping in a fancy clothing store?

If you find yourself being profiled, what can you do to take care of yourself and minimize the damage done by such prejudice?

⮑ Consider having students journal for a couple of minutes while they think about these questions. After the journaling, if you have time, do partner shares or go right to a whole-group discussion, whichever method you think will bring the best engagement in the issues.

Keep in Mind

Profiling, redlining, and employment color-coding are practices that people of color, immigrants, people in poverty, and others must cope with every day, including in school. When there is a power differential between them and someone making a judgment, they have to be particularly careful.

My mother prepared me. She told me that people would decide certain things about me based on the color of my skin and that I needed to be very careful. If a policeman stops me, for example, I needed to be very polite (whatever he said), not anger him in any way, not resist. It was too dangerous and I could get really hurt if I tried to talk back or defend myself. (College teacher)

"There are very few African-American men in this country who haven't had the experience of being followed when they were shopping in a department store. That includes me. There are very few African-American men who haven't had the experience of walking across the street and hearing the locks click on the doors of cars. That happens to me—at least before I was a senator. There are very few African Americans who haven't had the experience of getting on an elevator and a woman clutching her purse nervously and holding her breath until she had a chance to get off. That happens often.

"....On the other hand, in families and churches and workplaces, there's the possibility that people are a little bit more honest, and at least you ask yourself your own questions about, am I wringing as much bias out of myself as I can? Am I judging people as much as I can, based on not the color of their skin, but the content of their character?"[28] (President Barack Obama, July 19, 2013 in a public statement before the press)

As for the targets of discrimination, they can take care of themselves by being highly conscious of the bias realities in contemporary American life and by developing a critical consciousness. The same careful thinking that can identify logical fallacies and rhetorical manipulations can name discrimination when it occurs. This is part of what it takes for many disadvantaged students to do well in school. (See more discussion on this topic below in Advisory 18.)

"Beyond those individual characteristics of academic achievement and cultural competence, students must develop a broader sociopolitical consciousness that allows them to critique the cultural norms, values, mores, and institutions that produce and maintain social inequities. If school is about preparing students for active citizenship, what better citizenship tool than the ability to critically analyze the society?"[29]

Ask Yourself

In your experience, how important is appearance in influencing how people treat you?

ADVISORY 17 ▶ CPR

Advisory goal: Become aware of what it takes to shape the future

Greeting

Fist Tap Greeting: students greet using Basic Greeting format (*Good morning,_____,* around the circle), adding a gentle bump of fists with each partner.

Share

Partner Share: *Share about a time when you weren't confident, but you tried your best to do well or win at something.* Give a time limit for each share and issue a warning halfway through to ensure balanced sharing/listening in each pair. Volunteers share out.

> Good Morning, Everyone!
>
> Today I'll read you an excerpt from a book by Walter Dean Myers called <u>Handbook for Boys: A Novel</u>. It's about a sixteen-year-old boy named Jimmy who works in a barber shop and learns there how to be more in control of his future. Be ready tomorrow to report on your Friends with a Difference project. You have about 24 hours to complete it.

Activity

***Handbook for Boys: A Novel* by Walter Dean Myers:** Read the following summary of the novel, then guide a discussion about the courage to strive for something you want for yourself or for the world, even though it will be difficult to achieve.

Jimmy is a sixteen-year-old boy serving six months of probation. The terms of the probation include that he be under the supervision of Duke, the owner of a barbershop in Jimmy's neighborhood in Harlem. Jimmy works at the barbershop part time and engages in conversations with Duke about life and how to manage it for success.

Duke is 68 years old, and he owns the barbershop. He went to college and studied biology, but he ended up opening the barbershop, the best opportunity available to him at the time. When his wife died, Duke planned to use the money from selling her beauty salon business to help some kids from the neighborhood go to college. Jimmy is a candidate for one of the scholarships—if he can learn an important lesson about life that Duke teaches boys not to let circumstances rule their lives: "Pick your own road."[30] Duke wants Jimmy and other boys who have been in trouble to realize that the decisions they make and the actions they take could be designed *by them* to move them toward a good future.

Jimmy begins to understand what Duke is trying to teach him: "You've been saying that the way a lot of people mess up their lives is by being spectators instead of taking care of business, right?"[31] Jimmy begins to take care of business, and to help other boys do the same.

Reflection

Describe a time when you or someone you know took a chance and stretched to accomplish something important.

What is something you'd be willing to take a chance and go for?

⊃ Students can journal for a couple of minutes while they think about these questions. Do partner shares or go right to a whole-group discussion.

Keep in Mind

Disadvantaged students have hard work to do

Some people are forced into heroism very young. Students who grow up in poverty, or speaking a language other than English, or whose culture is very different from that of most American schools, must work much harder than others to achieve academically and socially. They must move each day between their worlds, using their mindsets to believe in their own growth, working for it, and refusing to be side-tracked.

In *Handbook for Boys,* many boys in Jimmy and Duke's Harlem neighborhood have been in trouble. In the introduction, Myers writes, "I've lived long enough to see some of my childhood friends finish school, enjoy successful careers, and even retire. Others I've seen end up in jails, or working far below what I had thought was their capacity.... Speaking with young inmates is heartbreaking, especially when you see that they are often bright, articulate young people who should have done more with their lives." He noticed that many of those who had failed thought of success as a matter of chance, something that happened for people who had "natural advantages." "There are teenagers who have fallen behind academically, don't see a way to catch up, and stop trying. They often adapt to a lesser lifestyle, one far below their potential, and far less satisfying."[32]

The home and neighborhood cultures and everyday ways of behaving (the "style") of these boys differed markedly, from the cultural expectations set by adults in school and perhaps from the dominant student style in school. This story suggests (as does research) that as educators, to help students living in poverty succeed, we need a high awareness of the extra work they have to do to adjust their ways of being so they fit in. Much depends on this adjustment. If they do not overcome the cultural gaps, or if they resist rather than adapt to the school culture, they will fail. Looking from the other side, if we educators do not help bridge those cultural gaps, if we do not help them adapt, we, too, will fail.

Participating comfortably in two cultures at the same time is a tall order. Adaptive resistance—resisting the erasure of one's own culture while adapting to the dominant culture—can be a student's scaffold for succeeding in school without abandoning his home culture.

Researchers and theorists have explored how students of color can adapt successfully to the school culture in the following ways.

Developing self-awareness: Example of African American "racial" identity that supports success

A high level of self-awareness, including awareness of your cultural roots and the relative position of your culture in the larger society, strengthens the ability to work successfully in school and in the world.

A socially-contextualized model of an African American "racial" identity that supports success includes three characteristics. Achieving African Americans are aware of and have strategies for (1) identifying with and embracing their culture, (2) coping with racism, and (3) achieving by connecting personal effort to personal success.[33]

1) They identify with and embrace their culture

Every individual needs to acknowledge and enjoy the person he or she is. Identifying proudly with your culture, loving its members, and enjoying being together doing what you do in the way you do it are all self-affirming.[34]

I'm mixed blood, with an African-American mother and a Latino father. My dad didn't want to talk about being Cuban—he wanted us to concentrate on being American. But I listened to my mom tell stories of her great-grandparents and slavery and Reconstruction and began to understand what it meant to be African American. I immersed myself in African-American culture. I went to a predominantly African-American college. When we were 17 years old, we were proud to wear an Afro hairstyle, and even today, having straight hair feels disloyal. I identify myself as African American. (Middle level teacher)

Open your eyes and realize it's me
Don't be disturbed by the image you see
My name is Elon, and I think I'm pretty
Yes I'm black, and independent at that
Open your eyes and realize it's me!

—High school student

2) They cope with racism: they are aware of and can analyze bias and discrimination (an objective mindset)

Students who know their ethnic history are better prepared to cope with discrimination and prejudice. If these matters are discussed frankly in school, young people are better known and understood.

For example, in some homes and schools parents and/or teachers teach the history and sociology of the lives of African Americans in the United States. They talk about the facts of racism, from slavery to contemporary practices like redlining, employment color coding, and racial profiling. Children are taught the whole story, its causes and effects, its history and contemporary realities. They are not naïve. They know what they're up against, and are prepared to confront it.[35]

I don't think too many black kids grow up not knowing they're black. But they can't listen to the words given to us about ourselves by people who dominate us—they're suspect. What we need to talk about isn't slavery—it's how we talk to one another today, how we treat each other. Some students understand this. When I told my high school daughter one day about some untrue rumors that were being spread about me, she reassured me: "They just don't like that you're a loud, black woman, mom." (Middle-level social studies teacher)

"Dr. King explains that there are three evils here on earth that would hold us back from world peace. The three evils are war, poverty, and racism. And he also explained that as long as these three evils exist in the world, there would never be world peace. We are a group of youth in north Minneapolis who gave these three evils some thought and came to realize that they are the very things that are not only present in our world but in our own community, affecting ourselves, our families, and our friends." (Keeping the Legacy Alive: North Community Youth Speak Up)[36]

3) They see themselves as achievers and strive for success (a growth mindset)

The growth mindset is the belief that you have what it takes to succeed in school and in life if you make the effort. Such a mindset is much more likely to develop when parents and teachers believe in young people, and believe that if they work at it, they will succeed.

I Am

The Hope in my community
The cope in times of difficulty
The joke to those who ridicule me
Kicked open the doh and colored the ice in hockey
I am the kid with high expectations from my family.
—High school student

Dan's grandmother was raising him and his two siblings because his parents were drug users. Dan was not strong intellectually, but he had the will to keep making an effort to succeed, because, as he said, he didn't want to be like his mom and dad. He was an eighth grade student, but because his basic skills were low I had to have him work with seventh graders, with the promise that I'd move him to the eighth grade group as soon as he could handle the work. We set a goal of December. He worked very hard. He showed his work in progress to me every step of the way so he could get it right: "What do I need to do?" he would ask every time. He didn't make it by December, but by February he was doing eighth grade work. (Seventh-eighth grade math teacher)

For my father, being an immigrant meant taking a stand for success. The ethic was, "You will be working for it, but you will get an education. Whatever you do, you're going to be good at it—the best you can be." That still drives me. I gave him my college diploma for a year to carry around and show people. And seeing the beam in my father's eye when my older brother went to college too was great. (Middle grades teacher)

Ask yourself

What adaptations to school culture were required of you as a student? What adaptations are required of you as a teacher?

ADVISORY 18 ▶ CPR

Advisory goal: Recognize the value in getting to know someone who is significantly different from you

Greeting:

High Five Greeting: In sequence around the circle, students greet each other with a high five. *Hi, Jim.* (high five) Reply: *Hi, Brenda.* (high five)

> Welcome, Friends!
> Today we'll reflect on our Friends with a Difference project. Get ready to describe how it went for you and any <u>insights</u> you gained from the experience.

Share

Talking Cards Share: Lead reflection on the completed Friends with a Difference project. Students respond to each of the following questions in on a separate card:

1. What did you anticipate that the experience of spending time with someone different from you would be like? Was the experience the way you thought it would be?

2. What was enjoyable about getting to know your "friend with a difference"?

3. What was awkward or uncomfortable about it?

4. What understanding or insight did you gain from the experience?

Collect the cards as they complete their answers, and label and sort the cards into four piles, one for each question. Organize students into four groups. Give each group one of the four sets of cards. Groups look over the responses and cluster similar answers together to prepare to report to the whole group at the next meeting (combine responses with similar meanings).

⮑ Complete your own set of four Talking Cards, reflecting on your experience getting to know someone different from you.

Activity

Helium Hoop: Provide a hula hoop or a lightweight stick for each group of five to eight players. All group members place both index fingers under the hoop or stick held at waist level (the hoop or stick is parallel to the ground). They lower the object to the floor while keeping their fingers under it. The results will be uplifting (the hoop rises)!

Keep in Mind

We tend to be attracted to people who are like them: "... people are genetically inclined to choose as social partners those who resemble themselves at a genetic level."[37] It takes extra effort to associate with people who seem different. The effort could pay off in less tension and conflict and more enjoyment and equity among the diverse people with whom we share our lives in our community, our country, and our world.

Ask yourself

Did you gain something from your Friends with a Difference experience?

ADVISORY 19 ▶ CPR

Advisory goal: Recognize the value in getting to know someone who is significantly different from you

Greeting

Name Card Greeting: Students' names are written on note cards and placed face down in the middle of the circle. One at a time, each student takes a card and greets (or greets and exchanges seats with) the student whose name is on the card.

> *Good Morning, Decision-makers!*
>
> *It's Four Corners time! The statement has to do with <u>affirmative action</u>. You will take an assigned stand and then your own stand, to practice thinking hard when we give our opinions.*

➲ This is a good greeting to use to mix things up if students have begun to sit in the same seats and/or next to the same people.

Share

Talking Cards reporting: Groups from the Talking Cards activity at the previous meeting share out to the whole group. You read aloud one of the four questions below, and the appropriate group reads aloud the responses to the question.

➲ At the end of the sharing, ask students to respond with a show of hands to these questions:

Raise your hand if you feel that our school would benefit if many people intentionally made friends with people different from them.

Raise your hand if you would again seek out a person different from you to get to know.

Activity

Four Corner Thinking: Affirmative Action: Designate the four corners of the room as: *strongly agree, somewhat agree, somewhat disagree, strongly disagree*. Read aloud the definition of affirmative action:

Affirmative action: Policies or programs designed to create equity in employment, housing, and education. Affirmative action laws and policies (some mandated by government, some voluntary) counter practices that have discriminated against certain groups (especially minorities and women) for a long time. When an organization implements affirmative action, it actively seeks to increase the presence in its organization of members of certain groups.

Pose the statement: *Schools, government, and businesses should use affirmative action to make up for past discrimination and to diversify.*

First round: Assign numbers one through four randomly and evenly to students and have them go to the corresponding corner. Volunteers from each corner explain their positions, regardless of their personal opinion on the statement.

Second round: This time students *choose* and move to the corner of the room that best fits their opinion. Volunteers from each corner explain their positions.

Reflection

Was it difficult to defend a position that you didn't choose? What might be the advantages of doing so?

Keep in Mind

Affirmative action is known as "positive discrimination" in the United Kingdom and as "employment equity" in Canada and other places. Another definition: "'Affirmative action' means positive steps taken to increase the representation of women and minorities, especially in the areas of college admissions and government employment, from which they have been historically excluded. When those steps involve *preferential* selection—selection on the basis of race, gender, or ethnicity—affirmative action generates intense controversy."[38]

There is tension between favoring certain Americans today because of injustices done them historically as well as today, versus equal opportunity for all Americans, based exclusively on individual merit. The matter is complicated by many factors, including the tendency to judge merit through a cultural-clouded lens. In June, 2013, the United States Supreme Court ruled 7 to 1 that a Texas appeals court should reconsider a case under a demanding standard: colleges and universities must operate with a very high standard for using affirmative action: they must be able to demonstrate that "available, workable race-neutral alternatives do not suffice" before taking account of race in admissions decisions. (Majority opinion written by Justice Anthony Kennedy, "Held: Because the Fifth Circuit did not hold the University to the demanding burden of strict scrutiny articulated in Grutter and Regents of Univ. of Cal. v. Bakke, 438 U. S. 265, its decision affirming the District Court's grant of summary judgment to the University was incorrect.")[39]

Ask yourself

Where do you stand on requiring colleges and universities as well as government (local, state, national) to enroll or hire historically disadvantaged people of color and women?

ADVISORY 20 ▶ CPR

Advisory goal: Increase understanding of what courage is and how it feels to be courageous

Greeting

Name Everyone Greeting: A student greets everyone in the room individually by name and with eye contact. Each student returns the greeting. The greeter may remain where she is as she greets, or she may walk around the circle, greeting each student from a closer perspective.

> Greetings, Courageous People!
>
> Is someone willing to step up and greet each person in our group individually? We'll be talking about courage today, so be thinking about a time when <u>circumstances</u> demanded courage from you.

Share

Partner Share: *Describe a time when you were courageous.* Volunteers share out about a time when their *partners* were brave.

Activity

Words for Courage: Keeping share partners together, assign one of the quotes about courage below to half the group and the other to the other half. Partners must have the same quote.

"It takes a great deal of bravery to stand up to your enemies, but a great deal more to stand up to your friends."[40] (*Harry Potter and the Sorcerer's Stone*, by J.K. Rowling)

"Courage is about doing what you're afraid to do. There can be no courage unless you're scared. Have the courage to act instead of react." (Oliver Wendell Holmes)

Partners say what their quote means to them, and perhaps give an example. Volunteers share out. Partners then collaborate to make their own statement about courage in their own lives. Use the starting phrase, *Courage is...* students complete the thought with a specific example, such as:

- Courage is walking into the locker room when you've made a mistake that cost the team a win.

- Courage is telling your friend he is being biased about someone else.

Partners write their examples about courage on a note card and post it on a chart or the board. Two volunteers read aloud the results.

Keep in Mind

Help students understand that acting in the face of your fear and embarrassment is true courage. It requires that you overcome an internal pull to do nothing or to avoid a situation. It means your courage is sufficient to take you past your misgivings, your concern for being liked by your friends, your fear of being wrong, or fear that you will regret a decision to stick your neck out.

Ask yourself

What was a moment of courage in your life?

ADVISORY 21 ▶ CPR

Advisory goal: Know the value and characteristics of effective acknowledgments

Greeting

One-Minute Mingle Greeting: Each person greets as many students by name as possible in one minute. Model how to efficiently complete a greeting, including maintaining eye contact, before moving on to the next person.

> *Good Morning, Generous People!*
> *Today you get to spread the love by writing a card to someone you admire for their <u>empathy</u> toward others, no matter who those others are.*

Share

Whip Share: *What's the value in acknowledging someone for something caring that they have done? How do you feel when someone expresses appreciation to you?* Each student offers a brief response to one or both of the questions; responses quickly "whip" around the circle.

⮌ It helps to write the questions on the board, so nobody asks, "What were the questions again?"

Activity

Write a card to someone you know and admire: Inspire students to write meaningfully: *Get ideas about what to say by making a list of what you like about this person and why you like that characteristic. Be as specific as possible, with details that add color to what you say and show that you really mean it.* Coach students to choose someone with whom they have a personal relationship. Students can hand deliver or mail their cards.

Keep in Mind

Vague compliments like "Great job, Jack!" "Nice work, Sal." don't mean much. A meaningful acknowledgment is specific and descriptive. It specifies the work or aspects of the person that you admire, and describes vividly what was excellent and why (e.g., "Lamar, your story kept me wondering all the way through what was going to happen. The characters were so interesting and the events so clearly described that I never lost interest.")

Ask yourself

What compliments have you given recently that were specific and descriptive?

ADVISORY 22 ▶ CPR

Advisory goal: Appreciate the safety and fun of a caring community

Greeting/Share

Meet and Greet Greeting and Share: *What is a compliment you have given or received? Was it meaningful to you? Did it describe with specifics what you admired?*

Students stand, form groups of three, greet each other, then talk about the topic. To foster inclusion, encourage groups to invite into their cluster those who are having difficulty finding a group, even if it means creating a group of four.

> Hello, Kind Folks!
>
> Acknowledgments and thank you's are ways to express caring and admiration for others. Today we'll get a little <u>inane</u> about spreading the love. Let's play Honey, Do You Love Me?

Activity

Honey, Do You Love Me? Form two teams. One student (the initiator) from one side walks to the other team and asks one of the students (the responder), *Honey, do you love me?* The response is, *Honey, I love you, but I just can't smile.* If the responder smiles or laughs while saying this, he is "recruited" and moves to the other team. If the responder does not laugh, the initiator is recruited by that team. The game continues until all students are on one side (or until you decide to stop playing).

Keep in Mind

After all these conversations, some easy, some very hard, if we've been successful, students have come to know and care about one another more. Watch how students behave during Honey, Do You Love Me? to see if they seem to trust and care about one another,

Ask yourself

What was a compliment you received that you still remember? What made it memorable?

ADVISORY 23 ▶ A+

Advisory goal: Appreciate the price we pay for indulging in "isms"

Greeting

One-Minute Mingle Greeting: Each person greets as many students by name as possible in one minute.

Activity

Stay and Stray: Cost of isms Write on each of six index cards one of the following isms: racism, heterosexism, classism, sexism, ableism, ageism. Divide students into six groups. Each group randomly picks a card from the six and creates a chart on that "ism" with the following information or make charts ahead of time:

1. Things you might see, hear, read about, etc. that could indicate an "ism," e.g., a building without handicapped access or reference to Europeans "settling the West" in an American history book.

2. One action an individual or group could take to counteract the "ism," e.g., speaking out directly against it or writing a letter to a publisher. Refer to Giraffe Stories for inspiration, page 297.

Groups have about ten minutes to work on their charts. Stop here if time runs out and finish at the next meeting.

Stay and Stray circulation among charts: One member of the group *stays* with the group's chart to explain it to visitors and get feedback. The others *stray* to look at the other charts. Allow two or three minutes at each chart. Groups end up at their own charts.

Reflection

Exit Card: Ask students to answer one or both of the following questions on index cards. Students hand their cards to you as they exit the classroom.

What characteristics do the "isms" seem to all have in common?

What is one action you could take to reduce the impact of an "ism"?

⮑ These cards can give you a sense of whether students understand the isms. You can read the action suggestions at the next meeting.

Keep in Mind

The "isms" share certain qualities: they are founded on narrow-minded, biased thinking and they damage both the people upon whom they are imposed and those who indulge in them. They are the ultimate expression of lose-lose thinking. This is a good reason to work hard to avoid them, correct our language if and when we slide into one of them, and coach students to do the same.

Ask yourself

Have you increased your awareness of bias and the dangers of "isms" during these meetings?

ADVISORY 24 ▶ CPR

Advisory goal: Gain insight into personal growth

Greeting

Fist Tap Greeting: Students greet each other around the circle silently or with *Good morning,_____,* adding a gentle fist bump.

Share

Partner Share on Self-interview responses:
Read your responses for the first self-interview and compare them to the answers you just wrote. When you and your partner have finished reading and comparing your two self-interviews, discuss the differences and similarities between your earlier and later versions and between your responses and those of your partner. Volunteers share out differences and similarities they noticed.

> Good Morning, Clear Thinkers!
>
> Today we will revisit the self-interviews we did at the beginning of our talks about cultural diversity and getting along.
> <u>Do Now:</u> Pick up a copy of the Self-interview Questions and fill it out.

➲ Give students the envelopes with their first self-interviews from Perspective One, Advisory 17, and provide a blank interview form for today's activity. Be sure to participate in this activity.

Activity

Something's Different (variation of Something's Changed): Four students stand in the center of the circle. The observers have one minute or less to observe their appearance in detail. The group of four leaves the room, and each makes one quick change in appearance (e.g., tucks in shirt, rolls up sleeves, switches a ring from one hand to the other). When they return, the group tries to name all the changes made.

➲ A quicker activity to use if time is short is Simultaneous Clap (page 75).

Keep in Mind

Some students may find few or no changes in their self-interview responses. As the leader, you can comment on changes you have noted in students as individuals, but especially as a group, from the beginning of the year to now. Share personal changes that your self-interview revealed.

Think ahead about whom you want to acknowledge specifically and descriptively: for their contributions to the discussions and the activities, for taking the *Face to Face Advisories* process seriously, for participating authentically, for sticking their necks out, and for whatever else you have observed. You can tell a story, remind them of funny and serious moments, and thank them for what they have contributed to each other and to you. If time is short, acknowledge students in the next meeting—it is devoted to acknowledgments.

Ask yourself

What change do you perceive, if any, between your own first and second self-interviews?

ADVISORY 25 ▶ A+

Advisory goals: Declare an action you will take to make the community more inclusive and friendly. Acknowledge each other

Greeting

Handshake Greeting: Students stand and greet with *Good morning, _____,* and a handshake.

Share

Snowball Share: *What action will you take to make our school more inclusive?*

Each student writes an answer on a piece of paper, crumples it up, and tosses it into the middle of the circle. Then each student picks up a "snowball" and reads to him/her self. Students form pairs and read aloud and discuss what was written in their snowballs.

> *Peace, Friends!*
> *Whatever we do to help people get along better, one thing is sure: we'll have a better chance of having a peaceful, equitable world if we work together. As John Lennon told us, "A dream you dream alone is only a dream. A dream you dream together is a reality."*

⮑ Tell students ahead of time that this is not a time for jokes and not a time to opt out. Remind them that small gestures (e.g., a smile or greeting in the halls) can make a difference for some, can help them feel more accepted and connected.

Activity

Tap Someone Who Acknowledgment: Students sit in a circle, eyes closed. Choose four "Tappers." Tappers open their eyes and stand; others keep their eyes closed.

Choose from categories below (or create your own) to complete the phrase *Tap someone who....* Tappers move quietly around the room gently tapping the shoulders of students they feel fit each category. Give ample time for tapping before announcing a new category. Play can continue for several categories. Select new tappers after three categories.

⮑ Tappers remain anonymous. Watch for people peeking when you select tappers (students should keep their heads down as well as their eyes closed), and have them sit out a round.

⮑ At the end of Tap Someone Who, save a few minutes to acknowledge students for the effort they have put into the conversations and activities in *Face to Face Advisories*, if you haven't already done so (see Keep in Mind for the previous meeting, Advisory 25).

Acknowledgment categories: Tap someone who...

is a good listener
has stuck his/her neck out
is fair-minded
is a logical, clear thinker
includes others
will invent something
is truthful

is a good friend

you would like to get to know better

helped you recently

would make a good (politician, comedian, leader, etc.)

has made you laugh

you'd like to have lunch with

you admire

you would like to have an adventure with

has taught you something

Keep in Mind

Before inviting students to take a stand for an inclusive, just society, acknowledge the difficulty of the challenge. It is crucial that pitfalls and breakdowns are perceived as opportunities to become more creative and effective problem-solvers. It is realistic to anticipate breakdowns, but just as realistic to be prepared to turn them into opportunities for leadership and accomplishment. We take a stand that we can and will do this.

This kid was hard to figure out. Demaine was tough. He wanted to be top dog, the alpha male of the classroom. When we were making a decision about something, he tried to push everyone to do it his way. He was Mr. Macho, and I kept working with him about this tendency. I didn't see any changes, but I am committed to the idea that every student can change and grow. One day Tshua, a Hmong student who was generally quiet, shared about a drive-by shooting on his block. He was obviously shaken by it and scared. Demaine stood up, walked across the circle and hugged him! "Man," he said quietly, "It's gonna be OK." That was a moment to make the biggest skeptic believe in human possibility. There was the toughest guy in the class gently hugging another boy right there in front of everyone! (Middle-level teacher)

Ask yourself

What satisfactions and growth have you experienced from these face to face advisories?

[1] Horace Mann, baccalaureate address, Antioch College, *Life and Works of Horace Mann*, vol. 1, ed. Mary Tyler Peabody Mann (Boston: Walker, Fuller & Co., 1865), 575.

[2] "12th Annual Report to the Massachusetts State Board of Education (1848)," *Life and Works of Horace Mann*, vol. 3, ed. Mary Tyler Peabody Mann (Boston: Walker, Fuller & Co., 1865), 669.

[3] Edmund Burke, *The Works of the Right Honourable Edmund Burke*, vol. 1 (Boston: John West and O.C. Greenleaf, 1807) 526.

[4] "Arn Chorn Pond: Everyone Has a Story," Facing History and Ourselves, http://www.facinghistory.org/video/arn-chorn-pond-everyone-has-story.

[5] Sonia Nieto, What Keeps Teachers Going (New York: Teachers College Press, 2003), 128.

[6] "Giraffe Heroes Database," The Giraffe Heroes Project, http://www.giraffe.org/option,com_sobi2/Itemid,53/.

[7] Eileen Landay and Kurt Wootton, *A Reason to Read: Linking Literacy and the Arts* (Cambridge: Harvard Educational Press, 2012), 30.

[8] David Nash Ford, "Knights of the Round Table," Britannia, http://www.britannia.com/history/arthur/knights.html.

[9] Chretian de Troyes, "Lancelot of the Cart" *Arthurian Romances*, trans. W.W. Comfort (London: Everyman's Library, 1914).

[10] "The Honor Program," United States Military Academy West Point, http://www.usma.edu/scpme/SitePages/Honor.aspx.

[11] "Honor Code," Middlebury College, http://www.middlebury.edu/academics/administration/newfaculty/handbook/honorcode.

[12] "Girl Scouts Promise and Law," Girl Scouts of the United States, http://www.girlscouts.org/program/basics/promise_law/.

[13] Zeno Franco and Philip Zimbardo, "The Banality of Heroism," Greater Good Science Center, University of California, Berkeley, Fall/Winter 2006-07, http://greatergood.berkeley.edu/article/item/the_banality_of_heroism.

[14] Agathe Maier Glaser, Simeon, Meyer, Sara, and Jack Glaser, *Agathe's Stories: A Child's Journey from Germany to America* (Blurb.com, 2011), 38-39.

[15] "The Righteous Among the Nations," Yad Vashem, http://www.yadvashem.org/yv/en/righteous/about.asp.

[16] University of Southern California Shoah Foundation Institute for Visual History and Education, http://sfi.usc.edu.

[17] The quotation stems from Niemöller's lectures during the early postwar period. Different versions of the quotation exist.

[18] "Martin Niemöller: Biography," United States Holocaust Memorial Museum, http://www.ushmm.org/wlc/en/article.php?ModuleId=10007391.

[19] Jesús Colón, Puerto Rican in New York and Other Sketches (New York: International Publishers, Inc, 1982), 115. © International Publishers, Inc./New York. Used with permission.

[20] Debra J. Pepler and Wendy Craig, "Making a Difference in Bullying (Report #60)," Queen's University, Kingston, Ontario, Canada, 9, http://www.melissainstitute.org/documents/MakingADifference.pdf.

[21] Nancy Garden, "Parents' Night," in *Am I Blue: Coming Out from the Silence*, ed. Marion Dane Bauer (New York: HarperCollins, 1994), 139.

[22] Ibid., 144.

[23] "Mix It Up Schools," Teaching Tolerance, http://www.tolerance.org/mix-it-up/map.

[24] "The 2011 National School Climate Survey: The Experiences of Lesbian, Gay, Bisexual and Transgender Youth in Our Nation's Schools," GLSEN, http://www.glsen.org/sites/default/files/2011%20National%20School%20Climate%20Survey%20Full%20Report.pdf.

[25] "10 Steps for Starting a GSA," Gay-Straight Alliance Network, http://www.gsanetwork.org/ http://www.gsanetwork.org/resources/building-your-gsa/10-steps-starting-gsa>.

[26] "Tips for Teachers- Ally Yourself with LGBT Students," Teaching Tolerance, http://www.tolerance.org/toolkit/tips-teachers-ally-yourself-lgbt-students   http://www.tolerance.org/toolkit/tips-teachers-ally-yourself-lgbt-students.

[27] Robert Sylwester, *The Adolescent Brain: Reaching for Autonomy*, (Thousand Oaks: Corwin Press, 2007), 21-22.

[28] Frank James, "Obama Explains Black America to White America," National Public Radio, http://www.npr.org/blogs/itsallpolitics/2013/07/19/203706929/obama-explains-black-america-to-white-america.

[29] Gloria Ladson-Billings, "But That's Just Good Teaching!: The Case for Culturally Relevant Pedagogy," Theory into Practice, 34, no. 3 (Summer 1995): 162.

[30] Walter Dean Myers, *Handbook for Boys: A Novel* (New York: HarperCollins, 2002), 75.

[31] Ibid., 193.

[32] Ibid., preface.

[33] Daphna Oyserman, L. Gant, and J. Ager, "A Socially Contextualized Model of Racial Identity: Possible Selves and School Persistence," *Journal of Personality and Social Psychology* 69 (1995): 1216-1232.

[34] Dorinda J. Carter Andrews, "Achievement as Resistance: The Development of a Critical Race Achievement Ideology Among Black Achievers," in *Education for a Multicultural Society*, ed. Kolajo Paul Afolabi, Candice Bocala, Raygine C. DiAquoi, Julia M. Hayden, Irene A. Liefshitz, and Soojin Susan Oh (Cambridge: Harvard Educational Review, 2011), 176-7; 188; 189.

[35] Ibid.

[36] "Keeping the Legacy Alive: North Minneapolis Youth Speak Up!" *Developmental Designs* YouTube channel, www.youtube/developmentaldesigns.org.

[37] J. Philippe Rushton and Trudy Ann Bons, "Mate Choice and Friendship in Twins: Evidence for Genetic Similarity," *Psychological Science* 16, no. 7(2005): 555.

[38] Robert Fullinwider, "Affirmative Action," *Stanford Encyclopedia of Philosophy* (Winter 2011), http://plato.stanford.edu/archives/win2011/entries/affirmative-action/.

[39] Justice Anthony Kennedy, "Fisher v. University of Texas at Austin, 570 U. S. (2013): __." There is a blank space for the page number(s) because the case will be published after this book's publication. Until its publication, the case has only the Supreme Court's docket number.

[40] J.K. Rowling, *Harry Potter and the Sorcerer's Stone* (New York: Scholastic Inc, 2013), 306.

Appendix

SOCIAL-EMOTIONAL LEARNING IN *FACE TO FACE ADVISORIES*

The Illinois State Board of Education Learning Standards: Social/Emotional Learning, one of the most comprehensive sets of social-emotional learning (SEL) standards in the United States, includes target outcomes related to all five of the *Face to Face Advisories* Perspectives. Here is a non-exhaustive list of social-emotional skills included in the Illinois performance descriptors, with advisories that address them. Note: an advisory is identified by its number within a Perspective, e.g., Advisory 8 in Perspective One is noted as P1-8.

Illinois Performance Descriptors for Social-Emotional Learning, Grades 6-8	FACE TO FACE ADVISORY
Goal 1: Develop self-awareness and self-management	
Analyze the effort my family or other adults have made to support my success in school	P1-8
Recognize outside influences on development of my personal characteristics (e.g., body image, self-esteem, behavior)	P1-4, 5
Evaluate how my physical characteristics have contributed to decisions I have made (e.g., what sports I play, what activities I participate in, etc.)	P1-8
Analyze how others in my life have helped me resist negative influences	P5-8
Reflect on a time when I overcame an obstacle to accomplish something that was important to me	P5-18
Goal 2: Use social-awareness and interpersonal skills to establish and maintain positive relationships	
Recall a situation where my behavior impacted the feelings of others either positively or negatively	P3-25
Describe how classmates who are the subject of rumors or bullying might feel	P3-8
Ask open-ended questions to encourage others to express themselves	CPR/A+ format
Paraphrase the perspectives of people on both sides of conflict	P3-14
Recognize actions that hurt others	P3-18
Acknowledge the contributions of others	P5-25
Provide support to others who are experiencing problems	P5-6
Analyze why parties on both sides in a conflict feel as they do	P4-24
Identify ways to advocate for others	P5-24, 26
Identify unwelcome teasing or bullying behaviors	P3-24

Describe stereotyping and its negative impact on others	P5-24
Explain how a lack of understanding of social and cultural differences can contribute to intolerance	P3-7
Explain why bullying or making fun of others is harmful to myself or others	P2-1
Analyze the consequences of ignoring the rights of other people	P2-3
Analyze why students who are different may be teased or bullied	P3-5
Demonstrate respect for members of various ethnic and religious groups	P1-12
Investigate the traditions of others (e.g. memorize phrases from other languages, familiarize myself with the music or cuisine of other cultures)	P1-13-16
Listen respectively to opposing points of views on controversial issues	CPR/A+ format
Practice reflective listening	CPR/A+ format
Encourage others and recognize their contributions	P1-13
Practice strategies for maintaining positive relationships (e.g., pursuing shared interests and activities, spending time together, giving and receiving help, practicing forgiveness)	CPR/A+ format
Learn to maintain an objective, non-judgmental tone during disagreements	P3-17
Use self-reflection to determine how to stop the spread of gossip	P5-9
Participate in setting and enforcing class rules	CPR/A+ format
Recognize that conflict is a natural part of life	P3-7
List characteristics of friends who are a healthy influence and friends who are an unhealthy influence	P3-3

Goal 3: Demonstrate decision-making skills and responsible behaviors in personal, school, and community contexts.

Recognize the impact of unethical or destructive behavior on family, friends, or loved ones	P2-2
Identify how my actions have affected others through journaling and otherwise	CPR/A+ format
Analyze how media advertising influences consumer choices	P4-16
Analyze how a literary character or historical figure considered societal and ethical factors in making important decisions	P1-P5
Collect information about how groups are working to improve the community	P5-5
Describe the roles of voluntary organizations in a democratic society	P5-5
Explain how my decisions and behaviors affect the well being of my school and community	P5-12
Work with other students to plan and implement a service project in our school	P5-26

Illinois State Board of Education. *Performance Descriptors Social-Emotional Learning Grades 6-12.* http://www.isbe.state.il.us/ils/social_emotional/pdf/descriptors_6-12.pdf (accessed August 16, 2013). The Illinois standards align with the SEL goals defined by the Collaborative for Academic, Social, and Emotional Learning (CASEL).

NATIONAL CENTER FOR EDUCATION STATISTICS

The cost for students of color who live in poverty shows up clearly and in statistics about school success and failure.

• Poverty and "race" are closely connected in the United States. In 2007, 18% of American children lived in poverty, but 34% of African-American children, 33% of American Indian/Alaskan Native children, and 27% of Hispanic children did. At the same time, 10% of European-American children lived in poverty, and 11% of Asian-American children.

• High-school graduation rates in 2007 were on average 74%; and 91% of Asian Americans graduated and 80% of European Americans. Hispanic, American Indian, and African-American students' graduation rates that year were 62%, 61%, and 60% respectively.

• The average percentage of students retained one grade level or more in 2007 was 11%, but 21% of African-American students were held back, compared to 9% of white students and 3% of Asian-American students.

• 43% of African-American students were suspended at least once in 2007, as were 22% of Hispanic students, compared to 16% of European-American students and 11% of Asian-American students.

• Only 1% of European-American students were expelled from school in 2007, compared to 13% African-American students.

• 43 American teenage girls per thousand gave birth in 2007. Almost twice that number, 82 per thousand, Hispanic teenage girls did so. 64 per thousand African-American teenage girls had babies, and 59 per thousand Native American girls, compared to 27 and 17 per thousand respectively for European-American and Asian-American teenagers. (On average, only 40% of teenage mothers complete high school.[2])

• 5% European-American students and 21% of Hispanic students dropped out of school in 2007.

Students' achievement scores went down in proportion to the rate of all of these indicators. On the *National Assessment of Educational Progress* mathematics test results in 2009, European Americans and Asian/Pacific Islanders were the top scorers with 73 and 68% of them respectively scoring at or above the Basic level. Only 44% of Hispanics, 43% of American Indians/Alaskan Natives, and 38% of African-American adolescents achieved the Basic level.

[1] Susan Aud, Mary Ann Fox, Angelina KewalRamani, "Status and Trends in the Education of Racial and Ethnic Minorities," National Center for Education Statistics (NCES) (July 2010) http://nces.ed.gov/pubs2010/2010015.pdf.

[2] Lisa Shuger, "Teen Pregnancy and High School Dropout: What Communities Can Do to Address These Issues," The National Campaign to Prevent Teen and Unplanned Pregnancy and America's Promise Alliance (2012) http://www.thenationalcampaign.org/resources/pdf/teen-preg-hsdropout.pdf.

GLOSSARY

Following are definitions for vocabulary used in *Face to Face Advisories* meetings that are central to exploring issues of identity, prejudice, and discrimination. Definitions draw on Merriam Webster (mw.com) and Dictionaryreference.com.

Stereotype: a simplistic opinion of a group of people felt to be "other;" usually uncomplimentary.

Prejudice: a hostile opinion about a "racial," religious, or national group, usually based on stereotypes.

Bias: the tendency to hold a certain opinion or prejudice, rather than think open-mindedly.

Intolerance: rigid refusal to consider a certain group of people as equals; implementation of bias.

Discrimination: treatment of a person based on a category to which that person appears to belong rather than on fact or on individual merit; intolerance of a person's self-definition if it conflicts with one's bias.

Bigotry: entrenched habit and practice of discrimination against certain people.

Inequity: customary, routine, or institutional practice of injustice and unfairness against a certain group.

Class: For purposes of this book, members of a particular social or economic stratum.

Sexual orientation: inclination of an individual with respect to sexual behavior.

Ethnic: pertaining to or characteristic of a people, especially a group sharing a common and distinctive culture including religion, language, history, country of origin and/or ancestors' origin

Ethnicity: ethnic identity or affiliation.

"Race": a basis widely used for categorizing people, primarily according to skin tone and ancestors' assumed place of origin. A biological basis for the concept of race was challenged in 1998 by the American Anthropological Association, which considers it merely a social mechanism invented during the 18th century to distinguish as biologically separate groups populations brought into contact in colonial America: European Americans, Native Americans, and African Americans.

Diversity: variety

Minority: people grouped by a characteristic such as skin color or other superficial trait, often subjected to discrimination in hiring, housing, education, and other areas.

Culture: behaviors and beliefs characteristic of a particular social or ethnic group.

Multicultural: culturally integrated, with every culture equally respected.

Integrated: free of discrimination, every person equal with every other person.

Inclusive: not excluding any particular or identifiable person or group of people.

Scapegoat: someone who is blamed for others' bad behavior; often, the victim is blamed, i.e. "she brought it on herself."

Institutionalized discrimination: discrimination practiced routinely, consciously or unconsciously, intentionally or unintentionally, in a school, workplace, neighborhood, city, or other organization.

Culturally specific: related to or characteristic of a particular culture as opposed to others.

Caste mentality: a habit of forming opinions about people based on perceived wealth, education, race, or other characteristics.

Narrow-minded: having a closed mind.

Defamation: harming the reputation of someone by libel or slander.

Gossip: talk about a person who is not present; talk that spreads rumors about someone; almost always negative or critical of the person spoken of.

Derogatory: detracting from the character or standing of someone or something, like an idea.

Isms

Racism: discrimination based on skin color, usually favoring people with lighter skin tone.

Ageism: prejudice or discrimination against a particular age-group, especially the elderly.

Sexism: discrimination based on a person's sex, usually against women.

Chauvinism: attitude of superiority toward members of the opposite sex, usually men toward women.

Jingoism: expression of extreme nationalism, usually accompanied by belligerence.

Xenophobia: fear and/or hatred of people considered to be foreigners.

Heterosexism: discrimination against homosexuals.

Homophobia: fear and/or hatred of homosexuals.

Anti-Semitism: discrimination against or prejudice or hostility toward Jews.

Classism: discrimination against or prejudice or hostility toward members of a certain social or economic class.

Ableism: discrimination against or prejudice or hostility toward people with mental or physical disabilities.

GREETINGS INDEX

Find greeting descriptions by name and their first appearance in the book.

LANGUAGE GREETINGS

Language Variations on "Good morning" and "Hello"

You can list and model and practice the greeting language possibilities ahead of time to facilitate pronunciation.

Japanese: *Ohayou gozaimasu* ("Oh-hi-oh goes eye moss") Good morning

Spanish: *Buenos dias* ("BWEH-nohs DEE-ahs") Good morning

Spanish: *Hola* ("OH-lah") Hello

Spanish: *Bienvenidos* ("B'YEN-veh-NEE-dohs") Welcome

Swahili: *Jambo* ("JAHM-bo") Hello

German: *Guten morgen* ("GOO-ten MOR-gen") Good morning

German: *Guten tag* ("GOO-ten tog") Good day

Fijian: *Bula* ("mbula") Hello

Fijian: *Ni sa yadra* ("NI sah yan dra") Good morning

Hebrew: *Shalom* ("Shah-LOME") Peace

Hebrew: *Boker tov* ("BOH-ker tohv") Good morning

Polish: *Dzien dobre* ("Jean dough-bree") Good morning

French: *Bonjour* ("Boh-JOOR") Hello

Arabic: *Sabaah el kheer* ("Sabah el khair") Good morning

Hindi: *Namaste* ("NA-mas-tay") Hello

Italian: *Ciao* ("Chow") Hello

Italian: *Buon giorno* ("Boowone JOR-no") Good morning

Hawaiian: *Aloha* ("Ah-LOW-ha") Love, peace, compassion

Arabic: *Salaam aleichem* ("Sah-LAHM a-LEH-kem") Peace to all

Ojibwe: *Boozhoo* ("Boo-ZHU") Hello

Language Variations on "Good Morning, Friend"

Spanish: *Buenos dias, amigo/amiga* ("BWEH-nohs DEE-ahs, ah-ME-go/ah-ME-ga") *Good morning, friend* (male/female)

Spanish: *Hola, compadre* ("OH-lah, com-PAH-dray") Hello, friend/buddy

French: *Bonjour, mon ami/amie* ("Boh-JOOR, moan ah-MEE") Hello, friend (male/female)

Hebrew: *Shalom, chaver* ("Shah-LOME, ha-VER") Peace, friend

Hindi: *Namaste, dost* ("NA-mas-tay dust") Hello, friend

Italian: *Buon giorno, amico/amica* ("Boowone jJOR-no, a-MEE-co/a-MEE-ca") Good morning, friend (male/female)

CHEERS

The Alligator

Stretch both arms straight out as if to make an alligator's jaws; at the signal do one big clap.

The Beatnik

Students cross arms in front of themselves and snap fingers in unison.

The Clam

Interlock fingers; at the count, clap palms of hands together.

High Five

Pass a high five around the circle.

Invent Your Own

The best cheers are those the students create. Have them design cheers that relate to the purpose of the acknowledgment. For example, to acknowledge somebody for helping her on the phone with homework, the student could mime picking up a phone, dialing, and saying, *Thank you, homework help line!*

The Noiseless Cheer

Hearing-impaired people use this to acknowledge others. Place open hands, palms out, beside ears and shake them.

Round of Applause

Clap while moving your hands in a circle.

Two Snaps Up

As a group, start with hands waist high. At the count, raise hands to shoulder height and snap once. Then lower hands back to waist level. Raise hands again to shoulder height and snap once.

About the Author

Linda Crawford founded Origins and is now Lead Program Developer there. She has taught kindergarten through graduate school, and she was principal of an arts-integrated elementary school for five years. She has led professional-development seminars and workshops for educators for nearly thirty years. She is co-founder of the *Developmental Designs* approach to integrated social and academic learning for adolescents, and is the author of *The Advisory Book: Building a Community of Learners Grades 5-9; Classroom Discipline: Guiding Adolescents to Responsible Independence; To Hold Us Together: Seven Conversations for Multicultural Understanding; Lively Learning: Using the Arts to Teach the K-8 Curriculum;* books and videos for multicultural education through the arts; and numerous articles on the integration of social and academic learning. She has a BS in English Education from the University of Wisconsin and an MA in English Literature from the University of Minnesota.

Index

ORIGINS DEVELOPMENTAL DESIGNS®

The Origins Program is a nonprofit educational organization and the creator of the *Developmental Designs*™ approach to teaching and learning. The approach consists of highly practical strategies designed to integrate social and academic learning for adolescents, increase motivation and self-management, and strengthen connections to school.

Developmental Designs Teaching Practices

Advisory—The Circle of Power and Respect (CPR) and Activity Plus (A+) meeting structures build community, social skills, and readiness for learning.

Goals Setting—Students declare a personal stake in school to anchor their learning in a meaningful commitment to growth.

Social Contract—Based on their personal goals, students design and sign an agreement that binds the community to common rules.

Modeling and Practicing—Nothing is assumed; all routines are practiced. Social competencies are learned by seeing and doing.

The Loop—Ongoing, varied reflective planning and assessments ensure continuous, conscious growth.

Empowering Language—Gesture, voice, and words combine to create a rigorous, respectful climate for building responsible independence.

Pathways to Self-control—When rules are broken, teachers have an array of strategies, such as redirections, loss of privilege, and take a break. Self-management grows without loss of dignity.

Problem-solving Strategies—Students and teachers use social conferencing, problem-solving meetings, and other structures to find positive solutions to chronic problems.

Practices for Motivating Instruction—Student choice, bridging, structured interaction, and other practices help connect young adolescent needs and the school curriculum, so that students are deeply engaged in learning.

Power of Play—Play is designed to build community, enliven students, and restore their focus, ensuring more time on task.

Additional *Developmental Designs* Resources

The Advisory Book: Building a Community of Learners Grades 5-9, Revised

Linda Crawford

Discover how advisory meets adolescents' developmental needs through two meeting formats and 200+ activities, greetings, and shares. Includes a year's worth of ready-to-use advisories on themes, such as getting acquainted, social skills, and bullying.

304-page soft cover book, 978-0-938541-21-9

Classroom Discipline: Guiding Adolescents to Responsible Independence

Linda Crawford and Christopher Hagedorn

Build a classroom climate where students practice positive behavior, help develop daily routines, and endorse expectations. Proactively guide behavior with engaging instruction. Teach self-management and minimize escalation when you redirect rule breaking.

304-page soft cover book, 978-0-938541-13-4

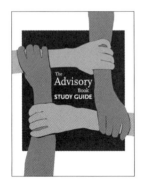

The Advisory Book Study Guide

This companion to *The Advisory Book* steers you chapter by chapter as you read it as a team. Together, you will deepen your understanding of the advisory formats and learn how to embed them in your school.

72-page soft cover book, 978-0-938541-14-1

Classroom Discipline Study Guide

A professional development guide and read-along for *Classroom Discipline*. Enrich your staff and team meetings and create consistent, positive behavior across classrooms. Includes meeting outlines and leader instructions.

84-page soft cover book, 978-0-938541-18-9

The Circle of Power and Respect Advisory Meeting DVD

See CPR in action! Watch students thoroughly engaged in advisory greetings, sharing, and games. Hear educators discuss their process and success with CPR.

70-minute DVD and viewing guide, 978-0-938541-16-5

Modeling and Practicing Classroom Routines DVD

Watch educators model expectations and get students on board to create an orderly learning environment. See success in common classroom routines, including: transitions, small group work, and waiting for assistance.

38-minute DVD and viewing guide, 978-0-938541-19-6

Tried and True Classroom Games and Greetings

A dozen acknowledgments and cheers, 50 games and greetings, and more! Energize, engage, and connect adolescents through the power of play.

72-page ring bound, 978-0-938541-15-8

Order at www.developmentaldesigns.org or call (800) 543-8715   M-F: 9-5, CT

WORKSHOPS • CONSULTING • BOOKS & RESOURCES